FOR SONIA

Life partner, inspiration, teacher, best friend

Contents

Acknowledgments

These acknowledgments must perform double duty. In writing this book, I have depended upon countless acts of support, generosity, and guidance. But perhaps more important, in engaging with the challenges of our global society and deeply divided world, I have depended upon steadfast colleagues, teachers, and leaders. This is an important opportunity for me to thank them for a lifetime of collegiality and support.

I naturally begin with my family, wife Sonia, daughters Lisa and Hannah, and son Adam. This has been a family effort, through two decades of redefining "vacation" as listening to Dad give another lecture in a sweltering room in a village in East Africa. Sonia has been my guide, inspiration, teacher of differential diagnosis, and partner and coauthor in development studies. My kids, I'm proud to say, have seen all corners of the developing world and have taken up the challenge of global development themselves. Their wonderment at what we see together is my inspiration to fight for the future for them. In all of this family effort, the wisdom of my father-in-law, Walter Ehrlich, the good sense of my mother, Joan Sachs, and the avid interest of my sister, Andrea Sachs, all played a tremendous role in keeping us on the right track. So too has the enduring moral compass of my late father, Theodore Sachs, who devoted his great lawyerly gifts and energies to the struggle for social justice.

For twenty years I have been blessed to be welcome in all parts of the world and to have colleagues who joined me in understanding the local conditions and challenges and in fitting those challenges into the broader global canvas. My earliest colleagues in Bolivia were Daniel Cohen and Felipe Larraín, lifelong companions in intellectual forays. David Lipton left the IMF to join me in work in Latin America and Eastern Europe and then went on to a scintillating role in international political economy during the Clinton administration. Wing Woo has tutored me on Asia for a quarter century and has been my guide, coauthor, and coadviser in many valuable efforts. Nirupam Bajpai has been steadfast and accurate as a keen observer, scholar, coauthor, and adviser on all aspects of India's remarkable reforms during the past decade.

The best way to become a successful economic adviser is to advise successful governments. I've been extremely fortunate to do that. My earliest adventure was in Bolivia, under the remarkable leadership of the late President Victor Paz Estenssoro and his top economic aide and later president, Gonzalo Sánchez de Lozada. Both taught me about the practical politics of successful economic reforms and the value of honesty and love of country in achieving broader political successes. In Poland, Larry Lindenberg played the pivotal role in introducing me to Solidarity's remarkable leaders, including Adam Michnik, Jacek Kuron, Bronislaw Geremek, and of course Lech Walesa. Leszek Balcerowicz, the brave and brilliant leader of Poland's reforms, made us all look good. I admire Poland's long-serving president, Alexander Kwasniewski, and remain in his debt for the honor he bestowed upon Lipton and me in awarding us one of Poland's highest civilian awards, the Commanders Cross of the Order of Merit. President Janez Drnovsek of Slovenia not only taught me about the tangled politics of the Balkans during the past two decades, but also inspired me with his leadership and honored me with the chance to contribute to Slovenia's birth as an independent country. In Russia, I want to thank my advisory partner Anders Aslund and pay special tribute to three reformers who struggled bravely against the odds: Yegor Gaidar, Boris Fedorov, and Grigory Yavlinsky.

My work in Africa has been blessed by help and guidance from a large number of colleagues and African leaders. I am especially grateful to Calestous Juma, Dyna Arhin-Tenkorang, Wen Kilama, Charles Mann, and Anne Conroy. My ardent hopes for Africa are fueled by the powerful and visionary leadership that I have seen in abundance throughout the continent, in contrast to the typical uninformed American view about Africa's governance. In particular I would like to thank Africa's new generation of democratic leaders who are pointing the way, including former President Alberto Chissano of Mozambique, President Mwai Kibaki of Kenya, President John Agyekum Kufuor of Ghana, President Olusegun Obasanjo of Nigeria, former Vice President Justin Mulawesi of Malawi, President Festus Mogae of Botswana, President Abdoulaye Wade of Senegal, and Prime Minister Meles Zenawi of Ethiopia.

The world is held together, however precariously, by the vision, leadership, and struggle of its leaders who are committed to a world of justice, equality, and rule of law. The greatest of these is UN Secretary-

General Kofi Annan, whose quiet resolve has helped to keep the world from falling over the precipice in recent years. Another great leader is Gro Harlem Brundtland, who gave me the honor to serve the World Health Organization during her tenure as WHO director general. The WHO Commission on Macroeconomics and Health helped to show the way toward scaling up basic investments for the poor. My fellow commissioners are incomparable leaders in their respective fields, including Manmohan Singh, India's current prime minister; Richard Feachem, director of the Global Fund to Fight AIDS, TB, and Malaria; Supachai Panitchkadie, the director general of the World Trade Organization; and Harold Varmus, director of Memorial Sloan-Kettering Cancer Center.

The UN agencies are filled with talented and dedicated leaders, and I have been honored to work closely with them in recent years: Mark Malloch Brown, administrator of UNDP, who has championed the UN Millennium Project from the start; Joseph Chamie, director of the UN Population Division; Zephirin Diabre, deputy administrator of UNDP and my guide to the economies of the African Sahel; former IMF managing director and current president of Germany, Horst Kohler, who during his stint at the IMF pressed the case for more global justice in resource allocation; Anna Tibaijuka, the remarkable Tanzanian-born leader of UN Habitat; Klaus Topfer, the relentlessly talented head of the UN Environmental Program; and Jim Wolfensohn, the brave and energetic leader of the World Bank. I am also grateful for the marvelous collegiality of World Bank Chief Economists Nick Stern and François Bourguignon, and IMF Chief Economist Raghuram Rajan.

Many of the specific ideas on how to end global poverty have emerged from the work of the UN Millennium Project, which I am honored to direct and from which I have drawn amply in this book. This project would have slid off the rails from the start without the unerring, beyond-the-call-of-duty leadership of John McArthur, my day-to-day colleague in the effort. John and I, in turn, have depended upon a spectacular secretariat, including Chandrika Bahadur, Stan Bernstein, Yassine Fall, Eric Kashambuzi, Margaret Kruk, Guido Schmidt-Traub, Erin Trowbridge, and round-the-clock assistants Alberto Cho, Michael Faye, Michael Krouse, Luis Javier Montero, Rohit Wanchoo, and Alice Wiemers.

The leaders of the UN Millennium Project Task Forces, and allied scientists and policy experts, are my teachers and guides through the interconnected fields of agronomy, water management, climate, energy systems, disease control, and other areas of central concern for poverty reduction and long-term development. Happily, many of these marvelous world-class scientists are my colleagues at the Earth Institute at Columbia University. I am happy to give special thanks to Columbia colleagues Deborah Balk, Wallace Broecker, Bob Chen, Lynn Friedman, James Hansen, Klaus Lackner, Upmanu Lall, Roberto Lenton, Marc Levy, Don Melnick, Vijay Modi, John Mutter, Cheryl Palm, Allan Rosenfield, Josh Ruxin, Pedro Sanchez, Peter Schlosser, Joseph Stiglitz, Awash Teklehaimonot, Ron Waldman, Paul Wilson, and Stephen Zebiak, who have played such a key role in expanding my understanding of the challenges of sustainable development. Columbia University's inspiring president, Lee Bollinger, has strongly backed the Earth Institute in this and its other endeavors, and for that I am grateful. I also thank all of the task force coordinators and task force members for making the UN Millennium Project the extraordinary effort that it has been.

None but the incomparable Bono has opened the eyes of millions of fans and citizens to the shared struggle for global equality and justice. I am grateful to Bono for his foreword to the book, for his gifted leadership in connecting worlds that would otherwise remain separate, and for reaping the energies and commitments of those newly forged connections. Bono's close associates, Jamie Drummond and Lucy Matthews, are incomparable stars in global civil society. They make miracles each day in pushing the agenda of global development to the forefront of often indifferent and unaware global leaders. Other miracle workers in promoting global justice who have generously helped me in my own activities include world-class philanthropist and financier George Soros and public health pioneers Paul Farmer, Jim Kim, and Bruce Walker.

It is a cliché to say that this book would not have been possible but for . . . and sometimes such clichés are all too true. Margarethe Laurenzi, skilled writer and editorial assistant from the very start of this project, provided incomparable support, expert suggestions, and editorial feedback that kept us on track and on time. Gordon McCord is an invaluable special assistant regarding all aspects of my work at the Earth Institute and the UN Millennium Project, including detailed work on all parts of this book. Gordon is also without doubt an upcoming global leader of his generation in the challenges of sustainable development. Winthrop Ruml joined the team from Harvard in mid-2004 and has been a key member of the project since arriving at the Earth Institute. Martha Synnott managed my office during the two decades of the events described in this book, until 2003. Ji Mi Choi offered invaluable help the following year, and now Heidi Kleedtke manages the controlled chaos that permits me to combine the obligations at the UN, the Earth Institute, and far-flung projects and programs throughout the world.

Several colleagues and friends read the manuscript with great care and creativity, heading off mistakes, misunderstandings, or problematic gaps. I especially thank Diane Asadorian, Nirupam Bajpai, David Lipton, Will Masters, Staci Warden, Wing Woo, and Jeannie Woo for their generous time and thoughtful suggestions. I also thank Bob Edgar and his colleagues at the National Council of Churches USA for answering questions on the Christian tradition's commitment to reducing global poverty.

Andrew Wylie, literary agent nonpareil, helped me to conceive of this book—its structure and logic as a way to broaden the world's understanding of our generation's opportunity to end extreme poverty. Scott Moyers, my editor at The Penguin Press, provided the steady, clear, professional guidance and support to see the project through to fruition, including the enormous skilled teamwork at Penguin Press to make such a masterful production effort. I'm grateful to both.

F o r e w o r d

Two men asleep beside each other on a long journey into Africa, literally and thankfully above the thunderclouds. One is fairly clean shaven, papers strewn around him. Matte black suit, eyes slightly hollowed from no sleep, thoughts too big even for his big head. The other is a more bohemian mess. Unshaven, unkempt, he can't just have been up for days, his boyish face says years. An advertisement for why air miles can be bad for your health. When he wakes, an air hostess asks for his autograph. Confused and amused, he points to the geek in the black suit lying among the papers. That's me. Let me introduce myself. My name is Bono and I am the rock star student. The man with me is Jeffrey D. Sachs, the great economist, and for a few years now my professor. In time, his autograph will be worth a lot more than mine.

Let me tell you how we started this journey. It goes back to before Jeff Sachs had become director of the Earth Institute at Columbia University. Before he moved to New York to become UN Secretary-General Kofi Annan's special adviser. It goes back to when Jeff gave me the third degree from the Kennedy School of International Development at Harvard University in Cambridge, Massachusetts. My great friend Bobby Shriver had advised me to meet him in order to know what I was talking about before I went up to Capitol Hill to lobby on behalf of Jubilee 2000 for the cancellation of the LDC's (least developed countries') debt to the rich countries of the OECD (Organization for Economic Cooperation and Development) as part of the millennium celebrations. I would enter the world of acronyms with a man who can make alphabet soup out of them. Soup you'd want to eat. Soup that would, if ingested properly, enable a lot more soup to be eaten by a lot more people.

Hunger, disease, the waste of lives that is extreme poverty are an affront to all of us. To Jeff it's a difficult but solvable equation. An equation that crosses human with financial capital, the strategic goals of the rich world with a new kind of planning in the poor world.

I'm a singer with an ear for a melody. Great ideas have a lot in common with a great melody. A certain clarity, inevitability, memorability . . . you can't get them out of your head, they nag at you. . . . The ideas in this book are not exactly sing-a-long but they have a hook you won't forget: the end of poverty. It's a challenge that's hard to ignore.

Jeff is hard to ignore. At speaking events I've had to walk on after this man (it's like the Monkees going on after the Beatles). His voice is louder than any electric guitar, heavier than heavy metal. His passion is operatic, he's physically very present, animated. There is wildness to the rhetoric but a rigor to the logic. God may have given him a voice with an amplifier built in, but it's the argument that carries the day.

He's not just animated; he's angry. Because he knows that a lot of the crisis in the developing world can be avoided. Staring at people queuing up to die three to a bed, two on top and one underneath, in a hospital just outside of Lilongwe, Malawi, and knowing this doesn't have to be so is too much for most of us. I am crushed. He is creative. He's an economist who can bring to life statistics that were, after all, lives in the first place. He can look up from the numbers and see faces through the spreadsheets, families like his own that stick together on treks to the far ends of the world. He helps us make sense of what senseless really means: fifteen thousand Africans dying each and every day of preventable, treatable diseases—AIDS, malaria, TB—for lack of drugs that we take for granted.

This statistic alone makes a fool of the idea many of us hold on to very tightly: the idea of equality. What is happening in Africa mocks our pieties, doubts our concern, and questions our commitment to that whole concept. Because if we're honest, there's no way we could conclude that such mass death day after day would ever be allowed to happen anywhere else. Certainly not in North America, or Europe, or Japan. An entire *continent* bursting into flames? Deep down, if we really accept that their lives—African lives—are equal to ours, we would all be doing more to put the fire out. It's an uncomfortable truth.

This book is about the alternative—taking the next step in the journey of equality. Equality is a very big idea, connected to freedom, but an idea that doesn't come for free. If we're serious, we have to be prepared to pay the price. Some people will say we can't afford to do it. . . . I disagree. I think we can't afford *not* to do it. In a world where distance no longer determines who your neighbor is, paying the price for equality is not just heart, it's smart. The destinies of the "haves" are intrinsically linked to the fates of the "have-nothing-at-alls." If we didn't know this already, it became too clear on September 11, 2001. The perpetrators of 9/11 might have been wealthy Saudis, but it was in the collapsed, poverty-stricken state of Afghanistan that they found succor and sanctuary. Africa is not the front line in the war against terror, but it soon could be.

"The war against terror is bound up in the war against poverty." Who said that? Not me. Not some beatnik peace group. Secretary of State Colin Powell. And when a military man starts talking like that perhaps we should listen. In tense, nervous times isn't it cheaper—and smarter—to make friends out of potential enemies than to defend yourself against them?

We wish things were different. But wishful thinking is not just unhelpful here; it's dangerous. The plan Jeff lays out is not only his idea of a critical path to accomplish the 2015 Millennium Development Goal of cutting poverty by half—a goal signed up to by all the world's governments. It's a handbook on how we could finish out the job. On how we could be the first generation to outlaw the kind of extreme, stupid poverty that sees a child die of hunger in a world of plenty, or of a disease preventable by a twenty-cent inoculation. We are the first generation that can afford it. The first generation that can unknot the whole tangle of bad trade, bad debt, and bad luck. The first generation that can end a corrupt relationship between the powerful and the weaker parts of the world which has been so wrong for so long.

In Jeff's hands, the millstone of opportunity around our necks becomes an adventure, something doable and achievable. His argument is clear. We converge from our different starting points . . . he from markets, I from placards. Luckily we agree you need both. However, for all of the book's cogency, you won't find an answer to the most important question of all. It falls outside regressions, theorems, field work and lands fairly, squarely on our shoulders. We *can* be the generation that no longer accepts that an accident of latitude determines whether a child lives or dies—but *will* we be that generation? Will we in the West realize our potential or will we sleep in the comfort of our affluence with apathy and indifference murmuring softly in our ears? Fifteen thousand people dying needlessly every day from AIDS, TB, and malaria. Mothers, fathers, teachers, farmers, nurses, mechanics, children. This is Africa's crisis. That it's not on the nightly news, that we do not treat this as an emergency—that's *our* crisis.

Future generations flipping through these pages will know whether we answered the key question. The evidence will be the world around them. History will be our judge, but what's written is up to us. Who we are, who we've been, what we want to be remembered for. We can't say our generation didn't know how to do it. We can't say our generation couldn't afford to do it. And we can't say our generation didn't have reason to do it. It's up to us. We can choose to shift the responsibility, or, as the professor proposes here, we can choose to shift the paradigm.

BONO, 2004

Introduction

This book is about ending poverty in our time. It is not a forecast. I am not predicting what will happen, only explaining what can happen. Currently, more than eight million people around the world die each year because they are too poor to stay alive. Our generation can choose to end that extreme poverty by the year 2025.

Every morning our newspapers could report, "More than 20,000 people perished yesterday of extreme poverty." The stories would put the stark numbers in context—up to 8,000 children dead of malaria, 5,000 mothers and fathers dead of tuberculosis, 7,500 young adults dead of AIDS, and thousands more dead of diarrhea, respiratory infection, and other killer diseases that prey on bodies weakened by chronic hunger. The poor die in hospital wards that lack drugs, in villages that lack antimalarial bed nets, in houses that lack safe drinking water. They die namelessly, without public comment. Sadly, such stories rarely get written. Most people are unaware of the daily struggles for survival, and of the vast numbers of impoverished people around the world who lose that struggle.

Since September 11, 2001, the United States has launched a war on terror, but it has neglected the deeper causes of global instability. The $450 billion that the United States will spend this year on the military will never buy peace if it continues to spend around one thirtieth of that, just $15 billion, to address the plight of the world's poorest of the poor, whose societies are destabilized by extreme poverty and thereby become havens of unrest, violence, and even global terrorism.

That $15 billion represents a tiny percentage of U.S. income, just 15 cents on every $100 of U.S. gross national product, or GNP. The share of U.S. GNP devoted to helping the poor has declined for decades, and is a tiny fraction of what the United States has repeatedly promised, and failed, to give. It is also much less than the United States should give, both to solve the crisis of extreme poverty and thereby to provide for U.S. national security. This book, then, is about making the right choices—choices that can lead to a much safer world based on a true reverence and respect for human life.

I have spent the past twenty years working with heads of state, finance and health ministers, and villagers in dozens of countries in all parts of the world. I have visited and worked in more than a hundred countries with around 90 percent of the world's population. The cumulative experience of seeing the world from many vantage points has helped me to appreciate the real circumstances on our planet—the causes of poverty, the role of rich-country policies, and the possibilities for the future. Gaining a proper perspective on these issues has been my struggle and challenge for two decades. Nothing else in my intellectual life and political engagement has been as rewarding.

I have been fortunate to have observed, and contributed to, some real successes—the end of hyperinflations, the introduction of new stable national currencies, the cancellation of unpayable debts, the conversion of moribund communist economies to dynamic market-based economies, the start-up of the Global Fund to Fight AIDS, TB, and Malaria, and modern drug treatment for impoverished HIV-infected people. I have increasingly understood the yawning gap between what the rich world claims to be doing to help the poor and what it is actually doing. I have also gradually come to understand through my scientific research and on-the-ground advisory work the awesome power in our generation's hands to end the massive suffering of the extreme poor, and thereby to make our lives safer in the process.

In the following pages, I will explain what I have witnessed and learned in societies as varied as Bolivia, Poland, Russia, China, India, and Kenya. You will see that all parts of the world have the chance to join an age of unprecedented prosperity building on global science, technology, and markets. But you will also see that certain parts of the world are caught in a downward spiral of impoverishment, hunger, and disease. It is no good to lecture the dying that they should have done better with their lot in life. Rather, it is our task to help them onto the ladder of development, at least to gain a foothold on the bottom rung, from which they can then proceed to climb on their own.

Am I an optimist? Optimism and pessimism are beside the point. The key is not to predict what will happen, but to help shape the future. This task is a collective one—for you as well as for me. Although introductory economics textbooks preach individualism and decentralized markets, our safety and prosperity depend at least as much on collective decisions to fight disease, promote good science and widespread education, provide critical infrastructure, and act in unison to help the poorest of the poor. When the preconditions of basic infrastructure (roads, power, and ports) and human capital (health and education) are in place, markets are powerful engines of development. Without those preconditions, markets can cruelly bypass large parts of the world, leaving them impoverished and suffering without respite. Collective action, through effective government provision of health, education, infrastructure, as well as foreign assistance when needed, underpins economic success.

Eighty-five years ago the great British economist John Maynard Keynes pondered the dire circumstances of the Great Depression. From the depths of despair around him, he wrote in 1930 of the *Economic Possibilities for Our Grandchildren*. At a time of duress and suffering, he envisioned the end of poverty in Great Britain and other industrial countries in his grandchildren's day, toward the end of the twentieth century. Keynes emphasized the dramatic march of science and technology and the ability of advances in technology to underpin continued economic growth at compound interest, enough growth indeed to end the age-old "economic problem" of having enough to eat and enough income to meet other basic needs. Keynes got it just right, of course: extreme poverty no longer exists in today's rich countries, and is disappearing in most of the world's middle-income countries.

Today we can invoke the same logic to declare that extreme poverty can be ended not in the time of our grandchildren, but in *our* time. The wealth of the rich world, the power of today's vast storehouses of knowledge, and the declining fraction of the world that needs help to escape from poverty all make the end of poverty a realistic possibility by the year 2025. Keynes wondered how the society of his grandchildren would use its wealth and its unprecedented freedom from the age-old struggle for daily survival. This very question has become our own. Will we have the good judgment to use our wealth wisely, to heal a divided planet, to end the suffering of those still trapped by poverty, and to forge a common bond of humanity, security, and shared purpose across cultures and regions?

This book will not answer this question. Instead, it will help to show the way toward the path of peace and prosperity, based on a detailed understanding of how the world economy has gotten to where it is today, and how our generation could mobilize our capacities in the coming twenty years to eliminate the extreme poverty that remains. I hope that by showing the contours of that promising path, we will be more likely to choose it. For now, I am grateful for the chance to share what I have seen of the world and of the economic possibilities for our time.

One

A GLOBAL FAMILY PORTRAIT

MALAWI: THE PERFECT STORM

It is still midmorning in Malawi when we arrive at a small village, Nthandire, about an hour outside of Lilongwe, the capital. We have come over dirt roads, passing women and children walking barefoot with water jugs, fuel wood, and other bundles. The midmorning temperature is sweltering. In this subsistence maize-growing region of an impoverished landlocked country in southern Africa, households eke out survival from an unforgiving terrain. This year has been a lot more difficult than usual because the rains have failed, probably the result of an El Niño cycle. Whatever the cause, the crops are withering in the fields that we pass.

If the village were filled with able-bodied men who could have built small-scale water harvesting units on rooftops and in the fields to collect what little rain had fallen in the preceding months, the situation would not be as dire as it is this morning. But as we arrive in the village, we see no able-bodied young men at all. In fact, older women and dozens of children greet us, but there is not a young man or woman of working age in sight. Where, we ask, are the workers? Out in the fields? The aid worker who has led us to the village shakes his head sadly and says no. They are nearly all dead. The village has been devastated by AIDS, which has ravaged this part of Malawi for several years now. There are just five men between twenty and forty years of age left in the village. They are not there this morning because they are all attending the funeral of a fellow villager who died of AIDS the day before.

The presence of death in Nthandire has been overwhelming in recent years. The grandmothers whom we meet are guardians for their orphaned grandchildren. Each woman has her own story of how her sons and daughters have died, leaving her to bear the burden of raising and providing for five or ten, sometimes fifteen, orphaned grandchildren. These women have reached an age where, in more prosperous places, they would be the revered matriarchs enjoying a well-earned rest from a lifetime of toil. But there is no break now, no chance for even a moment's respite, because the grandmothers of this village, and countless others like it, know that if they let up for a moment, these young children will die.

The margin of survival is extraordinarily narrow; sometimes it closes entirely. One woman we meet in front of her mud hut has fifteen orphaned grandchildren, as shown in photograph 1. As she begins to explain her situation to us, she first points to the withered crops that have died in the fields next to her hut. Her small plot, perhaps a half hectare (a little more than an acre) in all, would be too small to feed her family even if the rains had been plentiful. The problems of small farm size and drought are compounded by yet another problem: the soil nutrients have been depleted so significantly in this part of Malawi that crop yields reach only about one ton of maize per hectare with good rains, compared with three tons per hectare that would be typical of healthy soils.

A half a ton of grain from a half-hectare field would not be sufficient for proper nutrition and would provide precious little, if any, market income. This year, because of the drought, she will get almost nothing. She reaches into her apron and pulls out a handful of semirotten, bug-infested millet, which will be the basis for the gruel she will prepare for the meal that evening. It will be the one meal the children have that day.

I ask her about the health of the children. She points to a child of about four and says that the small girl contracted malaria the week before. The woman had carried her grandchild on her back for the ten kilometers or so to the local hospital. When they got there, there was no quinine, the antimalarial medicine, available that day. With the child in high fever, the grandmother and grandchild were sent home and told to return the next day.

In a small miracle, when they returned the next day after another ten-kilometer trek, the quinine had come in, and the child responded to treatment and survived. It was a close call, though. When malaria is untreated over the course of a day or two, a child may slip into cerebral malaria, followed by coma and then death. More than one million African children, and perhaps as many as three million, succumb to malaria each year. This horrific catastrophe occurs despite the fact that the disease is partly preventable—through the use of bed nets and other environmental controls that do not reach the impoverished villages of Malawi and most of the rest of the continent—and completely treatable. There is simply no conceivable excuse for this disease to be taking millions of lives each year.

Our guide to Nthandire is a Christian aid worker, a dedicated and compassionate Malawian working for a local nongovernmental organization (NGO). He and his colleagues work against all odds to help villages such as this one. The NGO has almost no financing available and survives from meager contributions. Its big effort in the village, including this particular household, is to provide a piece of plastic tarpaulin to put under the thatch of each hut's roof. The tarp keeps the children from being completely exposed to the elements, so that when the rains do come, the roof will not leak on the fifteen grandchildren sleeping below. This contribution of a few cents per household is all the aid organization can muster.

As we proceed through the village, other grandmothers share similar stories. Each has lost sons and daughters; those who remain fight for survival. There are only poor in this village. No clinic nearby. No safe water source. No crops in the fields. And notably, no aid. I stoop down to ask one of the young girls her name and age. She looks about seven or eight, but is actually twelve, stunted from years of undernutrition. When I ask her what her dreams are for her own life, she says that she wants to be a teacher, and that she is prepared to study and work hard to achieve that. I know that her chances of surviving to go on to secondary school and a teacher's college are slim under the circumstances in which she lives. Attending school now is a hit-and-miss affair. Children are in and out of school with illness. Their attendance depends on how urgently they are needed at home to fetch water and firewood, or to care for siblings or cousins; on whether they can afford to buy supplies, a uniform, and pay local fees; and on the safety of walking several kilometers to the school itself.

We leave the village and fly later that day to the second city of the country, Blantyre, where we visit the main hospital in Malawi, Queen Elizabeth Central Hospital. There we experience our second shock of the day. This hospital is the place where the government of Malawi is keen to begin a treatment program for the roughly nine hundred thousand Malawians infected with the HIV virus and currently dying of AIDS because of lack of treatment. The hospital has set up a walk-in clinic for people who can afford to pay the dollar a day cost of the antiretroviral combination therapy, based on Malawi's arrangements with the Indian generic drug producer Cipla, which has pioneered the provision of low-cost antiretroviral drugs to poor countries. Since the government is too impoverished to be able to afford a dollar a day for all those in need, the program has begun for those few Malawians who can afford to pay out of pocket. At the time of our visit, this treatment site is providing anti-AIDS drugs on a daily basis to about four hundred people who can afford it—four hundred people in a country where nine hundred thousand are infected. For the rest, there is essentially no access to anti-AIDS medicines.

We duck into a conference room with the doctor who is overseeing the outpatient service and medical wards. He describes to us the small miracles of the patients on anti-AIDS drug treatment. The response has been dramatic. The success rate of the medicines is nearly 100 percent. The HIV strains do not exhibit drug resistance because the Malawian people have never had access to the drugs before. The doctor also reports that his patients' adherence to this twice-daily regimen has been very high. His patients surely want to stay alive. In short, the doctor is extremely pleased with the results.

Just as his briefing is encouraging us, the doctor stands up and suggests that we visit the medical ward, which lies just across the hall. "Medical ward" is, in fact, a shocking euphemism, because in truth it is not a medical ward at all. It is the place where Malawians come to die of AIDS. There is no medicine in the medical ward. The room has a posted occupancy rate of 150 beds. There are 450 people in the ward. These 450 people are fit into a room with 150 beds by putting three people in or around each bed. In most cases, two people are lying head to toe, toe to head—strangers sharing a death bed. Alongside or underneath the bed there is somebody on the ground, sometimes literally on the ground or sometimes on a piece of cardboard, dying beneath the bed.

The room is filled with moans. This is a dying chamber where three quarters or more of the people this day are in late-stage AIDS without medicines. Family members sit by the bed, swabbing dried lips and watching their loved ones die. The same doctor who is treating patients across the hall is the doctor in charge of this service. He knows what could be done. He knows that each of these patients could rise from the deathbed but for the want of a dollar a day. He knows the problem is not one of infrastructure or logistics or adherence. He knows that the problem is simply that the world has seen fit to look away as hundreds of impoverished Malawians die this day as a result of their poverty.

I have come to know Malawi relatively well after several visits. A few years earlier, I had been contacted by the vice president of Malawi, Justin Mulawesi, a remarkably fine individual, a dignified, eloquent, and popular figure in what is against all odds a multiparty democracy. The odds are long because democracy is bound to be fragile in an impoverished country where incomes are around 50 cents per person per day, or around $180 per person per year, and where the stresses of mass disease, famine, and climate shock are pervasive. Amazingly, the Malawians have done it, while the international community has largely stood by through all of this suffering.

Vice President Mulawesi himself has lost several family members to AIDS. The first time we talked about AIDS, he spoke to me through mournful eyes about his new responsibilities as head of the National AIDS Commission. He has led a team of experts to design a national AIDS strategy that could begin to meet this horrific challenge. That team has traveled throughout the world—to Harvard, Johns Hopkins, Liverpool, the London School of Hygiene and Tropical Medicine, and the World Health Organization—to discuss ideas for scaling up the fight against AIDS.

Malawi actually put together one of the earliest and best conceived strategies for bringing treatment to its dying population, and gave an enormously thoughtful response to the challenges of managing a new system of drug delivery, patient counseling and education, community outreach, and the financial flows that would accompany the process of training doctors. On that basis, Malawi made proposals to the international community to help Malawians try to reach about a third of the total infected population (about three hundred thousand people) with anti-AIDS drug treatment within a five-year scale-up period.

Yet international processes are cruel. The donor governments—including the United States and Europeans—told Malawi to scale back its proposal sharply because the first proposal was "too ambitious and too costly." The next draft was cut back to a mere hundred thousand on treatment at the end of five years. Even that was too much. In a tense five-day period, the donors prevailed on Malawi to cut another 60 percent from the proposal, down to forty thousand on treatment. This atrophied plan was submitted to the Global Fund to Fight AIDS, TB, and Malaria. Incredibly, the donors that run that fund saw fit to cut back once again. After a long struggle, Malawi received funding to save just twenty-five thousand at the end of five years—a death warrant from the international community for the people of this country.

Carol Bellamy of UNICEF has rightly described Malawi's plight as the perfect storm, a storm that brings together climatic disaster, impoverishment, the AIDS pandemic, and the long-standing burdens of malaria, schistosomiasis, and other diseases. In the face of this horrific maelstrom, the world community has so far displayed a fair bit of hand-wringing and even some high-minded rhetoric, but precious little action.

BANGLADESH: ON THE LADDER OF DEVELOPMENT

A few thousand miles away from this perfect storm is another scene of poverty. This is poverty in retreat, where the fight for survival is gradually being won, although still with horrendous risks and huge unmet needs. This struggle is being waged in Bangladesh, one of the most populous countries in the world, with 140 million people living in the flood plains of the deltas of the two great rivers, the Brahmaputra and the Ganges, that flow through Bangladesh on their way to the Indian Ocean.

Bangladesh was born in a war for independence against Pakistan in 1971. That year, it experienced massive famine and disarray, leading an official in Henry Kissinger's State Department to famously label it an "international basket case." Bangladesh today is far from a basket case. Per capita income has approximately doubled since independence. Life expectancy has risen from forty-four years to sixty-two years. The infant mortality rate (the number of children who die before their first birthday for every 1,000 born) has declined from 145 in 1970 to 48 in 2002. Bangladesh shows us that even in circumstances that seem the most hopeless there are ways forward if the right strategies are applied, and if the right combination of investments is made.

Still, Bangladesh is not out of the grip of extreme poverty. Although it has escaped the worst of the ravages of famine and disease in the past generation, it faces some profound challenges today. A few months after my visit to Malawi, I was up at dawn one morning in Dhaka, Bangladesh, to see a remarkable sight: thousands of people walking to work in long lines stretching from the outskirts of Dhaka and from some of its poorest neighborhoods. Looking more closely, I noticed that these workers were almost all young women, perhaps between the ages of eighteen and twenty-five. These are the workers of a burgeoning garment industry in Dhaka who cut, stitch, and package millions of pieces of apparel each month for shipment to the United States and Europe.

Over the years, I have visited garment factories all over the developing world. I have grown familiar with the cavernous halls where hundreds of young women sit at sewing machines, and men at cutting tables, where the fabrics move along production lines and the familiar labels of GAP, Polo, Yves Saint Laurent, Wal-Mart, J. C. Penney, and others are attached as the clothing reaches the final stages of production. There is nothing glamorous about this work. The women often walk two hours each morning in long quiet files to get to work. Arriving at seven or seven-thirty, they may be in their seats for most of the following twelve hours. They often work with almost no break at all or perhaps a very short lunch break, with little chance to go to the lavatory. Leering bosses lean over them, posing a threat of sexual harassment. After a long, difficult, tedious day, the young women trudge back home, when they are again sometimes threatened with physical assault.

These sweatshop jobs are the targets of public protest in developed countries; those protests have helped to improve the safety and quality of the working conditions. The rich-world protesters, however, should support increased numbers of such jobs, albeit under safer working conditions, by protesting the trade protectionism in their own countries that keeps out garment exports from countries such as Bangladesh. These young women already have a foothold in the modern economy that is a critical, measurable step up from the villages of Malawi (and more relevant for the women, a step up from the villages of Bangladesh where most of them were born). The sweatshops are the first rung on the ladder out of extreme poverty. They give lie to the Kissinger state department's forecast that Bangladesh is condemned to extreme poverty.

On one visit to Bangladesh, I picked up an English-language morning newspaper, where I found an extensive insert of interviews with young women working in the garment sector. These stories were poignant, fascinating, and eye-opening. One by one, they recounted the arduous hours, the lack of labor rights, and the harassment. What was most striking and unexpected about the stories was the repeated affirmation that this work was the greatest opportunity that these women could ever have imagined, and that their employment had changed their lives for the better.

Nearly all of the women interviewed had grown up in the countryside, extraordinarily poor, illiterate and unschooled, and vulnerable to chronic hunger and hardship in a domineering, patriarchal society. Had they (and their forebearers of the 1970s and 1980s) stayed in the villages, they would have been forced into a marriage arranged by their fathers, and by seventeen or eighteen, forced to conceive a child. Their trek to the cities to take jobs has given these young women a chance for personal liberation of unprecedented dimension and opportunity.

The Bangladeshi women told how they were able to save some small surplus from their meager pay, manage their own income, have their own rooms, choose when and whom to date and marry, choose to have children when they felt ready, and use their savings to improve their living conditions and especially to go back to school to enhance their literacy and job-market skills. As hard as it is, this life is a step on the way to economic opportunity that was unimaginable in the countryside in generations past.

Some rich-country protesters have argued that Dhaka's apparel firms should either pay far higher wage rates or be closed, but closing such factories as a result of wages forced above worker productivity would be little more than a ticket for these women back to rural misery. For these young women, these factories offer not only opportunities for personal freedom, but also the first rung on the ladder of rising skills and income for themselves and, within a few years, for their children. Virtually every poor country that has developed successfully has gone through these first stages of industrialization. These Bangladeshi women share the experience of many generations of immigrants to New York City's garment district and a hundred other places where their migration to toil in garment factories was a step on the path to a future of urban affluence in succeeding generations.

Not only is the garment sector fueling Bangladesh's economic growth of more than 5 percent per year in recent years, but it is also raising the consciousness and power of women in a society that was long brazenly biased against women's chances in life. As part of a more general and dramatic process of change throughout Bangladeshi society, this change and others give Bangladesh the opportunity in the next few years to put itself on a secure path of long-term economic growth. The countryside that these women have left is also changing quickly, in part because of the income remittances and ideas that the young women send back to their rural communities, and in part because of the increased travel and temporary migration between rural and urban areas, as families diversify their economic bases between rural agriculture and urban manufacturers and services.

In 2003, my colleagues at Columbia and I visited a village near Dhaka with one of the leaders of an inspiring nongovernmental organization, the Bangladeshi Rural Advancement Committee, now known universally as BRAC. There we met representatives from a village association, which BRAC had helped to organize, in which women living about an hour outside the city were engaged in small-scale commercial activities—food processing and trade—within the village and on the roads between the village and Dhaka itself. These women presented a picture of change every bit as dramatic as that of the burgeoning apparel sector.

Wearing beautiful saris, the women sat on the ground in six rows, each with six women, to greet us and answer questions. Each row represented a subgroup of the local "microfinance" unit. The woman in the front of the row was in charge of the borrowing of the whole group behind her. The group in each line was mutually responsible for repayments of the loans taken by any member within the line. BRAC and its famed counterpart, Grameen Bank, pioneered this kind of group lending, in which impoverished recipients (usually women) are given small loans of a few hundred dollars as working capital for microbusiness activities. Such women were long considered unbankable, simply not creditworthy enough to bear the transaction costs to receive loans. Group lending changed the repayment dynamics: default rates are extremely low, and BRAC and Grameen have figured out how to keep other transaction costs to a minimum as well.

Perhaps more amazing than the stories of how microfinance was fueling small-scale businesses were the women's attitudes to child rearing.

When Dr. Allan Rosenfield, dean of Columbia University's Mailman School of Public Health and one of the world's leading experts on reproductive health, asked the women how many had five children, no hands went up. Four? Still no hands. Three? One nervous woman, looking around, reluctantly put her hand in the air. Two? About 40 percent of the women. One? Perhaps another 25 percent. None? The remainder of the women. Here was a group where the average number of children for these mothers was between one and two children.

Rosenfield then asked them how many they wanted in total. He again started at five—no hands. Four? No hands. Three? No hands. Two? Almost all the hands went up. This social norm was new, a demonstration of a change of outlook and possibility so dramatic that Rosenfield dwelt on it throughout the rest of our visit. He had been visiting Bangladesh and other parts of Asia since the 1960s, and he remembered vividly the days when Bangladeshi rural women would typically have had six or seven children.

The jobs for women in the cities and in rural off-farm microenterprises; a new spirit of women's rights and independence and empowerment; dramatically reduced rates of child mortality; rising literacy of girls and young women; and, crucially, the availability of family planning and contraception have made all the difference for these women. There is no single explanation for the dramatic, indeed historic, reduction in desired rates of fertility: it is the combination of new ideas, better public health for mothers and children, and improved economic opportunities for women. The reduced fertility rates, in turn, will fuel Bangladesh's rising incomes. With fewer children, a poor household can invest more in the health and education of each child, thereby equipping the next generation with the health, nutrition, and education that can lift Bangladesh's living standards in future years.

Bangladesh has managed to place its foot on the first rung of the ladder of development, and has achieved economic growth and improvements of health and education partly through its own heroic efforts, partly through the ingenuity of NGOs like BRAC and Grameen Bank, and partly through investments that have been made, often at significant scale, by various donor governments that rightly viewed Bangladesh not as a hopeless basket case but as a country worthy of attention, care, and development assistance.

INDIA: CENTER OF AN EXPORT
SERVICES REVOLUTION

If Bangladesh has one foot on the ladder, India is already several steps up the ladder. The young woman whose computer screen I peered over, in an information technology center in Chennai, is a prototypical employee of the new India. She is twenty-five years old and a graduate of a local teacher's college where she obtained a two-year degree following high school. Now she works as a transcriber of data for a new Indian information technology (IT) company operating in the capital of the southern state of Tamil Nadu. Chennai is a center of India's IT revolution, one that is beginning to fuel unprecedented economic growth in this vast country of one billion people. The IT revolution is creating jobs that are unknown in Malawi and still largely unthinkable in Bangladesh, but that are becoming the norm for educated young women in India.

This company has a remarkable arrangement with a hospital in Chicago, where doctors dictate their charts and transmit them by satellite to India as voice files at the end of each work day in Chicago. Because of the ten-and-a-half-hour time zone difference, the end of each work day in Chicago is the beginning of another in Chennai. When the voice files are received, dozens of young women who have taken a special course in medical data transcription sit in front of computer screens with headphones in place and speedily type in the medical charts of patients almost ten thousand miles away. I listened, for a short bit, to the transcription. The workers there know the medical jargon much better than I do because of their intensive training course and experience. They earn about $250 to $500 a month, depending on their level of experience, between a tenth and a third of what a medical data transcriber might earn in the United States. Their income is more than twice the earnings of a low-skilled industrial worker in India and perhaps eight times the earnings of an agricultural laborer.

The entrepreneur who started up this firm has close relatives in the United States who made the business connections on the U.S. side. Now the business is thriving. It is moving from data transcription to financial record keeping, and soon into financial consulting and advising for American companies, as well as back-office processing operations, or BPO in the new jargon of the global economy. Its employees work in gleaming buildings with broadband Internet facilities, satellite hook-ups, and videoconferencing capability for the heads of operations who have to be in face-to-face contact with their counterparts in the United States. They have access to hygienic facilities. They are women whose mothers, typically, were the first in the family to become literate and to gain a foothold in the urban economy (perhaps as seamstresses in the sweatshops), and whose grandmothers were almost without a doubt rural laborers in the overwhelmingly village economy of two generations before.

India is vast. Many parts of India, particularly in the north, are still caught in the same back-breaking rural poverty that grips Malawi and parts of Bangladesh. Much of urban India resembles Dhaka. Only a few leading "growth poles" share the cutting-edge feel of IT-driven Chennai. Throughout the Ganges Valley of northern India, home to two hundred million Indians living in the vast plains of India's greatest river, the IT revolution has been slow to emerge, if it has emerged at all. Yet so powerful are the new trends in India, not only in IT but also in textiles and apparel, electronics, pharmaceuticals, automotive components, and other sectors, that the overall economic growth of India is reliably now 6 percent or more per year. India is beginning to nip at the heels of China's growth rates, and investors around the world are warming to the notion of establishing operations, from IT to manufacturing to research and development, in the fast-growing Indian economy.

Progress is hard enough to achieve in the world without being perceived as a danger. One of the ironies of the recent success of India and China is the fear that has engulfed the United States that success in these two countries comes at the expense of the United States. These fears are fundamentally wrong and, even worse, dangerous. They are wrong because the world is not a zero-sum struggle in which one country's gain is another's loss, but is rather a positive-sum opportunity in which improving technologies and skills can raise living standards around the world. Not only are the Indian IT workers providing valuable goods and services to United States consumers, but they are also sitting at terminals with Dell computers, using Microsoft and SAP software, Cisco routers, and dozens of other empowering pieces of technology imported from the developed countries. As India's economy grows, its consumers opt for a growing array of U.S. and European goods and services for their homes and businesses.

CHINA: THE RISE OF AFFLUENCE

Following another visit to India, I continued on to Beijing, China, where economic development is speeding ahead at full throttle. Beijing has emerged not only as a major capital of the developing world, but also as one of the world's economic capitals. It is now a booming city of eleven million. Annual income has surpassed $4,000 per capita, and the Chinese economy continues to soar at above 8 percent growth per annum.

On one particular night, I was the guest of two young couples, truly young urban professionals, who took me to one of the trendiest nightspots of the city. I tried to listen to them over the operatic duet taking place on the stage, a kind of retrochic performance in which a Mao-era revolutionary opera was being performed for a room filled with very well-dressed young business executives. Every table had at least one, and usually half a dozen, cell phones lying on it in case any of the hotshot young businessmen and -women received calls from clients or the office. As I peered at the opera out of a corner of my eye, my hosts showed me the new cell phones they had just purchased that were also digital cameras. They demonstrated them by sending a picture of me from one phone to the other. This was a gadget that I had not yet seen back home.

I would not have been so stunned had I been in London or New York or Paris or Tokyo. But I was in a country that twenty-five years ago was still emerging from the chaos of the Cultural Revolution and decades of turmoil under Mao Tse-tung. Within a single generation, China has become one of the most important economies and trading powers of the world.

These young Chinese men and women have the chance to attain tremendous affluence, to travel the world, and to enjoy the other benefits of the high living standards available to them because of the powers of globalization. China's great advance during the past twenty-five years reflects the fact that within two decades, it has gone from being a virtually closed society and economy to one of the great export powers of the world. Its exports have been fueled by a vast inflow of foreign investment and technology, which brought the money to build modern factories together with the machinery and techniques to run them, in combination with relatively low-cost Chinese workers who are increasingly proficient in skills of all sorts. The result has been the rise, in one industry after another, of highly competitive enterprises that have increased China's exports from around $20 billion in 1980 to around $400 billion in 2004.

ASCENDING THE LADDER OF ECONOMIC DEVELOPMENT

What do these four widely divergent images of the globe show us? We see an almost unimaginable divide between the richest and poorest parts of the world, with all the gradations in between. We glimpse the pivotal roles that science and technology play in the development process. And we sense a progression of development that moves from subsistence agriculture toward light manufacturing and urbanization, and on to high-tech services. In Malawi, 84 percent of the population lives in rural areas; in Bangladesh, 76 percent; in India, 72 percent; and in China, 61 percent. In the United States, at the other upper end of the development spectrum, it is just 20 percent. Services account for under 25 percent of employment in Malawi, whereas in the United States, they account for 75.

If economic development is a ladder with higher rungs representing steps up the path to economic well-being, there are roughly one billion people around the world, one sixth of humanity, who live as the Malawians do: too ill, hungry, or destitute even to get a foot on the first rung of the development ladder. These people are the "poorest of the poor," or the "extreme poor" of the planet. They all live in developing countries (poverty does exist in rich countries, but it is not extreme poverty). Of course, not all of these one billion people are dying today, but they are all fighting for survival each day. If they are the victims of a serious drought or flood, or an episode of serious illness, or a collapse of the world market price of their cash crop, the result is likely to be extreme suffering and perhaps even death. Cash earnings are pennies a day.

A few rungs up the development ladder is the upper end of the low-income world, where roughly another 1.5 billion people face problems like those of the young women in Bangladesh. These people are "the poor." They live above mere subsistence. Although daily survival is pretty much assured, they struggle in the cities and countryside to make ends meet. Death is not at their door, but chronic financial hardship and a lack of basic amenities such as safe drinking water and functioning latrines are part of their daily lives. All told, the extreme poor (at around 1 billion) and the poor (another 1.5 billion) make up around 40 percent of humanity.

Another 2.5 billion people, including the Indian IT workers, are up yet another few rungs, in the middle-income world. These are middle-income households, but they would certainly not be recognized as middle class by the standards of rich countries. Their incomes may be a few thousand dollars per year. Most of them live in cities. They are able to secure some comfort in their housing, perhaps even indoor plumbing. They can purchase a scooter and someday even an automobile. They have adequate clothing, and their children go to school. Their nutrition is adequate, and some are even falling into the rich-world syndrome of unhealthy fast food.

Still higher up the ladder are the remaining one billion people, roughly a sixth of the world, in the high-income world. These affluent households include the billion or so people in the rich countries, but also the increasing number of affluent people living in middle-income countries—the tens of millions of high-income individuals in such cities as Shanghai, São Paolo, or Mexico City. The young professionals of Beijing are among the fortunate one sixth of the world enjoying twenty-first-century affluence.

The good news is that well more than half of the world, from the Bangladesh garment worker onward, broadly speaking, is experiencing economic progress. Not only do they have a foothold on the development ladder, but they are also actually climbing it. Their climb is evident in rising personal incomes and the acquisition of goods such as cell phones, television sets, and scooters. Progress is also evident in such crucial determinants of economic well-being as rising life expectancy, falling infant mortality rates, rising educational attainment, increasing access to water and sanitation, and the like.

The greatest tragedy of our time is that one sixth of humanity is not even on the development ladder. A large number of the extreme poor are caught in a poverty trap, unable on their own to escape from extreme material deprivation. They are trapped by disease, physical isolation, climate stress, environmental degradation, and by extreme poverty itself. Even though life-saving solutions exist to increase their chances for survival—whether in the form of new farming techniques, or essential medicines, or bed nets that can limit the transmission of malaria—these families and their governments simply lack the financial means to make these crucial investments. The world's poor know about the development ladder: they are tantalized by images of affluence from halfway around the world. But they are not able to get a first foothold on the ladder, and so cannot even begin the climb out of poverty.

WHO AND WHERE ARE THE POOR?

There are many definitions, as well as intense debates, about the exact numbers of the poor, where they live, and how their numbers and economic conditions are changing over time. It is useful to start with what is agreed, and then to mention some of the areas of debate. As a matter of definition, it is useful to distinguish between three degrees of poverty: extreme (or absolute) poverty, moderate poverty, and relative poverty. Extreme poverty means that households cannot meet basic needs for survival. They are chronically hungry, unable to access health care, lack the amenities of safe drinking water and sanitation, cannot afford education for some or all of the children, and perhaps lack rudimentary shelter—a roof to keep the rain out of the hut, a chimney to remove the smoke from the cook stove—and basic articles of clothing, such as shoes. Unlike moderate and relative poverty, extreme poverty occurs only in developing countries. Moderate poverty generally refers to conditions of life in which basic needs are met, but just barely. Relative poverty is generally construed as a household income level below a given proportion of average national income. The relatively poor, in high-income countries, lack access to cultural goods, entertainment, recreation, and to quality health care, education, and other perquisites for upward social mobility.

The World Bank has long used a complicated statistical standard—income of $1 per day per person, measured at purchasing power parity—to determine the numbers of extreme poor around the world. Another World Bank category, income between $1 per day and $2 per day, can be used to measure moderate poverty. These measures feature prominently in public policy circles, and most recently were estimated by World Bank economists Shaohua Chen and Martin Ravallion. They estimated that roughly 1.1 billion people were living in extreme poverty in 2001, down from 1.5 billion in 1981. Figure 1a shows the distribution of the world's extreme poor by region. Each bar signifies the number of poor in the region, with the first bar indicating the number in 1981, the

Figure 1a: Numbers of Extreme Poor

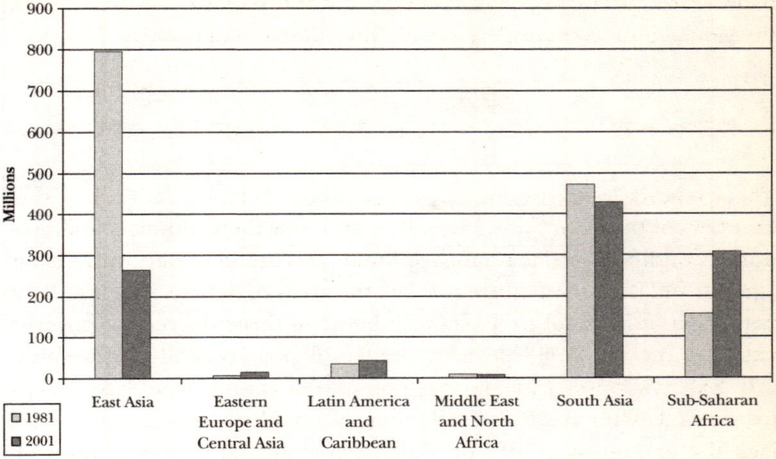

Source: Data from Chen and Ravallion (2004).

second bar, in 2001. The overwhelming share of the world's extreme poor, 93 percent in 2001, live in three regions: East Asia, South Asia, and sub-Saharan Africa. Since 1981, the numbers of extreme poor have risen in sub-Saharan Africa, but have fallen in East Asia and South Asia.

Figure 1b repeats the same measurement, but now shows the proportion of the region's population in extreme poverty, rather than the absolute number. Almost half of Africa's population is deemed to live in extreme poverty, and that proportion has risen slightly over the period. The proportion of the extreme poor in East Asia has plummeted, from 58 percent in 1981 to 15 percent in 2001; in South Asia the progress has also been marked, although slightly less dramatically, from 52 percent to 31 percent. Latin America's extreme poverty rate is around 10 percent, and relatively stuck; Eastern Europe's rose from a negligible level in 1981 to around 4 percent in 2001, the result of the upheavals of communist collapse and economic transition to a market economy.

Figures 2a and 2b show the calculations for the moderate poor, those living between $1 and $2 per day. East Asia, South Asia, and sub-Saharan Africa continue to dominate the picture, with 87 percent of the world's 1.6 billion moderately poor. The numbers of moderate poor in East Asia and South Asia have actually risen as the poorest households

Figure 1b: Proportion Living in Extreme Poverty

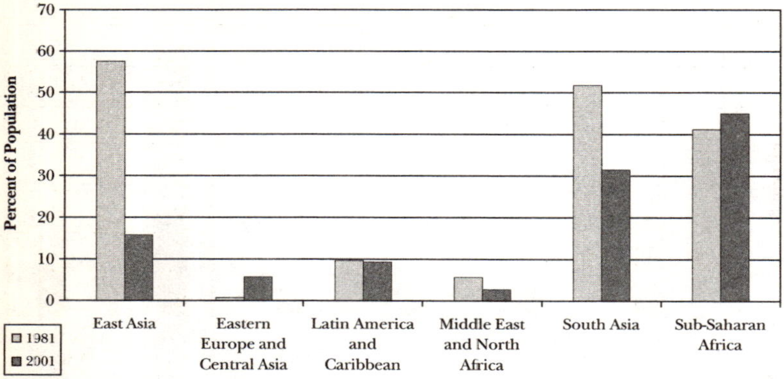

Source: Data from Chen and Ravallion (2004).

have improved their circumstances from extreme poverty to moderate poverty. Some 15 percent of Latin Americans live in moderate poverty, a rate that has been fairly constant since 1981.

Map 1 gives us yet another perspective on these data, on a country-by-country basis. Each country is shaded according to the proportion of the population living in extreme poverty and moderate poverty. A country as a whole is deemed to suffer from extreme poverty if the proportion of the population in extreme poverty is at least 25 percent of the total. A country is categorized as suffering from moderate poverty if it is not in extreme poverty, but at least 25 percent of the households are extremely poor or moderately poor, that is, living under $2 per day. Most of the countries of sub-Saharan Africa are in extreme poverty (and even more would be in this category but for lack of reliable data), as are the countries of South Asia. East Asia and Latin America include many countries in moderate poverty, but also many that have risen beyond moderate poverty in recent decades.

The precision of the World Bank figures have been questioned in heated debates. The World Bank has relied on household surveys, while other researchers have relied on national income accounts, which tend to show somewhat faster progress in the reduction of Asian poverty. The details need not detain us here, except to say that the general picture remains true in either case: extreme poverty is concentrated in East Asia,

Figure 2a: Numbers of Moderate Poor

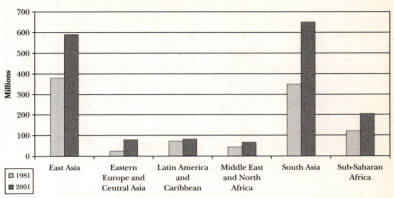

Source: Data from Chen and Ravallion (2004).

Figure 2b: Proportion Living in Moderate Poverty

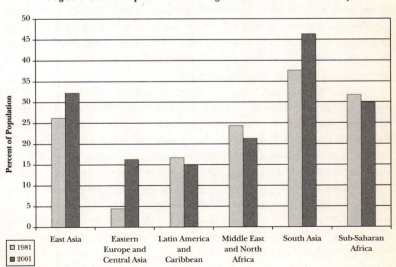

Source: Data from Chen and Ravallion (2004).

South Asia, and sub-Saharan Africa. It is rising in Africa in absolute numbers and as a share of the population, while it is falling in both absolute
numbers and as a proportion of the population in the Asian regions.

We will have many occasions to discuss the specific circumstances of
the poorest of the poor. They are mainly in rural areas, though with a
growing proportion in the cities. They face challenges almost unknown
in the rich world today—malaria, massive droughts, lack of roads and
motor vehicles, great distances to regional and world markets, lack of
electricity and modern cooking fuels—challenges that are at first harrowing to contemplate, but on second thought encouraging, precisely
because they also lend themselves to practical solutions.

OUR GENERATION'S CHALLENGE

The very hardest part of economic development is getting the first
foothold on the ladder. Households and countries at the very bottom of
the world's income distribution, in extreme poverty, tend to be stuck.
Countries already on the ladder of development, such as Bangladesh
and India, are generally making progress, even if it is uneven and sometimes painfully slow. Our generation's challenge is to help the poorest
of the poor to escape the misery of extreme poverty so that they may begin their own ascent up the ladder of economic development. The end
of poverty, in this sense, is not only the end of extreme suffering but also
the beginning of economic progress and of the hope and security that
accompany economic development.

When I speak of the "end of poverty," therefore, I will be speaking of
two closely related objectives. The first is to end the plight of one sixth of
humanity that lives in extreme poverty and struggles daily for survival.
Everybody on Earth can and should enjoy basic standards of nutrition,
health, water and sanitation, shelter, and other minimum needs for survival, well-being, and participation in society. The second is to ensure
that all of the world's poor, including those in moderate poverty, have a
chance to climb the ladder of development. As a global society, we
should ensure that the international rules of the game in economic management do not advertently or inadvertently set snares along the lower
rungs of the ladder in the form of inadequate development assistance,
protectionist trade barriers, destabilizing global financial practices,

poorly designed rules for intellectual property, and the like, that prevent the low-income world from climbing up the rungs of development.

The end of extreme poverty is at hand—within our generation—but only if we grasp the historic opportunity in front of us. There already exists a bold set of commitments that is halfway to that target: the Millennium Development Goals (MDGs), the eight goals that all 191 UN member states unanimously agreed to in 2002 by signing the United Nations Millennium Declaration. These goals are important targets for cutting poverty in half by the year 2015, compared with a baseline of 1990. They are bold but achievable, even if dozens of countries are not yet on track to achieve them. They represent a crucial midstation on the path to ending extreme poverty by the year 2025. And the rich countries have repeatedly promised to help the poor countries to achieve them through increased development assistance and improved global rules of the game.

These, then, are the economic possibilities of our time:

- To meet the Millennium Development Goals by 2015

- To end extreme poverty by 2025

- To ensure well before 2025 that all of world's poor countries can make reliable progress up the ladder of economic development

- To accomplish all of this with modest financial help from the rich countries, more than is now provided, but within the bounds of what they have long promised.

To meet these challenges, we first have to understand how we got to where we are, for in that understanding we will also find the way forward.

Two

THE SPREAD OF
ECONOMIC PROSPERITY

The move from universal poverty to varying degrees of prosperity has happened rapidly in the span of human history. Two hundred years ago the idea that we could potentially achieve the end of extreme poverty would have been unimaginable. Just about everybody was poor, with the exception of a very small minority of rulers and large landowners. Life was as difficult in much of Europe as it was in India or China. Our great-great-grandparents were, with very few exceptions, most likely poor and living on a farm. One leading economic historian, Angus Maddison, puts the average income per person in Western Europe in 1820 at around 90 percent of the average income of Africa today. Life expectancy in Western Europe and Japan as of 1800 was about forty years.

A few centuries ago, vast divides in wealth and poverty around the world did not exist. China, India, Europe, and Japan all had similar income levels at the time of European discoveries of the sea routes to Asia, Africa, and the Americas. Marco Polo marveled at the sumptuous wonders of China, not at its poverty. Cortés and his conquistadores expressed astonishment at the riches of Tenochtitlán, the capital of the Aztecs. The early Portuguese explorers were impressed with the well-ordered towns of West Africa.

THE NOVELTY OF MODERN
ECONOMIC GROWTH

If we are to understand why a vast gap between rich and poor exists to-day, we must return to the very recent period of human history when this divide emerged. The past two centuries, since around 1800, consti-tute a unique era in economic history, a period the great economic his-torian Simon Kuznets famously termed the period of modern economic growth. Before then, indeed for thousands of years, there had been vir-tually no sustained economic growth in the world, and only gradual in-creases in the human population. The world population had risen gradually from around 230 million people at the start of the first millen-nium in A.D. 1, to perhaps 270 million by A.D. 1000, and 900 million people by A.D. 1800. Real living standards were even slower to change. According to Maddison, there was no discernible rise in living standards on a global scale during the first millennium, and perhaps a 50 percent

Figure 1: World Population

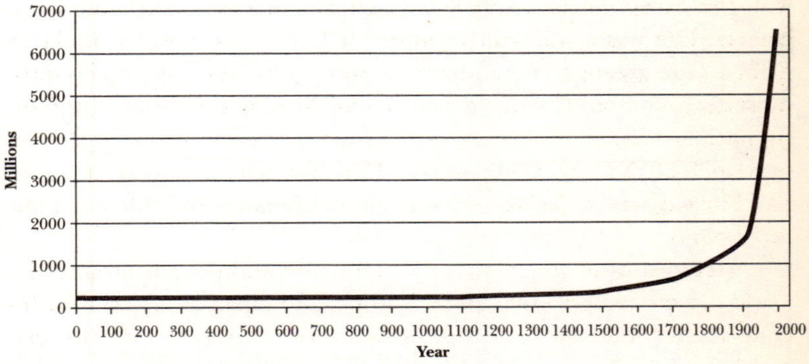

Source: Data from Maddison (2001).

increase in per capita income in the eight-hundred-year period from A.D. 1000 to A.D. 1800.

In the period of modern economic growth, however, both popula-tion and per capita income came unstuck, soaring at rates never before seen or even imagined. As shown on figure 1, the global population rose more than sixfold in just two centuries, reaching an astounding 6.1 billion people at the start of the third millennium, with plenty of momentum for rapid population growth still ahead. The world's average per capita income rose even faster, shown in figure 2, increasing by around nine times between 1820 and 2000. In today's rich countries, the economic growth was even more astounding. The U.S. per capita income increased almost twenty-five-fold during this period, and Western Europe's increased fifteen-fold. Total worldwide food production more than kept up with the booming world population (though large numbers of chronically hungry people remain until today). Vastly improved farm yields were achieved on the basis of technological advances. If we combine the increases in world population and world output per person, we find that total economic activity in the world (the gross world product, or GWP) rose an astounding forty-nine times during the past 180 years.

Figure 2: World Average per Capita Income

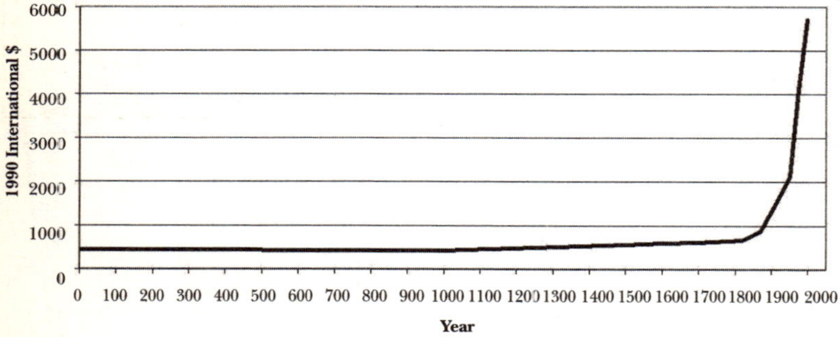

Source: Data from Maddison (2001).

The gulf between today's rich and poor countries is therefore a new phenomenon, a yawning gap that opened during the period of modern economic growth. As of 1820, the biggest gap between the rich and poor—specifically, between the world's leading economy of the day, the United Kingdom, and the world's poorest region, Africa—was a ratio of four to one in per capita income (even after adjusting for differences in purchasing power). By 1998, the gap between the richest economy, the United States, and the poorest region, Africa, had widened to twenty to one. Since all parts of the world had a roughly comparable starting point in 1820 (all very poor by current standards), today's vast inequalities reflect the fact that some parts of the world achieved modern economic growth while others did not. Today's vast income inequalities illuminate two centuries of highly uneven patterns of economic growth.

Figure 3: GDP per Capita by Region in 1820 and 1998

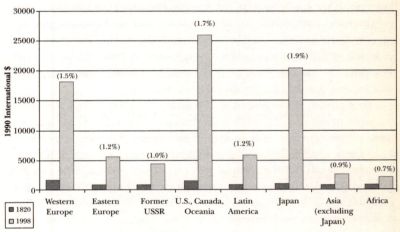

Source: Data from Maddison (2001): average annual growth rate in parentheses.

This inequality is evident in the bar chart in figure 3. The height of the first bar indicates the level of per capita income in 1820, and the second in 1998, using Maddison's estimates. The number in parentheses at the top of the second bar is the average annual growth rate of the region (between 1820 and 1998). Three main points stand out:

• All regions were poor in 1820

• All regions experienced economic progress

• Today's rich regions experienced by far the greatest economic progress

What do I mean by "highly uneven" economic growth across regions between 1820 and 1998? Even small differences in annual economic growth rates, if sustained for decades or centuries, eventually lead to huge differences in the levels of economic well-being (as measured here by the average per capita income in a society). The per capita gross national product of the United States, for example, grew at an annual rate of around 1.7 percent per year during the period 1820 to 1998. This led to a twenty-five-fold increase in living standards, with per capita incomes rising from around $1,200 per person in 1820 to around $30,000 today (in 1990 dollars). The key for the United States to become the world's richest major economy was not spectacularly fast growth, such as China's recent achievement of 8 percent growth per year, but rather steady growth at a much more modest 1.7 percent per year. The key was consistency, the fact that the United States maintained that income growth rate for almost two centuries.

By contrast, the economies of Africa have grown at an average of 0.7 percent per year. This difference may not seem like much compared with 1.7 percent per year in the United States, but over a period of 180 years a small difference in annual growth leads to huge differences in income levels. With growth of 0.7 percent per annum, Africa's initial income (roughly $400 per capita) increased by little more than three-fold, to roughly $1,300 per capita as of the year 1998, compared with an almost twenty-five-fold increase in the United States. Today's twenty-fold gap in income between the United States and Africa, therefore, results from a three-fold gap as of 1820, which was magnified seven times by the difference in annual growth rates of 1.7 percent in the United States versus 0.7 percent in Africa.

The crucial puzzle for understanding today's vast inequalities, therefore, is to understand why different regions of the world have grown at different rates during the period of modern economic growth. Every region began the period in extreme poverty. Only one sixth of the world's population achieved high-income status through consistent economic growth. Another two thirds have risen to middle-income status with more modest rates of economic growth. One sixth of humanity is stuck in extreme poverty, with very low rates of economic growth during the whole period. First we must understand why growth rates differ over long periods of time so that we can identify the key ways to raise economic growth in today's lagging regions.

Let me dispose of one idea right from the start. Many people assume that the rich have gotten rich *because* the poor have gotten poor. In other words, they assume that Europe and the United States used military force and political strength during and after the era of colonialism to extract wealth from the poorest regions, and thereby to grow rich. This interpretation of events would be plausible if gross world product had remained roughly constant, with a rising share going to the powerful regions and a declining share going to the poorer regions. However, that is not at all what happened. Gross world product rose nearly fiftyfold. Every region of the world experienced some economic growth (both in terms of the overall size of the economy, and even when measured per person), but some regions experienced much more growth than others. The key fact of modern times is not the *transfer* of income from one region to another, by force or otherwise, but rather the overall *increase* in world income, but at a different rate in different regions.

This is not to say that the rich are innocent of the charge of having exploited the poor. They surely have, and the poor countries continue to suffer as a result in countless ways, including chronic problems of political instability. However, the real story of modern economic growth has been the ability of some regions to achieve unprecedented long-term increases in total production to levels never before seen in the world, while other regions stagnated, at least by comparison. Technology has been the main force behind the long-term increases in income in the rich world, not exploitation of the poor. That news is very good indeed because it suggests that all of the world, including today's laggard regions, has a reasonable hope of reaping the benefits of technological advance. Economic development is not a zero-sum game in which the winnings of some are inevitably mirrored by the losses of others. This game is one that everybody can win.

On the Eve of Takeoff

Until the mid-1700s, the world was remarkably poor by any of today's standards. Life expectancy was extremely low; children died in vast numbers in the now rich countries as well as the poor countries. Many waves of disease and epidemics, from the black death of Europe to smallpox and measles, regularly washed through society and killed mass numbers of people. Episodes of hunger and extreme weather and climate fluctuations sent societies crashing. The rise and fall of the Roman Empire, for famed twentieth-century historian Arnold Toynbee, was much like the rise and decline of all other civilizations before and since. Economic history had long been one of ups and downs, with growth followed by decline rather than sustained economic progress.

John Maynard Keynes wrote about this virtual stagnation of human economic progress in his 1930 essay on the *Economic Possibilities for Our Grandchildren*:

> From the earliest times from which we have record, that, say, the two thousand years before Christ, down to the beginning of the eighteenth century, there was no really great change in the standard of living of the average man living in the civilized centers of the earth. Ups and downs, certainly visitations of plague, famine and war, golden intervals, but no progressive violent change. Some periods perhaps fifty percent better than others, at the utmost a hundred percent better in the four thousand years that ended, say, in A.D. 1700.

He also pinpointed technology as the reason for this long-term stasis:

> The absence of important technological inventions between the prehistoric age and comparatively modern times is truly remarkable. Almost everything which really matters, and which the world possessed at the commencement of the modern age, was already known to man at the dawn of history: language, fire, the same domestic animals which we have today, wheat, barley, the vine and the olive, the plow and the wheel, the oar, the sail, leather, linen and cloth, bricks and pots, gold and silver, copper, tin, and lead—and iron was added to the list before one thousand B.C.—banking, statecraft, mathematics, astronomy, and religion. There is no record when we first possessed these . . .

What changed was the onset of the Industrial Revolution, supported by a rise in agricultural productivity in northwestern Europe. Food yields rose with systematic improvements in agronomic practice, including the management of soil nutrients through improved crop rotations. The dramatic breakthrough came in England around 1750, when Britain's nascent industry first mobilized new forms of energy for production at scales that had never before been achieved. The steam engine marked the decisive turning point of modern history. By mobilizing a vast store of primary energy, fossil fuels, the steam engine unlocked the mass production of goods and services on a scale beyond the wildest dreams of the preindustrial era. Modern energy fueled every aspect of the economic takeoff. Food production soared as fossil fuel energy was used to produce chemical fertilizers; industrial production skyrocketed as vast inputs of fossil fuel energy created equally vast powerhouses of steel, transport equipment, chemicals and pharmaceuticals, textile and apparels, and every other modern manufacturing sector. By the early twentieth century, the service industries, including modern information and communications technologies, were powered by electrification, itself a breakthrough of the fossil-fuel age.

As coal fueled industry, so, too, industry fueled political power. The British Empire became the global political manifestation of the Industrial Revolution. Britain's industrial breakthrough, unique in the world as of the early nineteenth century, created a huge military and financial advantage that allowed Britain to expand its control over one sixth of humanity at the peak of the empire during the Victorian era.

Why was Britain first? Why not China, which was the world's technological leader for about a thousand years, between A.D. 500 and A.D. 1500? Why not other centers of power on the European continent or in Asia? This question is much debated among economic historians, but a few good answers are evident, and they provide clues to the deeper underpinnings of the Industrial Revolution.

First, British society was relatively open, with more scope for individual initiative and social mobility than most other societies of the world. The fixed social orders of the feudal era had weakened enormously or disappeared entirely by 1500, at a time when serfdom was still the rule through much of Europe. Even more rigid social hierarchies, such as India's caste system, were common in other parts of the world.

Second, Britain had strengthening institutions of political liberty. Britain's parliament and its traditions of free speech and open debate were powerful contributors to the uptake of new ideas. They were also increasingly powerful protectors of private property rights, which in turn underpinned individual initiative.

Third, and critically, Britain became one of the leading centers of Europe's scientific revolution. After centuries in which Europe was mainly the importer of scientific ideas from Asia, European science made pivotal advances beginning in the Renaissance. Modern physics emerged from the astronomical discoveries of Copernicus, Brahe, Kepler, and Galileo. With Britain's political openness, speculative scientific thinking was given opportunity to thrive, and the scientific advances on the Continent stimulated an explosion of scientific discovery in England. The decisive breakthrough came with Isaac Newton's *Principia Mathematica* in 1687, one of the most important books ever written. By showing that physical phenomena could be described by mathematical laws, and by providing the tools of calculus to discover those laws, Newton set the stage for hundreds of years of scientific and technological discovery, and for the Industrial Revolution that would follow the scientific revolution.

Fourth, Britain had several crucial geographical advantages. First, as an island economy close to continental Europe, Britain enjoyed low-cost sea-based trade with all parts of Europe. Britain also had extensive navigable river ways for internal trade and enjoyed a highly favorable environment for agriculture, with a combination of plentiful rainfall, an ample growing season, and good soils. Another crucial geographical advantage was Britain's proximity to North America. The new settlements in North America provided vast new territories for food production and raw materials such as cotton for British industry, and they were the safety valve that facilitated the exodus of impoverished people from the British countryside. As England's own agricultural productivity grew, with more food produced by fewer people, millions of landless poor went to North America.

In his seminal 1776 work, *The Wealth of Nations,* Adam Smith referred to Britain's natural advantages:

> England, on account of the natural fertility of the soil, of the great extent of the sea-coast in proportion to that of the whole country, and of the many navigable rivers which run through it and afford the conveniency of water carriage to some of the most inland parts of it, is perhaps as well fitted by nature as any large country in Europe to be the seat of foreign commerce, of manufactures for distant sale and of all the improvements which these can occasion.

Fifth, Britain remained sovereign and faced lesser risk of invasion than its neighbors. Being an island helped considerably, much the same way that Japan's insular geography allowed it to escape invasion despite numerous attempts from the Asian mainland. Indeed, with a one-century lag, Japan was to play a role similar to Britain's as the leader of Asia's takeoff to modern economic growth on the other side of the Eurasian land mass.

Sixth, Britain had coal, and with the invention of the steam engine, coal freed society from energy constraints that had limited the scale of economic production throughout human history. Before coal, economic production was limited by energy inputs, almost all of which depended on the production of biomass: food for humans and farm animals and fuel wood for heating and certain industrial processes. Wind power could also be harnessed for sea transport, and wind and water power could be harnessed for some industrial processes. None of these energy sources, however, could unleash the potential for mass production that coal did.

Britain's advantages, in summary, were marked by a combination of social, political, and geographical factors. British society was relatively free and politically stable. Scientific thinking was dynamic. Geography enabled Britain to benefit from trade, productive agriculture, and energy resources in vast stocks of coal. Other parts of the world were not as fortunate to have this confluence of favorable factors. Their entry into modern economic growth would be delayed. In the most disadvantaged environments, modern economic growth has been delayed until today.

The Great Transformation

The combination of new industrial technologies, coal power, and market forces created the Industrial Revolution. The Industrial Revolution, in turn, led to the most revolutionary economic events in human history since the start of agriculture ten thousand years earlier. Suddenly, economies could grow beyond long-accustomed bounds without hitting the biological constraints of food and timber production. Industrial production grew rapidly, and the power of economic growth spilled out from Great Britain to all parts of the world. Societies the world over were fundamentally changed, often tumultuously.

The Industrial Revolution, and the modern economic growth that followed, has changed the way people live in every fundamental sense: where and how they live, what kind of work or economic activity they perform, how they form families. In Britain first, and then elsewhere, industrialization meant a shift of people from overwhelmingly agrarian activities to industrial activities, giving rise to urbanization, social mobility, new gender and family roles, a demographic transition, and specialization in labor.

Modern economic growth is accompanied first and foremost by *urbanization,* that is, by a rising share of a nation's population living in urban areas. There are two basic reasons why economic growth and urbanization go hand in hand. The first is rising agricultural productivity. As food production per farmer rises, an economy needs fewer and fewer farmers to feed the overall population. As food production per farmer rises, food prices fall, inducing farmers and especially their children to seek employment in nonfarm activities. The second is the advantage of high-density urban life for most nonfarm economic activities, especially the face-to-face demands of commerce and other parts of the service sector. Sparsely populated rural areas make good economic sense when each household needs a lot of land for farm production. But they make little sense when people are engaged mainly in manufacturing, finance, commerce, and the like. Once the labor force is no longer engaged mainly in food production, it is natural that the bulk of the population will relocate to cities, drawn by higher wages that in turn reflect the higher productivity of work in densely settled urban areas.

Modern economic growth has also produced a revolution in *social mobility.* Established social rankings—such as the fixed hierarchical divisions between peasants and gentry, or within the Indian caste structure, or in the social orders of nobility, priests, merchants, and farmers that characterized many traditional Asian societies—all unravel under the forces of market-based modern economic growth. Fixed social orders depend on a static and largely agrarian economic setting where little changes in living standards or technologies from one generation to the next. They cannot withstand the sudden and dramatic bursts of technological change that occur during modern economic growth, in which occupations and social roles shift dramatically from one generation to the next, rather than being inherited by sons from fathers and daughters from mothers.

One aspect of changing social mobility requires special note, the change in *gender roles.* Traditional societies tend to be strongly differentiated in gender roles, with women almost always getting the short end of the deal. In settings where the total fertility rate—the average number of children per woman—is typically at least five, and often much higher, women spend most of their adult lives rearing children. Traditionally homebound, women live lives of back-breaking labor on the farm, endless walking to collect fuel wood and water, and child rearing. With modern economic growth, this dynamic changes. Women can avail themselves of urban-based employment, as in the case of the young women in the apparel factories of Dhaka, leading them ultimately toward social and political empowerment.

The changes in living conditions and economic activities lead to new realities in *family structure* as well. The age of marriage is typically delayed, and sexual relations are transformed, with greater sexual freedom much less directly linked to child rearing. Fewer generations of family members live under one roof. And crucially, the desired number of children changes remarkably as families move from rural to urban settings. In rural societies, large families are almost always the norm. In urban societies, families choose to have fewer children. This is the crux of the demographic transition, one of the most fundamental of all social changes during the era of modern economic growth.

One more crucial element occurs with deep structural change: the *division of labor* increases, as people become more and more specialized in their skills. The talents of a poor rural farmer in Africa today, or in Scotland at the time of Adam Smith, are truly marvelous. These farmers typically know how to build their own houses, grow and cook food, tend to animals, and make their own clothing. They are, therefore, construction workers, veterinarians and agronomists, and apparel manufacturers. They do it all, and their abilities are deeply impressive.

They are also deeply inefficient. Adam Smith pointed out that specialization, where each of us learns just one of those skills, leads to a general improvement of everybody's well-being. The idea is simple and powerful. By specializing in just one activity—such as food raising, clothing production, or home construction—each worker gains mastery over the particular activity. Specialization makes sense, however, only if the specialist can subsequently trade his or her output with the output of specialists in other lines of activity. It would make no sense to produce more food than a household needs unless there is a market outlet to trade that excess food for clothing, shelter, and so forth. At the same time, without the ability to buy food on the market, it would not be possible to be a specialist home builder or clothing maker, since it would be necessary to farm for one's own survival. Thus Smith realized that the division of labor is limited by the extent of the market (that is, by the ability to trade), whereas the extent of the market is determined by the degree of specialization (and hence, productivity).

THE SPREAD OF MODERN ECONOMIC GROWTH

Modern economic growth first emerged in England because of the confluence of favorable conditions. However, these conditions were not unique to England, and once the Industrial Revolution was under way, the same combination of modern technologies and social organization could spread to other parts of the world. What started in one corner of Northern Europe would eventually reach almost the entire planet. In doing so, the forces of modern economic growth propelled a general increase in global production of unprecedented dimensions.

On paper, the transition to modern economic growth might appear to be an unambiguous and straightforward benefit for the world. After all, new technologies enabled society to harness energy and ideas that raised labor productivity (economic output per person) to levels never before imagined. This productivity brought about a rise in living standards of unprecedented scale. Yet the transition was more tumultuous than not, involving vast social struggles and often war. Before turning to the historical record, it is worth considering for a moment why the transition was so difficult in so many places.

Most important, modern economic growth was not only a question of "more" (output per person) but also "change." The transition to modern economic growth involved urbanization, changing gender roles, increased social mobility, changing family structure, and increasing specialization. These were difficult transitions, involving multiple upheavals in social organization and in cultural beliefs. In addition, the spread of modern economic growth was also marked by a systematic and repeated confrontation between the world's newly rich countries and the world's still poor countries. Since modern economic growth occurred at such different rates in different places, it created an extent of inequality of global wealth and power that was unique in human history. Britain's industrial dominance—the result of Britain's lead in industrialization—gave it a unique military dominance as well, which it in turn converted to empire. More generally, Europe's early industrialization in the nineteenth century ended up fueling a vast European empire throughout Asia, Africa, and the Americas.

Finally, the vast differences in power contributed to faulty social theories of these differences that are still with us today. When a society is economically dominant, it is easy for its members to assume that such dominance reflects a deeper superiority—whether religious, racial, genetic, cultural, or institutional—rather than an accident of timing or geography. Thus the inequality of power and economics of the nineteenth century in favor of Europe was accompanied by the spread of new forms of racism and "culturism," which offered pseudoscientific justifications for the vast inequalities that had opened. These theories in turn justified brutal forms of exploitation of the poor through colonial rule, dispossession of the properties and lands of the poor by the rich, and even slavery.

Still, despite these difficulties, the basic underlying forces that propelled the Industrial Revolution could be and were replicated elsewhere. As they were replicated, multiple sites of industrialization and economic growth took hold. Like a chain reaction, the more places that were undergoing this change, the more they interacted with each other and thereby created the bases for yet more innovations, more economic growth, and more technological activity. Britain's industrialization spread to other markets in several ways: by stimulating the demand for exports from Britain's trading partners, by supplying those trading partners with British capital to make investments in infrastructure (for example, ports and railroads), and by spreading technologies first pioneered in Britain.

This diffusion of modern economic growth occurred in three main forms. The first, and in some ways, most direct spread of the Industrial Revolution was from Britain to its colonies in North America, Australia, and New Zealand. All three regions are in temperate zones with conditions for farming and other economic activities similar in many ways to those of Britain. It was therefore relatively straightforward to transplant British technologies, food crops, and even legal institutions into these new settings. These new homes of modern economic growth were literally a "New England," in the case of the North American seacoast, or a "Western offshoots" in the phrase of Angus Maddison. Ideologically, the imperial powers and colonizers considered North America and Oceania to be empty places, despite the presence of native inhabitants in both regions. By slaughtering, cornering, or removing these native inhabitants from their lands, England's new colonizers fueled a huge expansion of population and subsequent economic growth of North America and Oceania.

A second form of diffusion took place within Europe itself, broadly in a process that ran from Western Europe to Eastern Europe and from Northern Europe to Southern Europe during the nineteenth century. Northwestern Europe started with certain advantages over Eastern and Southern Europe. First, northwestern Europe is on the Atlantic side of the continent, and therefore had benefited more than Eastern Europe from the great explosion of ocean-based trade with the Americas and Asia. Second, northwestern Europe generally had more favorable natural resources, including coal, timber, rivers (for water-powered mills), and rainfall. Third, northwestern Europe generally benefited from a more benign disease environment, less vulnerable to tropical and subtropical diseases like malaria. Fourth, for a host of reasons, some understood and others much debated, the political and social conditions were more favorable. Serfdom had essentially disappeared in much of northwestern Europe by the seventeenth century, whereas serfdom and other social rigidities were far more intact in the south and east. Germany and Italy were still not nation states by the start of the Industrial Revolution, and they suffered from extremely high barriers to trade among competing principalities.

When the Industrial Revolution began, and especially when it began to spread in the midst of and after the Napoleonic Wars, the obstacles to development in Southern and Eastern Europe began to diminish. Serfdom was abolished, fitfully, often violently, across Europe. Constitutional governance was introduced. Railways were established to link European regions. Ideas and technologies flowed with ever greater speed and were backed by ever larger amounts of financial capital. By the end of the nineteenth century, industrialization was making itself felt throughout all of Europe.

The third diffusion involved the spread of modern economic growth from Europe to Latin America, Africa, and Asia. The process was tumultuous everywhere, involving the confrontation of an increasingly industrialized and rich Europe with nonindustrialized, largely rural, and militarily weak societies in other parts of the world. Some were ancient civilizations with grand traditions, like China or Japan; some were sparsely populated regions like those in much of tropical Africa. But the great drama that ensued almost everywhere was the turmoil of confrontation between these different societies, economies, and cultures. Even when it raised living standards, modern economic growth brought fundamental change to social organization and painful clashes with the more powerful Europeans.

The confrontation between rich and poor was very stark because the gap of wealth also meant the gap of power, and power could be used for exploitation. Europe's superior power was used repeatedly to compel actions by the weaker societies on behalf of the richer overlords. European imperial powers forced Africans to grow cash crops they chose. Colonial authorities imposed head taxes, compelling Africans to work in mines and on plantations, often hundreds of miles from their families and homes. European investors and governments commandeered natural resources, including mineral wealth and vast woodlands in Africa and Asia. Private European companies maintained private armies in the colonies to ensure compliance with company "law," knowing as well that their national governments would back them up with military force in extremis.

The Cascade of Technological Change

Living standards began to rise in many parts of the world, even with all this brutality and suffering in places that had succumbed to colonial rule, and even in places where colonial masters, rather than the local populations, grabbed much of the increased economic output. Often the climb out of extreme poverty was very gradual and fitful, set back by war and famine. Occasionally it was rapid, such as Japan's economic takeoff and industrialization in the last quarter of the nineteenth century.

I believe that the single most important reason why prosperity spread, and why it continues to spread, is the transmission of technologies and the ideas underlying them. Even more important than having specific resources in the ground, such as coal, was the ability to use modern, science-based ideas to organize production. The beauty of ideas is that they can be used over and over again, without ever being depleted. Economists call ideas nonrival in the sense that one person's use of an idea does not diminish the ability of others to use it as well. This is why we can envision a world in which everybody achieves prosperity. The essence of the first Industrial Revolution was not the coal; it was how to use the coal. Even more generally, it was about how to use a new form of energy. The lessons of coal eventually became the basis for many other energy systems as well, from hydropower, oil and gas, and nuclear power to new forms of renewable energy such as wind and solar power converted to electricity. These lessons are available to all of humanity, not just for the first individuals who discovered them.

The first wave of the Industrial Revolution was the development of the steam engine and related technologies, including the organization of large-scale factory production, new machinery in the textile and apparel sector, and new techniques to produce steel. A second wave of technological breakthroughs came in the middle of the nineteenth century with the rail, and even more notably the telegraph, which offered the first instantaneous telecommunications around the world, a phenomenal breakthrough in the ability to diffuse information on a large scale.

The second technological wave also included ocean steamers, global-scale trade, and two huge infrastructure projects: the Suez Canal, completed in 1869, which significantly shortened the trade time between Europe and Asia, and the Panama Canal, completed in 1914, which dramatically reduced the trade time between the U.S. eastern seaboard and destinations in the western United States, much of Latin America, and East Asia. Epidemics of yellow fever and malaria that killed thousands of workers delayed the first attempt to build the canal in the 1880s. Once scientists understood that mosquitoes were transmitting those killer diseases, the canal builders made a full-fledged effort to control the mosquito breeding alongside the construction of the canal and thereby completed the project in 1914.

The third wave of technological advance involved electrification of industry and urban society at the end of the nineteenth century, including Edison's invention of the incandescent bulb and other electronic appliances. Edison, Westinghouse, and others championed large power plants that could bring electricity into homes, office buildings, and factories by wire, which was the defining new infrastructure of the early twentieth century. The development of the internal combustion engine was also critical, as was the pivotal advance in the chemical industry, mainly in Germany, with the new process for taking atmospheric nitrogen and converting it into ammonia for fertilizer (the Haber-Bosch process). This use of fossil fuel energy to create nitrogen-based fertilizers was the breakthrough advance in raising food production in the twentieth century, enabling a great proportion of humanity, though still not all of it, to overcome chronic hunger and the risks of famine that had forever plagued humankind.

These waves of technological advance diffused around the world through the spread of trade and foreign investment; with it, economic prosperity spread to other parts of the world as well. But so, too, did the global system of European political domination. This domination reflected the vast inequality of power that grew out of Europe's head start in industrialization, a head start that we have seen is rooted in an advantageous confluence of politics, geography, and resource base.

By the early twentieth century, Europe largely dominated the world. European empires controlled essentially all of Africa and large parts of Asia, and loomed large in financing and organizing Latin America's trade as well. This was the first age of globalization, an era of global trade, an era of global communications over telegraph lines, an era of mass production and industrialization—in short, what would seem to be an era of inevitable progress. And it was globalization under European domination. It was viewed as not only economically unstoppable, but also as the natural order of things. This imagined natural order gave rise to the infamous "white man's burden," the right and obligation of European and European-descended whites to rule the lives of others around the world, which they blithely did with a contradictory mix of naïveté, compassion, and brutality.

The Great Rupture

At the beginning of the twentieth century, globalization was viewed as so inevitable that some thought war itself was probably passé, and certainly so irrational that no right-thinking leader in Europe would ever take his country to war. In 1910, a leading British pundit, Norman Angell, wrote *The Great Illusion,* which rightly argued that national economies had become so interdependent, so much part of a global division of labor, that war among the economic leaders had become unimaginably destructive. War, Angell warned, would so undermine the network of international trade that no military venture by a European power against another could conceivably lead to economic benefits for the aggressor. He surmised that war itself would cease once the costs and benefits of war were more clearly understood.

Angell tremendously underestimated the irrationalities and social processes that lead to devastating outcomes, even when they make no sense. Angell was therefore half right: war had become much too dangerous to use for economic gain. But it didn't stop war from happening.

The year 1914 began the great rupture of the twentieth century, even more dramatic a rupture than World War II would prove to be.

Why was World War I so dramatic and so traumatic? It ended the era of European-led globalization. Its death toll was staggering, and it led to several cataclysmic events that cast their shadow over the rest of the century. The first side effect was that it destabilized the Russian czarist regime, unleashing the Bolshevik revolution. A relatively backward Russia, which had been the last country in Europe to come out of serfdom, fell into turmoil under the fiscal and human burdens of war. Vladimir Lenin and a small group of conspirators were able to seize power with very little popular support and institute a revolutionary doctrine that sent Russia on a seventy-five-year detour of enormous brutality and economic waste. At their maximum extent, the communist doctrines that Lenin and Joseph Stalin instituted in Russia ensnared roughly a third of the world's population, including the former Soviet Union, China, the Eastern European states under Soviet domination, Cuba, North Korea, and other self-styled revolutionary states aligned with the Soviet Union.

Another great consequence of World War I was the prolonged financial instability it created in Europe after the war. The war created a morass of interlocking financial and economic problems, including the mountain of debt incurred by combatant countries; the destruction and dismembering of the Ottoman and Hapsburg empires and their replacement by small, unstable, and feuding successor states; and the Allied claims for reparation payments from Germany, which embittered the next generation of Germans and was one of the rallying points for Hitler's rise to power.

John Maynard Keynes understood that the world as he knew it had been brought to an end after World War I. In his famous essay on *The Economic Consequences of the Peace*, Keynes masterfully captured all that had been lost:

> What an extraordinary episode in the economic progress of man that age was which came to an end in August 1914! The greater part of the population, it is true, worked hard and lived at a low standard of comfort, yet were, to all appearances, reasonably contented with this lot. But escape was possible, for any man of capacity or character at all exceeding the average, into the middle and upper classes, for whom life offered, at a low cost and with the least trouble, conveniences, comforts, and amenities beyond the compass of the rich-

est and most powerful monarchs of other ages. The inhabitant of London could order by telephone, sipping his morning tea in bed, the various products of the whole earth, in such quantity as he might see fit, and reasonably expect their early delivery upon his doorstep; he could at the same moment and by the same means adventure his wealth in the natural resources and new enterprises of any quarter of the world, and share, without exertion or even trouble, in their prospective fruits and advantages; or he could decide to couple the security of his fortunes with the good faith of the townspeople of any substantial municipality in any continent that fancy or information might recommend. He could secure forthwith, if he wished it, cheap and comfortable means of transit to any country or climate without passport or other formality, could despatch his servant to the neighbouring office of a bank for such supply of the precious metals as might seem convenient, and could then proceed abroad to foreign quarters, without knowledge of their religion, language, or customs, bearing coined wealth upon his person, and would consider himself greatly aggrieved and much surprised at the least interference. But, most important of all, he regarded this state of affairs as normal, certain, and permanent, except in the direction of further improvement, and any deviation from it as aberrant, scandalous, and avoidable.

As Keynes stressed, in a message for our time, the end of this era was simply unimaginable:

> The projects and politics of militarism and imperialism, of racial and cultural rivalries, of monopolies, restrictions, and exclusion, which were to play the serpent to this paradise, were little more than the amusements of his daily newspaper, and appeared to exercise almost no influence at all on the ordinary course of social and economic life, the internationalisation of which was nearly complete in practice.

The economic instability that followed World War I led to the Great Depression of the 1930s and then to World War II. The linkages are subtle and debated in detail, but undeniable in basic fact. The overhang of bad debts, shrunken trade within Europe, and overstretched budgets of the European powers meant that inflation, stabilization, and austerity were the orders of the day throughout the 1920s. The European countries duly climbed one by one back to the gold standard, viewed at the time as the guarantor of long-term financial stability. Alas, the return to the gold standard did little more than exacerbate the conditions that had prevailed in the 1920s. Most important, the gold standard and its "rules of the game" for monetary management made it difficult if not impossible for the major economies to escape from a slide into deep depression in the early 1930s. The Great Depression, in turn, triggered a calamitous spread of trade protectionism and the rise of Nazism in Germany and military rule in Japan.

By the end of World War II, the pre-1914 global system had gone to pieces. International trade was moribund. National currencies were not convertible one to another, so even the basic payments mechanisms for international commerce had broken down. Mercifully, the age of European imperialism was also coming to an end, although it would take decades longer, and many wars, for it to end decisively. Still, standing on the ruins of World War II, the benefits of a global marketplace—with a global division of labor, a peaceful spread of technology, and open international trade—looked long gone, buried under the rubble of two world wars and a great depression.

RECONSTRUCTING A GLOBAL ECONOMY

Much work between the end of World War II in 1945 and the end of the Soviet Union in 1991 went into reconstructing a new global economic system. The immediate struggle was physical reconstruction: to repair or rebuild the roads, bridges, power stations, and ports that underpinned national economic production and international trade. Yet the "plumbing" of the international economy also needed to be reconstructed, with currency arrangements and rules for international trade that would permit the market-based flow of goods and services, and the productivity gains that would emerge from a renewed global division of labor. This reconstruction effort took place in three steps.

First, the countries already industrialized as of 1945—Europe, the United States, Japan—reconstructed a new international trading system under U.S. political leadership. Step by step, these countries reestablished currency convertibility (in which businesses and individuals could buy and sell foreign exchange at market rate) in order to create a payments system for international trade. The European currencies became convertible again in 1958. The yen became convertible again in 1964. At the same time, these countries agreed to reduce the trade barriers, including high tariffs and quotas, which they had put in place in the chaos of the Great Depression. The trade barriers came down in several rounds of international trade negotiations handled under the auspices of the General Agreement on Tariffs and Trade (GATT), a set of rules that constituted the forerunner to today's World Trade Organization. The rich world, soon called the first world, succeeded in reconstructing a market-based trading system. With it came a burst of rapid economic growth, a powerful recovery after decades of war, blocked trade, and financial instability.

The restoration of trade in the first world did not, however, mean the restoration of a global economy. The divisions in the world economy after 1945 went deeper than currency inconvertibility and trade barriers. By the end of the World War II, the world had become starkly divided in political terms that mirrored the economic ruptures. These divisions would last for decades and are only now being healed.

The second world was the socialist world, the world first forged by Lenin and Stalin in the wake of World War I. The second world remained cut off economically from the first world until the fall of the Berlin Wall in 1989 and the end of the Soviet Union in 1991. At its peak, the second world included around thirty countries (depending on the criteria for inclusion), and included about a third of humanity. The overriding characteristics of the second world were state ownership of the means of production, central planning of production, one-party rule by communist parties, and economic integration within the socialist world (through barter trade) combined with economic separation from the first world.

The third world included the rapidly rising number of postcolonial countries. Today we use the term *third world* simply to mean poor. Earlier on, the third world had a more vivid connotation as a group of countries emerging from imperial domination that chose neither to be part of the capitalist first world nor the socialist second world. These were the true third-way countries. The ideas at the core of the third world were: "We will develop on our own. We will nurture industry, sometimes through state ownership, sometimes by giving subsidies and protection to private business, but we will do it without foreign multinationals. We will do it without open international trade. We do not trust the outside world. We want to stay nonaligned. The first world countries are not our heroes; they were our former colonial powers. The second world leaders are not to be trusted either. We do not want the Soviet Union to swallow us. Therefore, politically we are non-aligned, and economically we are self-sufficient."

Thus, the post–World War II world evolved on three tracks. The fundamental problem, however, was that the second world and third world approaches did not make economic sense, and they both collapsed under a pile of foreign debt. Second world central planning was a bad idea, and so, too, was third world autarky, in both cases for reasons that Adam Smith had explained. By closing their economies, both the second world and third world countries also closed themselves off from global economic progress and the advance of technology. They created high-cost local industries that could not compete internationally even when they chose to try. The closed nature of these societies, in which domestic businesses were sheltered from competition, fostered a great deal of corruption. The nonaligned third world countries lost the chance to participate in the technological advance of the first world mainly because they did not trust the first world. They were understandably intent on protecting their hard-won sovereignty, even when that sovereignty was not really at risk.

My own work as an economist began at a time when the second world and the third world economies were already economically moribund, and were falling into a deepening spiral of economic chaos. The early manifestations of that crisis, typically, were rising levels of foreign debt and increasing rates of inflation. My early work centered on macroeconomic stabilization—the end of high inflation—and this work brought me into contact with countries that were isolated from first world markets and technology. This early work involved technical monetary economics, but it brought me face to face with the more basic and fundamental choices of how countries should relate economically to the broader world.

By the early 1990s, the overwhelming majority of countries of the second world and third world were saying, "We need to be part of the global economy once again. We want our sovereignty; we want our self-determination, but we will abandon Leninist-Stalinist central planning because it doesn't work. And we will abandon the idea of self-imposed autarky, because economic isolation makes no more sense for a country than it does for an individual." In essence, one of my roles from the mid-1980s onward was to help countries to become sovereign members of a new international system. I repeatedly dealt with three big questions: What is the best way back to international trade? How do we escape from the barnacles of bad debts and inefficient industry? How do we negotiate new rules of the game to ensure that the emerging global economy would truly serve the needs of all of the countries of the world, not only the richest and most powerful?

TWO HUNDRED YEARS OF MODERN ECONOMIC GROWTH

I have touched lightly and briefly on two hundred years of modern economic growth—complete with change, turmoil, conflict, and ideology. What has this era of modern economic growth brought the world? Higher living standards than were imaginable two centuries ago, a spread of modern technology to most parts of the world, and a scientific and technological revolution that still gains strength. Living standards are much higher in almost all places than they were at the start of the process, the major exception being the disease-ravaged parts of Africa.

But modern economic growth has also brought phenomenal gaps between the richest and poorest, gaps that were simply impossible when poverty gripped all of the world. The era of modern economic growth has bequeathed us an economic picture of the world as seen in map 2, where each country is shaded according to its per capita GDP (measured in purchasing-power adjusted prices) as of 2002. The rich world (above $20,000 in per capita income) is shaded green, and includes the United States, Canada, Western Europe, Japan, Australia, and New Zealand. The countries in the middle-income range (between $4,000 and $20,000) are shaded in yellow, and include most of East Asia (such as Korea and Singapore), Central Europe, the former Soviet Union, and Latin America. Countries within the upper end of the low-income range (between $2,000 and $4,000) are shaded in orange, and include parts of South America, South Asia, and East Asia. The poorest countries (below $2,000) are shaded in red, and are concentrated in sub-Saharan Africa and South Asia. There is, of course, a striking similarity between this map of average GNP per person and the map showing the proportion of households in poverty (map 1): the low-income countries are, notably, the countries with high proportions of moderate and extreme poverty.

So why does a vast gulf divide one sixth of humanity today in the richest countries from the one sixth of the world barely able to sustain life? The richest countries were able to achieve two centuries of modern economic growth. The poorest did not even begin their economic growth until decades later, and then often under tremendous obstacles. In some cases, they faced the brutal exploitation of dominant colonial powers. They faced geographical barriers (related to climate, food production, disease, energy resources, topography, proximity to world markets) that had not burdened the early industrial economies like Great Britain and the United States. And they made disastrous choices in their own national policies, often until the past decade. All of this left them without the good fortune of two centuries of rapid economic growth, instead growing only sporadically during a few years.

The key point for these countries is that there are practical solutions to almost all of their problems. Bad policies of the past can be corrected. The colonial era is truly finished. Even the geographical obstacles can be overcome with new technologies, such as those that control malaria or allow for large crop yields in marginal production areas. But as there is no single explanation for why certain parts of the world remain poor, there is also no single remedy. As I shall stress repeatedly in the pages ahead, a good plan of action starts with a good differential diagnosis of the specific factors that have shaped the economic conditions of a nation.

Three

WHY SOME COUNTRIES
FAIL TO THRIVE

Of the world's population of 6.3 billion, roughly 5 billion people have reached at least the first rung of economic development. Five sixths of the world's population is at least one step above extreme poverty. Morever, approximately 4.9 billion people live in countries where average income—measured by GDP per person—increased between 1980 and 2000. An even larger number, roughly 5.7 billion people, live in countries where life expectancy increased. Economic development is real and widespread. The extent of extreme poverty is shrinking, both in absolute numbers and as a proportion of the world's population. That fact is why we can realistically envision a world without extreme poverty as soon as 2025.

Precisely because economic development can and does work in so many parts of the world, it is all the more important to understand and solve the problems of the places where economic development is not working, where people are still off the ladder of development, or are stuck on its lowest rungs. To understand why economic growth succeeds or fails, we first need a conceptual framework that can account for changes over time in GDP per person. I have already discussed some of the factors that promote long-term development, but here I address them more systematically, including a discussion of why the process of economic development breaks down in many places, especially the poorest places. Perhaps it would be clearest to begin with a very specific case: a single farm household.

THE GROWTH OF HOUSEHOLD INCOME

Consider a household consisting of a husband, wife, and four children (two daughters and two sons) living on a two-hectare farm. The household grows maize and provides for its own shelter in an adobe hut. Being extremely poor, the family consumes its own maize harvest and earns no other cash income during most years. The children collect fuelwood in the vicinity of the farm for cooking, and fetch drinking water from a nearby spring.

This year the household produces two tons of maize per hectare, or four tons in total. Even though the household eats its own maize, the statisticians in the government will assign this household an income based on the market value of the maize. Suppose that each ton of maize sells in the local market for $150 per ton. The household's imputed annual income will be $600 ($150 per ton times four tons), or $100 per capita ($600 divided by six people). The government will add this figure to other household incomes to calculate the country's gross national product.

The family's income per capita can increase in at least four ways the following year.

Saving

The household might decide to consume only three out of the four tons of maize, and take one ton to market. With the $150, the household invests in livestock (perhaps chickens or sheep or a bull or dairy cow). The livestock generate a new stream of income, whether from improved food yields by using the bull for manure and animal traction, or the cow for sales of milk, or the animals for meat, eggs, or hides. In economic jargon, the saving has led to capital accumulation (in the form of livestock), which in turn has raised household productivity.

Trade

In a different scenario, the household learns from a neighboring farmer that it has the right kind of farmland, climate, and soil to produce vanilla beans, with a much higher income. After some deliberation, the household decides to shift to vanilla as a cash crop. The next year the household earns $800 in vanilla, and uses $600 to buy four tons of grain for food. As more vanilla farmers arise in the region, a new group of trading firms also forms, specializing in shipping and storage of vanilla, food, and farm inputs.

This pattern exemplifies Adam Smith's insight into the two-way link from specialization to expanded markets back to increased specialization. The farm household specializes in high-value vanilla farming because it lives in favorable ecological conditions for vanilla trees. It relies on the market to trade with other households, which instead specialize in producing food. As incomes rise, and the "extent of the market" increases, to use Smith's phrase, there is room for further specialization, in this case in transport services. Later on, economic activities will be further divided among firms specializing in housing construction, clothing manufacturing, road maintenance, plumbing, electricity, water and sanitation systems, and so forth.

Technology

Alternatively, an agricultural extension officer teaches the farm household how to manage the soil nutrients in a new and improved manner by planting special nitrogen-fixing trees that replenish the vital nitrogen nutrients of the soil, and to multiply the benefits by using improved grains. The new cereal varieties are faster maturing and pest resistant, and they flourish with the replenished soil nutrients. As a result, the crop yield rises in a single year to three tons of maize per hectare, or six tons in total. The income per capita therefore rises to $150 (three tons per hectare times two hectares at $150 per ton divided by six people).

Resource Boom

The farm household is able to move to a much larger and more fertile farm after the government's success in controlling the breeding of black flies, which spread African river blindness. Suddenly there are thousands of hectares of new farmland and a significant expansion of production capacity as a result. Incomes rise and hunger falls as each household in the newly opened region is able to triple its previous food output.

These four pathways to higher income are the main ways that economies grow, albeit in much more complicated settings than I have just described. In actual economies, a rise in gross domestic product (GDP) per capita is typically the result of most or all of these four processes simultaneously at work: saving and capital accumulation, increasing specialization and trade, technological advance (and a resulting rise in output for a given amount of inputs), and greater natural resources per person (and a resulting increase in the level of output per person). Although I have illustrated these pathways to rising income at the level of an individual household, in fact each of these processes operates through the interactions of thousands or millions of households linked together by markets and collective actions through public policies and public investments.

What, instead, could lead to a *reduction* of household income per capita? In general, an economy can rewind the clock, moving backward rather than forward. Here are a number of ways that this might happen.

Lack of Saving

Suppose that the household is chronically hungry and, therefore, consumes all of the four tons of maize, leaving nothing to sell to the market and no income to use to purchase a new plow. In fact, during the year, the existing plow breaks down. Next year's crop falls below four tons, and household income per person declines. The broken plow counts as capital depreciation, or a fall in the amount of capital available per worker.

Absence of Trade

In another case, suppose the household hears about the vanilla opportunity, but is unable to make use of it. There may be no road linking the farm and the regional market, so it is not possible for the household to market the vanilla or to use the proceeds to buy food. As a result, the household passes up the opportunity to specialize in a cash crop and stays with the food crop on which it depends to stay alive. Trade can similarly be hampered, or blocked altogether, by violence (which impedes the reliable shipment of goods), monetary chaos (so that money is not a reliable medium of exchange), price controls, and other forms of government intervention that may impede specialization and trade.

Technological Reversal

What if, as often happens in rural Africa, the children lose their mother and father to HIV/AIDS? The oldest child takes charge, but has not yet had time to master proper farming techniques. The next crop fails, and the children must depend on other households in the village. The family income has declined to zero because the level of technological knowledge has actually declined. Technological know-how is not automatically inherited. Each new generation must learn technological expertise.

Natural Resource Decline

To illustrate another possibility, not only is there no additional land, but part of the existing farmland gives way to environmental decline. Specifically, the household has not been able to afford fertilizer and does not know about nitrogen-fixing trees, so the nitrogen in the farmland is seriously depleted. The result is that only one hectare remains in production, and household annual income falls to a devastating $50 per capita (two tons times $150 per ton divided by six).

Adverse Productivity Shock

A natural disaster, perhaps a flood, drought, heat wave, frost, pests, or disease in the household (for example, a bout of malaria), or some combination, wipes out household income for the year.

Population Growth

A generation passes. The parents die, and the two hectares are divided between the two sons. Each son now has a wife and four children. Assuming that crop yields of two tons per hectare remain unchanged, household income per capita has declined by half because the size of the population living on the same farm has doubled. This experience has been prevalent in rural Africa's in the most recent generations.

These simple illustrations show the many ways that even a simple one-household "economy" may grow, as well as the many ways that the household economy can decline. The first task of a development specialist looking at the conditions in any particular country is to understand which of these various processes is working and which is not. Knowing that an economy is in decline is not enough. We must know why the economy is failing to achieve economic growth if we are to take steps to establish or reestablish it.

WHY COUNTRIES FAIL TO ACHIEVE ECONOMIC GROWTH

The most common explanation for why countries fail to achieve economic growth often focuses on the faults of the poor: poverty is a result of corrupt leadership and retrograde cultures that impede modern development. However, something as complex as a society's economic system has too many moving parts to presume that only one thing can go wrong. Problems can occur in different parts of the economic machine and can sometimes cascade, bringing the machine to a near halt.

In economic growth, eight major categories of problems can cause an economy to stagnate or decline. I have witnessed these kinds of disasters in many parts of the world. Each has its own different appropriate course of treatment; therefore, a good diagnosis is crucial.

The Poverty Trap: Poverty Itself as a Cause of Economic Stagnation

The key problem for the poorest countries is that poverty itself can be a trap. When poverty is very extreme, the poor do not have the ability—by themselves—to get out of the mess. Here is why: Consider the kind of poverty caused by a lack of capital per person. Poor rural villages lack trucks, paved roads, power generators, irrigation channels. Human capital is very low, with hungry, disease-ridden, and illiterate villagers struggling for survival. Natural capital is depleted: the trees have been cut down and the soil nutrients exhausted. In these conditions the need is for more capital—physical, human, natural—but that requires more saving. When people are poor, but not utterly destitute, they may be able to save. When they are utterly destitute, they need their entire income, or more, just to survive. There is no margin of income above survival that can be invested for the future.

This is the main reason why the poorest of the poor are most prone to becoming trapped with low or negative economic growth rates. They are too poor to save for the future and thereby accumulate the capital per person that could pull them out of their current misery. Table 1 shows the rate of gross domestic saving as a share of GDP for countries at different income levels. Clearly, the poorest of the poor have the lowest saving rate because they are using their income merely to stay alive.

Table 1: Saving Rates in Developing Countries by Income Level in 2002, in % of GDP	
Upper-Middle-Income Countries	25%
Lower-Middle-Income Countries	28%
Low-Income Countries	19%
Least-Developed Countries	10%

Source: World Bank (2004).

In fact, the standard measures of domestic saving, based on the official national accounts, overstate the saving of the poor because these data do not account for the fact that the poor are depleting their natural capital by cutting down trees, exhausting soils of their nutrients, mining their mineral, energy, and metal deposits, and overfishing. These forms of natural capital are not monitored in the official national accounts data and, as a result, their "depreciation" or depletion is not recognized as a form of negative saving. When a tree is cut down and sold for fuelwood, and not replanted, the earnings to the logger are counted as income, but instead should be counted as a conversion of one capital asset (the tree) into a financial asset (money).

Physical Geography

Even if the poverty trap is the right diagnosis, it still poses the question of why some impoverished countries are trapped and others are not. The answer often lies in the frequently overlooked problems of physical geography. Americans, for example, believe that they earned their wealth all by themselves. They forget that they inherited a vast continent rich in natural resources, with great soils and ample rainfall, immense navigable rivers, and thousands of miles of coastline with dozens of natural ports that provide a wonderful foundation for sea-based trade.

Other countries are not quite so favored. Many of the world's poorest countries are severely hindered by high transport costs because they are landlocked; situated in high mountain ranges; or lack navigable rivers, long coastlines, or good natural harbors. Culture does not explain the persistence of poverty in Bolivia, Ethiopia, Kyrgyzstan, or Tibet. Look instead to the mountain geography of a landlocked region facing crushing transport costs and economic isolation that stifle almost all forms of modern economic activity. Adam Smith was acutely aware of the role of high transport costs in hindering economic development. He stressed, in particular, the advantages of proximity to low-cost, sea-based trade as critical, noting that remote economies would be the last regions to achieve economic development:

> As by means of water-carriage a more extensive market is opened to every sort of industry than what land-carriage alone can afford it, so it is upon the sea-coast, and along the banks of navigable rivers, that industry of every kind naturally begins to sub-divide and improve itself, and it is frequently not till a long time after that those improvements extend themselves to the inland part of the country.

Other kinds of geographical distress are also at play. Many countries are trapped in arid conditions with low agricultural productivity or vulnerability to prolonged droughts. Most of the tropics have ecological conditions that favor killer diseases like malaria, schistosomiasis, dengue fever, and dozens of others. Sub-Saharan Africa, in particular, has an ideal rainfall, temperature, and mosquito type that make it the global epicenter of malaria, perhaps the greatest factor in slowing Africa's economic development throughout history. Jared Diamond, in his wonderful book *Guns, Germs, and Steel,* gives a magnificent account of how geography helped shape the early stages of human civilization. He offers scintillating insights into how the Americas, Africa, Europe, and Asia differed in terms of indigenous crop species, animals for domestication, ease of transport, possibilities for the spread of technology, disease ecology, and other geographically related factors in economic development. Some of these factors, of course, became much less or not at all important with the advent of modern transportation and communications and the resulting transfer of crops and animal species across different regions of the world.

Fortunately, none of these conditions is fatal to economic development. It is time to banish the bogeyman of geographical determinism, the false accusation that claims about geographical disadvantage are also claims that geography single-handedly and irrevocably determines the economic outcome of nations. The point is only that these adversities require countries to undertake additional investments that other, more fortunate, countries did not have to make. Roads can be built from a landlocked country to a port in another country. Tropical diseases can be controlled. Arid climates can be overcome with irrigation. Adverse geography poses problems that can be solved, typically through physical investments and good conservation management. But adverse geography raises the costs of solving the problems of farming, transport, and health, and thereby makes it much more likely that a country will be caught in a poverty trap.

Fiscal Trap

Even when the private economy is not impoverished, the government may lack the resources to pay for the infrastructure on which economic growth depends. Governments are critical to investing in public goods and services like primary health care, roads, power grids, ports, and the like. The government may lack the financial means to provide these public goods, however, for at least three reasons. First, the population itself may be impoverished, so taxation of the population is not feasible. Second, the government may be inept, corrupt, or incapacitated, and thereby unable to collect tax revenues. Third, the government may already be carrying a tremendous load of debt (for example, debt carried forward from an earlier decade), and must use its limited tax revenue to service the debt rather than to finance new investments. This third case is often called a debt overhang. Debt from the past crushes the prospects for growth in the future. In such circumstances, debt cancellation may be the only way to give the country a fresh start on a path of economic development.

Governance Failures

Economic development requires a government oriented toward development. The government has many roles to play. It must identify and finance the high-priority infrastructure projects, and make the needed infrastructure and social services available to the whole population, not just a select few. The government must create an environment conducive to investments by private businesses. Those investors must believe that they will be allowed to operate their business and to keep their future profits. Government must exercise self-restraint in demanding bribes or side payments. Governments must also maintain internal peace and safety so the safety of persons and property is not unduly threatened, maintain judicial systems that can define property rights and honestly enforce contracts, and defend the national territory to keep it safe from invasion.

When governments fail in any of these tasks—leaving huge gaps in infrastructure, or raising corruption to levels that impair economic activity, or failing to ensure domestic peace—the economy is sure to fail, and often to fail badly. Indeed, in extreme cases, when governments are unable to perform their most basic functions, we talk about "state failures," which are characterized by wars, revolutions, coups, anarchy, and the like. We will see later on that state failures are often not only the cause of economic disaster, but also the last stage of it. State failure and economic failure can chase each other in a dizzying and terrifying spiral of instability.

Cultural Barriers

Even when governments are trying to advance their countries, the cultural environment may be an obstacle to development. Cultural or religious norms in the society may block the role of women, for example, leaving half of the population without economic or political rights and without education, thereby undermining half of the population in its contribution to overall development. Denying women their rights and education results in cascading problems. Most important, perhaps, the demographic transition from high fertility to low fertility is delayed or blocked altogether. Poor households continue to have six or seven children because the woman's role is seen mainly as child rearing, and her lack of education means that she has few options in the labor force. In these settings women often lack basic economic security and legal rights; when they are widowed, their social circumstances turn even more dreadful, and they are left completely impoverished without hope for improvement.

Similar cultural barriers may apply to religious or ethnic minorities. Social norms may prevent certain groups from gaining access to public services (such as schooling, health facilities, or job training). These minorities may be blocked from entering universities or public sector jobs. They may face harassment in the community, including boycotts of their businesses and physical destruction of property. In extreme circumstances, as occurred in East Africa with the Indian community, wholesale "ethnic cleansing" may ensue, with many fleeing for their lives.

Geopolitics

It takes two to trade. Trade barriers erected by foreign countries can impede a poor country's economic development. These barriers are sometimes political, as when a powerful country imposes trade sanctions on a regime that it does not like. These sanctions may aim to weaken or topple a despicable regime, but often they simply impoverish the population of the targeted country without toppling the regime. Many factors in addition to trade that may affect a country's development can be manipulated from abroad for geopolitical reasons.

Lack of Innovation

Consider the plight of inventors in an impoverished country. Even if these inventors are able to develop new scientific approaches to meet local economic needs, the chances of recouping investments in research and development through later sales in the local market are very low. The local purchasing power to buy a new product is tiny, and will not provide for sufficient profits if an invention is successfully brought to market, even if the impoverished country has state-of-the-art patent legislation. The problem is not the property rights to the invention, but the size of the market.

There is, therefore, a huge difference between rich and poor countries in their tendency to innovate. Rich countries have a big market, which increases the incentive for innovation, brings new technologies to market, further raises productivity and expands the size of the market, and creates new incentives for innovation. This momentum creates, in effect, a chain reaction, which economists call endogenous growth. Innovation raises the size of the market; a larger market raises the incentives for innovation. Therefore, economic growth and innovation proceed in a mutually reinforcing process.

In the rich countries of North America, Western Europe, and East Asia, the process of massive investment in research and development, leading to sales of patent-protected products to a large market, stands at the core of economic growth. Advanced countries are typically investing 2 percent or more of their gross national product directly into the research and development process, and sometimes more than 3 percent of GDP. That investment is very sizable, with hundreds of billions of dollars invested each year in research and development activities. Moreover, these investments are not simply left to the market. Governments invest heavily, especially in the early stages of R and D (more in R, research, than in D, development, although government finance is present at both stages).

In most poor countries, especially smaller ones, the innovation process usually never gets started. Inventors do not invent because they know that they will not be able to recoup those large, fixed costs of developing a new product. Impoverished governments cannot afford to back the basic sciences in government labs and in universities. And the scientists do not stay. The result is an inequality of innovative activity that magnifies the inequality of global incomes. Although today's low-income countries have 37 percent of the world's population and 11 percent of the world's GDP (adjusted for differences in purchasing power), these countries accounted for less than 1 percent of all of the U.S.-registered patents taken out by inventors in the year 2000. The top twenty countries in patenting, all high-income countries, account for 98 percent of all patents.

Over the span of two centuries, the innovation gap is certainly one of the most fundamental reasons why the richest and the poorest countries have diverged, and why the poorest of the poor have not been able to get a foothold on growth. The rich move from innovation to greater wealth to further innovation; the poor do not. Fortunately, there are a few opportunities for innovation, although these are not as robust as we would hope.

The first is the diffusion of technology. Even when countries are not inventors of technology, they can still be beneficiaries through the importation of technology. All countries today, without exception, are using personal computers, and cell phones are reaching most parts of the world as well, even very poor places. Innovations can be imported through consumer goods, capital imports by business (in the form of machinery, for example), foreign direct investment (in which a high-tech firm sets up a factory in a poor country), or textbooks, word of mouth, and reverse engineering. History is replete with examples in which new capital goods and blueprints were simply pilfered and brought to a new location.

However, the importation of technology can be frustrated in the poorest of the poor countries. These countries may be too poor to purchase the capital goods, and they may be unattractive as places for foreign investment, given their lack of infrastructure. But there is often a much deeper problem. Many of the key breakthroughs in technology developed in the rich countries are relevant for the particular ecological conditions of the rich countries, and are not especially useful in the tropical, or arid, or mountain environments where so many of the extreme poor live today. The massive investments in biomedical research in the rich countries, more than $70 billion, largely overlook the challenges of tropical diseases such as malaria. Rich-country funding is, not surprisingly, aimed at rich-country diseases.

Many poor East Asian countries were initially successful in raising technology not so much through home-grown innovation as through their success in attracting foreign investors who brought the technologies with them. As early as the late 1960s, Texas Instruments, National Semiconductor, and Hewlett Packard, among others, set up operations in Singapore, Penang Island (Malaysia), and other parts of East Asia. They saved a lot of money but also introduced what were otherwise very poor economies to sophisticated scientific technology and advanced management processes. If a poor country can become an attractive place for high-technology enterprises to conduct part of their production activities, then they can become a home, even at a low level of development, to quite sophisticated production and management techniques. Under the right circumstances, hosting such activities on the home turf can then lead to a diffusion of knowledge, and participation in modern production, so that those benefits can then be transferred to domestic firms.

The process even works in technologically humbler sectors like apparel. When foreign investors such as Wal-Mart, J. C. Penney, Yves Saint Laurent, and others outsource their production to Dhaka, they bring in the latest fashion designs and integrate the local production unit into a global supply chain. The local production units do the cutting, stitching, labeling, and packaging of the merchandise, which is designed and ultimately destined for the United States and Europe. These factories become important training grounds for climbing the technology ladder, moving from basic technology up to the next steps. A cutting and stitching company may take 100 percent of the fashion design orders from abroad at the beginning, but later on, once it gets the hang of it, it may start hiring its own designers, and start selling not only the labor of the assembly operation, but also the designs. That progression has happened over and over again throughout the world.

What prevents this process from taking hold everywhere in the world? Eventually it can, but in the early stages the process almost always starts right at a port. The accompanying maps, 3 and 4, show the locations of multinational companies in the electronics sector and in textiles and garment manufacturing, illustrating the coastal location of these firms, especially in their operation in the poor countries. Hinterlands have lagged far behind in their ability to attract these kinds of industries.

It is no coincidence that booming sites for foreign investment—such as Penang Island (Malaysia), Singapore, Taiwan, Hong Kong, and Mauritius—are all islands on the Asia-Europe trade route. It is no coincidence that China's leading economic city, Shanghai, sits right on the coast at the mouth of the Yangtze River. It is no coincidence that Mexico's assembly sector is right along the Rio Grande River, since Mexico's economically relevant "coast" is its border with the United States. The same geographical advantages are seen in many other places that have received substantial foreign investments in recent years. Wroclaw, Poland, and Bratislava, Slovakia, and Lada Bolislav, Czech Republic, and Lubljiana, Slovenia, have all reaped an extra bonus of jobs and technology transfer by virtue of their proximity to Western European markets.

The Demographic Trap

Most countries have experienced a significant decline in fertility rates in recent decades. Half the world, including all of the rich world, is at or near the so-called replacement rate of fertility, in which each mother is raising one daughter on average to "replace" her in the next generation. The replacement rate is two children, one of whom, on average, is a girl. (In fact, the replacement rate is a little bit above two, to take into account the possibility that the daughter will not survive to reproductive age.) The poorest of the poor countries, by contrast, are stuck with fertility rates of five or more. On average, a mother is raising at least two girls, and in some cases three girls or more. In those circumstances, national populations double each generation.

However, the demographic transition has occurred in most parts of the world. Moreover, although Western Europe's demographic transition took a century or more, the transition among developing countries in the twentieth century has occurred over decades or just a few years. In Bangladesh, the total fertility rate fell from 6.6 in 1975 to just 3.1 in 2000, as we saw plainly with the BRAC microfinance group in the village

Figure 1: Fertility and Economic Development

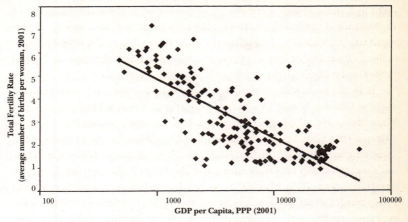

Note: X axis is on a logarithmic scale.
Source: Calculated using data from World Bank (2004).

outside of Dhaka. In Iran following the 1979 Islamic revolution, the transformation was even faster, from 6.7 in 1980 to just 2.6 in 2000. The Iranian revolution, it seems, brought a generation of young girls into the schools, and this boom in girls' literacy has translated rapidly and dramatically into the desire for fewer children.

One reason for a poverty trap is a demographic trap, when impoverished families choose to have lots of children. These choices are understandable, yet the results can be disastrous. When impoverished families have large numbers of children, the families cannot afford to invest in the nutrition, health, and education of each child. They might only afford the education of one child, and may send only one son to school. High fertility rates in one generation, therefore, tend to lead to impoverishment of the children and to high fertility rates in the following generation as well. Rapid population growth also puts enormous stresses on farm sizes and environmental resources, thereby exacerbating the poverty.

As with the other obstacles to economic growth, the demographic trap is avoidable. Girls' education would allow women to more easily join the labor force, increasing their earning power and the "cost" of staying home to bear children. Education, law, and social action can empower women to more easily make fertility choices (instead of having those choices made solely by husbands or others in the family). Children can be treated for disease to better ensure their survival, meaning that parents can have fewer children, feeling secure that they will survive to take care of their parents in old age. Family planning and reproductive health services can be provided even in very poor communities. All of this requires money, however, and money is lacking in the poorest economies.

Figure 1 shows how the total fertility rate in the year 2001 compares with the country's national income per person. The total fertility rate, and hence the population growth rate, is stunningly high especially in the poorest parts of the world. Here is the demographic trap in vivid perspective: the poorest places, many with the greatest obstacles to modern economic growth, are also the places where families have the most numbers of children, and where the populations continue to soar. High population growth leads to deeper poverty, and deeper poverty contributes to high fertility rates.

WHERE GROWTH HAS FAILED

Map 5 shows all of the countries in the world where per capita GDP declined during the twenty-year period between 1980 and 2000. Notice that not one single rich country in North America, Western Europe, or East Asia failed to achieve economic growth! All of the problems lie in the developing world. Forty-five countries had negative growth in GDP per capita. (Only countries with a population of at least two million people in 1980 were examined in order to avoid the idiosyncrasies of some very small countries.)

It is illuminating to divide the world's economies into the following six categories, depending on their per capita income in 1980:

- All low-income countries

- Middle-income oil exporters

- Middle-income postcommunist countries

- Other middle-income countries

- High-income oil exporters

- All other high-income countries

Table 2: Country Classifications in 1980

		Negative Economic Growth		Positive Economic Growth		Totals	
Low-Income Countries		Angola Bolivia Burundi Cameroon Central African Rep. Congo, Dem. Rep. Côte d'Ivoire Ecuador Ethiopia Guatemala Haiti Honduras Jordan	Kenya Madagascar Mali Nicaragua Niger Nigeria Peru Philippines Rwanda Sierra Leone Togo Zambia	Bangladesh Benin Burkina Faso Cambodia Chad Chile China Dominican Rep. Egypt El Salvador Ghana Guinea India Indonesia Iran Jamaica Korea, Rep. Lao PDR Malawi	Malaysia Morocco Mozambique Nepal Pakistan Papua New Guinea Senegal Sri Lanka Sudan Syria Tanzania Thailand Tunisia Turkey Uganda Vietnam Yemen Zimbabwe	25 (-)	37 (+)
Middle-Income Countries	Post-Soviet Countries	Armenia Belarus Croatia Georgia Kazakhstan Kyrgyz Rep. Latvia Lithuania	Moldova Romania Russia Tajikistan Turkmenistan Ukraine Uzbekistan	Albania Bulgaria Czech Republic	Hungary Poland Slovak Rep.	15 (-)	6 (+)
	Fuel Exporters	Algeria	Venezuela			2 (-)	0 (+)
	Other Middle Income	South Africa	Paraguay	Argentina Brazil Colombia Costa Rica Greece Hong Kong	Lebanon Mexico Portugal Singapore Spain Uruguay	2 (-)	12 (+)
High-Income Countries	Non-Fuel Exporters			Australia Austria Belgium Canada Denmark Finland France Germany Israel	Italy Japan Netherlands New Zealand Norway Sweden Switzerland United Kingdom United States	0 (-)	18 (+)
	Fuel Exporters	Saudi Arabia				1 (-)	0 (+)

Source: Calculated using data from World Bank (2004). Includes only countries with population greater than 2 million in 1980.

The accompanying table 2 lists the countries in each category, divided into two columns: those that experienced positive economic growth and those that experienced outright economic decline. The numbers of countries in each category are shown in the two columns at the right of the table. There are several key points. First, the biggest problem with economic decline is indeed in the poorest countries, especially but not only in sub-Saharan Africa. The second observation is that except for oil-exporting and ex-Soviet countries, all high-income countries achieved economic growth, as did most middle-income countries. The only growth failure among high-income countries occurred in Saudi Arabia, an oil-exporting country. Among the middle-income countries, the vast proportion of growth failures were in the oil-exporting and postcommunist countries. In the rest of the middle-income countries, twelve out of fourteen countries enjoyed positive economic growth.

The economic declines in the oil-producing and postcommunist countries reflect very unusual circumstances. The oil-rich states are, of course, not impoverished countries, but instead are middle-income and high-income countries where the economic activity depends overwhelmingly on oil exports. These economies rise and fall in line with the "real" price of oil, that is, the price of oil relative to the price of imported goods such as machinery and consumer goods. The real price of oil soared during the 1970s, leading to the massive growth in living standards of these economies, but during the 1980s and 1990s, the oil price fell sharply, leading to a collapse of living standards. If there is a lesson here, it is that an economy dependent on a single product (or a small number of products) for export is bound to experience high volatility as the relative price of the product fluctuates in world markets. Since oil is highly volatile, the real income of the oil economies has similarly been highly volatile.

The economic decline in postcommunist countries is even more of a special case. These countries have experienced a one-time decline in GDP per capita as they changed over from a failed communist system to a market economy. Even in the cases of the strongest of the so-called transition economies—the Czech Republic, Hungary, and Poland—there was a period of sharp reduction in GDP per capita for a few years as old heavy industries linked to the Soviet economy declined or disappeared in bankruptcy and new sectors took time to develop. The result was what economists called a transition recession. By the late 1990s, the postcommunist countries had resumed economic growth, but from a lower GDP per capita than before the Soviet collapse.

Figure 2: Cereal Yield and Growth
Among Low-Income Countries

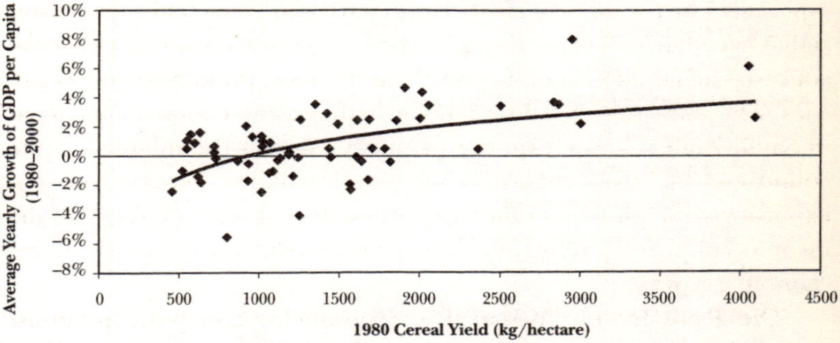

Source: Calculated using data from World Bank (2004).

WHY SOME POOR COUNTRIES GREW AND OTHERS DECLINED

Poor countries have a significant chance of falling into a poverty trap. Out of the fifty-eight nonoil countries with per capita incomes below $3,000, twenty-two (or 38 percent) experienced an outright decline. Yet the thirty-six other countries enjoyed economic growth. How is it that some very poor countries escaped the ravages of a poverty trap while the rest did not? Comparing those countries that made it and those that did not, the success stories show certain characteristics. The most important determinant, it seems, is food productivity. Countries that started with high cereal yields per hectare, and that used high levels of fertilizer input per hectare, are the poor countries that tended to experience economic growth. Countries that began with very low yields in 1980 are the countries that tended to experience economic decline between 1980 and 2000. Figure 2 illustrates this point: among low-income countries, high cereal yields in 1980 (measured on the horizontal axis) are associated with high economic growth rates (measured on the vertical axis).

The poverty trap is mainly a rural phenomenon of peasant farmers caught in a spiral of rising populations and stagnant or falling food production per person.

Table 3: East Asia and Sub-Saharan Africa in 1980	East Asia	Sub-Saharan Africa
Cereal yield (kg/hectare)	2016	927
Irrigated land (% of cropland)	37	4
Share of crop area planted to modern varieties (%)	43	4
Adult literacy rate (%)	70	38
Infant mortality rate (per 1000 live births)	56	116
Total fertility rate (births per woman)	3.1	6.6

Source: Calculated using data from World Bank (2004).

The biggest difference between Africa and Asia is that Asia has had high and rising food production per capita during recent decades, whereas Africa has low and falling food production per capita. The Asian countryside is densely populated, with a relatively extensive road network that can carry fertilizer to the farms and farm output to the markets. Farmers use fertilizers and irrigation, and food yields are high. Donor agencies gave ample support to the development of new high-yield varieties in Asia. Under these conditions Asian farmers were able to adopt high-yield crop varieties that produced the famous Green Revolution of rising food production per farmer. The African countryside is much less densely populated, with an absence of roads to transport fertilizers and crops. Farmers do not use fertilizer on food crops, and depend on rainfall rather than irrigation. Donors have woefully underfunded the scientific efforts toward improved varieties appropriate for African conditions. Under these much harsher conditions, Africa's farmers were not able to benefit much, if at all, from the Green Revolution development of high-yield varieties of food crops. Although both Asia and Africa were very poor in 1980, Asian agriculture was significantly outperforming African agriculture, as shown in table 3. This performance has provided a platform for Asia's extraordinary growth since then.

There are other tendencies apparent in the data. The Asian countries that experienced growth started in 1980 with better social conditions: higher literacy, lower infant mortality, and lower total fertility rates. They were, therefore, less prone to fall into a demographic trap of rapidly rising populations pressing on a limited amount of farmland. Once again, the Asian peasants were somewhat better off than their African counterparts. Another tendency is that poor countries with large populations seem to have done better than poor countries with smaller populations. The larger population probably increased the size of the domestic market, making it more appealing to foreign and domestic investors. Perhaps it was easier to introduce key infrastructure such as roads and power supplies in countries with larger populations, since these infrastructure networks are characterized by large initial costs of construction that are more easily financed by larger and more densely populated economies.

WHY LATIN AMERICA'S MIDDLE-INCOME COUNTRIES FAILED TO THRIVE

The poverty trap of the poorest countries is less puzzling, in some ways, than the stagnation that gripped a number of countries in Central and South America during the 1980s and 1990s. Table 2 shows that countries like Ecuador, Guatemala, Paraguay, and Peru experienced outright economic declines. These are not, in general, destitute countries, though they have destitute populations within them. How can we account for their development failures?

I take up that question in more detail later. It will suffice here to note three characteristics of these economies. First, all of these economies face particular geographical difficulties. Ecuador and Peru are Andean countries, with populations divided between a lowland tropical environment and a mountainous highland environment. Transport conditions are hazardous and expensive. Paraguay, of course, is landlocked. Guatemala is a mix of mountains and low-lying tropical rain forests. Second, the Central American and Andean societies suffer from sharp social divisions, typically along ethnic lines. The European-descended population tends to be much richer than the indigenous and mestizo (mixed) populations. Europeans conquered the native populations, repressed them in many ways, and were generally uninterested in investing in their human capital until very recently. Politics have therefore been highly conflict laden and often violent. Third, these countries are all vulnerable to extreme external shocks, both natural and economic. Natural hazards include earthquakes, droughts, floods, and landslides. Economic hazards include the huge instabilities in international prices for the leading commodity exports of these countries, such as copper, fish meal, coffee, bananas, and other agricultural and mining products.

CONTINUING EXTREME POVERTY IN THE MIDST OF ECONOMIC GROWTH

Even among the poor countries in Asia that experienced marked economic growth, extreme poverty often continues to afflict significant parts of the population. Economic growth is rarely uniformly distributed across a country. China's coastal provinces, linked to world trade and investment, have grown much more rapidly than the hinterland to the west of the country. India's southern states, also deeply integrated in world trade, have experienced much faster economic development than the northern regions in the Ganges valley. Thus, even when average economic growth is high, parts of a country may be bypassed for years or decades.

Another reason for persistent poverty is the failure of government. Growth may enrich households linked to good market opportunities, but it may bypass the poorest of the poor even within the same community. The very poor are often disconnected from market forces because they lack the requisite human capital—good nutrition and health, and an adequate education. It is vital that social expenditures directed at human capital accumulation reach the poorest of the poor, yet governments often fail to make such investments. Economic growth enriches households, but it is not taxed sufficiently to enable governments to increase social spending commensurately. Or even when governments have the revenue, they may neglect the poorest of the poor if the destitute groups are part of ethnic or religious minorities.

A third possible reason for continued poverty in the midst of growth is cultural. In many countries, women face extreme cultural discrimination, whether or not those biases are embedded in the legal and political systems. In South Asia, for example, there are an overwhelming number of case studies and media reports of young women facing extreme undernutrition within the household even when there is enough to go around. The women, often illiterate, are poorly treated by in-laws and lack the social standing and perhaps legal protections to ensure their own basic health and well-being.

In short, there are myriad possibilities for the persistence of poverty even in the midst of economic growth. Only a close diagnosis of particular circumstances will allow an accurate understanding. Policy makers and analysts should be sensitive, however, to geographical, political, and cultural conditions that may each play a role.

THE GREATEST CHALLENGE: OVERCOMING THE POVERTY TRAP

When countries get their foot on the ladder of development, they are generally able to continue the upward climb. All good things tend to move together at each rising rung: higher capital stock, greater specialization, more advanced technology, and lower fertility. If a country is trapped below the ladder, with the first rung too high off the ground, the climb does not even get started. The main objective of economic development for the poorest countries is to help these countries to gain a foothold on the ladder. The rich countries do not have to invest enough in the poorest countries to make them rich; they need to invest enough so that these countries can get their foot on the ladder. After that, the tremendous dynamism of self-sustaining economic growth can take hold.

Economic development works. It can be successful. It tends to build on itself. But it must get started.

Four

CLINICAL ECONOMICS

The rich world dominates the training of Ph.D. economists, and the students of rich-world Ph.D. programs dominate the international institutions like the International Monetary Fund (IMF) and the World Bank, which have the lead in advising poor countries on how to break out of poverty. These economists are bright and motivated. I know. I have trained many of them. But do the institutions where they work think correctly about the problems of the countries in which they operate? The answer is no. Development economics needs an overhaul in order to be much more like modern medicine, a profession of rigor, insight, and practicality.

In some ways, today's development economics is like eighteenth-century medicine, when doctors used leeches to draw blood from their patients, often killing them in the process. In the past quarter century, when impoverished countries have pleaded with the rich world for help, they have been sent to the world's money doctor, the IMF. The main IMF prescription has been budgetary belt tightening for patients much too poor to own belts. IMF-led austerity has frequently led to riots, coups, and the collapse of public services. In the past, when an IMF program has collapsed in the midst of social chaos and economic distress, the IMF has simply chalked it up to the weak fortitude and ineptitude of the government. Finally, that approach is beginning to change. The IMF, thank goodness, is searching for more effective approaches vis-à-vis the poorest countries.

It has taken me twenty years to understand what good development economics should be, and I am still learning. Fortunately for me, and for the countries where I have worked, I realized from the very start of my advisory activities that my formal training was not adequate to the task. While I had learned an important set of tools in my advanced studies, I had not learned the contexts in which to apply them. I had also been led to believe that the standard economics tools were adequate if they were properly used. It took me a long time to understand the urgent need to bring additional tools and procedures to bear if impoverished and crisis-struck countries are to surmount their difficulties.

I propose a new method for development economics, one that I call clinical economics, to underscore the similarities between good development economics and good clinical medicine. On numerous occasions during the past twenty years, I have been invited to take on an economics patient—a crisis-ridden economy—in order to prescribe a course of treatment. Over the years I have marveled at how that experience is akin to that of my wife Sonia's clinical practice of pediatrics. I have watched in awe, often in the middle of the night, how she approaches a medical emergency or complicated case with speed, efficacy, and amazing results. Development economics today is not like modern medicine, but it should strive to be so. It can improve dramatically if development economists take on some of the key lessons of modern medicine, both in the development of the underlying science and in the systematization of clinical practice, the point where science is brought to bear on a particular patient.

SOME LESSONS OF CLINICAL MEDICINE

A doctor is called in the middle of the night. A child has spiked a high fever. What to do? This is akin to a call I received in mid-1985, when Bolivia had spiked the high fever of hyperinflation. Medical science and practice offer a set of rigorous procedures for addressing the fever. There are five main lessons of clinical medicine relevant to clinical economics.

Lesson 1 is that *the human body is a complex system*. Ancient Greek medicine talked about illness resulting from an imbalance of the four bodily fluids. Perhaps this was a good stab at matters more than two thousand years ago, but we know much better today. The human body involves biological and biochemical processes of incredible complexity. The division of human physiology into a large number of interconnected systems—nervous, circulatory, respiratory, digestive, endocrine, immune, reproductive, and so forth—just scratches the surface of the underlying biological processes. The sources of disease can involve infectious agents, environmental hazards, genetic abnormalities, and malnourishment, among other causes, and complex combinations of these factors.

The complexity of the human system has many implications beyond the mere fact that lots of things can go wrong. Most important, one failure can lead to a cascade of additional failures. A fever resulting from an infectious agent can lead to brain seizures caused by the fever rather than the infection itself. Heart failure can result in kidney failure, which in turn can lead to liver failure as the kidney fails to remove certain dangerous toxins from the body. A loss of blood can cause virtually every system to fail as the body falls into shock. Emergency room doctors must struggle to keep each basic system functioning at a minimum level, not only for its own sake but also to prevent a downward spiral of catastrophes that shut down other critical systems. Once that downward spiral starts, it might be hard to reverse, so complex and rapid are the interconnected failures.

Lesson 2 is that *complexity requires a differential diagnosis*. A doctor seeing a child with a high fever for the first time knows that fevers can be caused by many different factors. The doctor's first impulse is to find out which is the cause in the particular case. Some causes of fever are dangerous; others are not. Some are treatable; others are not. Some require urgent attention; others do not (except, perhaps, to raise the comfort level of the child). Fevers may result from various kinds of infection (bacterial, fungal, viral, protozoan), trauma, autoimmune disease, cancers, poisoning, and other causes. Since fever is a symptom, rather than a specific disease, a proper course of treatment requires the doctor to identify the true underlying cause of the symptom.

The doctor works through a checklist to get to the right answer. My wife may ask an hour of questions, and then prescribe a battery of laboratory tests before passing along any judgment. On other occasions, the cause can be pretty clear. An earache accompanying the fever is a pretty good giveaway that the underlying condition is the common otitis media (ear infection), especially if the child's older sibling had an earache earlier in the week, since that particular malady travels rapidly among children in classrooms and families. The doctor's checklist is not randomly ordered. There are a few principles that determine the order in which the doctor proceeds with an investigation. First, confronted with a child with high fever, my wife looks immediately to see whether the child's neck is stiff—a warning sign for meningitis as the underlying cause of the fever. This is one of the few conditions that can kill a feverish child almost immediately. If the child's neck is indeed stiff, my wife orders the child to the emergency room before asking other questions. The principle, in this case, is that diagnosis should not unduly delay the treatment, a good lesson for the IMF, we will see later, which sometimes studies problems to death while an economy collapses.

Another principle is one of applied epidemiology. The doctor should think first about the most likely conditions, not the most obscure. A child who comes in with fever does not immediately invoke fears of cancer, even though cancer can cause fever. The overwhelming proportion of cases result from infection, and those likely causes should be examined first. As doctors say, "When you hear hoof beats, think of horses, not zebras." (A doctor in Washington should indeed think about horses. A doctor in Kenya, however, might be wise to think first of zebras!) Epidemiologists also remind us that a patient may be suffering from more than one condition at a time, and that these diseases might indeed be interrelated.

Lesson 3 is that *all medicine is family medicine.* It is not enough to identify the disease in a child. In order to treat the child's disease successfully, it is important to understand the social setting. Are the parents capable of providing treatment? Is the mother herself suffering from disease, or extreme poverty, abuse, or some other condition that would prevent her from following through on a recommended course of treatment for her child? Is a child's injury truly an accident or rather a sign of mistreatment? When a mother is hysterical over the phone about the condition of her child, is that likely to be a trustworthy account or merely the latest in a series of overreactions? Upon receiving a late-night phone call, my wife would save the life of a child with the comment to me, "That's an unusually desperate concern of this particular mother, who is typically understated. I think I'll send the child directly to the emergency room." And sure enough, a condition of meningitis would be caught in time.

Lesson 4 is that *monitoring and evaluation are essential* to successful treatment. Doctors keep charts so that they know where the patient has been. Even a careful initial diagnosis can be wrong. Lab tests can give false positives or false negatives. A child can suffer from multiple underlying conditions, so that even a correct diagnosis of one of them is a partial account of the true underlying reasons for illness. Only careful monitoring, evaluation, testing, and retesting can ensure a safe passage to health in many cases. Good clinicians therefore hold each diagnosis not as sacrosanct, but as the best-maintained hypothesis of the moment. The hypothesis might well be confirmed, but the doctor is prepared to shift ground if the evidence calls for a new approach.

Lesson 5 is that *medicine is a profession,* and as a profession requires strong norms, ethics, and codes of conduct. The Hippocratic oath is not a mere curiosity to remind doctors of the ancient lineage of their profession. Even if it is not read literally, and after two thousand years it should not be, the oath underscores to all newly trained doctors that they have entered a hallowed occupation, a great and distinctive calling with very high ethical responsibilities. The doctor has a unique relationship with a patient, one that gives the doctor an entry into the most private conditions of an individual and family. The doctor literally has life and death sway, and it is not hard to take advantage of that sway for money or other forms of personal gain. The oath reminds doctors that they must not abuse the privilege of their positions. They must offer judgments in the interests of the patient, not for personal gain. And they must keep abreast of new scientific findings, including new procedures and medicines, to ensure the highest quality care that they can manage.

DEVELOPMENT ECONOMICS AS CLINICAL ECONOMICS

The challenge of making policy recommendations for an economy, especially a poor and unstable economy, shares many of the challenges of clinical medicine. Yet the practice of development economics is not yet up to the task. Economists are not trained to think like clinicians, and are rarely afforded clinical experience in their advanced training. A graduate student in an American Ph.D. program in economics may very well study the development crisis in Africa without ever setting foot in the country or countries under study. An adviser may hand over a data set, say for Nigerian households, and ask the student to do a statistical analysis without the benefit of context, history, or direct observation. Years later, the student may have the opportunity to show up in Nigeria for the first time.

The five key lessons of clinical medicine have clear counterparts in good economics practice as well. First, economies, like individuals, are complex systems. Like the circulatory, respiratory, and other systems of a human being, societies have distinct systems for transport, power, communications, law enforcement, national defense, taxation, and other systems that must operate properly for the entire economy to function appropriately. As with a human being, the failure of one system can lead to cascades of failure in other parts of the economy. When the U.S. government asked Bolivia to eradicate its peasants' coca crops in the late 1990s, the result was a deepening of rural poverty. When the government sought to respond to the rising rural poverty with social and development programs, the crisis became a fiscal crisis. When outside donor agencies, including the U.S. government, failed to help Bolivia with the fiscal crisis, the crisis became one of civil disorder, with the police, army, and peasants battling in the streets. Eventually the government was toppled, and Bolivia entered a new period of extended instability.

Second, economists, like medical clinicians, need to learn the art of differential diagnosis. Medical pathology textbooks are now often two thousand pages, and even those may cover just one of the key physical systems. Doctors know that lots of things can go wrong, and that a particular symptom such as high fever might reflect dozens, or hundreds, of underlying causes. The IMF, by contrast, has focused on a very narrow range of issues, such as corruption, barriers to private enterprise, budget deficits, and state ownership of production. It has also presumed that each episode of fever is just like the others, and has trotted out standardized advice to cut budgets, liberalize trade, and privatize state-owned enterprises, almost without regard to the specific context. The IMF has overlooked urgent problems involving poverty traps, agronomy, climate, disease, transport, gender, and a host of other pathologies that undermine economic development. Clinical economics should train the development practitioner to home in much more effectively on the key underlying causes of economic distress, and to prescribe appropriate remedies that are well tailored to each country's specific conditions. When in Afghanistan or Bolivia, the IMF should think automatically about transport costs; when in Senegal, attention should turn to malaria.

Third, clinical economics, like clinical medicine, should view treatment in "family" terms, not just individual terms. It is not enough to tell Ghana to get its act together if Ghana faces trade barriers in international markets that prevent it from selling its goods and services to world markets; if Ghana is burdened by an unpayable mountain of debt inherited from previous decades; if Ghana requires urgent investments in basic infrastructure as a precondition for attracting new investors; if Ghana is burdened by refugee movements and disorders emanating from neighboring countries. In short, for the IMF and World Bank to tell Ghana to liberalize its trade, balance its budget, and attract foreign investors may be fine and good, but it will be ineffectual if not combined with trade reforms in the rich countries, debt cancellation, increased foreign financial assistance for investments in basic infrastructure, and support to the West African region as a whole to maintain peace. In the case of a country, the entire world community is part of the family. That is an assumption of the Millennium Development Goals, and especially the concept of a global partnership to achieve the goals, but it is not yet part of real clinical practice.

Fourth, good development practice requires monitoring and evaluation, and especially a rigorous comparison of goals and outcomes. When goals are not being achieved, it is important to ask why, not to make excuses for past advice. Under current development practice, the IMF and World Bank have rarely taken on specific development objectives as the standards for judging country performance, and by extension, their own advice. Instead, countries are judged on the basis of policy inputs, not outputs. A government may be told to cut its budget deficit by 1 percent of GDP. It is judged on whether or not it carries out that measure, not on whether the measure produces faster growth, or a reduction of poverty, or a solution to a debt crisis. The result is a descent into formalistic debates on whether or not a particular policy has been carried out, not on whether the policy was the right one in the first place. The current situation reminds me too much of the fable of the farmer whose chickens are dying. The local priest gives one remedy after another—prayers, potions, oaths—until all of the chickens are dead. "Too bad," says the priest, "I had so many other good ideas."

Fifth, the development community lacks the requisite ethical and professional standards. I am not suggesting that development practitioners are corrupt or unethical; such cases are rare. Rather, the development economics community does not take on its work with the sense of responsibility that the tasks require. Providing economic advice to others requires a profound commitment to search for the right answers, not to settle for superficial approaches. It requires a commitment to be thoroughly steeped in the history, ethnography, politics, and economics of any place where the professional adviser is working. It also requires a commitment to give honest advice, not only to the country in question, but to the agency that has hired and sent the adviser. Not every problem facing the impoverished world is homegrown, nor will all solutions be found in good governance, belt tightening, and further market reforms. True solutions will also require deeper debt relief, greater development assistance, more open trade with the rich countries, and the like. Any IMF or World Bank official, as well as any academic development practitioner, has the responsibility to speak truth not only to the policy makers within the impoverished country, but to the policy makers of the rich and powerful countries as well.

WHERE ECONOMIC DEVELOPMENT PRACTICE HAS GONE WRONG

Clinical economics is needed to replace the past twenty years of development practice, known widely as the structural adjustment era. This era, ushered in by the conservative turn in the United States under President Ronald Reagan and in the United Kingdom under Prime Minister Margaret Thatcher, was based on a simplistic, even simpleminded, view of the challenge of poverty. The rich countries told the poor countries: "Poverty is your own fault. Be like us (or what we imagine ourselves to be—free market oriented, entrepreneurial, fiscally responsible) and you, too, can enjoy the riches of private-sector-led economic development." The IMF-World Bank programs of the structural adjustment era were designed to address the four maladies assumed to underlie all economic ills: poor governance, excessive government intervention in the markets, excessive government spending, and too much state ownership. Belt tightening, privatization, liberalization, and good governance became the order of the day.

There were some truths in the structural adjustment agenda. Many poor countries that had fallen into economic crisis by the early 1980s were there as a result of profound economic mismanagement. Too many countries had chosen closed trading systems. The second world and third world strategies had failed, and needed to be reoriented to a global, market-based international economic system. But the policy and governance problems in the poorest countries were only part of the story, and in many places not the central part. It should have been possible to tend to the problems of closed trading systems and excessive nationalization of industry without ignoring the problems of malaria and AIDS, mountain geographies, and inadequate rainfall. But alas, such a multifaceted approach did not enter the policy debate until very recently.

Sadly, there were self-serving and ideological aspects of the structural adjustment era's failures of advice and insufficient help. The self-serving aspect is clear. The responsibilities for poverty reduction were assumed to lie entirely with the poor countries themselves. Increased foreign financial assistance was deemed not to be needed. Indeed, foreign aid per person in the poor countries plummeted during the 1980s and 1990s. Aid per person in sub-Saharan Africa, for example, expressed in constant 2002 dollars, fell from $32 per African in 1980 to just $22 per African in 2001, during a period in which Africa's pandemic diseases ran rampant, and needs for increased public spending were stark. Donors thought they had done everything they could, with any remaining problems caused by issues beyond their responsibility.

The ideological aspects of the advice are plain enough. Conservative governments of the United States, United Kingdom, and elsewhere used international advising to push programs that found no support at home. Many African countries have heard an earful from the World Bank over the past two decades about privatizing their health services, or at least charging user fees for health and education. Yet most of the high-income-country shareholders of the World Bank have health systems that guarantee universal access, and all have education systems that ensure access to public education.

DIFFERENTIAL DIAGNOSIS FOR POVERTY REDUCTION

The Millennium Development Goals (MDGs) offer the world a chance to do better vis-à-vis the poorest countries after twenty years of failed structural adjustment policies. The MDGs state real goals that provide not only benchmarks for aid but also milestones for assessing the advice of the international agencies as well. The failures to meet the MDGs are failures of the rich countries as well as the poor, since both are responsible for their success. The fact that the MDGs are not being met throughout Africa, the Andean region, and Central Asia tells us that the problems are more than simply those of governance. Many governments in these regions have shown boldness, integrity, and intelligence. Yet development continues to fail. A clinical economics approach will point the way to a better strategy.

The key to clinical economics is a thorough differential diagnosis, followed by an appropriate treatment regimen. In the course of a physical exam, the doctor runs through pages of questions: "Are you taking medications?" "Do you have allergies?" "Have you been operated on recently?" "Do you have a family history of the following diseases?" The clinical economist must do the same. In table 1, I describe a seven-part diagnostic checklist that should be part of the "physical exam" of any impoverished country.

The Extent of Extreme Poverty

The first set of questions involves the extent of extreme poverty. The clinical economist should make a set of poverty maps, using available or newly commissioned household surveys, geographic information systems data, national income accounts, and other information. What proportion of households live in extreme poverty? What proportion of households lack access to basic needs in schooling, health care, water and sanitation, electricity, roads, nutrition? What is the spatial distribution of poverty? Is poverty mainly urban or rural, and is it concentrated in a few regions or distributed evenly throughout the country? How does poverty relate to demographic conditions of the household (female- or male-headed household, number of children, health of household members) and to its asset ownership and economic activities (landless poor, smallholder farmer, commerce, industry, and so on)?

In the course of mapping poverty, the clinical economist should also identify key risk factors that may exacerbate poverty in the coming years. What are the demographic trends (births, deaths, internal and international migration) that may affect the numbers and distribution of the extreme poor? What environmental shocks and trends (sea level changes, coastal erosion, deforestation, land degradation, depletion of water aquifers, biodiversity loss) might impinge on poverty? What climate shocks (El Niño, long-term warming, chronic drought, extreme weather events) are likely to affect public health, disease, and agricultural productivity? What changes in infectious disease incidence and prevalence may weigh on the national or regional economies? How

Table 1. Checklist for Making a Differential Diagnosis

I. Poverty Trap

Poverty mapping

Proportion of households lacking basic needs

Spatial distribution of household poverty

Spatial distribution of basic infrastructure (power, roads, telecoms, water and sanitation)

Ethnic, gender, generational distribution of poverty

Key risk factors

Demographic trends

Environmental trends

Climate shocks

Disease

Commodity price fluctuations

Others

II. Economic Policy Framework

Business environment

Trade policy

Investment policy

Infrastructure

Human capital

III. Fiscal Framework and Fiscal Trap

Public sector revenues and expenditures by category

Percent of GNP

Absolute levels in comparison with international norms

Tax administration and expenditure management

Public investment needs to meet poverty reduction targets

Macroeconomic instability

Overhang of public sector debt

Quasi-fiscal debt and hidden debt

Medium-term public sector expenditure framework

IV. Physical Geography

Transport conditions

Proximity of population to ports, international trade routes, navigable waterways

Access of population to paved roads

Access of population to motorized transport

Population density

Costs of connectivity to power, telecoms, roads

Arable land per capita

Environmental impacts of population-land ratios

Agronomic conditions

Temperature, precipitation, solar insolation

Length and reliability of growing season

Soils, topography, suitability for irrigation

Interannual climate variability (e.g., El Niño)

Long-term trends in climate patterns

Disease ecology

Human diseases

Plant diseases and pests

Animal diseases

V. Governance Patterns and Failures

Civil and political rights

Public management systems

Decentralization and fiscal federalism

Corruption patterns and intensity

Political succession and longevity

Internal violence and security

Cross-border violence and security

Ethnic, religious, and other cultural divisions

VI. Cultural Barriers

Gender relations

Ethnic and religious divisions

Diaspora

VII. Geopolitics

International security relations

Cross-border security threats

War

Terrorism

Refugees

International sanctions

Trade barriers

Participation in regional and international groups

might world-market fluctuations in key commodities affect extreme poverty and prospects for economic growth?

Economic Policy

The second set of questions involves the economic policy framework. These are more traditional questions, but they should be addressed systematically. What is the cost of doing business in the country (and in different regions within the country)? What is the coverage of key infrastructure (power, water, roads, transport services), focusing on subnational regions, both urban and rural, as well as national averages? How are costs affected by the lack of infrastructure? What is the trade policy framework, and how are trade barriers impinging on the costs of production, especially for export-oriented businesses? What are the incentives in place for potential domestic and foreign investors, and how does the incentive system compare with the incentives in place in competitor countries? Is the government investing adequately in human capital through programs on nutrition, public health, disease control, education, and family planning?

The Fiscal Framework

The third set of questions homes in on the fiscal framework, since the budget must carry much of the burden of key investments in infrastructure and social services. What are the current levels of budget spending and public revenues? These should be measured both as a percent of GDP and in dollars per person. The share of public spending in GDP in various categories (health, education, infrastructure) gives a sense of the level of effort that a country is making to reduce poverty. The absolute spending, in dollars per person, gives a sense of the adequacy of the spending to ensure basic needs and to support the escape from a poverty trap. To what extent is the government hampered by an overhang of public sector debt inherited from the past? How much would debt relief contribute to the capacity of the government to expand public services? Are there hidden or off-balance-sheet lines on the public sector, such as debts of the central bank, or hidden losses of the commercial banking system that will have to be covered by the government's budget?

Physical Geography and Human Ecology

The fourth category of questions involves the physical geography and human ecology (meaning the interface of society with the physical environment). Economists are surprisingly untrained in this area, despite its fundamental importance in diagnosing and overcoming extreme poverty. What are the transport conditions in the country, on average and by subregion? How much of the population is proximate to seaports and airports, navigable rivers, paved roads, and rail services? What are the costs of transporting freight (such as fertilizers, food crops, machinery, industrial products) within the country and internationally, and how do those costs compare with competitor countries? What is the distribution of population between coastal and interior areas, rural and urban settlements, and densely and sparsely populated areas? How does population density in various parts of the country affect the costs of infrastructure, for example bringing the population into road, rail, power, and telecom grids?

How are agronomic conditions affected by the physical environment? What is the length of the growing season, and how does that affect crop choice, nutrition, and income levels? What are the patterns of soils, topography, hydrology, and land use affecting crop yields, suitability for irrigation, and costs of land improvements? How are agronomic conditions affected by interannual climate variability linked, for example, to the El Niño fluctuations? How are agronomic conditions affected by long-term trends such as global warming and changes in precipitation patterns, like the evident decline in rainfall in the African Sahel?

How are ecosystem functions changing, and perhaps degrading, over time? Is deforestation threatening the functioning of ecosystems (for example, by exacerbating flooding and land degradation) and the livelihoods of the poor (for example, by exhausting the supplies of fuel wood)? Is the loss of biodiversity threatening ecosystem functions (for example, by reducing the pollination of agricultural products)? Are invasive species affecting the fertility of the land and fisheries? Is the introduction of toxins into the environment threatening the air and drinking water?

How does the ecology affect the burden of disease and its change over time? Malaria is a disease heavily conditioned by climate and mosquito species. Is malaria transmission epidemic or endemic (year-round), and is it changing over time as a result of population movements and climate change? What are the key patterns of animal disease that may have major effects on agricultural productivity (such as African sleeping sickness, a classic example)? What plant pests and diseases pose the gravest threats to livelihoods, international trade, and human health?

Patterns of Governance

The fifth category of the differential diagnosis involves patterns of governance beyond the specifics of the budget process and detailed economic policies. History has shown that democracy is not a prerequisite for economic development. On the other hand, a regime that is despotic, arbitrary, and lawless will easily destroy an economy. Is there a rule of law, or only the arbitrary command of a dictator? Do the systems of public management—for registering businesses, trading property, defending contracts, bidding for government tenders—work effectively? Are public services such as water and sanitation, power, and basic health and education efficiently provided (given the resources at hand), or are they subject to massive waste and fraud? Is corruption rampant, and at what levels of government? Is the succession of power from one government to the next regularized, or subject to the whim and abuse of the current rulers? Are public services run on behalf of a narrow elite, a subregion of the country, or particular ethnic groups?

Cultural Barriers to Economic Development

The sixth category of issues involves possible cultural barriers to economic development. Is the society torn apart by class, caste, ethnicity, religion, or gender inequity? Do women and girls face severe discrimination in personal rights (for example, sexual and reproductive choices) and access to public services (education, health facilities, family planning services)? Are women deprived either legally or informally of the right to own and inherit property? Can women participate with substantial equality of opportunity in the economy beyond home production? Do cultural norms and practices define limits to the economic opportunities of minority groups? Is interethnic violence rampant? What role, if any, is played by a diaspora, such as the offshore Chinese and Indian communities, in terms of investment, remittances, and social networking?

Geopolitics

The final category of the differential diagnosis involves geopolitics, the country's security and economic relations with the rest of the world. Is the country part of a security bloc that might define or limit its economic possibilities? Is the country subject to international sanctions, and if so, what are the consequences of the sanctions for economic development? Are there critical cross-border security threats, such as refugee movements, terrorism, or cross-border warfare? Do the contiguous neighbors cooperate regarding cross-border infrastructure? Is there an effective regional trade group, and if so, is it supporting an overall expansion of trade or merely a diversion of trade from nonmembers? What trade barriers in the rich world seriously impede development prospects?

The checklist is long. Answers to these questions cannot be ascertained in a fifteen-minute checkup at a clinic, nor, in practice, can they be addressed by a single international agency like the IMF. The answers must be systematic, continually updated, and put into a comparative framework for sound analysis. Many institutions, both within the low-income countries and internationally, should cooperate to address these diagnostic issues. Not only the IMF and World Bank, but also the specialized United Nations institutions such as the World Health Organization, UNICEF, the Food and Agriculture Organization, and many others, should cooperate in the diagnostics.

EDUCATION OF AN ECONOMIST

A differential diagnosis is the beginning, not the end, of the process. The next steps, of course, are to design programs and institutions to address the critical barriers to poverty reduction that are identified through the differential diagnosis. These strategies will be much more effective if the right questions are asked from the start. Questions, I trust, that will be evident later in this book.

It took me a long time to appreciate the need for a new approach to development economics. I did not have the benefit of hindsight—or a comprehensive diagnostic checklist—when I went on my first economic house call. In fact, when I arrived in La Paz, Bolivia, in July 1985, I had almost no checklist at all. I was there for a specific problem in a specific place. I had no idea that during the trip I would be involved with the very issues that were to become the centerpiece of my research and practical work for the next twenty years. These were issues that, much to my surprise, I had not been truly trained to address.

Five

BOLIVIA'S HIGH-ALTITUDE HYPERINFLATION

As with many events in my career, it was an accidental path that first brought me to the tarmac of the La Paz airport, thirteen thousand feet above sea level. I had first seen extreme poverty up close during my first visit to India in 1978, but my early academic work was very much about the U.S. and European economies, not the problem of extreme poverty and the puzzle of why it persists in a world of increasing wealth.

In the early 1980s, development economics was a fringe topic in U.S. Ph.D. programs, studied mainly by students from the poor countries. Although I was interested in the questions of development, my formal training focused on international economics, especially international finance. When I joined the Harvard faculty as an assistant professor in the fall of 1980, I was working mainly on problems of the rich countries, and on the flows of international financial capital between the rich and poor countries. When the developing-country debt crisis hit in 1982, I began to write theoretical papers on how to account for the onset of the debt crisis. I studied some of the historical precedents for such debt crises, particularly the Great Depression, and some of the mechanisms used to help extricate countries from bankruptcy. Little did I know that I would be the first to apply these mechanisms in the 1980s.

My work was theoretical and statistical, rather than immediately practical. At the time, I thought that I knew just about everything that needed to be known about the subject. As a young faculty member, I lectured widely to high acclaim, published broadly, and was on a rapid academic climb to tenure, which I received in 1983 when I was twenty-eight.

And then my life changed. A note arrived from a former Bolivian student of mine who asked if I would come to a seminar on campus to be given by a group of visiting Bolivians. The student, David Blanco, had been the finance minister of Bolivia in the 1970s. He had delighted me during my first year of teaching when he had introduced himself as a former finance minister, and said that he was taking the course to try to understand exactly what he had done while in office!

I was scheduled to give a development seminar at the World Bank soon after the scheduled seminar, and I thought hearing about Bolivia might bolster my knowledge. Of the Harvard faculty who were invited, only two of us showed up. It was probably one of the luckiest things that ever happened to me. A young Bolivian, Ronald McLean, who was a Kennedy School graduate and would later become mayor of La Paz and my dear friend, stood up and opened the seminar with the most mesmerizing portrait of Bolivia's hyperinflation that I could have imagined. His talk, I still remember, opened with a scene of the burgeoning black market for foreign exchange in which huge stacks of Bolivian pesos were being traded for dollars at an ever more frenetic pace in a street market on Avenida Camacho in La Paz, the capital city.

For a finance specialist like myself, Bolivia's crisis was riveting. I had studied the German hyperinflation of 1923, as well as some of the other hyperinflations. Those long-ago events were legends to economics students. We chuckled and groaned at Keynes's quips about those hyperinflations (always order two beers at the start, lest their price go up while you are sitting at the bar; take buses rather than taxis, because in a bus you pay at the start; and so forth). But we never expected to come across real hyperinflation other than in the history books.

Many academic economists in the early 1980s had been using the hyperinflations of the 1920s as bases for theoretical analyses of some of the current debates in macroeconomics, so I had read some recent papers. At one point in the seminar I raised my hand and took issue with a statement that had been made. Walking to the blackboard with great confidence, I said, "Here's how it works." After I put down the chalk, a voice at the back of the room said, "Well, if you're so smart, why don't you come to La Paz to help us?" I laughed. And he called out again, "I mean it." This was Carlos Iturralde, a key political figure who in the coming years became a friend and eventually minister of foreign relations and ambassador to the United States.

The group told me that they wanted an economic adviser. I was taken aback. I did not know exactly where Bolivia was in South America, and I certainly did not know whether it was safe or wise for me to get involved. I told them that I would get back to them. The next morning I told them that although I had never done anything like help a country, I would be willing to give it a shot if they were really interested. I also told them I would not work for their political party, but only for a government after the forthcoming elections. I did not want to get involved in partisan politics, since I knew it would prevent me from being effective. Throughout my work in Bolivia and elsewhere, this approach has allowed me to advise governments of different political parties as a trusted, impartial outsider.

The group agreed they would call me again if they won the elections. That was May. In early July, I got a call from Ronnie McLean. "We've won the election; pack your bags." I asked a colleague, French economist Daniel Cohen, and a graduate student, Felipe Larraín, to join me. We embarked for La Paz on July 9, 1985.

Designing a Stabilization Plan

From the moment I walked off the plane, I began to understand what real economic development was about. It was the beginning of twenty years of grasping the need for a new clinical economics, one up to the task of helping countries such as Bolivia. All I had with me at the start was an empty notebook and a few articles on hyperinflation. Fortunately, I had a basic theoretical understanding of what we would be up against.

First, I understood the basic monetary forces that led to hyperinflation. The government was printing money to finance a large budget deficit. Initially I did not understand the origins and dynamics of the budget deficit, nor the politics of the budgetary process. But I did understand that the Bolivian government was not creditworthy enough to sell bonds to the private sector at home or abroad. Instead, it had to sell its bonds directly to the Central Bank of Bolivia (or BCB in its Spanish acronym) in return for fresh cash to pay the army, miners, and teachers. The Bolivian hyperinflation was in this sense no different from others from economic history. Like those before it, the government was printing money to pay its bills, and as it printed the money it was driving down the value of the currency—and driving up the price of goods.

As the government paid the salaries, the injection of new pesos into circulation fueled the precipitous rise of prices. With each injection of Bolivian currency, people would take their pesos to the black market to buy dollars. The price of a dollar in terms of pesos soared: about 5,000 pesos per dollar in June 1983, about 10,000 pesos per dollar by January 1984, about 50,000 pesos per dollar by June 1984, about 250,000 pesos per dollar by December 1984, and 2 million pesos per dollar by July 1985, when a team of three inexperienced economists arrived. The goods in the shop by this time carried dollar price tags, even though the purchases were still made in pesos. A one-dollar item, therefore, cost almost 2 million pesos in July 1985, up from 5,000 pesos just two years earlier. In the single year between July 1984 and July 1985, prices had risen by more than 3,000 percent (thirty times).

Second, I knew that the end of a hyperinflation tended to be very rapid, and would occur as soon as the peso could be stabilized relative to the dollar. This would happen when a government could end its dependency on borrowing from the BCB. The concept of a sudden end to a 24,000 percent inflation was not intuitive. Some people thought that if you stopped the hyperinflation abruptly, it would necessarily lead to economic collapse. They thought that a better way would be to try to reduce the inflation gradually from several thousand percent per year to several hundred percent the next year, to a couple hundred percent the third year, and so on. Although no hyperinflation had ever been stopped that way, some of the consultants to the outgoing government had recommended such a policy.

Within a couple of days of arriving, I was asked to give a talk to the Bolivian-American Chamber of Commerce, and I went armed with my theoretical and historical knowledge. I displayed a figure from a recent paper by Thomas Sargent to stress that Germany's hyperinflation had ended in one day, November 20, 1923, and that I predicted the same for Bolivia. The crowd was startled, and delighted, at the prospect.

My small team, bolstered by assistance from Bolivian colleagues, started doing the numbers. We looked for a package of fiscal measures that could quickly wean the government away from its dependence on Central Bank financing of the deficit. We soon realized in discussions with our Bolivian colleagues and in looking through the books that the budgetary key lay in the price of oil. Government revenues depended heavily on taxes on hydrocarbons, mainly paid by the state petroleum company, YPFB. The YPFB set the price of oil and gasoline (in pesos). Generally, the oil price was changed only every few months, so the price of oil fell sharply in comparison with other prices and in terms of the U.S. dollar during the period in which the peso price was held constant. The low price of oil, in turn, was destroying the budget.

Here's an illustration: Suppose that the gasoline price is temporarily set at 250,000 pesos per liter on a day when the peso-dollar exchange rate is 1 million pesos per dollar. The U.S. dollar price of gas is therefore $0.25 per liter. Now suppose that the exchange rate depreciates by 50 percent per month. In thirty days, a U.S. dollar will cost 1.5 million pesos. In sixty days, it will cost 2.25 million pesos. If the peso price of gasoline remains unchanged for sixty days (not uncommon back in 1984 and 1985), the price of a liter in dollars will fall to just $0.11 (250,000 pesos per liter multiplied by $1 per 2.25 million pesos). Since the government budget depends on oil taxes, the tax base has collapsed.

The actual situation regarding oil prices was more dramatic than the illustration. By August 1985, the U.S. dollar price of a liter of gasoline in Bolivia had plummeted to around $0.03 per liter. Whole truckloads of gasoline were being smuggled over the border to Peru. The budget revenues had collapsed. The budget deficit was on the order of 10 percent of GDP, all financed by printing money (technically by "borrowing" the money from the BCB). We calculated that if the price of gasoline (and other fuels) was raised around tenfold, back to the actual world price of around $0.28 per liter, this increase by itself would close most of the budget deficit. A package of other measures on the spending and revenue side could close the rest.

My team therefore proposed a sharp one-time increase in oil prices as the key element in stopping the hyperinflation, combined with a package of other fiscal measures. Our Bolivian colleagues viewed skeptically the idea that a massive increase in oil prices could end the hyperinflation rather than trigger yet another acceleration. To the untrained eye, indeed, it seemed preposterous to propose price *increases* as the key to price stability. It made sense only in the context of a theoretical understanding of the problem, which diagnosed hyperinflation as being caused by the underlying monetary and budget conditions. In a way, I was taken aback by the skepticism. This part of the problem, after all, seemed rather straightforward. John Maynard Keynes, I decided, had it right in 1923 when he noted how little the process of inflation was understood, and how hyperinflation was all the more destructive as a result:

> There is no subtler, no surer means of overturning the existing basis
> of society than to debauch the currency. The process engages all the
> hidden forces of economic law on the side of destruction, and does
> it in a manner which not one man in a million is able to diagnose.

We wrote our report in two weeks and left La Paz on July twenty-fourth. Though we had come on the assurance that our friends were about to take power following the elections, in fact the electoral results proved to be a deadlock, which meant that the next president would be selected by the congress, not the outright vote. Back in Boston I received word that the political party with whom I had worked, the ADN, had not won. As of August sixth, the new president would be Victor Paz Estenssoro, of the opposing MNR party. I had met Paz Estenssoro's key economic advisers, especially a leading businessman, Gonzalo ("Goni") Sánchez de Lozada. I had no idea whether I would have any relationship at all with the new government, although I was happy to hear that the ADN had shared a copy of our stabilization plan with the new president and his team.

In fact, the new president moved quickly. He asked Goni to lead the effort to write a plan for bold and broad-based economic reforms, including but well beyond currency stabilization. The draft plan was revolutionary, calling for Bolivia to move from a statist and closed economy—typical of third world countries of the day—to a market-based, open economy. The plan prefigured the changes that would take place later in the decade in Eastern Europe, albeit on a more limited scale. The plan included the ideas about stabilization—including the central tactic of raising energy prices—but went well beyond stabilization to issues that our team had not even discussed.

As a wily politician, back as president for his fourth time since 1952, Paz Estenssoro pulled off something that only an experienced backroom dealer could accomplish. With Goni's plan in hand, he brought the new cabinet to the presidential palace and told them, "Nobody leaves. No one talks to the press. We're going to debate and then agree on an economic strategy. And we're all going to sign it. If you want to resign, you can resign. But otherwise, you're in the government, and you're going to be part of this." They debated around the clock for the better part of three days, and adopted what became known in Bolivia as Supreme Decree 21060, a blueprint not only for ending the hyperinflation but also for a thoroughgoing transformation of Bolivia's economy.

The program was initiated on August twenty-ninth, starting with a sharp rise in oil prices. As gasoline prices soared (a *gasolinazo* in Latin American slang), the budget deficit closed. Money poured into the state oil company and from the state oil company into the budget coffers. The sudden end of the budget deficit led to an immediate stabilization of the exchange rate. Since prices were set in dollars and paid in pesos, the sudden stabilization of the Bolivian peso-U.S. dollar exchange rate meant an equally sudden stability in peso prices. Within a week, the hyperinflation was over.

Figure 1 shows the monthly price level for the period 1982 (at the onset of the hyperinflation) until 1988. We see the sudden stop in the rise of the price level in September 1985. Figure 2 shows the same thing in finer resolution, on a week-to-week basis during August and September of 1985. There would be tense moments in the early months of the stabilization program, and a near collapse of the stability at the end of 1985, but the hyperinflation as it turned out was over for good. It had lasted for three years, and was ended in a day.

Had events proceeded quietly from that point on, I might never have had a further engagement with Bolivia. Sooner rather than later, however, I came to understand that Bolivia's hyperinflation, and the budget deficit that had caused it, were symptoms of much deeper ills.

Figure 1: Bolivian Prices, 1982–1988

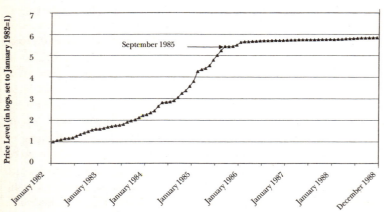

Source: Data from Instituto Nacional de Estadística, accessed online on August 27, 2004 from
http://www.udape.gov.bo

My understanding of Bolivia was quite superficial at the time—good enough to help assess how a stabilization plan could be launched, but not good enough to understand why the hyperinflation had occurred in the first place, and why a long cascade of wrenching changes lay ahead. Circumstances were far more fragile and difficult than I imagined.

CRACKS IN THE EDIFICE

On October 24, 1985, the London Metal Exchange suspended trading on tin, marking the beginning of a crash in prices. Over the next nine months, tin prices plummeted by about 55 percent after the tin cartel, of which Bolivia was a member, went bankrupt and was no longer able to buy tin stockpiles to hold the price at the earlier targeted rate. Bolivia was a tin exporting country, and the state-owned tin mines were an important source of jobs, political support, social support for workers, and taxes. Thus another huge hole opened in the deficit of this impoverished and stricken country, and what had been an early start to stability was suddenly thrown onto the shoals once again. Soon afterward, I got a call: President Paz Estenssoro wanted me to return to Bolivia.

By then I was more familiar with Bolivia's economic history. Amazingly, I had found an obscure book in Harvard's library written by George Eder, a foreign economic adviser to the Bolivian government in 1956, who advised the Bolivians on ending the high inflation that had

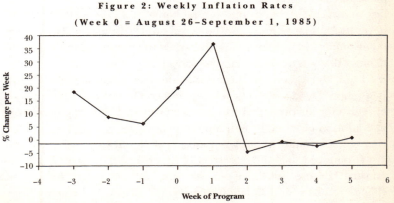

Figure 2: Weekly Inflation Rates
(Week 0 = August 26–September 1, 1985)

Source: Data from Morales and Sachs (1990).

followed Bolivia's 1952 Revolution. George Eder had set up a government committee for economic stabilization and had advised the committee. Eder had had lots of good ideas. Even the cast of characters was familiar, including Victor Paz Estenssoro himself, who had led the 1952 revolution and was Bolivia's president betweem 1952 and 1956.

When I returned to La Paz, I met Paz Estenssoro for the first time, and presented him with a memo on recommendations that harked back to 1956. The president was quite taken with the memo, and asked if I would continue as his adviser. I accepted, knowing it would give me the chance to watch the continuing drama, make suggestions, and learn from the experience. I went home, planning to return in a couple of months.

At Christmastime, a month later, I got another urgent call: the hyperinflation was back. Could I return immediately? I arrived immediately after the new year. On a brief stop in Lima, I heard the news that Bolivian Planning Minister Guillermo Bedregal had resigned, and on his way out had called for a 50 percent increase in wages so that Bolivians could keep up with a new explosion of prices. It sounded as if the hyperinflation was off and running once again. I knew that a new round of hyperinflation would trigger a new cycle of political instability. Upon arriving in La Paz, I went straight from the plane to the Central Bank. Sure enough, there had been a tremendous spike in the money supply in December.

A technical team at the Central Bank explained that the budget has to cover two monthly salaries in December as part of the Christmas package. This could have been accommodated through better monetary management, but as one central banker told me wistfully, "We've never had a finance minister who lasted two Christmases." The government simply did not know how to handle the extra monthly wage in a manner that was not financially explosive!

I quickly worked out a trick after the fact. I said that the Central Bank should sell its foreign exchange reserves into the currency market in return for the pesos that had just been issued. This foreign exchange operation would thereby mop up the newly issued pesos. The peso exchange rate would strengthen, peso prices would stop rising, and the just-announced wage increases could be obviated. This approach was unusual because Bolivia risked throwing away its scarce foreign exchange reserves for a situation that seemed already to be going down the drain. I thought that it was worth the risk, however. A return to hyperinflation would have been devastating. I took the idea to Goni, who was just then becoming the new planning minister. Goni bought the idea. We went to the president, who also accepted it.

The foreign exchange operation began. Just as monetary theory said, the exchange rate stabilized and then started to strengthen. This time was the first in a long while that the Bolivian currency had actually strengthened. The president announced, "There will be no wage increase. We are committed to stability and will make sure that our monetary policy is consistent with that." So the government took a strong line and won a lot of credibility with the public as a result. After this skirmish the hyperinflation was never to return, even as a threat.

The turnaround succeeded, at which point, ironically, I was called to the International Monetary Fund in Washington to explain why I was encouraging the Bolivian government to "waste" its scarce foreign exchange reserves. I explained the logic. The IMF could not see it and felt that the sale of foreign exchange was unwarranted. The opposition came too late. The operation was already finished and had succeeded. I happily left Washington on the evening flight, having had my first skirmish with the IMF. I was coming to realize that "official advice" coming from Washington could have its weak points. Little did I know at the time!

Consolidating the Victory over Hyperinflation

I also began to discover that there is no moment of peace in such crises. Bolivia had four huge obstacles that remained before the stabilization was finally consolidated. First, the October 1985 collapse of tin prices was eating away at the budget and macroeconomic stability. The tin mines were no longer profitable. The mining sector was throwing the entire budget into a huge deficit. The Bolivians undertook a massive cutback of the tin-mining labor force, one that was shocking in scale and heartrending for those affected. Almost five sixths of the tin workers eventually lost their jobs. An era of large-scale tin mining in Bolivia had ended with the collapse of the tin cartel.

The second obstacle was facing up to the debt crisis. The Bolivian government was bankrupt. It could not service its foreign debts owed to international banks and to foreign governments, and had, in fact, suspended payments more than a year earlier. Now that Bolivia had stabilized, the IMF was pressing for a resumption of debt servicing. I felt that such a step at this point would simply send Bolivia into political crisis and back to hyperinflation. It would require politically explosive and socially unacceptable burdens on Bolivia's poor through further cuts in government spending and further increases in taxation (if those were even possible to collect). Upon my strong advice, and Goni's strong concurrence, Bolivia said no to the IMF: it would not restart debt servicing. Bolivia's opposition to the resumption of debt servicing, and its insistence on debt cancellation, helped to set in motion the process of debt cancellation for the poorest countries.

How the debt debate played out was another eye-opener for me. The IMF team and I opened the debate one evening in Goni's living room. I held forth vigorously that renewed debt servicing would crush the living standards of already impoverished people, and would also destabilize the country politically. The IMF, on its side, said that there was no alternative; debt service must resume. After a heated exchange, we agreed to continue the debate the next day at lunch. As lunch started, I gave a little sermon about how renewed debt servicing was completely inappropriate, and how debt crises in the past had been resolved by substantial reductions in the debt through one contrivance or another. Indeed, Bolivia and many other countries had defaulted in the 1930s and had had their debts canceled in the 1940s. I announced, rather brazenly, that this was just the way it was going to have to be again in the 1980s.

The IMF team, of course, had instructions to the contrary. The Reagan administration had not yet acknowledged the need for debt cancellation, and was apparently content to squeeze Bolivia, if only to set an example for other much larger debtors, such as Argentina, Brazil, and Mexico. As I was talking, the IMF mission chief turned redder and redder. He was deeply annoyed to hear this kind of radical talk by an adviser. Finally, in exasperation, he said, "That is unacceptable, Professor Sachs. We will never send such a program to our board for approval." To my further protests, he then declared, "When I get home, I will call Bill Rhodes, who will also say that this is completely unacceptable." I nearly fell out of my seat because Bill Rhodes was a senior Citibank executive with responsibility for Latin American debt. Here was the IMF mission chief, in a broken country with hungry people, closed mines, hyperinflation, and disarray, saying that Citibank would have a veto over an IMF policy on debt cancellation.

I paused, and then replied scornfully, "Oh, now I really do understand. Let me explain to my Bolivian friends what you've just said. You are going to call Citibank to find out whether Bolivia's policies are appropriate? So the IMF's debt strategy is going to be determined by the international banks?" He became furious, closed his book and stood up, declared the meeting over, and walked out of the room with everyone scrambling behind him. The amazing fact, however, was that after that the IMF never again asked Bolivia to repay its debts. I think they were taken aback by their acknowledgment that the creditor governments that controlled the IMF were setting debt policies according to the wishes of major international banks rather than the dictates of good macroeconomic policy and international commitments to the needs of extremely poor countries. The IMF had finally acknowledged that Bolivia was truly broke, and needed to have its debt written down if it was going to get back on its feet.

From that point on, Bolivia remained in suspension of its debt. In 1987, I helped Bolivia to negotiate a debt cancellation agreement with its major commercial bank creditors, which became a template for later debt-cancellation operations. The concept was radical, but it was the only sensible and realistic way to face the economic circumstances of the country. It has made sense in the long term for the creditors as well as the debtors, since—when applied wisely—it has allowed countries to get back on their feet and either repay part of the debt (where that is possible) or at least be less of a burden to the international system in terms of future foreign assistance. The strategy of debt cancellation has now been applied in dozen of countries, but far too often the international community has been too late and too grudging in the debt relief to enable really impoverished, debt-torn countries to reestablish economic growth and development.

John Maynard Keynes, as usual, had many important things to say about debt servicing. In the period following World War I, Keynes understood and wrote brilliantly about the political economy of societies in deep economic distress. He understood that there was little advantage in pushing countries over the brink, either by demanding war reparations from Germany or the repayment of wartime debts to the allied victors of the war. Keynes warned that political systems could snap. In *The Economic Consequences of the Peace,* he boldly called for the cancellation of the post–World War I claims in an eloquent plea that I would find invaluable three quarters of a century later.

It might be an exaggeration to say that it is impossible for the European Allies to pay the capital and interest due from them on these debts, but to make them do so would certainly be to impose a crushing burden. They may be expected, therefore, to make constant attempts to evade or escape payment, and these attempts will be a constant source of international friction and ill-will for many years to come. . . .

There will be a great incentive to [the debtors] to seek their friends in other directions, and any future rupture of peaceable relations will always carry with it the enormous advantage of escaping the payment of external debts. If, on the other hand, these great debts are forgiven, a stimulus will be given to the solidarity and true friendliness of the nations lately associated. The existence of the great war debts is a menace to financial stability everywhere. . . .

We shall never be able to move again, unless we can free our limbs from these paper shackles. A general bonfire is so great a necessity that unless we can make of it an orderly and good-tempered affair in which no serious injustice is done to anyone, it will, when it comes at last, grow into a conflagration that may destroy much else as well.

Keynes warned that the failure to address the debt crisis could eventually lead to calamity, as indeed overtook Europe with the rise of Bolshevism and Nazism:

The bankruptcy and decay of Europe, if we allow it to proceed, will affect every one in the long-run, but perhaps not in a way that is striking or immediate.

The third critical obstacle was tax reform, the great drama of the spring of 1986. It was time for Bolivia's upper class to contribute to the tax system. I pushed friends within the government and political supporters of the government. Many of Bolivia's richest landowners could not quite understand why their thousand-hectare cattle ranches also needed to be taxed. The political debate was touch and go, but in the end, the tax reforms passed and they helped to consolidate a fairer fiscal base. Bolivia remains a place of great inequality. But the country took a step forward to greater fairness in 1986, and one that was extremely important in maintaining monetary stabilization and political civility in the country.

The final major initiative that year was to establish an emergency social fund that could address at least some of the urgent social conditions of the country. I was beginning to understand that the end of hyperinflation did not mean the end of suffering or extreme poverty. Far from it. I said ruefully to the government's economic team that if they were brave, heroic, steadfast, earnest, and honest, they could hope to turn their impoverished, hyperinflationary country into an impoverished country with stable prices. The end of the hyperinflation would at least provide the foundation for economic development.

Goni Sánchez de Lozada understood that Bolivia would have to reinvent itself, since tin mines could never again offer prosperity. But transformations and reinventions take time. Until then, Bolivians had to survive. People needed jobs, health care, and schools for their children. Canceling the debt was part of the answer. Working hard for more foreign aid was another piece. And finding new ways to direct emergency help to the poorest people was absolutely essential. One day in Goni's office we were brainstorming and hit on the idea of establishing an emergency social fund that would direct money to the poorest communities to help finance local infrastructure like water harvesting, or irrigation, or road improvements. I picked up the phone and called the World Bank. Katherine Marshall, the head of the Bolivia team at the Bank immediately responded, "You're right, let's do this." Within a very short period of time we were able to get the emergency social fund started with World Bank backing. The fund offered a bit of a safety net—jobs, village-level infrastructure—in extraordinarily difficult and fragile circumstances.

My last intensive involvement in Bolivia in this period came a year later when a U.S. military effort to interdict Andean drug trade hit Bolivia very hard. The arrival of U.S. military forces sent Bolivia's drug-traffickers scurrying. A financial crisis quickly ensued. Goni and I decided to seize the opportunity by pushing for a much deeper eradication of the coca crops (which provide coca leaf used in the manufacture of cocaine). We believed that if the United States would invest meaningfully in alternative development options for the tens of thousands of organized, politically mobilized *cocaleros* (coca cultivators), it would be possible to shift Bolivia to other agricultural and manufacturing exports.

Goni and I got together a group of anthropologists, agriculture specialists, and coca cultivation experts to work out a program to use increased foreign assistance to offer realistic economic alternatives to coca production, partly to help move people out of coca-growing regions with alternative employment, and partly to substitute other crops.

As with many other cases, the U.S. government ended up adopting some of these ideas, gradually and fitfully, over the next fifteen years. It did so, as so often happens, only after dividing the scope of U.S. funding by ten. The United States, then and now, was looking for the cheap way out, trying to push the costs onto the very poorest people, never making enough of an investment to underwrite a solution.

I went with Goni to Washington to present the analysis. The U.S. lack of support for Bolivia was appalling. In essence, Goni was told there was no money available to accomplish anything other than through military means. The worst meeting of all was with George Shultz, secretary of state at the time, who spent half an hour explaining to the Bolivian planning minister how the United States had budget problems and that there was just no money to help the Bolivians. This lecture came from a country whose per capita income was perhaps thirty times higher than Bolivia's, at a time when Bolivia was doing the United States' bidding on coca interdiction at great risk to its own economic and political stability.

WAKING UP TO GEOGRAPHY

Perhaps three years into my work in Bolivia, I received a wake-up call on economic realism in the course of a conversation with David Morawetz, a genial and insightful World Bank consultant. Morawetz was an international trade expert who had written a wonderful book on the collapse of Colombia's textile and apparel sector in the 1970s. He was attuned to the practicalities of business. The bank had sent him to address one major issue: what could Bolivia export after tin and coca?

Morawetz began the conversation with a straightforward observation: "This is a landlocked country, up in the Andean mountains, facing incredibly high transport costs. The only products that Bolivia has ever been able to export are commodities with a very high value per unit weight because only those commodities can successfully overcome the high transport costs." Morawetz observed that as a nation, Bolivia had been born in the Spanish colonial period first as a silver exporter, then as a gold exporter. It experienced a rubber boom in the middle of the nineteenth century, the tin boom early in the twentieth century, a brief hydrocarbons boom in the 1960s and 1970s, and the coca boom in the 1980s. All of Bolivia's exports were indeed commodities with a very high value per weight. "What can this country export now?"

Morawetz's point about Bolivia's geographical distress was truly (and incredibly) something new for me. Of course I knew that Bolivia was landlocked and mountainous. The mountain vistas added immeasurably to Bolivia's charm, the high altitude to my chronic shortness of breath in La Paz, and the landlocked status to Bolivia's lingering suspicions and hard feelings concerning Chile, which had stripped away Bolivia's coastal territory in 1884. Yet I had not reflected on how these conditions were key geographical factors, perhaps the overriding factors, in Bolivia's chronic poverty. In all of my training, the ideas of physical geography and the spatial distribution of economic activity had not even been mentioned.

Problems of geographic distress became a centerpiece of my thinking over the next fifteen years because once I started thinking about the economic forces of geography, it was hard not to think about it. Countries are shaped profoundly by their location, neighborhood, topography, and resource base. Adam Smith had thought widely about it, but I had not read Adam Smith for years. My conversation with Morawetz really got me thinking, and I realized that almost all the international commentary and academic economic writing about Bolivia neglected this very basic point. It bothered me greatly that the most basic and central features of economic reality could be overlooked by academic economists spinning their theories from thousands of miles away.

Fortunately, in my first foray into country advising, this serious mistake did not cause too much disruption. My assignment had been largely about ending a hyperinflation and reestablishing a fiscal and financial base for economic development. Monetary theory, thank goodness, still worked at thirteen thousand feet above sea level. My basic insights about how to end a hyperinflation and how to overcome a debt crisis still worked. When I turned my attention from stabilization to development, however, a renewed focus on physical geography and its economic consequences became crucial.

EARLY LESSONS IN CLINICAL ECONOMICS

Bolivia gave me my first insights into the problems of economic development. I began to understand vividly how much I would have to learn to be able to give sound guidance on critical issues of development. I would never again be an economist who could neglect a crucial "detail" about a country, such as its being mountainous or landlocked or at war with a neighbor. I became ever more attuned to a country's resource base, climate, topography, political relations with neighbors, internal ethnic and political divisions, and proximity to world markets. In short, I started realizing that I needed to be a clinician with the skills of differential diagnosis. I was not yet thinking explicitly in these terms, but the general notion that I was an economist making house calls began to take hold.

I learned several specific points that would prove useful in the future.

- Stabilization is a complex process. Ending a large budget deficit may be the proximate step, but controlling the underlying forces that caused the budget deficit is a more complex and longer-term process. Many factors in Bolivia had to change to consolidate its new price stability: domestic oil prices, the closure of unprofitable tin mines, reform of domestic taxation, debt cancellation, and social funds to reduce the crisis of extreme poverty.

- Macroeconomic tools are limited in their power. Even with the success of macroeconomic stabilization, Bolivia continued to experience great long-term difficulties because of its intrinsic problems: its geography; the great social and economic inequalities that divide the country; and regional political relations fraught with difficulty, particularly with Chile, Brazil, and Argentina.

- Successful change requires a combination of technocratic knowledge, bold political leadership, and broad social participation. Without technocratic knowledge, there would have been no successful stabilization or debt cancellation. Without the strong leadership of President Victor Paz Estenssoro and Goni Sánchez de Lozada, the very same plans would have failed.

- Success requires not only bold reforms at home but also financial help from abroad. Bolivia needed to make bold, coherent, and complex reforms. The international community needed to give adequate aid and debt cancellation.

- Poor countries must demand their due. Bolivia would have suffered years of further anguish from external debt had Goni and I not pushed relentlessly for a cancellation of Bolivia's debts. The IMF, certainly, was not coming to Bolivia's rescue. Perhaps because of my inexperience, I believed that a very different approach to debt reduction was not only needed but also possible. This outlook proved to be correct. Since then, I have strived to be clear about what is needed, and have paid much less attention to what I am told is "politically possible." When something is needed, it can and must become possible!

Table 1: Bolivian Progress Since 1985		
	1985	**2002**
GDP per capita (constant 1995 $)	835	940
Adult literacy rate (% of people ages 15 and above)	74	87
Primary school enrollment (%)	91	94
Secondary school enrollment (%)	29	67
Tertiary school enrollment (%)	21	39
Infant mortality rate (per 1,000 live births)	87	56
Under-5 child mortality rate (per 1,000)	122	71

Note: Where 1985 or 2002 data are not available, table shows nearest available year.
* Source: Data from World Bank (2004).

Bolivia has improved significantly since 1985, with social and political stability, constitutional rule, low inflation, and positive per capita economic growth (albeit growth that has been much too slow to consolidate public support), major improvements in literacy and school enrollment, and major reductions in infant and child mortality rates. Table 1 shows some of these improvements. During the early 1980s, the path of per capita income was on a steep decline; after stabilization there was a significant increase, shown by the V-shaped curve in figure 3. Goni Sánchez de Lozada was much praised for this turnaround, and won election as president, serving from 1993 to 1997. Bolivia's growth, however, stagnated at the end of the 1990s and the first years of the new century, part of a generalized economic crisis throughout South America.

Bolivia remains poor and divided to this day. Stabilization and open markets did not end poverty, even a generation later. Deep ethnic divisions remain. After Sánchez de Lozada won a second round of the presidency in 2002, protests exploded in 2003 over the government's acquiescence to U.S. demands to eradicate coca production and over the government's plans to sell natural gas to the United States. Sadly, in the midst of violence and bloodshed, Sánchez de Lozada was forced to resign. Despite the notable achievements since 1985, the burden of geography and the relative neglect by the United States and other donor countries still weigh very heavily on Bolivia, as does the continuing economic crisis throughout the rest of the Andean region.

Figure 3: Bolivian Income

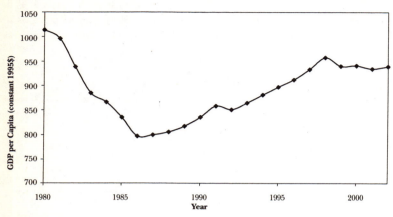

Source: Data from World Bank (2004).

The story of Bolivia thus shows the successes of macroeconomic reforms as well as their deep limitations. Price stability and market reforms reestablished growth, but the growth was too little and too uneven in its impact to lift the entire population from extreme poverty. The economic transformation in Bolivia remains only partially accomplished. Bolivia has gotten one foot on the development ladder, but the step up to the next rung has been excruciatingly slow and uncertain.

Bolivia's successes in the mid-1980s in stabilization and the restoration of growth attracted international notice for my evolving ideas on debt relief, stabilization, and social programs. I was invited to work with national leaders in Argentina, Brazil, Venezuela, and Peru, and I rapidly got to know more about the history, physical geography, social conditions, and economic trends of South America. This work, in turn, led to an unexpected call and invitation to Poland in early 1989 that began another chapter in my career.

Six

POLAND'S RETURN
TO EUROPE

In early 1989, I got a call out of the blue from Krzysztof Krowacki, an official in the Polish embassy in Washington, to ask if he could visit me at my office at Harvard. I agreed. I did not know what it was about, but it would turn out to be an invitation to participate in the epochal events starting to unfold in Eastern Europe.

A few days later, Krowacki was in my office explaining the economic disasters that had hit his country, and asking whether the advice I was giving in Latin America might be of relevance to Poland. He described a country in deep trouble: Poland had long ago partially suspended its international debt payments, the economy was suffering from high and rising inflation, and there was a deepening political crisis. He said that the government wanted to make reforms.

Poland had long been known as the most liberal of the communist states, but after the rise of Solidarity in 1980 and the military crackdown the year afterward, it was the only Soviet-dominated country of Eastern Europe under martial law. But even during martial law between 1981 and 1989, Poland was a kind of freewheeling, almost chaotic country and economy, with tremendous black marketing and smuggling. Although many people were arrested and jailed, there were still dissident voices being heard.

I listened with fascination to my guest for more than an hour. We talked about the developing-country debt crisis and what I had recommended in South America. At the end of the discussion he asked me if I would be willing to go to Poland to discuss these issues with some of his colleagues. I told him that I was interested in the events in Poland and that I had visited Wroclaw, Poland, in 1976, soon after worker strikes and protests in that city. I had followed Polish affairs and events in Eastern Europe with great interest, in part because my wife and her family had emigrated from Czechoslovakia.

That said, I politely declined his invitation, explaining that I did not choose to work for the communist government. I was a great fan of Lech Walesa's, who was still under house arrest. If a time came when there was a chance to talk both to the government and to a legalized Solidarity, I would be interested in doing so. When we parted, I said, "If anything changes, if martial law is lifted, please give me a call. I'd love to go."

Four weeks later Krowacki called me back and said, "Professor Sachs, you said to call if anything changes. Well, it turns out the government is going to legalize Solidarity in a round-table agreement in early April." This was amazing news. I did not quite take it at face value, since these things are never sure until they actually happen. But I said, "If this is really going to happen, count me in. Please make sure that when I arrive, I see both the government and the Solidarity economists. I want to see if there is some way that my knowledge and experience can help to bridge the gap between the two sides."

POLAND'S DEMOCRATIC REVOLUTION

I arrived in Warsaw on April 5, 1989, after attending a short conference in Moscow. A professional economist at the Trade Institute was my host. I gave a talk about debt management, met with a couple of the economists from the Solidarity movement as planned, and drove by the palace where the negotiations were being completed for the signing of the round-table agreement. I left that evening. It was a one-day visit, but I had a sense of history in the making.

A few weeks later I got a call from the remarkable investor and philanthropist George Soros, who said that he was in touch with some of the Solidarity leadership and with the government, and was taking a trip to Poland. Would I accompany him on the trip to meet with these groups? I told him that, strangely enough, I had recently had discussions in Warsaw and that I had an open invitation to return. Soros understood that his financial backing could help leverage democratization throughout Eastern Europe. His timely grants of fax machines, photo-copiers, airplane tickets, and much more had an unparalleled catalytic effect on the democratic revolutions throughout Eastern Europe. In May 1989, I went with Soros, and we met with government officials and again with the Solidarity economists.

During that spring, everybody had expected a continuation of com-munist rule. Still, there was growing economic chaos, and a desperate urge to find some kind of political and social equilibrium in which re-forms could go forward. No one knew what to do. The economy was broken; planning had collapsed; black markets, inflation, and extreme shortages were pervasive. At the conclusion of the trip, I told the Soli-darity group and the Polish government that I would be willing to be-come more involved to help address the deepening economic crisis. I asked George Soros if his Stefan Batory Foundation would cover the costs of a small team. I invited a friend, former student, and coauthor David Lipton, then at the IMF, to work with me. We began our advisory work still not having any inkling of what was about to happen.

Poland's political turning point was June 4, 1989. On the same day as the Tiananmen massacre in China, Poland held its first partially free elections in a half century. According to the round-table agreement, two things happened: first, an upper chamber of the parliament was added to create a new senate. And second, one third of the seats of the lower chamber, the Sejm, went up for election. Solidarity swept both cham-bers, winning ninety-nine of the hundred Senate seats, and all 35 per-cent of the lower chamber up for election. The result was a political earthquake: a partial political opening and a public scream in unison, "We want the communists out."

The next two months were the most remarkable of my professional life. When I returned to Poland soon after the election, a young and dy-namic activist, Grzegorz ("Larry") Lindenberg, took Lipton and me to meet, one by one, the leading strategists of the Solidarity movement: Bronislaw Geremek, Jacek Kuron, and Adam Michnik. All three men are giants in the worldwide struggle for human rights; all three played a pivotal role in ending the cold war divisions of Europe.

Early one evening I sat down with Geremek, who asked me what I thought Solidarity should do at that point. We began several hours of discussion. I told Geremek that the elections had given Solidarity a man-date to govern. I did not want to be naive, I hastened to add, given the repeated tragedies of Eastern Europe's recent history, including Soviet-led crackdowns in East Germany in 1953, Hungary in 1956, and Czechoslovakia in 1968, not to mention martial law in Poland. Still, the election results were unambiguous.

Geremek demurred. I could see the weight of history on his deeply furrowed brow. Aside from the practical difficulties of any form of power sharing in Eastern Europe, Geremek doubted that Solidarity could actually manage the economy, which was in a state of complete disarray if not freefall. He wondered whether it would be better for Solidarity to participate from the political sidelines, giving advice—perhaps through a Solidarity-run economics committee of the newly elected Senate—but not attempting to take responsibility for a mess that was not Solidarity's making and that was not easily remedied.

Now it was my turn to demur. I disputed the idea that an economy could be steered from the sidelines, that Solidarity could play its historic role through a Senate committee. I explained the trials and tribulations of managing a stabilization program. I explained how the real life of economic reform, as in Bolivia, was "one damned thing after another." I explained how steering an economy through the gales of hyperinflation and a foreign debt crisis was a treacherous task. I also explained why I thought that Solidarity could succeed. Economic reforms work, I insisted. The public was with Solidarity. Now was the time to act.

After several hours, Geremek slowly rose. "I feel terrible after this discussion because I think you're right. Maybe we don't have a choice."

Geremek suggested that Lipton and I go next to see Jacek Kuron. We met in his apartment in the early evening a few days later. We entered Kuron's small apartment and made our way to the study, where Kuron sat at a crowded desk in a room filled with books piled high on the table and everywhere else. He took out the first of many packs of cigarettes that he would smoke that evening, and a bottle of alcohol. He barely spoke English, and understood just a little bit more. He smiled and said, "Okay, so why are you here?"

"Well, I was asked to see you to talk about how Poland can get out of this mess." "Okay then," he replied with Larry serving as interpreter, "what do you say?" I started weaving a story about what economic reform in Poland might really mean. I said that Poland needed to become a "normal" country once again with a normal economy. The revolutionaries of Eastern Europe, including Kuron, had carried the banner of a "Return to Europe." They were not utopians or would-be inventors of a new social system. They simply demanded that Poland and its neighbors should become part of a united "normal" Europe again. In economic terms, that meant a mixed economy like Poland's neighbors to the west.

I continued to improvise, sketching out an economic strategy for Poland's return to Europe, drawing a bit on my experience in Bolivia, since that country had "returned" to the world economy after decades of self-imposed protectionism. I also compared Poland's situation with that of Spain's and Portugal's in the 1970s, after their long periods of military rule under Franco and Salazar, respectively. Those countries had been isolated economically and politically, and then had found their way back to the heart of Europe through economic and political reforms. Their return to Europe had been marked by considerable economic achievement, with high rates of economic growth and success in attracting job-creating foreign investment from the rest of Europe.

I said that the essence of Poland's return to Europe would be to trade on a market basis with Europe; to have people, and goods, and companies moving to and from Europe; and to have Poland adopt the laws, institutions, and governance patterns of Western Europe, so that sooner rather than later—perhaps on a five-year timetable—Poland could become a member of the European Community (the European Union, established in 1992, was still three years away). To get there, however, would also require a decisive stabilization program, since the immediate crisis was one of shortages, black markets, and spiraling hyperinflation. The mountain of unpayable foreign debt would also have to be reduced by negotiating the cancellation of part of the debt, as Bolivia had just accomplished in 1987.

This conversation took place well before there was a Solidarity-led government, so I was improvising. Every couple of minutes Kuron would hit the table and say, "Tak, rozumiem! Tak, rozumiem!"—"Yes, I understand! Yes, I understand!" Smoke was filling the room, and the bottle kept pouring. I talked and talked, probably for another three or four hours. I was drenched in sweat. I do not know how many packs of cigarettes he smoked that night, each stub being crushed into an ever filling ashtray. At the end of the evening, he said, "Okay, I understand this. We'll do it. Write a plan."

I thought to myself, "This is exciting. He liked the ideas." I said, "Mr. Kuron, we will go home and fax you something within a week or two about these ideas." He hit the table. "No! We need the plan now." I said, "What do you mean?" "I need this tomorrow morning." Lipton and I looked at each other. And Kuron said again, "I need this tomorrow morning." It was probably half past eleven at night. Larry said, "Okay, we'll go over to the *Gazeta* office. There's a computer there. You can type out a plan." Larry Lindenberg was business manager of *Gazeta Wyborcza,* the newly legalized Solidarity newspaper, under the leadership of the new editor in chief, Adam Michnik.

A PLAN TO ESTABLISH A MARKET ECONOMY

We arrived at midnight in the newsroom, recently converted from a kindergarten classroom. I sat at the keyboard, and Lipton and I began to write a plan for the transformation of Poland from a socialist economy in the Soviet orbit to a market economy within the European Community. We worked through the night until dawn, at which point we printed out a fifteen-page paper with key concepts and a planned chronology of reforms. It was the first time, I believe, that anyone had written down a comprehensive plan for the transformation of a socialist economy to a market economy. It briefly touched on the questions of trade, exchange rates, price liberalization, convertibility of the currency, stabilization, industrial policy, debt cancellation, and a bit on privatization, which was the area of greatest uncertainty.

Our proposal was for a dramatic, quick transformation to a market economy—a leap across the institutional chasm—with market forces to be introduced even before widespread privatization could be achieved. Our hypothesis, which proved to be correct, was that the state-owned enterprises would function somewhat like regular businesses if they were allowed to operate according to market forces, despite the fact that they were bureaucratic entities without owners other than the state. We stressed that sooner rather than later the state would have to find real owners for these enterprises, through various methods of privatization.

In an economic shorthand that was to be repeated many times in the coming years, our program, in essence, was described as resting on five pillars:

- Stabilization—ending the high inflation and establishing a stable, convertible currency

- Liberalization—allowing markets to function by legalizing private economic activity, ending price controls, and establishing the necessary commercial law

- Privatization—identifying private owners for assets currently held by the states. These assets might be privatized in the form of entire enterprises, or piecemeal (machinery, buildings, land), depending on the circumstances

- Social Safety Net—pensions, health care, and other benefits for the elderly and the poor, especially to help cushion the transition

- Institutional Harmonization—adopting, step by step, the economic laws, procedures, and institutions of Western Europe in order to be a successful candidate for the European Union (still the European Community as of 1989)

Poland's challenges had some similarities to the problems in Latin America, but also some profound differences. The similarities were mainly macroeconomic. Like Latin America, Poland had high inflation, a large budget deficit, and a large overhang of foreign debt. As in parts of Latin America, Poland's currency was unstable and not freely convertible at the official exchange rate, so there was a huge gap between the official exchange rate and the black market rate. That gap, in turn, led to massive smuggling and tax evasion.

The differences were perhaps even more important. Poland was a literate and ethnically homogeneous society. The ethnic and class tensions that divided Bolivia were, mercifully, not present. Poland was also not impoverished. Yes, its infrastructure was in a dilapidated state and needed a massive overhaul; its air and water were polluted after decades of energy-intensive industrialization and lack of environmental control; and its Soviet-era factories were uncompetitive in Western markets. But still, Poland was largely urban, literate, and equipped with basic infrastructure (roads, electricity, piped water and sewerage, seaports and airports). Geography was also favorable. Poland's proximity to Germany, for once in its modern history, would be a big plus because it would ease the two-way trade between Poland and the largest economy in Western Europe. (In the past, the same proximity had meant repeated invasions and conquest by outside forces.)

The biggest difference with Latin America, by far, was that Polish society knew where to head: toward Western Europe. Before 1945, Poland had been a market economy, and part of the reforms would be to dust off the commercial codes of the 1930s. Another part would be to adopt the more modern commercial laws that were the shared legal base of the European Community. In its quest to return to Europe, Poland also had a worthy role model, at least in part: Spain, after the death of the dictator Francisco Franco.

In important ways, Spain and Poland shared a similar position in Europe. Both are Catholic countries of around forty million people. Both are in the periphery of the continental European economy, roughly equidistant from the heartland of the Rhine industrial region, with Spain to the south and Poland to the east, as shown in map 6. As such, both were late industrializers in Europe.

In 1955, the per capita GDPs of the two economies were roughly of equal size: Spain was at $516 per capita; Poland at $755. Both countries had been damaged by war (civil war in Spain's case); Poland was newly under the political control of the Soviet Union. Spain gradually liberalized, even while Franco was still alive, and then accelerated its integration with Europe after Franco's death in 1975. It finally became a member of the European Community in 1986. Spain's return to Europe had done wonders for its economic growth. Spain attracted Western European tourists and investments, and enjoyed an export boom to its neighboring countries, thereby becoming one of Europe's fastest growing economies. By 1989 Spain's per capita GDP was roughly four times that of Poland.

My explicit hope and belief was that Poland could enjoy a Spanish type of boom to start making up for nearly forty years of lost time. As we wrote the plan, there was one big uncertainty, however. What would happen to the old heavy industry built in Poland on the basis of trade and energy links with the Soviet Union? We were soon to find out. The start of the transition involved a large reduction in production by the old industry. The first changes, therefore, saw a dramatic decline in industrial production as a shakeout of the old Soviet-era enterprises occurred. It was two years into the reform, in 1991, when a recovery in GNP began to occur. Fortunately, that recovery would soon gain momentum and carry Poland above its 1989 GDP and industrial production levels, as is evident in figure 1.

Figure 1: GDP and Industrial Production in Poland

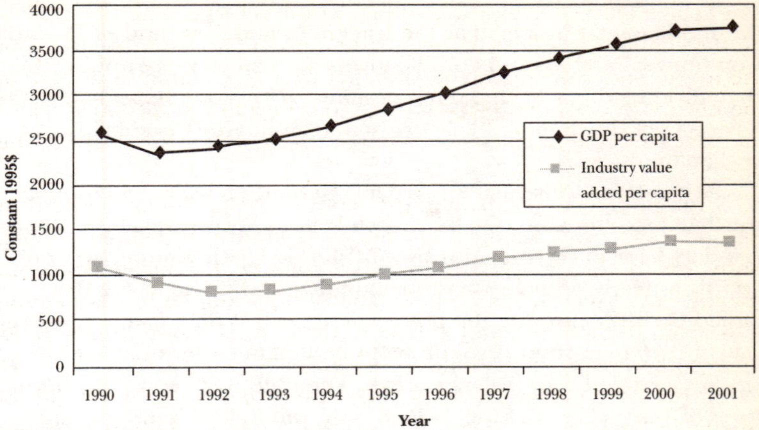

Source: Calculated using data from World Bank (2004).

Launching the Plan

We took the document to Jacek Kuron the next morning. "Good, this is good," said Kuron. "Go see Michnik." Adam Michnik, the *Gazeta* editor, was the third member of Solidarity's intellectual triumvirate. Brave and visionary, Michnik was as clear thinking as anyone I met in the democratic upheavals of Eastern Europe and the former Soviet Union.

I laid out the plan to him. We talked a bit. He kept saying, "I'm not an economist. I don't understand these things." At the end of our conversation he asked, "Will this work? That's what I want to know. Will this work?" I said, "Yes, this is going to work." He said, "Are you really confident that it's going to work?" I said, "This is good. This will work." Michnik said, "Okay, then you have filled in the last piece of my puzzle. I've known what to do politically. Now you tell me that there is an economic strategy as well. In that case, we're going to go for government."

Within a few days, Michnik wrote a lead editorial in the *Gazeta Wyborcza* that defined Poland's political transformation: "Wasza Prezydentura, Nasz Premier" ("Your Presidency, Our Prime Minister"). Power would be shared. Solidarity would form the government; the communists would keep the presidency and the "power ministries" (defense, interior, intelligence, police). It was a brilliant gambit, building confidence across an embittered half-century political divide. Michnik's compromise proposal was based not only on political realism, but also on the fundamental insight that the leaders of Solidarity and of Poland's Communist Party were all Polish patriots, with much more uniting them than dividing them. With the power ministries in communist hands, the Soviets were much more likely to assent to Solidarity's leadership in the civilian ministries.

At this point, Michnik, Kuron, and Geremek all advised Lipton and me that it was time for us to brief Lech Walesa. We got on a little plane a few days later to fly from Warsaw to Gdansk. Upon landing, we took a taxi to a nearly empty, cavernous building across the street from the famed Gdansk Shipyard, the place where Lech Walesa had jumped the wall in 1980 to start the revolution of freedom in Eastern Europe.

We were led into Walesa's office. The walls were covered with pictures of Martin Luther King, Jr., and John and Robert Kennedy, and various proclamations and awards. Out of the window we could see the great anchor at the shipyard entrance. Walesa came in and we greeted him. He began abruptly. "What are you doing here? What do you want?" I said, "Mr. Walesa, we're here to talk to you about the fact that Poland is slipping into hyperinflation. We have a plan for economic stabilization and reforms that we'd like to present." He immediately interrupted me. "I didn't come here for an abstract discussion; I want to know how we get banks into Gdansk."

I was nonplussed, but I pushed back firmly. "Mr. Walesa, hyperinflation is not an abstract issue. The current economic crisis could really destroy Polish society." I began to try to describe what I thought was happening. He listened, asked a question or two, and then said, "I want to know how we get foreign banks to come here. We've got good buildings here. We need banks. I want you to help me get a bank to Gdansk." I said, "Well, I'll certainly be working to try to help you with that." We discussed a little bit more, and he thanked us for coming, and we were led out. I was bewildered.

A few years later I was at the Belgian embassy in Moscow, speaking to a number of ambassadors. The Belgian ambassador pulled me aside, and said, "You'll be a little bit surprised to know that I was the next visitor to see Lech Walesa after you met him in the summer of 1989. I was Belgium's ambassador to Poland at the time." I expressed my amazement. He continued, "Well, Mr. Walesa said to me, 'I don't know what that fellow was talking about, but it sure sounded interesting.'"

As it turned out, I had many subsequent meetings with Lech Walesa. My admiration for Walesa was, and remains, sky-high. He was surely the inspiration that had brought me to Poland in the first place. Having been an electrician who jumped a shipyard wall and brought freedom to his country, Walesa had not had much time to learn macroeconomics. He clearly understood human nature and politics, however, and I learned a lot from him on both counts, as did the entire world. Walesa was a great president of Poland in the early 1990s and is one of the world's heroic freedom fighters.

Lipton and I flew back to the United States. About a week later, in mid-July, I talked with Michnik by phone. "So, what's going to happen?" Michnik responded, "It's okay; it's going to work." "What do you mean?" I asked. He said, "Gorbachev called us, and he's agreed with the proposed change." The Soviet Union was going to accept a Solidarity prime minister and a communist president. This decision was yet another of Gorbachev's extraordinary contributions to world peace and the end of the cold war. Gorbachev had actively helped to broker the arrival of Solidarity to power in Poland. Solidarity's rise to power was not a fait accompli grudgingly accepted by the Soviet leader. It was something Gorbachev promoted in the interest of peace.

Lipton and I returned to Poland in early August, and we introduced the reform plan to the Solidarity members of the Polish parliament. *Gazeta Wyborcza* also ran several big stories promoting the "Sachs Plan" as the way out of Poland's economic crisis. On August twenty-fourth, the day that Prime Minister Mazowiecki came to power, I was invited to speak to the Solidarity members of parliament. This was Poland's first day of political freedom in almost half a century. The national and international media were there, and as it turned out, so too were Senate Majority Leader Bob Dole and his wife, Elizabeth Dole.

Senator Dole spoke first. He brought the good wishes of the president of the United States and the American people. Dole wanted the Polish people to know that the American people stood with them in this moment of freedom. The United States would help to ensure that Poland was successful on its path to democracy and freedom. He sat down after prolonged applause. I was called to the podium next.

I started by saying that Poland's economic crisis was very deep, that a hyperinflation was brewing and the socialist system was collapsing. Poland was going to have to move with boldness and urgency to the market system. Then I said that there was one huge issue that was on everyone's mind: the crushing $40 billion of foreign debt that Poland owed to the world. Many people feared that this debt would become the real barrier separating Poland from Europe and from prosperity.

"I want to remind you of what Senator Dole just said. Senator Dole said that the American people are with you. I have no doubt that that's true. We Americans understand that after forty-five years of domination, Poland today marks one of the most important and positive events in modern history. Americans will be with you; Europe will be with you. So I'm sure Senator Dole agrees that Poland's debt should just be canceled. There's no way that the Soviet-era debt should in any way risk the freedom of the Polish people."

I then used the line that was often repeated afterward. I said, "Your debt crisis is over. All you have to do is send a postcard to your creditors: 'Thank you very much, but now we're in the age of freedom and democracy, and we can't pay you the Soviet-era debts.'" And I said, "Don't think about it again; it's done." A huge, thunderous applause erupted, not surprisingly, along with some shock.

After that evening there were a lot of people in Washington who tried to tell the new Polish leaders that I was dangerous. At least one well-placed Pole in Washington advised the prime minister to get me out of the country before I did real damage to Poland's economic reforms. I was worried, of course. Even though I felt that my concepts were right, my toehold as adviser was tenuous. Poland needed a decisive transformation to a market economy, combined with stabilization, currency convertibility, and debt cancellation. It was an attractive package of reforms that had a good chance of working despite the deepening crisis.

The next evening Lipton and I met the new prime minister, Tadeusz Mazowiecki. We were led in late at night to the Stalinesque Council of Ministers building. The prime minister greeted us wearily; his burden was evident. He was an older man, and the difficult months ahead were going to be exhausting. I didn't know what to expect of his approach to the economic crisis. In one sentence he dispelled my concerns and got it exactly right. He said to me, "I'm looking for Poland's Ludwig Erhard."

Ludwig Erhard had been the minister of economic affairs of postwar West Germany who decisively put the country on the path of market reform. He was a famously successful and bold economic manager who went on to become a somewhat less successful chancellor in the early 1960s. Erhard was especially famous for having ended price controls overnight in West Germany, a move that allowed goods to come back into the stores from the black markets. I had been recommending this kind of dramatic step, what would later be called shock therapy. Erhard had also been a major inspiration for Gonzalo Sánchez de Lozada in Bolivia.

We talked further. I described the ideas that I had, and he replied that the plans sounded very much like what he wanted to do. He needed to find someone who could really lead such a dramatic effort. He named a fellow whom I did not know, Leszek Balcerowicz. Balcerowicz ultimately headed the economic effort, and he was the true Ludwig Erhard of Poland—a brave, brilliant, and decisive leader.

Lipton and I met Balcerowicz two weeks later. I spent a few minutes describing our plan, with which he was already familiar. He then took out a large flow diagram and unfolded it on the table. He said, "We're going to do this, and we're going to do this dramatically fast." Balcerowicz was a professor at the Warsaw School of Economics and Planning. He was a respected, politically independent scholar who had received a master's degree in business at St. John's University in New York City. He spoke perfect English, understood the market economy, and was a long-distance runner. He would need this endurance for what lay ahead.

We began to work with Balcerowicz and his team to turn concepts into policies. It was one thing to sketch out some ideas, another to elaborate a program, and still another to construct a legislative, budgetary, and financial agenda. The details are overwhelming and unavoidable. That is why reforms cannot be led from the sidelines of parliament. Reforms have to be led by an executive team, with a real executive leader. Balcerowicz's first presentation of his plans would be in Washington, in late September 1989, at the annual IMF meetings. We helped draft the plan that he circulated to financial leaders at that occasion. It was an important moment. The world was waiting to hear what Poland planned to do.

Early one morning during the IMF meetings, I called Balcerowicz and said, "Leszek, I have an idea. I want to get you a billion dollars today. I want to raise money for a stabilization fund for the Polish currency, the Zloty Stabilization Fund. If we're going to make the Polish zloty a convertible currency, I think we should try to peg the zloty at a stable value right from the start of the reforms. To do that, Poland will need foreign exchange reserves, which could be put in a highly visible stabilization fund." Balcerowicz replied, "Do you think you could raise that money? If you can get a billion dollars, great."

As we had become accustomed to doing, Lipton and I set up a computer on Lipton's dining room table, and typed out a one-page memo explaining the idea of the $1 billion Zloty Stabilization Fund. The memo explained the concept of currency convertibility and stability as a linchpin of Poland's return to Europe. We then went to see Senator Dole. We explained the idea and he liked it. He invited us to return to his office in an hour to meet with General Brent Scowcroft, the National Security Adviser. We presented the concept to General Scowcroft, who also liked it. By the end of the day the plan had been accepted at the White House; and by the end of the week, the Bush administration had announced its support for the $1 billion Zloty Stabilization Fund, of which the United States would contribute $200 million and would seek $800 million in contributions from other governments. The fund was put together by the end of the year, and was in place at the start of Poland's reforms on January 1, 1990.

From Plan to Action

Poland's "big bang," or shock therapy as it came to be called, began on the first day of the new year. Virtually all price controls were eliminated. The currency was steeply devalued and then pegged at the new rate of 9,500 zlotys per dollar. The currency was backed by the Zloty Stabilization Fund, and the Central Bank of Poland announced that it was prepared to intervene in the foreign exchange market to keep the rate at 9,500 per dollar. A raft of new economic legislation went into effect, especially laws allowing private companies to open for business. Trade barriers with Western Europe were eliminated, and private traders were free to travel to and from Western European neighbors to buy and sell goods.

The first days were frightening. With the end of price controls, the pent-up excess demand of the socialist era caused a massive jump in prices, on the order of a fivefold increase. The price of a particular cut of meat, for example, might rise within days from 1,000 zlotys per kilo to 5,000 zlotys per kilo. In the prereform days, however, the 1,000-zloty price was mostly a fiction. Only those people who queued up early in the morning and were lucky to pick the right shops could get meat at that price, but most shoppers would find only empty store counters. If they really wanted to get meat, they would have to pay black market prices, which could be even higher than 5,000 zlotys per kilo. Thus what looked like a shocking fivefold jump in prices was, in many cases, an actual decline in prices if one compared the black market prices before January 1, 1990, with the free-market prices afterward. After the reforms, the goods were available in the shop counters, not the alleys of the black market. This change, too, lowered the cost of goods by lowering the time and effort that went into buying them.

Theory is one thing, and practice is quite another. Even though I was confident that the end of price controls on January 1, 1990, would put goods back into the shops, at affordable prices, the early days of 1990 were nerve-racking. I called Poland regularly from the United States. Larry Lindenberg was getting more and more nervous. "It's been a week, and we don't see any goods in the shops yet." And then, suddenly, the breakthrough came. "Jeff, there are goods in the stores! In fact, the department store down the block is having a sale, cutting the price that it was charging for some appliances. This is the first time in my adult life I've seen a sale. Something is starting to happen."

Indeed, within a few weeks the markets filled again. On our visits to Poland at the time, Lipton and I kept a reconnaissance on the availability of kielbasa in a shop around the corner from the Ministry of Finance. Throughout late 1989 there were no sausages available at all. By the middle of January, the sausages lasted until about eleven in the morning. A few weeks later, the sausages were amply available the entire day. An amazing shuttle trade also began between Germany and Poland. Poles would take their little cars and drive across the border to Germany to buy goods to sell in Poland. They would sell the goods out of the trunk of the car, convert the zlotys into deutsche marks (a conversion legal after the start of the year), and then use the deutsche marks for the next round of purchases. Others were selling Polish goods—such as processed meats—or Polish labor on construction sites in Western Europe, bolstering the flow of deutsche marks and other Western European currencies on the Polish market.

None of this trade made Poland rich overnight. The newly available goods were expensive, and incomes were low. Still, Poles stopped spending their daily lives searching for goods in the black market or queuing up for goods in front of empty shops. The freedom to trade would become an underpinning of economic growth during the coming years. There were, of course, some very sharp changes in consumption patterns, some highly desirable, others quite painful. One change for the better was in the composition of the Polish diet. Until 1990, the Polish diet had been overstuffed with fatty dairy products, the result of heavy subsidies for dairy farmers. At the start of 1990, the subsidies were eliminated, and the diet shifted toward fruit and vegetables and away from cholesterol-laden dairy products. Fruit that had simply been unavailable in Poland, such as bananas, was now available through the shuttle trade. The new diet led to a significant drop in heart disease within a few years.

The biggest dislocation, by far, came in Poland's large state-owned industrial enterprises. Many enterprises had survived only because of central planning. They were not manufacturing products that were marketable, especially when Western goods became readily available. Many were making products that had been sold to the Soviet Union, which was not much of a customer any longer. Most of heavy industry had relied for decades on the delivery of very cheap and plentiful Soviet energy to Poland. In the beginning of 1990, with the end of communist rule in Poland, the Soviet Union began selling oil and gas to Eastern Europe on a strictly market basis, leading to a huge drop in supplies. Poland's large heavy industrial firms were forced to scale back their workforce, and some closed their doors permanently. The greatest pain was endured by middle-aged workers in their forties and fifties who had been trained for a Soviet economy that no longer existed. Most of these laid-off workers ended up on the unemployment dole for a while, then on pensions after early retirement. History had cheated them of the training and knowledge for a full lifetime of productive employment.

Fortunately, foreign investment from Germany and other Western European countries began to pick up relatively early. In late 1989, I was asked to meet with a senior executive of Asea Brown Boveri in the Zurich airport as I was traveling back to Boston. She told me that the company was considering an investment in Poland: taking over a state-owned power turbine factory. She asked if I would meet with the board, and when I did, they were very surprised when I told them how optimistic I was about Poland. Fortunately, enough of the ABB leadership shared that optimism, and the proposed investment went ahead. It became very successful, and the company ended up selling power turbines all over the world through ABB's global production network. Its success was a clear example of how Poland's integration into the world economy could create jobs in Poland, raise the productivity of local industry, help integrate Poland into the European economy, and begin the long process of raising productivity and living standards.

In general, Western European firms began to invest in Eastern Europe after 1989, often setting up production facilities in order to export manufactured goods to Western European markets, taking advantage of the lower wages in the east. This same pattern fueled Spain's rapid economic

POLAND'S RETURN TO EUROPE

progress once it had become integrated with the European Community in the 1970s and 1980s. Geography, as usual, showed its power to shape economic events in the east. The farther a postcommunist country was from Western European markets, the lower the foreign direct investment (FDI) per person that flowed into the country. This is illustrated in figure 2. The distance of each postcommunist country's capital city from Stuttgart, in the heart of the European economy, is plotted on the horizontal axis, and the amount of foreign direct investment per person as of 1996 on the vertical axis. Though not a rigorous analysis, the downward sloping line shows a strong relationship: the closer to Western Europe, the higher the FDI.

Within two years, it was beginning to dawn on many people that Poland was out of disaster and, in fact, beginning to grow. That resurgence was the first case of postsocialist growth in all of the countries of Eastern Europe. A degree of optimism began to creep in, even in a milieu that was historically so riddled with pessimism. The real revival of optimism, however, awaited a solution to the foreign debt, which hung over Poland's future like a persistent storm cloud.

Figure 2: FDI and Location in Eastern Europe and former Soviet Union

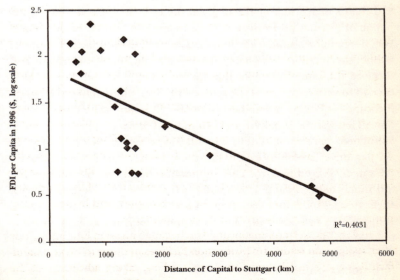

Note: Calculated using data from World Bank (2004).

ENDING THE STRANGLEHOLD
OF SOVIET-ERA DEBT

Balcerowicz was not going to be able to manage the strife and dislocation of wrenching economic reforms if the benefits of the reforms were
gobbled up by increased debt servicing. The gains from reform had to
accrue to the Polish people, not to Poland's foreign creditors, a basic
point of political economy that I had been stressing for many years
about Latin America and Eastern Europe. Balcerowicz decided to draw
the line, just as I had recommended. Poland would aim for a negotiated
cancellation of a significant part of its external debts to ensure that its
future was not held hostage to Soviet-era debts and that the Polish
people themselves would be the beneficiaries of their brave plunge into
democracy and a globally integrated market economy.

Alas, the negotiations would not be so simple. I heard repeatedly
from senior finance officials of the United States, Europe, and Japan
that the Western creditor nations would not forgive the debt of a European country. Bolivia was one thing, they argued, but Poland was quite
another. Then the breakthrough came, when Balcerowicz went to see
Helmut Kohl. Before he left, I suggested to Balcerowicz that it would be
helpful for him to read the 1953 London Agreement, in which the allied victors of World War II had given the new Democratic Federal Republic of Germany a fresh start by reducing the burden of pre–World
War II–era debts. In their meeting, as Chancellor Kohl started to object
to debt cancellation for Poland, Balcerowicz told him that Germany had
received the same treatment that he was asking for, and then he proceeded to summarize the 1953 settlement. Kohl ultimately agreed to do
the same for Poland as had been done for Germany, calling it a historic
time. That was the breakthrough. In the end, Poland received a cancellation of 50 percent of its debt, roughly $15 billion.

Countries are often told that if their debts are cancelled, they will
no longer be creditworthy. This argument is backward. If a country has
too much debt, it cannot be creditworthy. Rational investors will not
make new loans. If debt cancellation is warranted by financial realities,
is negotiated in good faith, and the country pursues sound economic
policies afterward, then debt cancellation raises creditworthiness rather
than reduces it. After all, a well-governed country with low debts can afford to take on new debts. Debt cancellation cannot be for a lark or
whim. It must not be a game to avoid past obligations. Debt cancellation

must reflect true social, economic, and political realities. Under those circumstances, a negotiated cancellation of debt can give new hope and new economic opportunities to the debtor country, and renewed credit-worthiness. This is exactly what happened with Poland, which returned to the capital markets in the 1990s.

Alas, Yugoslavia was not so fortunate. At the time that I was advising Poland, I was also asked to help Yugoslavia escape from a similar spiral of hyperinflation, excessive foreign debt, and socialist collapse. The last prime minister of federal Yugoslavia, Ante Markovic, launched a stabilization plan in January 1990 that I had helped to devise. That plan got off to a wonderful start and could actually have worked, but for Slobodan Milosevic's deliberate and disastrously successful moves to undermine the federal government and its economic program. Markovic needed bolstering in his struggle with Milosevic, who was at that point head of Serbia. Markovic appealed to the Western powers to postpone—not to forgive—Yugoslavia's debts. A postponement would have given financial breathing room and political prestige to Markovic, both of which would have strengthened the stabilization plan, whose success would have further strengthened him.

Yet while Milosevic gained strength in his battle to bring down Yugoslavia, the first Bush administration, the European Union, and the IMF refused even the modest request to reschedule Yugoslavia's debts. This refusal reflected, in my opinion, the stupidity of having foreign policy and international economic policy divorced from each other. Although Milosevic, not the West, must be blamed for the collapse of Yugoslavia, there was no effort of any sophistication to help hold the country together. The U.S. ambassador at the time, Warren Zimmerman, with whom I dealt briefly, wrote an account of the collapse of Yugoslavia, *Origins of a Catastrophe: Yugoslavia and Its Destroyers,* which arrived at the same conclusion.

LESSONS FROM POLAND'S REFORMS

By 2002, Poland was more than 50 percent richer in per capita terms than it had been in 1990, and it had logged the most successful growth record of any postcommunist country in Eastern Europe or the former Soviet Union. On May 1, 2004, fifteen years after the start of democracy, Poland became a member of the European Union. Poland has indeed returned to Europe. Its economic reforms have succeeded, even if the country faces many continuing challenges and decades more before it closes the income and wealth gaps with its richer neighbors in Western Europe.

I had first been invited to Poland because of my experience with Bolivia and its neighbors in South America. The lessons of Latin American stabilization and debt cancellation had indeed proved useful for Poland, as Krzysztof Krowacki hoped when he had first come to my office at Harvard in January 1989. I learned a vast amount after arriving in Poland, and the lessons were vital not only for understanding what was needed in Poland (and its neighbors) but also for understanding events and economic development strategies in Latin America and other parts of the world. Both the similarities and differences with Bolivia captivated me. I began to understand how a country's geography, history, and internal social dynamics shaped its economic performance. Clinical economics was beginning to evolve.

First, I realized more than ever how a country's fate is crucially determined by its specific linkages to the rest of the world. Bolivia's history, crises, and economic prospects all thoroughly reflected its situation as a mountainous, landlocked country making its living by exporting natural resources. Poland's history, crises, and economic prospects, by contrast, all thoroughly reflected its situation as a mainly low-lying plain sandwiched between Germany to the west and Russia to the east. Throughout the two centuries from 1763 to 1989, the long, flat Pomeranian plain had been among the worst, if not the very worst, plots of real estate on the planet. German and Russian armies had invaded Poland many times. Poland had disappeared from the map—consumed by its more powerful neighbors in the second half of the eighteenth century—only to reappear in 1919 as part of the peace settlement after World War I. But independence was not true freedom. Poland was invaded in the same month by Germany and the Soviet Union, in September 1939, the launch of World War II, and then it fell under Soviet domination between 1945 and 1989.

I believed that although Poland's geography had been perhaps the most adverse in the world for two centuries, it would likely prove to be among the most fortunate after 1989. With peace in Europe, that broad flat plain between Germany and Russia would be perfect for trucks carrying merchandise and cars carrying tourists, instead of tanks carrying conquering armies. Indeed, geography did work to Poland's advantage after 1989, with a boom of trade and foreign investment. ABB, Volkswagen, and dozens of other Western European companies viewed Poland as an enormously convenient base of operations for production for the European market. Poland thereby took in billions of dollars of foreign investment in ways that Bolivia, up in the mountains, could only dream about.

Second, I learned once again about the importance of a basic guiding concept for broad-based economic transformation, a concept powerful enough to frame the great debates in a society and give guidance to millions of individuals about the changes ahead. In Bolivia, the guiding concepts were democracy, the end of hyperinflation, and the reinvention of the country, from a tin and coca producer to something new. In Poland, the guiding principle, above all others, was the return to Europe. Western Europe, and particularly the European Community (and later the European Union), provided the reference point, the organizing principles, even the specific tasks ahead for Poland's transformation. Hardship and uncertainty would be tolerated in Polish society if the end point seemed reachable. Indeed, the promise of membership in the European Union was fulfilled fourteen years after the start of the reforms.

Third, and crucially, I saw again the practical possibilities of large-scale conceptual thinking. Poland needed a fundamental transformation from a moribund socialist economy to a market economy. The end point was clear, but the path was not. Certain facts seemed to stand in the way. Poland needed to integrate with the neighboring market economies, especially Germany's. For that it needed a stable, convertible currency for market-based trade. But convertibility of the zloty seemed a long way off, unless confidence in the zloty could be restored quickly. Hence the idea of the Zloty Stabilization Fund. Poland needed to reestablish creditworthiness, but the overhang of Soviet-era debt seemed to stand in the way; hence the idea of a negotiated debt cancellation. By showing how these specific policy initiatives fit into a grander vision, and with practical historical precedents (like Germany's debt agreement in 1953), I was able to sell the pragmatic approaches needed to clear away the stumbling blocks on Poland's way back to Europe.

Fourth, I learned not to take no for an answer. For almost two years I had been told by senior finance officials of the seven richest countries, the G7, that Poland's debts would not be cancelled. In the end, they were. Logic prevailed, as indeed it often does. Sometimes, however, logic fails, as it did in Yugoslavia, and as it did in important ways in the Russian reforms as well. Still, the experience of hearing no, no, no, eventually followed by yes, has deeply affected my view of policy advocacy. I do not take as a given what is considered politically impossible, but rather I am prepared to argue incessantly, and annoyingly, for what needs to be done, even when it is claimed to be impossible. That leads to some striking successes as well as some deep disappointments, something I would experience in the case of Russia's reforms.

Finally, Poland's experience further confirmed a fundamental lesson that I had seen clearly in Bolivia. By the time a society has fallen deep into crisis, it almost always needs some external help to get back on track. Countries are like individuals in trouble who need the help of their families, friends, counselors, and public programs, and can rarely simply pull themselves up by their bootstraps. Societies in crisis are subject to powerful forces of disarray. Even when leaders want to lead, societies may fracture nonetheless, slipping into violence, war, or anarchy, as Yugoslavia did in the early 1990s. Investors flee the country, not only because of fundamental weaknesses, but also because they see others fleeing as well. Disaster can become a self-fulfilling prophecy.

In these circumstances, outside help is vital on at least two accounts. First, the help may be needed to get the fundamentals right. Debt cancellation is a case in point. Second, the help may be needed to bolster confidence in the reforms. The Zloty Stabilization Fund is a clear example. Simply having $1 billion in the bank was enough to convince Poles that the zloty could be a stable and convertible currency (especially since the rest of macroeconomic policy was responsibly managed). Almost all countries have received important help at some point: The United States received French support during the War of Independence. Europe and Japan received extensive U.S. aid after World War II, as did Korea a decade later. Israel has received vast financial support from the United States. Germany and Poland had their debts canceled. We should be wary of excessive moralizing, or telling the poorest or the most vulnerable or crisis-struck peoples in the world simply to solve their own problems.

Seven

REAPING THE WHIRLWIND:

RUSSIA'S STRUGGLE FOR NORMALCY

After the exciting and difficult year in Poland from April 1989 to mid-1990, I planned to return to my academic work. I traveled regularly through Eastern Europe in 1990, and got to know more of the region and many of the new democratic leaders. Soon I began to meet some young Soviet economists who were interested in the transformation under way in Poland and the neighboring countries.

In the summer of 1990, David Lipton and I were invited to meet with the leadership of Gosplan, Russia's economic planning agency. We went to talk about Poland's reforms. We were told that we were the first foreigners ever to be invited to the top floor of Gosplan, which is replete with busts and portraits of Marx and Lenin and others of the communist pantheon. We gave detailed briefings to senior Soviet planners about the logic and key principles of market reforms. Gorbachev's perestroika was very much under way, but the economy was not responding, other than by falling deeper into black marketing, intensifying shortages, and the spiraling inflation that we had witnessed the previous summer in Poland.

The Soviet Union's cascading economic problems, at their core, reflected the breakdown of the socialist system, just as had occurred in Eastern Europe. But there were special immediate features that markedly exacerbated the Soviet crisis. Most important, the Soviet Union relied almost entirely on its oil and gas exports to earn foreign exchange, and on its own use of oil and gas in energy-intensive heavy industry to run the industrial economy. Starting in the mid-1980s, however, just as Gorbachev was coming to power, two big shocks hit the Soviet Union. First, the world price of oil plummeted, driving down the Soviet Union's export earnings. Second, Soviet oil production peaked and then began to fall sharply because of the depletion of old oil fields and a lack of investment in new, harder-to-reach fields in the tundra. The Soviet Union began to borrow from abroad, both to fill the gap left by falling export earnings and to try to modernize the economy. All of this was to no avail: the old system could not be salvaged. In the second half of the 1980s, the Soviet economy was caught in scissors of falling oil export earnings and rising external debt, as shown in figure 1. Oil earnings exceeded Soviet foreign net debt in 1985 ($22 billion versus $18 billion), but by 1989, debt had risen to $44 billion (on its way to $57 billion in 1991), while oil earnings had collapsed to a mere $13 billion. By 1991, the creditors (many of which were major German banks) stopped making loans and started demanding repayments, paving the way to economic collapse.

Figure 1: Russia's Scissors of Oil and Debt

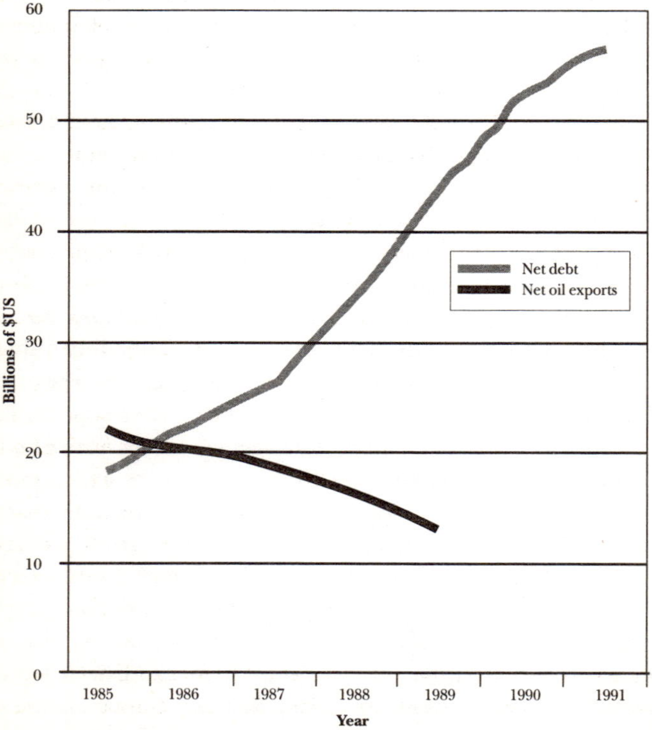

Source: Debt data from Aslund (1995); oil export revenue calculated from IMF (1991).

At that point, George Soros helped me to meet a young Soviet reformer, Grigory Yavlinsky, who was a new economic adviser to Mikhail Gorbachev. Yavlinsky explained to me that Gorbachev had sent him to Poland in early 1990 to observe the first days of Poland's reforms. Yavlinsky wrote back to Moscow that goods were coming back into Poland's shops and that there were important lessons for Gorbachev in what Poland was doing. Interestingly, when he tried to send that message back to Gorbachev through the Soviet embassy in Warsaw, the hard-line Soviet ambassador refused to transmit the message, so Yavlinsky carried it back personally to Gorbachev.

When I first met Yavlinsky, he was propounding the 400-Day Plan, an attempt at accelerated market reform in the Soviet Union, where such a call for radical market reforms was heatedly debated. Yavlinsky and I had had very good discussions early in 1991, and then he had come to Harvard that spring to work with Harvard's Graham Allison, MIT's Stanley Fischer, and me on what became known as the Grand Bargain. The idea of the Grand Bargain was that Gorbachev would attempt accelerated economic reforms and democratization, backed by large-scale financial assistance from the United States and Europe. The economic reforms would follow roughly along the lines of Poland's, tailored to the Soviet realities, and the democratization would include free elections in the republics, which at that point were still considered increasingly autonomous states within the union.

A flurry of political activity surrounded this work at Harvard. Allison tried to market the concept in Washington to the first Bush administration, but Bush's advisers did not buy the notion of large-scale financial assistance. Gorbachev had gone to the 1990 Houston G7 Summit looking for large-scale financial help, in part to service a growing mountain of external debts, but he did not get any traction. The Soviet crisis deepened markedly. Yavlinsky went back to Russia, and I went off to Europe for a much-needed summer vacation in August 1991. The first evening, though, I received a phone call to turn on CNN. The attempted putsch against Gorbachev was under way. It failed, but it gave Boris Yeltsin the upper hand in his political challenge to Gorbachev. Russia was soon to be an independent state, together with fourteen other successor states of an already moribund Soviet Union.

In November 1991, Boris Yeltsin asked Yegor Gaidar, a leading young Russian economist, to create an economic team. Gaidar invited me and David Lipton to a dacha outside of Moscow to work with the new economic team in putting together a reform plan for Russia. Russia was still a republic of the Soviet Union; but it seemed clear that it would soon gain its independence, and Yeltsin would become president of a sovereign state. The timing and the complexity of this transformation were mind-boggling. We spent several days at the dacha. With the experience of the Polish era and with the knowledge of economic events throughout Eastern Europe, we began a very long, intensive discussion about Russian reforms with the new team.

RUSSIA: A WORLD APART

The differences between Russia and what we had seen elsewhere were staggering. Everything in Russia was vastly more complex than in Poland: the scale of the problems; the extent of the socialist straitjacket on the society; the thousand years of autocracy; the eleven time zones in Russia alone; a population almost four times as large as Poland's; and profound geographical, cultural, religious, and linguistic differences within Russia and between Russia and the West. Even the knowledge of what a market economy meant was vastly greater in Poland than in Russia. Poland's minister of finance, Leszek Balcerowicz, had studied in the United States for two years and received a master's degree. No one in the Russian leadership had anything like that experience. Gaidar had spent just a few weeks in the West, and he was by far the most worldly of all of the emerging Russian leaders at the time.

Russia was truly a world apart. I realized that although Russia could not organize its reforms around the concept of the return to Europe as Poland had done, it could follow Yeltsin's call for Russia to be a "normal" power—one not seeking empire but embracing democracy and adopting a market economy. In the shadow of Russian history, normalcy was a riveting and revolutionary concept, but who in Russia truly knew what it meant? Nobody in Russia had ever lived under normalcy. Russians had lived under Stalin, seventy-five years of central planning, a thousand years of Russian autocracy, and centuries of serfdom in which the overwhelming majority of the population lived as peasants without freedom. Normalcy would not be so easy to achieve. I never once claimed it would be easy, only that it could be possible.

This transformation would be the hardest in modern history because the gap between where Russia was and where it needed to be—for domestic peace, stability, and economic development—was as vast as imaginable. All of Russia's basic economic and political institutions would need an overhaul. Russia's economic structure—the interconnections of factories, people, natural resources, and technology—had already reached a dead end. People were literally in the wrong places. They were in Siberia, living in large secret cities that had been created for military purposes. They were working in heavy industries utterly dependent on the massive use of oil and gas reserves, as if there was no limit to those resources. In 1989, for example, the Soviet Union produced 557 kilograms of steel per person, compared with just 382 kilograms in the United States, despite Russia's per capita income being less than one third of the United States in purchasing-power terms. Yet during that same period, the late 1980s and early 1990s, its oil and gas production was plummeting. Existing reservoirs were being depleted, and the Soviets were not investing adequately in new reservoirs in difficult locations, often in the tundra. According to estimates by the U.S. Energy Information Administration, overall Soviet oil production fell from 12 million barrels per day in 1989 to 10.3 million barrels in 1991.

No economic policy could be massive enough to relocate people, factories, and assets in a matter of days or weeks or even a few years. The transformation that Russia needed would be complex and contentious. The phrase shock therapy, a journalistic concoction to describe radical reform, was all wrong. There would be no single jolt to end Russia's tribulations. The initial shocks of price decontrol, currency convertibility, and market liberalization could help, as such measures did in Poland, but they would not solve the problems of underlying structural disarray, falling energy supplies, and a myriad of other interconnected crises. The reform measures, at their very best, would help to steer Russia onto a path of massive, generation-long economic and social transformation. Nevertheless, Russia would need considerable international help to pull all of this off successfully, including the now-familiar components of financial reserves for stabilization of the Russian currency, the ruble, and cancellation of part of the Soviet-era debt.

Could it work? I thought so. I certainly thought it was worth a try. What, after all, were the alternatives? Civil war? A quick descent into a new tyranny? Anarchy? A new conflict with the West? I took on the assignment of adviser to Gaidar and his team not because I was sure, or even confident, that the reforms would work, but rather because I thought they needed to be tried. They offered the best chance for peace, democracy, and economic prosperity.

My essential advice to Russia was to move quickly on the key reforms that were possible—such as stabilization and market liberalization—and to move definitively, although not overnight, on privatization. Aim for normalcy rather than uniqueness, we kept repeating. We also urged them to get all the external financial help possible. Gaidar shared this vision. He appointed a group of advisers from abroad, and asked us to prepare a strategy paper that could be presented to President Yeltsin in December. I became the main drafter and spokesman of the group, and we met twice with Yeltsin in December 1991 at the Kremlin.

In the second of the meetings, the morning of December eleventh, Yeltsin came in beaming, arms outstretched, and sat down as happy and as radiant as he could be. "Gentlemen, I want to tell you, indeed I can be the first to tell you, the Soviet Union is finished." He continued, "I just met in the next room with the Soviet generals, and they've agreed to the dissolution of the Soviet Union." Our work took on an added urgency. The Soviet Union was finished; Russia would soon be independent, and economic reforms would be launched within weeks.

Russia launched the reforms on January 2, 1992, two years to the day after Poland had launched its reforms. Gaidar became acting prime minister during 1992, until he was replaced as prime minister by Viktor Chernomyrdyn at the end of the year. By the end of the first week, the differences between Russia and Poland regarding social and political attitudes to reform had become clear. In Poland, the early days of reform were met with trepidation and grim acceptance. In Russia, the attacks on Gaidar and his team began immediately, including from within the cabinet and from his rival and eventual successor Chernomyrdyn, but more forcefully from leaders in the Russian Duma (parliament) who almost immediately called for Gaidar's resignation. It would be like that for years, with the reformers barely holding on to office and, even more rarely, to power. Most reforms were implemented only as pale shadows of what had been planned.

ATTEMPTS TO SECURE FOREIGN HELP

The question of foreign help for Russia was, for me, the dominant theme for the next two years. I believed that Russia needed something like what Poland had received, but scaled up by a factor of four to match its much larger economy and much greater challenge. I called repeatedly for a $15 billion per year aid program to enable Russia to stabilize the currency, introduce a social safety net for pensioners and other vulnerable groups, and to help restructure industry. I thought that $15 billion per year was not too much to ask, since it was a tiny fraction of 1 percent of the income of the rich world, and a tiny fraction of the annual spending for armaments to fight the cold war. If the end of the cold war could be secured, it would amount to a minuscule and worthwhile fraction of the peace dividend.

This view was not accepted in Washington. I did not realize the extent of its rejection until many years later because I always felt at the time that there was a fighting chance to get the aid in place. In a way, I had been spoiled by the against-the-odds successes that I had helped to achieve in Poland and Bolivia, where I had been told repeatedly that debts would not be cancelled or that various aid packages would not be forthcoming, only to see them fall into place with surprising speed. I had taken no to mean yes, but later.

I advocated three immediate actions by the West to support Russia's transformation:

- A stabilization fund for the ruble, as there had been for Poland

- An immediate suspension of debt payments, followed by deep cancellation of Russia's debts

- A new aid program for transformation, focusing on the most vulnerable social sectors of the Russian economy

Many critics later accused me of peddling a ruthless form of free-market ideology in Russia. That was not the case. My main activity for two years was an unsuccessful attempt to mobilize international assistance to help cushion the inevitable hardships that would accompany Russia's attempt to overcome the Soviet legacy.

The saga over a ruble stabilization fund provides a vivid case of Western obtuseness. The Polish case had proved the value of a stabilization fund. It had enabled Poland to move decisively and quickly to a convertible currency, which in turn was the financial linchpin of market-based international trade. The Zloty Stabilization Fund was so successful in bolstering confidence in the new currency that the Bank of Poland had never needed to draw on the fund to defend the zloty. (A few years later, the $1 billion was converted into budgetary support for other reform initiatives.) I argued that if Poland needed $1 billion, Russia needed a fund of around $5 billion. Initially, the IMF balked, partly on erroneous technical grounds (the IMF wanted to keep the Soviet ruble in circulation throughout the former Soviet Union, rather than replace it by separate national currencies), and also because of political resistance by the United States and other G7 leaders.

Ironically, by mid-1992, the concept of the stabilization fund had finally been approved by the G7, but it was never put into operation. By the time the fund had been accepted in principle by the G7, Gaidar had already lost momentum, the Central Bank was in the hands of opponents of the reforms, and, in practice, the G7 seemed content to have the proposal sit idle. In the midst of hyperinflation and political upheaval, timing is everything, and the timing of the stabilization fund was badly mishandled by the West.

There was one more major hiccup to address. In the Soviet system, the ruble had been used across the entire Soviet economy. With the Soviet Union now divided into fifteen successor states, there would need to be as many currencies. Otherwise, each state, with its own newly independent central bank, would aim to issue rubles. The only plausible alternative to fifteen separate national currencies was a single ruble backed by a single supranational central bank, akin to the European Central Bank. In the political conditions of 1992, however, that level of cooperation among the successor states was out of the question. They were fleeing from each other as fast as possible.

The conversion of the Soviet ruble into fifteen national currencies was a fairly complicated but still manageable technical operation, one that I thought could and should be carried out within the first six months of 1992. In the end, it took more than two years, partly because the IMF had huge objections to establishing separate national monies. The IMF analysts instead hoped to establish a cooperative approach to a shared currency, in which separate central banks would establish a common monetary policy. Their assessment was a diagnostic mistake, reversed by 1993, and one of many that they made in the early years of Russia's reforms.

As there had been in Poland in late 1989, there was great skepticism among Russian policy makers that the ruble would be convertible any time soon. The Russian Central Bank governor at the time, Georgy Matyukhin, said to me, "You know, I don't believe in any of this quick convertibility, but if you could get a $5 billion Ruble Stabilization Fund, of course I would support the policy," almost the same thing that the governor of the Central Bank of Poland had told me two years before. Matyukhin's position was, of course, a powerful reason for getting a stabilization fund established. Not only would it convince the public, but it would also convince the reform skeptics within the government itself, just as had happened in Poland!

I campaigned unsuccessfully for the Ruble Stabilization Fund in the early months of 1992, in growing incredulity and despair over the passivity and stubbornness of the IMF and G7 policies. In April 1992, I appeared on an evening news show about Russia with Secretary of State Lawrence Eagleburger, who offered me a ride back to town from the studio. On the ride back he said, "Jeff, I want to explain something to you. You know that stabilization fund you keep going on about? Suppose that I believe what you said. Suppose that I agree with you. Suppose that Leszek Balcerowicz, the Polish finance minister, was telling me the same thing last week. I want you to understand something. This is not going to happen." I was confused, especially given the premise that he agreed with the argument. "You know what year this is?" "Of course, it's 1992." "This is an election year. I want you to understand something. This is not going to happen this year. So, forget it."

Well, I admit, I did not believe him. Too many times a no had become yes. Eagleburger turned out to be half right: the proposal was delayed long enough to become moot. Eagleburger's message seemed to reflect processes under way in Washington. First, Patrick Buchanan was mocking President Bush for being a "foreign policy president," just the kind of attack to motivate the political advisers to oppose any major foreign policy initiative. Moreover, this period was when Richard Cheney, then the secretary of defense, and his deputy, Paul Wolfowitz, were drafting the controversial Defense Planning Guidance, which aimed to ensure long-term U.S. military dominance over all rivals, including Russia.

In my own thinking, I had treated Russia like Poland, only four times larger and perhaps ten times harder in structural and cultural terms. I had felt, like Yavlinsky and Gaidar, that Poland's reforms provided a valuable set of lessons and guideposts for Russian reforms, including the steps needed by the international community. I had supposed in 1991 and 1992 that the United States would be rooting for Russia's success as it had been rooting for Poland's. With hindsight, I doubt that this was ever the case. Poland was viewed by U.S. strategists, including those in the first Bush administration, as the eastern flank of the Western alliance. Poland was, unambiguously, a candidate for the European Union and indeed for NATO. Bolstering Poland was, therefore, unambiguously bolstering Western interests as well. I had believed that the same was true about Russia, but I now doubt that Cheney and Wolfowitz ever shared that perception. Russia was not destined to become a member of the European Community or European Union. Russia was certainly not a candidate for NATO. It was still a country with more than twenty thousand nuclear weapons. Given the zero-sum thinking that Cheney and Wolfowitz have propounded, it now seems plausible to me that bolstering Russia's quick recovery was viewed as inimical to U.S. interests by the White House of George H. W. Bush and the defense establishment.

The G7 treatment of Russia's Soviet-era debt was a similar debacle. I urged an immediate, unilateral suspension of debt servicing, pending a longer-term arrangement between Russia and its creditors. When Gaidar had his first meeting with the G7 finance deputies in late November 1991, David Mulford, who was a U.S. undersecretary of treasury, warned Gaidar, "Do not stop paying the debts. Keep paying." Other G7 deputies chimed in, warning Gaidar that shipments of emergency food relief could be suspended if Russia tried to stop servicing its foreign debt obligations. Worse still, the G7 negotiated a special "joint and several obligation" clause with the successor states, in which each pledged to make good, if necessary, on the overall Soviet-era debt. That led to a thicket of political and financial problems that took years to unravel. The G7 insistence on debt repayments was reckless and shortsighted. It simply guaranteed that Russia would be utterly drained of foreign exchange reserves by early 1992, which is exactly what happened by February 1992.

I have always found it ironic that Russia and R. H. Macy & Co., the department store, suspended debt servicing around the same day in February 1992. Macy's, however, had the benefit of U.S. bankruptcy law, which allowed it to obtain legal protection against its creditors, a formal standstill on debt servicing, and an almost immediate infusion of new market borrowing under the protection of bankruptcy law. (The U.S. bankruptcy code allows the new borrowing to have repayment priority over the old debt.) These protections under bankruptcy law kept Macy's intact and allowed it to regain its footing, thereby benefiting the creditors, who otherwise would have made a mad dash for the exits and ended up with less valuable claims on a defunct department store. Russia, by contrast, received none of those privileges. There was no legal protection against creditors, no legal standstill on debt servicing, and certainly no quick infusion of new working capital. Both Russia and its creditors suffered as a result.

As for grant assistance, the West announced in April 1992 a $24 billion aid package for Russia. It was one in an endless stream of misleading announcements that come from rich countries vis-à-vis poor countries. In truth, there was almost no real money for Russia in that announcement. Much of the money comprised short-term loans at market interest rates to enable Russia to buy goods it did not really want from American and European suppliers who had powerful political inroads with their governments. The $24 billion so-called aid package was in direct contrast to the Marshall Plan that had rebuilt Europe. Under the Marshall Plan, the United States gave grants to Europe, rather than short-term loans.

In the end, 1992 proved to be a dreadful year for Russia's reforms and reformers. After the first moment of price liberalization, the other reforms never really got under way, or they got under way only in a truncated form. Many price controls remained in place. International trade was only partly opened. The currency was only partly convertible. And worst of all, monetary stabilization was not achieved. Rampant inflation continued throughout the year. In part, this was the result of ongoing political pressures that prevented a more decisive monetary policy. In part, it was the result of the disastrous policies of the new Central Bank governor, Viktor Gerashchenko, whom I tagged at the time as "the world's worst Central Bank governor." It was also the result, however, of the IMF's failure to promote a Russian national currency. The reliance of fifteen sovereign countries on a shared Soviet-era ruble turned out to be a debacle, just as predicted. Since inflationary costs would be spread widely, each country had the incentive to issue credits, in other words, to "print money."

With inflation rampant in the final months of 1992—contrary to the early predictions and promises of Gaidar's economic team—Gaidar lost his political advantage. Yeltsin could not save him when the opponents of reforms began to howl for his head. In December 1992, Gaidar was replaced by the gray Soviet-era apparatchik Viktor Chernomyrdyn, who as energy minister had resisted reforms. When Gaidar left, I intended to resign from advising Russia. I was on a Christmas break when I got a call from Boris Fedorov, who had just been appointed finance minister. He was a young, tough, strong reformer who was calling to say that despite Chernomyrdyn's becoming prime minister, Fedorov would be serving as finance minister. Would I meet in Washington the following week?

We met in an office at the World Bank. Fedorov said that he had a big struggle ahead, and that he was intent on trying to keep the reforms on track. He was not very optimistic about Chernomyrdyn, and was even less optimistic about Gerashchenko. Fedorov asked if I would help him. Could I open a small office in the finance ministry and continue to serve as adviser? Despite the fact that Gaidar was out, and that the political situation was rather harrowing, I thought, once again, that it was worth the fight to help.

The year 1993 proved to be no better than 1992. The reformers were holding on by their fingernails. Fedorov lasted one year; he was thrown out by the end of 1993. Gaidar made a brief comeback toward the end of 1993. This time, he lasted about a month and a half, and in December 1993 was thrown out again. It was a year of struggling to prevent hyperinflation from taking off. For me, it was a year of trying to persuade the Clinton administration to do more than the Bush administration had done. Unfortunately, by the time President Clinton came to office, Gaidar and much of the reform team were already out of power. The new counterpart, Prime Minister Chernomyrdyn, was hardly an enthusiastic or reliable reformer.

Early on in the transition from the Bush to the Clinton administration, it was clear there would be no truly large-scale increase in help for Russia. Michael Mandelbaum, who had been one of Clinton's advisers on Russia during the election campaign, resigned from the Clinton team, saying he would not serve in the incoming administration. He explained to me that the Clinton team had decided against any large-scale program for Russia, and that it would continue to rely on IMF-led efforts. Clinton raised the levels of support for Russia and gave Yeltsin important political backing, but the headline figures for Russian aid were hyped. Too little aid came in a form useful for supporting budgetary needs like pensions and medical services. Much of it was merely in the form of commercial credits, and the IMF continued a ham-handed set of policies vis-à-vis Russia that curbed the efficacy of whatever help arrived.

More generally, the Clinton years were a period of falling foreign assistance budgets. The United States cashed in the peace dividend of reduced military outlays without investing in help for the world's poor and crisis-ridden regions. President Clinton tried to do more, especially toward the end of his term, but was hemmed in by a resistant Congress. Late in the administration he took up the cause of debt relief for the poorest countries and turned his attention to the fight against AIDS, which he has continued to champion since leaving the White House.

From my perspective in Russia, 1993 was another year of dashed hopes. I finally resigned at the end of 1993, when Gaidar and Fedorov were thrown out, again. My resignation was announced in January 1994, and that was the end of my involvement in Russia as a policy adviser. I continued for a year to do some research, and I helped the Ford Foundation to establish a research institute in Moscow. I have not been back to Russia since the beginning of 1995. My advisory role lasted for two short, harrowing years. I had little success in pushing forward the initiatives that I believed in, particularly the idea of using foreign financial support to cushion Russian reforms.

The West's failure to help had very high costs. The Russian people were optimistic at the beginning. They had become deeply cynical, and deeply demoralized, by the end of the 1990s. Democracy had a very bright chance in the early 1990s, with new institutions of free speech and a newly independent media. By the end of the decade, the optimism had vanished, and Russians were again searching for a strong leader with centralized power. When the reformers did not get the help they needed, they were replaced by gray apparatchiks and corrupt wealth seekers.

The worst occurred in 1995 and 1996, by which time I was watching from the sidelines. During those two years, Russian privatization became a shameless and criminal activity. Essentially, a corrupt group of so-called businessmen, who later became known collectively as Russia's new oligarchs, were able to get their hands on tens of billions of dollars of natural resource wealth, mainly the oil and gas holdings of the Russian state. The best estimates are that about $100 billion dollars of oil, gas, and other valuable commodities were transferred to private hands in return for perhaps no more than $1 billion of privatization receipts taken in by the treasury. Billionaires were created overnight, the proud (and newly rich) owners of Russia's oil and gas industry.

When the phony privatization process was announced, under a disreputable shares-for-loans scheme in which insiders would get access to company shares in return for making loans to the government, I tried to warn the U.S. government, the IMF, the Organization for Economic Cooperation and Development (OECD), and other G7 governments. I told them that I knew the players in this affair, and that the process was utterly disreputable. In the end, valuable state-owned resources would be plundered, and the Russian treasury would suffer greatly. Rather than using oil and gas income to support pensioners, for example, the energy-sector proceeds would now go straight into private pockets.

The West let this happen without a murmur. Many in the Clinton administration reportedly thought that shares for loans represented a clever deal: Yeltsin would give away the state's assets, and the cronies—the new oligarchs—would help finance Yeltsin's 1996 reelection. What a disastrously inefficient way to finance a reelection campaign! Probably tens of billions of dollars in value went out of the government's coffers, and a few hundred million dollars came back for the Yeltsin campaign.

In 1997, one of my colleagues in the Harvard Economics Department, Professor Andrei Shleifer, was discovered by the U.S. government to be making personal investments in Russia at the same time that he was on a U.S. government contract to advise the Russian leadership on privatization. This action, understandably, led to a public outcry. Having had no knowledge beforehand of Shleifer's activities, I rejected them then, and now, as unquestionably a breach of basic professional ethics. When the court eventually ruled on the matter in 2004, it found Shleifer guilty of defrauding the U.S. government. The court made clear that as an institution, Harvard had no way of knowing what Shleifer had been up to on his own account. I was annoyed, however, by Shleifer's behavior and by any implicit questioning of the integrity of those of us who had worked in Russia during the same period. Many of my colleagues on the Harvard faculty shared that feeling.

LESSONS FROM RUSSIA

Even a dozen years after the start of reforms, it is too early to make a final judgment about Russia's prospects for democracy and market economy. One recalls Chinese Premier Chou En-lai's quip when asked whether the French Revolution had been a success or failure: "It's too soon to say." We do not know yet whether Russia will become a "normal" country, with a functioning democracy and market economy. We do know, however, that many opportunities have been squandered. Russia could have stabilized much more easily if it had had the benefit of a stabilization fund, a debt standstill, a partial cancellation of debts, and a real aid program. The reformers would have been able to keep their place at the table of power. Corruption would have been less, and the oligarchs might never have become household names. And with oil and gas revenues flowing into the Russian treasury rather than private pockets, the situation of pensioners, the unemployed, and others depending on public revenues could have been ameliorated, and the country could have made the public investments needed to resume economic growth.

Still, despite the turmoil, much went right even as much went wrong. The world was lucky. Despite the upheavals of the 1990s and the lack of consequential help from outside, Russia remained at peace and in cooperation with the rest of the world. In Chechnya, violence flared at huge cost, and continues to rage, but matters could have been much worse. There were predictions of civil war, nuclear proliferation, pogroms, and more, yet none of those scenarios has come to pass.

Russia became a market economy, albeit one that remains lopsided toward primary commodities, especially oil and gas. Stabilization was only achieved at the end of the 1990s, after years of high inflation followed by a very sharp balance of payments crisis in 1998. After that, however, the economy began to grow, quite rapidly in fact, on the basis of high international energy prices and a devalued currency that promoted exports.

The biggest question is whether Russia will become a democracy, beating the odds and a history of a thousand years of authoritarianism. The tendencies toward authoritarian rule remain strong. Though President Vladimir Putin rules with the trappings of constitutionalism and multiparty democracy, he has also successfully centralized power, tamed the media, and muzzled the independent opposition. As always throughout Russian history, much remains murky. Putin's attack on the oligarchs in 2003 and 2004 can be viewed as an utterly appropriate challenge to ill-gotten wealth. Alternatively, it can be viewed as an attack on the kind of independent wealth that could challenge the supremacy of the state. It is probably a bit of both. Time will tell.

Russia, like Bolivia and Poland, bears the powerful imprint of its physical conditions, and thus adds another piece to our puzzle of global economic geography. Russia has two overwhelming geographical features that shape its fate. First, it is a huge landmass, the largest of any country in the world. Russia's population lives in the interior of Eurasia, mostly far from ports, navigable rivers, and international trade. Thus, throughout Russian history, the country has had only relatively weak economic engagements with the rest of the world. Second, Russia is a high-latitude country, marked by short growing seasons and an often forbidding climate. Population densities throughout Russian history have been low because food production per hectare has also tended to be low. As a result, during most of Russian history, more than 90 percent of the population lived as farmers in sparsely populated villages, producing food with very low yields. Cities were few and far between. The division of labor that depends on urban life and international trade were never dominant features of social life.

Adam Smith made the point vividly 228 years ago when he noted in *The Wealth of Nations,*

> All that part of Asia which lies any considerable way north of the Euxine and Caspian seas, the antient Scythia, the modern Tartary and Siberia, seem in all ages of the world to have been in the same barbarous and uncivilized state in which we find them at present. The sea of Tartary is the frozen ocean which admits of no navigation, and though some of the greatest rivers in the world run through that country, they are at too great a distance from one another to carry commerce and communication through the greater part of it.

Looking back, would I have advised Russia differently knowing what I know today? I would have been less optimistic about getting large-scale U.S. aid—especially with Richard Cheney and Paul Wolfowitz in leadership positions, with their visions of Russia as a continuing threat rather than a future trade and foreign policy partner. Knowing that, I would have been less sanguine about the chances for success. But would the advice have been different? To a large extent, the answer is no. I viewed external help as needed to cushion the reforms, but even without the foreign help, the reforms needed to be made. Without adequate aid, the political consensus around the reforms was deeply undermined, and the reform process was thereby compromised and put at increased risk of failure. But as for recommendations regarding budget balance, currency convertibility, international trade, and the like, these changes made sense with or without external aid. Most of the bad things that happened—such as the massive theft of state assets under the rubric of privatization—were directly contrary to the advice that I gave and to the principles of honesty and equity that I hold dear.

China had a much less tumultuous escape from its socialist economy, as I detail next, but China's meteoric economic rise is more the result of China's very different geography, geopolitics, and demography than a difference of policy choices.

Eight

CHINA:

CATCHING UP AFTER HALF A MILLENNIUM

By the early 1990s, I had begun to understand firsthand the contours of economic development and underdevelopment in Latin America, Eastern Europe, and the former Soviet Union, but my knowledge of Asia remained much too limited. I had traveled to Asia many times, and had lived in Japan during a sabbatical year in 1986. During that year, I met regularly with the new government of Corazon Aquino of the Philippines, and also traveled elsewhere in Asia. These visits deepened my resolve to understand the great Asian economic transformations that were gathering force, especially since those changes were transforming the entire world economy in the process. From 1992 to 2004, I was most fortunate to have several opportunities to work directly and intensively on Asia's economic reform challenges.

I was drawn to China for more specific reasons as well. Since 1978, China had undertaken dramatic market-based reforms. Without question, these reforms were achieving a spectacular success, helping to foster the fastest economic growth rates ever seen in a major economy. It became both a serious policy question and also an academic parlor game to make comparisons between the reforms in China and Russia. I had to understand why China was doing things differently, and whether there were deep lessons in what China was doing for Eastern Europe and the former Soviet Union, and perhaps vice versa. I began to travel regularly to China, starting in 1992, and became an adviser to the Chinese Economists Society, a group of Chinese scholars intensively studying China's economy in a comparative perspective. More recently, I have become an adviser to senior government officials on a range of policy issues, including China's public health system and the problems of economic development of China's remote western provinces.

I have always contemplated the challenges facing China with a special awe. China's population of 1.3 billion constitutes more than a fifth of humanity. Asia's population, in total, includes 60 percent of humanity. Asia's fate is truly the world's fate. But well beyond the sheer numbers of people involved, there is something deeply ironic about the basic economic fact that China and India are poor countries catching up with the high-income world. After all, both China and India are ancient civilizations that in important ways were far ahead of Europe not so many centuries ago. The rise of the West—the western part of the Eurasian landmass—was one of the great ruptures of human history, overturning a millennium or more in which Asia rather than Europe had the technological lead. Asia is not merely catching up with Europe and the United States; it is also catching up with its own past as a technological leader.

The centuries' long slide in relative income and the rapid catching up in recent decades is shown in figure 1, where I graph China's income

Figure 1: Per Capita Income in China Relative to Western Europe

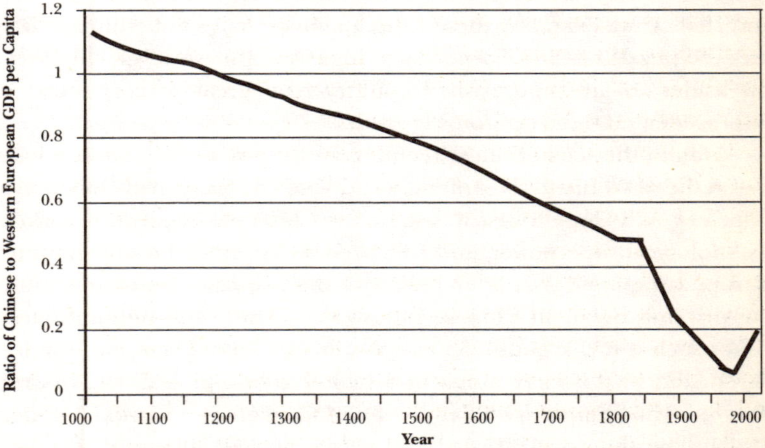

Source: Calculated from Maddison (2001).

per person relative to that of Western Europe over the truly long haul, one thousand years! The estimates, courtesy of economic historian Angus Maddison, may lack a bit of precision some centuries back, but they do show the basic stark facts. China was once in the lead. It lost the lead by 1500. It fell further behind as China stagnated while Europe took off. China actually fell backward not just in relative, but also absolute, terms between the mid-nineteenth and mid-twentieth centuries. By 1975, China's per capita income was a mere 7.5 percent of Western Europe's. Since then, and especially during the past quarter century, China has soared, reaching around 20 percent of Europe's income level by 2000. While this growth may not seem like much—and on the graph it doesn't look like much—it is of great historic importance. China is ending extreme poverty, and is on its way to reversing centuries of relative decline.

HOW CHINA LOST ITS LEAD

Where did China stumble, and why? That question is a useful starting point in contemplating why China is running so fast today, and what China must do to maintain this pace for decades to come. Certain dates stand out in China's economic history: 1434, 1839, 1898, 1937, 1949, and 1978. Understanding these dates, spanning half a millennium, clarifies the puzzle of China's epochal swings from the world's technological leader to an impoverished country to a great success story of unprecedented rapid economic growth.

Around the start of the sixteenth century, just after Columbus had found the sea route to the Americas and Vasco da Gama had circled the Cape of Good Hope to reach Asia by sea, China was clearly the world's technological superpower, and had been so for at least a millennium. Europe conquered Asia after 1500 with the compass, gunpowder, and the printing press, all Chinese innovations. There was nothing fated about such a turnaround. China's dominance, it appears, was squandered, and 1434 is increasingly understood to be a pivotal year. In that year, the Ming emperor effectively closed China to international trade, dismantling the world's largest and most advanced fleet of ocean vessels. Between 1405 and 1433, the Chinese fleet, under the command of the famed eunuch admiral, Zheng He, had visited the ports of the Indian Ocean all the way to East Africa, showing the flag, transmitting Chinese culture and knowledge, and exploring the vast lands of the Indian

Ocean region. Then, all at once, the imperial court decided that the voyages were too expensive, perhaps because of increased threats of nomadic incursions over China's northern land border. For whatever reason, the emperor ended ocean-going trade and exploration, closed down shipyards, and placed severe limitations on Chinese merchant trade for centuries to come. Never again would China enjoy technological leadership in naval construction and navigation, or command the seas even in its own neighborhood.

When Adam Smith wrote about China in his 1776 masterwork, he observed a country that was rich but static. China's dynamism was drained by its inward orientation and lack of interest in trade. Talk about the costs of trade protectionism! China had relinquished world leadership by turning inward. As Smith put it so succinctly and wisely:

> China seems to have been long stationary, and had probably long ago acquired that full complement of riches which is consistent with the nature of its laws and institutions. But this complement may be much inferior to what, with other laws and institutions, the nature of its soil, climate, and situation might admit of. A country which neglects or despises foreign commerce, and which admits the vessels of foreign nations into one or two of its ports only, cannot transact the same quantity of business which it might do with different laws and institutions.

The year 1839 is the next crucial marker of China's economic history. China's economic isolation ended that year, but very much the hard way. As had happened throughout the world, Europe's industrial prowess collided head on with every other civilization, battering down the walls, as Marx had predicted. In China, the European incursion was especially disastrous. Great Britain attacked China in 1839 to promote British narcotics trafficking, launching the first of the Opium Wars of 1839–42 to force China to open up to trade. Among other things, Britain insisted that China agree to the importation of opium that British commercial interests were producing and trading in India. British policy makers were interested in China's vast market, including solving the conundrum of how to pay for Britain's national craze: Chinese tea. The solution was ingenious and utterly destructive. Britain would sell opium to China and earn the wherewithal to purchase China's tea. It is as if Colombia waged war with the United States today for the right to sell cocaine.

In the second half of the nineteenth century, China began to achieve some commercial development, and even some incipient industrialization, under the effective control of the European powers. The collision between Europe and an inward-looking China was tumultuous and violent. It helped to trigger massive social upheavals, including domestic violence in the Taiping Rebellion, which claimed millions of lives. Pressure on China to reform its economy and political system continued to build through the decades. When Japan began its own process of rapid industrialization with a major revolution in 1868, known as the Meiji Restoration, the pressure on China intensified even more, and Japan became both a spur to reform and a source of advice.

The year 1898 is both symbolic and symptomatic of China's fate. That year was perhaps the final chance for the dying Ching dynasty to save itself from political collapse, and to spare China decades of turmoil. In that year, several young reformers, heavily influenced by Japan's success in capitalist transformation and industrialization, urged a hundred-day program of radical reforms in China. The empress dowager would have none of it. The reformers were arrested and murdered, except for a few who escaped to Japan. The episode was a grim warning for would-be economic reformers. Subsequent events show that China paid a fearful price for the failure of the reforms.

By the eve of revolution in 1911, China's regime had run out of legitimacy and money. It could not resist the encroachments of foreigners nor the pressures coming from Japan as well as Europe. Industrialization was under way in the major coastal cities, whose ports, pried open by European gunboats, had since become home to Japanese and European investors. Shanghai was already an industrial city, rising on the success of its textile exports to the world. The Ching dynasty collapsed under the hopeful calls of China's national revolution. But things did not go smoothly. The revolution itself failed to deliver political unity and economic reforms, and by 1916, China was falling into civil unrest and political disarray, with power increasingly divided among regional armies. Economic decline ensued. By Maddison's estimates, China was at 22 percent of the UK's per capita income in 1850, 14 percent as of 1900, and 19 percent as of 1930. In contrast, the corresponding proportions of Japan's per capita income were about 31 percent of the UK's in 1850, 25 percent in 1900, and 42 percent in 1930.

China's internal divisions and economic weakness provided the opportunity for military gain by its increasingly powerful and industrialized neighbor, Japan. In 1937, Japan invaded the Chinese mainland, six years after Japan had forcibly occupied the contested lands of Manchuria. The Japanese invasion was not only profoundly destructive and cruel, but it was also a crushing blow to the domestic political order in China. Invasion was followed by civil war, and then by the triumph of the insurgent communist forces under the leadership of Mao Tse-tung. In 1949, the People's Republic of China was established.

FROM TURMOIL TO TAKEOFF

Probably no country in the world, not even Russia, has experienced the extent of tumult and swings from misery to triumph, economically and socially, that China has since its revolution of 1949. The Maoist period, looking back, had a few huge successes, mainly a dramatic improvement in basic public health in the country, and many huge failures, especially socialist industrial development, which failed in ways similar to those of the Soviet economy's. The public health successes are striking, and deserve careful note, because they surely formed part of the foundation of China's economic boom after 1978.

At the time of independence, life expectancy was forty-one years and infant mortality (deaths before the first birthday for each 1,000 births) stood at an astounding 195. Women gave birth to an average of 6 children. By 1978, when market reforms began, life expectancy had risen to sixty-five years, infant mortality had declined to 52, and the total fertility rate stood at around 3. These successes reflected several major policy initiatives during the Maoist era. First, major public health campaigns reduced or eliminated the transmission of several infectious diseases, including malaria, hookworm, schistosomiasis, cholera, smallpox, and plague. Second, there was the innovation of the barefoot doctor, a community health worker for rural areas with basic training in essential health services, including the prevention and treatment of infectious diseases. Third, important improvements in basic infrastructure (roads, power, drinking water, and latrines) raised the safety of the physical environment. Fourth, major increases in crop productivity were achieved, in part through the introduction of high-yield crops during China's green revolution. Cereal yields, for example, went from 1.2 tons per hectare in 1961 to 2.8 tons per hectare in 1978, according to the official data.

China also had its share of tragic disasters caused by the madness of one-person rule. The two greatest of these disasters were the Great Leap Forward between 1958 and 1961 and the Cultural Revolution between 1966 and 1976. The Great Leap Forward was a mad scheme of Mao's to accelerate industrialization through the introduction of so-called back-yard steel mills. Millions of peasants throughout the country were told to stop planting and to start producing steel in tiny and ineffective, and totally misconceived, backyard mills. The policy ended up causing mass starvation, the news of which did not reach those in charge because of false reports and the fantasy world of the top leadership at the time, par-ticularly of Mao. Tens of millions of deaths resulted. The Cultural Revo-lution, which began in 1966, was Mao's decade-long attempt to create permanent revolution through upheaval in normal planning and bu-reaucratic processes. It turned Chinese society upside down, destroyed livelihoods, led to suicide and displacement, and disrupted for a decade or more the education of a whole generation of China's young people. Many of China's current scholars and leaders spent that decade in the countryside. It was Mao's death in 1976, the arrest of the Gang of Four

Figure 2: Economic Growth and Poverty Reduction in China

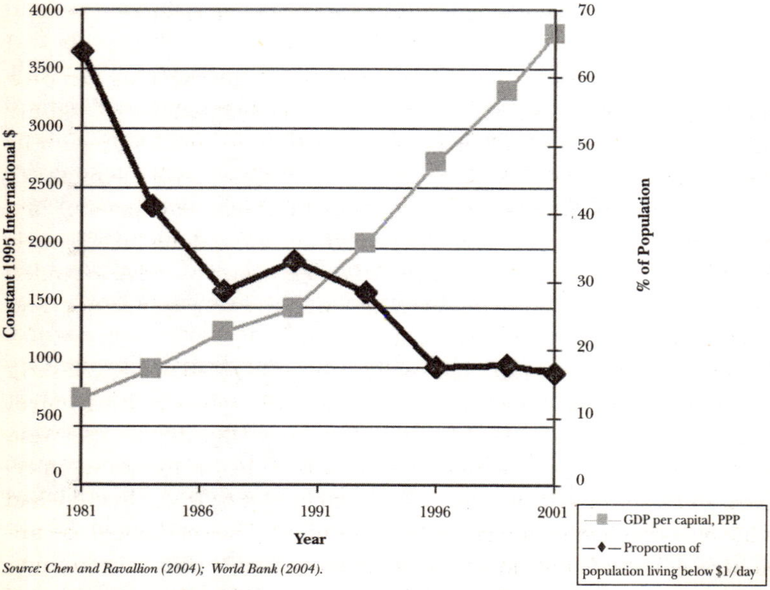

Source: *Chen and Ravallion (2004); World Bank (2004).*

in 1976, and Teng Hsiao-p'ing's ascension to power in 1978 that began the great opening of China.

Since 1978, China has been the world's most successful economy, growing at an average per capita rate of almost 8 percent per year. At that rate, the average income per person has doubled every nine years, and thus had increased almost eight-fold by 2003 compared with 1978. The reduction of extreme poverty in the country has been dramatic, as shown in figure 2. In 1981, 64 percent of the population lived on an income below a dollar a day. By 2001, the number was reduced to 17 percent. The engines of growth are still running strong, with per capita growth currently only slightly slower than a few years ago. It is typical for a fast-growing country like China to experience a gradual moderation of its growth over time, just as Japan did in the second half of the twentieth century. The basic reason is that much of the growth is catching up, specifically adopting the technologies of the leading innovative countries. As those technologies come into use, and the income gap is thereby narrowed with the leading countries, the opportunity for "easy" growth through the importation of technologies is narrowed.

CHINA'S TAKEOFF UP CLOSE

I was lucky to catch a glimpse of China at the start of the Teng era, on a short trip in 1981. China was still shaking off the Maoist legacy. Clothing was uniformly drab, mainly dark blue cotton tunics and pants worn by both men and women. Beijing was a sea of bicycles, with a handful of trucks and almost no personal cars. Peasant farmers were hawking cabbages at the roadside, a sign of both the new freedoms to sell their goods and the poverty of what they had to sell. Tourists were still guided to the special tourist shops, where they were invited to purchase low-quality, low-tech knickknacks and apparel.

By my next trip, in 1992, the changes were already startling. This trip was at the invitation of the Chinese Economists Society (CES), a group of remarkable young Chinese economists, mostly educated in the West, who were ardently trying to understand the best choices for economic reform and institutional change. Every member of the CES, it seemed, had a life history suitable for a great drama or novel. They embodied the turmoil of modern China. Most had come from middle-class backgrounds, children of doctors, teachers, and government officials. In the twisted logic of Maoism, these backgrounds were regarded with suspicion, and their families paid a heavy price during the Cultural Revolution. Parents lost their jobs and social standing; the children, with few exceptions, were sent for many years to the countryside, typically to become farm-hands in impoverished villages. Their formal educations were sus-pended. Many of their generation were never able to resume school.

The members of the CES were a select group, however. Almost all of the CES members had returned from the Cultural Revolution some-what self-taught in mathematics, languages, and even science, using books that had circulated informally among the displaced population. They sat for university exams at the end of the 1970s, as Teng was re-opening the universities after the Cultural Revolution. What a filter of talent! A few thousand students gained spots at universities among the hundreds of thousands who had competed. They sparkled in their stu-dent years, made their way to Ph.D. programs in the United States and Europe in the 1980s, and were now devoting their careers and lives to building China's economic takeoff and expanding the space for per-sonal freedom in the 1990s.

The 1992 CES Conference was on Hainan Island, one of China's new Special Economic Zones. Even the drive from the airport to the confer-ence site was mesmerizing. We arrived at night and drove for miles past campfires and torchlights on the side of the road. Each of these, we noted in amazement, was actually a building under construction, with the night shift hard at work, three or four floors up above the ground on precarious bamboo scaffolding. There was very little heavy equipment, and no crane in sight. The multistory buildings were going up by hand, and were they going up! I learned what a 9 percent growth rate means: an economy that is growing 24/7, with work shifts around the clock mak-ing up for lost time. In China's case, it was 550 years of lost time.

The conference participants had invited me to talk about the eco-nomic reforms that had just started in Eastern Europe and the former Soviet Union. They were voracious for information. The official Chi-nese press had scathingly bad-mouthed the Eastern European and post-Soviet reform processes, mainly because they were combining market reform with democratization. The Chinese leadership was intent on guiding its market reforms with a continuation of one-party rule. It was ironic, to say the least, that Poland's first partially free election, in 1989, had occurred on June fourth, the very same day as the Tiananmen crack-down. But there was more to the issue than mere propaganda or political posturing. China was booming in the course of its market reforms, whereas Eastern Europe and the former Soviet Union were experiencing a huge and very painful contraction of heavy industry. Had China chosen a superior reform path? What could it teach Eastern Europe? And what did China need to understand about the events in Europe and the former Soviet Union? These questions would engage me for years to come.

The standard take on these questions is one that I gradually discovered to be wrong both on the facts and in economic interpretation. The standard view is that China proceeded gradually, whereas Eastern Europe proceeded radically, indeed by shock therapy (that awful term that continued to follow me about). China's gradualism was humane; Eastern Europe's radicalism was dislocating. China, said many, had been wise to forestall democracy altogether, waiting until the economy was better placed to handle political freedom, whereas Eastern Europe had rushed headlong into democracy.

From the start, this line of thinking did not sit right with me for several reasons. First, I knew that Gorbachev had tried gradualism in the Soviet Union during the era of perestroika and, indeed, had modeled many of the Soviet reforms on the obvious successes in China. Yet that course had not worked. Similarly, Hungary had been famous for its "goulash socialism," another variant of gradual market reforms under one-party rule. As in the Soviet case, Hungary's gradual reforms had famously failed, for reasons definitively dissected by Hungary's leading economist, Janos Kornai. Conversely, China's much touted gradualism had shown episodes of breathtaking speed and radicalism, for example, during the initial phase of decollectivization of agriculture. Something more was at work in the different outcomes than simply a difference of throttle speeds!

Deciding to untangle the mystery through a detailed application of differential diagnosis, I did just that in a series of lectures and articles, most often in collaboration with my student and then coauthor Professor Wing Thye Woo of the University of California at Davis. Our analysis of the differences between the Soviet (and Eastern European) and Chinese cases was also greatly strengthened by our work with the late and brilliant Chinese economist and member of CES, Professor Xiaokai Yang of Monash University.

Our diagnosis began by noting a fundamental difference between the economies of Eastern European and the Soviet Union and the economy of China. As of 1978, when it began its market reforms, China was still a largely rural and agricultural economy. Roughly 80 percent of the population lived in rural areas, and 70 percent lived as peasant farmers. During the 1960s and 1970s, these peasants were organized in communes, with communal land tenure and communal pay. Individual families were not rewarded for their own efforts or investments in the land. Yields in the communes were extremely low, reflecting the absence of incentives at the household level. Only 20 percent of the population worked in cities, and about the same proportion of the labor force worked in state-owned enterprises of all sorts. These, too, were very inefficient. Workers were guaranteed their wages and benefits (including, for example, health care), and could not be laid off. They had, as the common expression put it, an "iron rice bowl" that could not be broken by an economic downturn.

Eastern Europe and the former Soviet Union were utterly different in structure. Unlike China, roughly 60 percent of the region's population lived in urban areas in 1978, whereas about 40 percent lived in rural areas. The industrial labor force was about 40 percent of the labor force, the service sector was another 40 percent, and the agricultural sector was only around 20 percent. Figure 3 compares China's and Russia's economic structures, showing the key difference in the percentage of the labor force engaged in agriculture and industry. In the Soviet-style economy, virtually 100 percent of the population worked in state-owned enterprises, as shown in figure 4. Even the farms were organized not as Chinese communes, but as state-owned enterprises with workers on salary. It could be said that 100 percent of the labor force in the Soviet system enjoyed the wheat-based equivalent of the iron rice bowl.

The difference in starting points made all of the difference. In both contexts the state enterprise sector posed an enormous challenge. With workers guaranteed their wages, jobs, and benefits, the state-owned enterprises were both inefficient and big drains on the budget. Only force, or the threat of force, kept down the workers' demands for wage increases, since the workers knew that they could press for higher wages without fear of layoffs or unemployment. Only subsidies from the budget and the state-owned banks allowed the state enterprises to keep operating and to cover implicit or explicit losses.

On the other hand, China's peasant commune sector was taxed by the state, rather than subsidized. The government bought all of the food from the farmers at low prices in order to subsidize the urban

Figure 3: Distribution of Employment by Sector in 1980

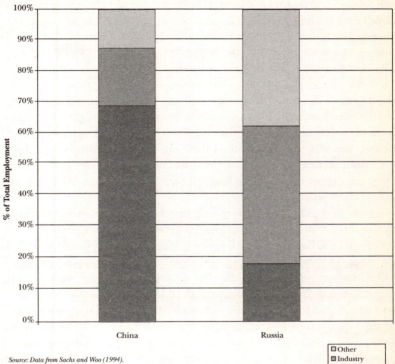

Source: Data from Sachs and Woo (1994).

☐ Other
☐ Industry
■ Agriculture

workers via low food prices. Moreover, the peasant farmers had no guarantees of incomes or benefits—in short, no iron rice bowl. As was true of China's peasants from time immemorial, they just wanted to be left alone by the state, rather than taxed by it. The communes were also very inefficient, with grain yields that were very low because of the lack of appropriate work incentives. The farmers' incomes did not depend on their own efforts or production, but rather on the overall commune output. The return to a "household responsibility" system, in which individual farm households farmed individual plots, with the benefits accruing mainly to those households, dramatically improved the work incentives.

China was able, therefore, to begin its reforms with a major burst of agricultural production and a radical market reform of the food sector.

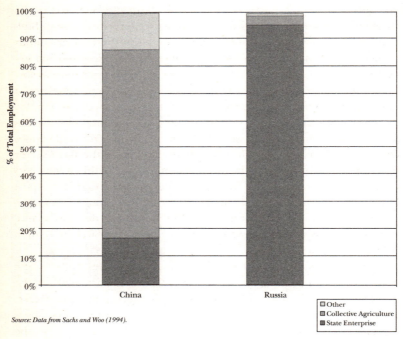

Figure 4: Distribution of Employment by
Type of Organization in 1984–1985

□ Other
▣ Collective Agriculture
■ State Enterprise

Source: Data from Sachs and Woo (1994).

Between 1977 and 1979, the commune system was spontaneously dismantled, not so much by top-down command, but by bottom-up action of villages across the country in the wake of the power vacuum after Mao's death. After decommunization spread like wildfire, it was validated by the Communist Party of China in 1979, but the real action was spontaneous.

There was nothing gradual about this change. This was shock therapy par excellence. Around seven hundred million individuals in farm households were suddenly farming on plots assigned to the household rather than to the commune. This new household responsibility system gave massive incentives to individual farmers to work harder, apply inputs with more care, and to obtain higher yields. Food yields boomed, and food supplies to the urban areas increased rather than decreased with decommunization. In short, the early stage of China's reforms was a burst of output that was "win-win" for both the rural and urban sectors.

The next steps of China's reforms, in the 1980s and early 1990s, were also rather swift and had highly positive results. First, the rural peasants were given the freedom to leave the farm and begin to work in rural industry, known as township and village enterprises (TVEs). Suddenly, millions of industrial jobs opened up in hundreds of thousands of these enterprises. Second, international trade and investment was liberalized, initially in specially designated free-trade zones, known as special economic zones (SEZs). Foreign investors saw moneymakers at hand. They could bring in foreign technology and capital to employ low-wage Chinese labor for the production of labor-intensive exports for world markets. Chinese workers flocked into the free-trade zones from the countryside. In effect, the liberalization of the farm sector freed up labor for the manufacturing export sector. Within a few years of the establishment of the free-trade zones, China began an export boom based on labor-intensive exports in garments, textiles, footwear, plastics, toys, and electronics assembly. Within just two decades, manufactured exports soared, from a few billion dollars in 1980 to more than $200 billion dollars by 2000.

The designation of a few favored free-trade zones had historic precedent in China's long history with world markets, particularly in the nineteenth century. It turned out that the special economic zones were, with a remarkable degree of overlap, the same sites of the initial opening of the Chinese economy in the mid-nineteenth century after the Opium Wars. The major difference between the early and the more recent period was that in the mid-1800s, China was under quasi-colonial rule, whereas the current episode was a matter of sovereign choice. This made the legitimacy of today's free-trade zones vastly greater and the reforms much deeper. The idea of using key centers of industrialization as a strategy of development, picking areas where the industrial investments would be encouraged, also has had a proven track record elsewhere in Asia, from Japan's successful economic development to the post–World War II successes of Korea, Taiwan, Hong Kong, Singapore, Penang Island (Malaysia), and many other parts of Asia.

The rest, as they say, is history. These zones took off. They combined very low-cost labor, availability of international technology, and an increasing and eventual torrent of investment funds, both from domestic savings, but increasingly in the 1990s, foreign direct investment.

That foreign direct investment had three components. Part of it was long-distance international capital flows from the financial and industrial centers of Europe and the United States. Another very important part was money from the offshore Chinese communities of Asia, the leaders of which were able to identify excellent business opportunities, frequently family centered. And a third part was what was called round-tripping money, money that was taken out of China, usually from state enterprise accounts, passed through Hong Kong financial intermediaries, and then reinvested in mainland enterprises. However it was done, the combination of low-cost laborers numbering hundreds of millions, modern technology, ample capital, and a safe and sound business environment produced one of the great moneymaking machines of modern history.

One area of China's reforms was indeed gradual: the state enterprise sector. China partly liberalized, but did not privatize, the state enterprises in the 1980s and 1990s. The government did not attempt to break the iron rice bowl, and the results were not good, as might have been predicted. Wages increased, profits decreased, and the burdens on the budget and banking sector multiplied. Still, the government kept the state enterprises in operation with few layoffs or ownership changes until state enterprise reforms began in earnest at the end of the 1990s. Only then did urban unemployment begin to rise with the layoffs of hundreds of thousands, and then millions, of state enterprise workers.

Gradualism, then, Chinese style, meant radicalism in rural reforms, a quick opening of the economy to trade, and only gradual reform of the state enterprises. In that sense, China saved the hardest for last in the sequence of reforms. This was a prerogative made possible by the structure of China's economy as of 1978.

COMPARING CHINA TO EASTERN EUROPE AND RUSSIA

Now consider the difference with Eastern Europe in 1989 or the Soviet Union in 1991. In both of these cases there was no nonstate-enterprise sector to be liberalized. Everybody had an iron rice bowl, and all enterprises were receiving subsidies from the state. The pressures on the budget and money supply were already enormous, and macroeconomic instability was at hand. Even worse, the Soviet Union and most of Eastern Europe were already overextended in international borrowing, so there was no fiscal relief at hand through new loans. On the contrary, the foreign creditors were demanding repayments from the Soviet Union.

Gorbachev tried Chinese-style gradualism between 1985 and 1990 by freeing the nonstate sector while preserving the iron rice bowl in the state enterprise sector. But the results were a disaster. Whereas China had 80 percent of the labor force outside state-owned enterprises, the proportion of workers in the Soviet context that were not dependent on the state was perhaps 1 percent. There was thus no surplus army of workers ready to join the nonstate sector, as in China's town and village enterprises or its free-trade zones. There was also no easily engineered jump in Soviet food production, since the Soviet state-owned farms (and nearly equivalent collective farms) could not be turned over to peasants as had been the case in China. The Soviet farms were capital-intensive, large-scale wheat-growing operations, not an agglomeration of small-scale family plots as were the Chinese communes. Soviet farmers, unlike China's farmers, did not want to be left alone by the state. They wanted and expected the guaranteed security of state-enterprise employment.

Thus when Gorbachev freed the nonstate sector and liberalized the state sector, only bad things happened. There was no surge in new sectors, but there was a surge in wage demands and losses in the state-owned enterprises. The budget deficit worsened measurably, and it was not offset either by a burst of nontraditional manufacturing for the local market (as in China's town and village enterprises) or a burst of exports (as in China's free-trade zones). Gradualism Soviet style, under the rubric of perestroika, was therefore fiscally destabilizing without the redeeming economic outcomes of China's reforms.

The differential diagnosis pointed to at least five structural differences between the Soviet and Eastern European economies on the one side and the Chinese economy on the other.

- The Soviet and Eastern European economies had massive foreign debts, whereas China did not.

- China had a large coastline that supported its export-led growth, whereas the Soviet Union and Eastern Europe did not have the benefit of large coastlines and the resulting low-cost access to international trade.

- China had the benefit of overseas Chinese communities, which acted as foreign investors and role models, whereas most of the Soviet Union and Eastern Europe did not have comparable overseas communities.

- The Soviet Union was experiencing a drastic decline in oil production at the outset of reforms, but China was not.

- The Soviet Union had gone much further down the road of industrialization, using technologies incompatible with Western (U.S., EU, and Japanese) technologies, whereas China remained at a low level of technology and could more easily adopt Western specifications.

All of these differences made reforms much tougher in Eastern Europe and the former Soviet Union than in China. None of this is to say that China's reforms were less than clever or that the Eastern European reforms were optimal. I have already indicated how things went terribly awry in Russia. It's just to say that glib comparisons between Russia and China are utterly unfounded. Not only could China's reforms not work in Russia, the irony is that Chinese-style gradualism was actually tried and failed in the Soviet Union in the second half of the 1980s.

CHINA'S GREATEST CHALLENGES

It would be nice to report that China's economic success is assured, and that the growth triumphs of recent years can be extended indefinitely. Although I am optimistic that China will indeed enjoy decades more of rapid growth, and thereby narrow the gap in per capita incomes that has developed over the course of several centuries, I am also aware of some significant challenges.

First, China's growth is not uniformly high. Like every other economy in the world, China's is shaped by its geography, in this case an east-west divide and a north-south divide. The east-west divide is striking. China's east coast is the Pacific Ocean, and some of the most important port cities in the world can be found there, including (from north to south) the ports of Tianjin, Shanghai, Guangzhou, Hong Kong, and Hainan Island. The coastal provinces have the advantage of proximity, both in time and transport costs, to major world markets by sea-based trade. China's western border is the Tibetan plateau, at 4,500 meters above sea level, and the deserts of Central Asia. Both are forbidding borders, with enormous transport costs and great distances to major world trading centers. It is not surprising that the western provinces have been growing much less rapidly than the eastern provinces, and that foreign investors focus their investments almost entirely on the eastern coastal provinces, as shown in map 7.

There is no easy answer to this divide. This is economic geography, and the east-west growth divide is natural. It won't go away. It will be addressed partly through an internal migration of job seekers leaving the west and heading east. This trend has already produced the largest migration occurring in the world today, with perhaps 150 million people having moved either permanently or seasonally between the interior and the coastal provinces. It will also be addressed in part through investments from the coastal provinces into the interior. These investments will help improve infrastructure, industrial development, and social development, through better schools and better health services.

Eastern Europe and the former Soviet Union also have an east-west divide, but there the western-most countries are closer to the major markets of the European Union. Just as China's eastern provinces have grown faster than the western provinces, so too have the countries of Eastern Europe that border the European Union grown faster than the countries of the former Soviet Union, which are much farther away.

The Chinese north-south divide is a little bit less conspicuous, but it is also very significant. The north is dry compared to the south. Water scarcity in the north of China will take on increasing economic and social significance in the years ahead. Already China is talking about spending tens of billions of dollars to divert rivers from the south to the north in three great canals whose costs, effectiveness, and ecological effects are hard to assess with precision, but the risks are very large.

A second major challenge for China is deciding on the role of the state sector in social and environmental protection in the context of market reforms. In some ways, China has overshot the mark in market reforms. When it dismantled the highly inefficient commune system in the countryside, it also disassembled the only rudimentary public health system that existed, which was also based on the commune structure. Since the 1980s, China's rural poor have had to depend on out-of-pocket payments for their health expenses. The results have been dire. Too many of the poor cannot afford the health care that they need. In some rural areas, infant mortality rates have increased in recent years, despite China's growing wealth. When the SARS epidemic hit in 2003, China discovered that it utterly lacked a functioning public health system in rural areas, one capable of surveillance and control of epidemic diseases. In short, in the coming years China will have to build a system of social protection, and most notably a system of public health care, especially in the rural areas.

In the same way, China will have to take much more seriously its system of environmental protection. With 1.3 billion people, likely to rise to 1.4 billion by midcentury, and with one of the world's highest population densities, the potential for the human destruction of China's ecosystems is profound. China already experiences profound costs of environmental stress, including enormous natural disasters such as flooding, massive costs to health from massive urban air pollution, and rapidly intensifying water demand in the dry north China plains. Moreover, China is likely to overtake the United States as the world's largest single contributor to man-made climate change as China's use of fossil fuels continues to soar. For both internal and international reasons, therefore, China will have to become a serious manager of environmental threats, a task that will require government leadership far beyond market reforms.

There is a third area of vital concern for China in the coming decades: political reform. I believe that China will achieve democratization, but it will not be a necessarily smooth process unless China's leadership understands that both domestically and internationally, democratization is vital to China's well-being. One reason for optimism, in general, is that as economic development takes place, the call for democratization and transparency grows. That phenomenon, although not universal, is very widespread, and it will definitely work in China. I say definitely because we have seen how powerfully that impulse succeeded in Taiwan, South Korea, and in other nearby cultures and countries. China will experience powerful forces for democratization from within as the rate of literacy and the level of private wealth grow, and as various interest groups in the society have more standing and greater eagerness to participate politically, in part to defend their property rights.

What is clear, though, is that China will need a different kind of political system. China's political system is perhaps the longest-standing state structure in the world: its roots can be directly traced to the administrative apparatus of the Han dynasty, almost 2,200 years ago. The idea of a centralized state, with power emanating from the top and extending down through bureaucracies at the regional, local, and, finally, village levels, has been the basic Chinese model since the unification of China in 202 B.C. What made the centralized state possible in China was a vast subcontinental-scale society of villages. The villages themselves looked a lot like each other across a very wide space: they were rice-growing communities of hundreds of millions of people, living in hundreds of thousands of villages, with common economic and cultural characteristics. In such a homogeneous setting, a centralized administrative strategy flourished, with orders going down from the top, percolating through various levels, and reaching the endpoints in communities very similar in their basic internal organization.

The success of China's centralized state will complicate democratization. It reigned for nearly two thousand years as a workable model of political organization. Over its long history, with only temporary exception, China remained a unified state, one with remarkably little internal violence for such a vast and populous area. Statecraft has had tremendous success because, after all, what is a measure of the success of statecraft? The ability of people to live together. Notwithstanding its startling achievement, though, it has not furthered China's accomplishment in economic development. The centralization of China contributed to nearly five hundred years of decisions from the top that had huge, negative economic repercussions. Such a process would have been impossible in Western Europe, where political and thus economic power was always decentralized.

Even with more than two thousand years of success, the central state has outlived its usefulness. Why? China's centralized apparatus, which extends over such a large area, is not compatible with the dynamism of a decentralized and diverse market economy and market-based society, which depends on migration, multiple bases of power and wealth, and regional diversity. This dynamism is already putting huge strains on Chinese statecraft.

Two millennia of social organization are being overturned by urbanization, with huge diversity in the kinds of economic activities that different parts of the country are pursuing. These different activities, together with diverse cultural, ethnic, and linguistic representation, give rise to different infrastructural, educational, and other needs. It is no longer possible to give one order from the top that will make sense for 1.3 billion people. Part of China's economic success in the last twenty years has been the empowerment of provincial and local governments to experiment at their levels by allowing for diversity, creating a more complex division of labor, and enabling mobility—in short, to see what works.

China's need for legitimate local government is greater than ever, because more decisions are being made at the local level. But if those important decisions are being made by people appointed from the top who cannot be effectively managed or who are not regarded as legitimate appointments by those below, the model breaks down. It is already breaking down, with much corruption in local and regional governments. The one-party system is losing adherence, and yet China wants to avoid internal disarray, even if it falls into conflict. The country's leaders need to avoid that, but also find ways to decentralize power.

I believe that a federal democratic system will be the most likely solution, but getting from here to there will be very tricky. There are early stirrings of democracy in China right now, for example, nonparty elections at the village level, where individuals stand for positions rather than represent organized political parties. Hu Jintao, the general secretary of the Communist Party, recently declared, "Democracy is the common pursuit of mankind, and all countries must earnestly protect the democratic rights of the people." There is a huge gap between words and action, but the gap is very likely to narrow meaningfully in the coming years.

The question is whether this change can be managed gradually and peacefully, or whether the hard-liners, corrupt officials, and sycophants of the one-party system will delay gradual change to the breaking point. A gradual evolution to democratic rule would be most desirable, and it is possible. The examples of Taiwan and Korea show that one can make a transition while maintaining national integrity and good economic performance at the same time. These are the political challenges that lie ahead for China.

CHINA'S HISTORIC OPPORTUNITY

China is likely to be the first of the great poverty-stricken countries of the twentieth century to end poverty in the twenty-first century. Its rate of extreme poverty has already plummeted, and the proportions continue to drop rapidly. Earlier I discussed China's centuries-long slide in relative income and the beginnings of its catching up. The turnaround in the past quarter century, although dramatic, looks modest set against the thousand-year history of decline. The good news for China and for the world, I strongly believe, is that the prospects for rapid catching up are the best they have been for centuries. In a short span of half a century, China can substantially narrow the existing gap. One rule of thumb among growth economists holds that the income gap between a

Figure 6: China's Prospects for Catch-up

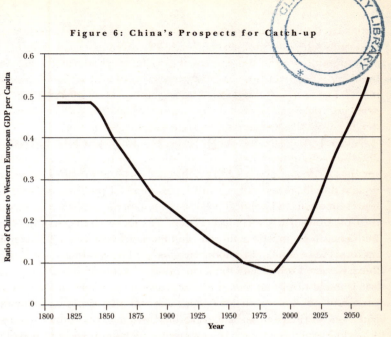

Source: Calculated using data from Maddison (2001) and author's projections.

rich and poor economy will tend to narrow by about 2 percent per year if all other things (geography, policy, and the like) are roughly the same. This narrowing occurs not because the richer country gets poorer, but because the lagging country is able to mobilize capital and technologies to promote faster growth. By this shorthand, we find the possibility for China in the first half of our new century shown in figure 6. By the year 2050, it is reasonable to suppose that China will reach around half of the Western European income average, restoring China's relative position at the start of the industrial era.

China's reforms are reshaping the global economy and global politics. Soviet reforms beginning in the 1980s and changes in India in the early 1990s were no doubt inspired in part by China's successes. As my engagement in China has deepened during the past decade, so too has my experience as an adviser and researcher in India. China has already demonstrated that a country of more than one billion can achieve unprecedented development. Many people around the world, including me, naturally wonder whether India will soon do the same. By 1994, I had begun to ponder that question intensively.

Nine

INDIA'S MARKET REFORMS:
THE TRIUMPH OF HOPE OVER FEAR

India began to introduce far-reaching market reforms in 1991. These reforms were similar, in important ways, to those that were sweeping China, Eastern Europe, and the former Soviet Union. In mid-1994, I was invited to New Delhi to meet with government members and to give a number of public lectures about globalization and economic reforms around the world. I was particularly thrilled with the opportunity to meet India's minister of finance, Dr. Manmohan Singh, a world-respected, Cambridge- and Oxford-trained development economist who was guiding India's economic reforms. Since then, I have had the honor and pleasure to work with Singh, India's prime minister since May 2004, and with other Indian leaders, including Prime Minister Atal Bihari Vajpayee, who held the office briefly in 1996 and again from 1998 to 2004.

I had first seen extreme poverty in 1978 on a month-long trip to India during my graduate studies. From my first day in India in 1978, I was utterly transfixed. India was visually breathtaking and jarringly incomprehensible: graceful women wearing colorful saris, teeming marketplaces, freely roaming cows, monkeys dashing from rooftop to rooftop, funeral processions inching through crowded bazaars, holy men in loincloths, temples of every variety, impoverished old people begging on the street corners, turbaned Sikhs. It posed the challenge of extreme poverty more starkly than I had ever before imagined. Why was this vast and ancient civilization so impoverished? What could be done about it? Would India be able to feed itself? On that trip I carried around the giant tome *Asian Drama,* by Nobel Laureate Gunnar Myrdal. I thought how extraordinarily lucky I would be if I could someday help to understand, even to help to solve, such problems.

Almost twenty years later I was back in India with a bit more preparation than the first time. By then I had seen much of the world, and had studied and participated in economic development problems for more than a decade. I was eager to make good on my personal commitments from graduate-school days to join, in some small way, the battle against India's extreme poverty. I was also an optimist. If China could rise from poverty at unprecedented rates, using globalization to boost technology, why couldn't India do the same? Of course it could, I told myself, and surely Manmohan Singh and his team would see to that.

Within a few days of my arrival in 1994, I confronted a new puzzle. Government leaders, including Singh and his team, were quite optimistic about India's reforms, and the business community was cautiously optimistic as well. The academics, however, were not. In lecture after lecture I heard skepticism from the economics professors. Poverty would worsen; growth would prove elusive. The skepticism was unnerving, but also eye-opening. It eventually made me appreciate the weight of history in India.

I was in the middle of giving a lecture at India's vibrant academic meeting ground, the India International Centre, waxing rhapsodic about the growth opportunities afforded by foreign direct investment. I looked at the doubting faces in the crowd, and then suddenly caught myself short. Here I was, glibly describing the wonders of foreign direct investment in a country that had actually lost its sovereignty to a private corporation! It was India's remarkable experience to have fallen victim to the British East India Company, a private joint-stock company, before succumbing to the British Empire itself. India's history during the seventeenth to nineteenth centuries was one of greed-driven private armies running roughshod over a great civilization. Globalization would not go down so easily among intellectuals keenly aware of the country's past tribulations.

THREE THOUSAND YEARS
OF INDIA AND THE WORLD

India's long, remarkable history bears heavily on it today. Historians hypothesized that India's traditional social structure, with its meticulous stratifications by caste, reflects the imprint of its formative history. Although much is obscure and heatedly contested about India's early history, recent genetic mapping of the Indian population suggests that the ancient Vedas may well tell an accurate tale of an indigenous Indian (Dravidian) population conquered by invading tribes from Central Asia who became the high-caste Brahmans. The Brahmans, some recent studies suggest, carry genetic markers closer to those of Central Asia and Asia Minor (Anatolia) than of Southern India. Caste differences and taboos may therefore reflect the earliest social relations of the conquerors and conquered. For whatever reasons, India is an unmatched mélange of cultures, ethnicities, languages, alphabets, and religions. Diversity is its first and overwhelming characteristic.

India's history offers a unique panorama of competing empires and conquests. Although India's population has been overwhelmingly Hindu from the time of the Vedas, India's rulers in the past millennium have more frequently been Muslims or Christians. The heavily populous regions of the Ganges River plains, long centered around Delhi and Agra, were conquered by Muslim invaders from the eleventh century onward. The famed Mogul emperors, builders of the Taj Mahal and Delhi's Red Fort, were Muslim invaders from Central Asia. These were the powerful rulers who were holding sway over northern India in 1602 when a small band of traders chartered by Queen Elizabeth I arrived at the Coromandel Coast near what is now the great city of Chennai, until recently known as Madras. While the Moguls dominated the Ganges River plains, an array of maharajahs, princes, and warrior kings ruled over the rest of the Indian subcontinent.

Through political genius and sheer ruthlessness, British forces gained the upper hand in India through a strategy of divide and conquer. How else could a small trading company from a country of perhaps 5 million people even contemplate creating a foothold, much less an empire, halfway around the world in a subcontinent of 110 million or more inhabitants? Step by step, from its inauspicious arrival in 1602 to the final conquest of the subcontinent in 1857, the British East India Company, backed by the British Crown, bamboozled and fought its way to power, siding first with one ruler and then another, double-crossing its allies and defeating its foes on the battlefield, buying, bribing, and fighting its way to complete control.

Exactly how this happened must surely be viewed as one of history's great perplexities. Yes, Britain had more advanced armaments. Britain commanded the seas in a way that India's rulers never attempted. Britain was the undisputed industrial world power of the nineteenth century. Yet when the East India Company began its expansion in the seventeenth century, India's population outnumbered Britain's by perhaps twenty-two to one, and they had the home court advantage. India also outstripped Britain as an industrial and manufacturing power. India's textiles and apparel were prized throughout the world, and its cloth exports constituted the vast bulk of the world's trade in textiles and apparel. Britain's ascent to power reflected not only its growing industrial and military prowess, but also the deep weaknesses in India's political and social structures. In political terms, an overextended Mogul empire began to disintegrate in the early eighteenth century, when it was unable to govern over the vast subcontinent and lacked support among the Hindu population. The Mogul empire dissolved into a growing number of sovereign successor states, and the British relentlessly manipulated these political divisions to their advantage. At the same time, India's remarkable social stratifications and caste hierarchies—so extreme that it was taboo for upper-caste Indians even to walk in the shadow of lower-caste or outcaste Indians—played an important role. A society without strong internal cohesion and camaraderie was much easier to conquer.

THE BRITISH RAJ AND ITS ECONOMIC LEGACY

The military conquests were combined with economic conquests. From the start of the eighteenth century to the end, Britain went from being an importer of Indian textiles and garments to a significant exporter to India. By the middle of the nineteenth century, Britain was the clothier of India, with British mechanized mills displacing millions of Indian hand-loom operators. The textbooks often paint this as a picture of market forces shaped purely by technological advance. The textbooks neglect to add, however, that Britain imposed trade restrictions on India's textile exports to Britain during the pivotal eighteenth century, giving itself time for its own less efficient manufactures to gain the upper hand. In short, Britain pursued an aggressive industrial policy to topple India's predominance in the textile trade.

Britain's military conquest of India was completed in 1857, at which point the East India Company, which was already under state control, formally transferred legal authority over India to the British Crown. India was, of course, the jewel of the British Empire, and much of Britain's foreign policy in the Middle East, Central Asia, and elsewhere was devoted to protecting that jewel. Britain also invested heavily on the Indian subcontinent, financing roads, rails, electricity grids, and telegraph connections to help develop the Indian economy from the late nineteenth century onward. Yet a proper reckoning of the British Raj must also consider the downsides of empire, which were severe.

Perhaps most important, the British Raj showed a disdain for educating the Indian population, both at the primary level and at the elite level. Although there were Indian elites such as Mohandas Gandhi and Jawaharlal Nehru who received world-class educations and who would go on to create an independent India, they were few in number. Under British rule, India remained a continent of illiterate peasants. At the time of independence, India's literacy was only 17 percent. Public health was also badly neglected. Life expectancy in 1947 was a mere 32.5 years. Britain also showed a disdain for Indian industrialization, at least the kind of industrialization that might threaten British industrial interests back home. The infrastructure was built to exploit India's raw materials, such as cotton for British mills, and not mainly to industrialize India itself. There were exceptions, once again, but they help to prove the rule. And as Angus Maddison notes, "The Indian capitalists who did emerge were highly dependent on British commercial capital and many sectors of industry were dominated by British firms, e.g. shipping, banking, insurance, coal, plantation crops and jute."

The greatest illustration of British imperial irresponsibility was its response to repeated famines and disease epidemics during the second half of the nineteenth century and the first half of the twentieth century. As recounted vividly in Mike Davis's stunning book *Late Victorian Holocausts,* India fell prey to repeated monsoon failures, which were probably linked to El Niño–Southern Oscillation (ENSO) climate fluctuations in the western Pacific. A monsoon failure would lead to drought and hunger one year and then to a severe malaria epidemic the next when the rains reappeared and a burst of mosquito abundance afflicted a weakened population. British infrastructure building—dams, irrigation channels, roads—exacerbated India's vulnerability to malaria by multiplying the breeding sites of the anopheles mosquitoes in proximity to human settlements.

The British cannot be blamed for the monsoon failures, or the increasing number of breeding sites. The role of mosquitoes in transmit-

PHOTOGRAPH 1

PHOTOGRAPH 2

PHOTOGRAPH 3

PHOTOGRAPH 4

PHOTOGRAPH 5

PHOTOGRAPH 6

PHOTOGRAPH 7

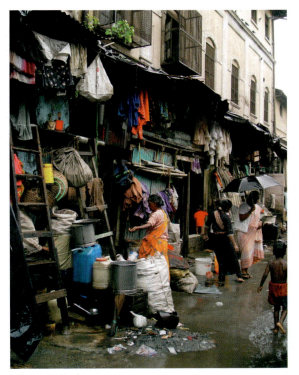

PHOTOGRAPH 8

Map 1: Moderate Poverty and Extreme Poverty

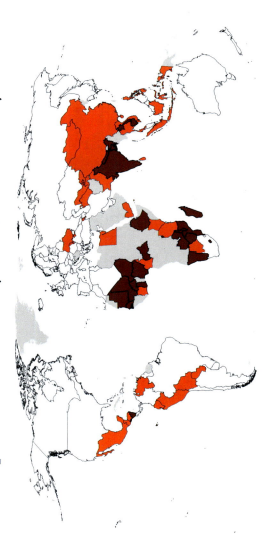

Moderate Poor (more than 25% of population lives below $2 per day)
Extreme Poor (more than 25% of population lives below $1 per day)
No Data

Source: Data from World Bank (2004).
Map uses most recent available data.

Map 2: Income per Capita in 2002
(PPP-adjusted, in current $)

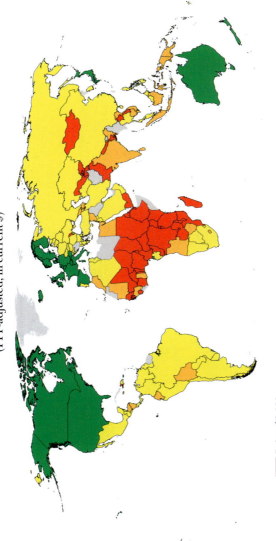

Below $2,000
$2,000–$4,000
$4,000–$20,000
Above $20,000
No Data

Source: Data from World Bank (2004).

Map 3: Distribution of Foreign Affiliates of the Largest Ten Electronics Multinational Companies, 1999

Production of Equipment and Parts

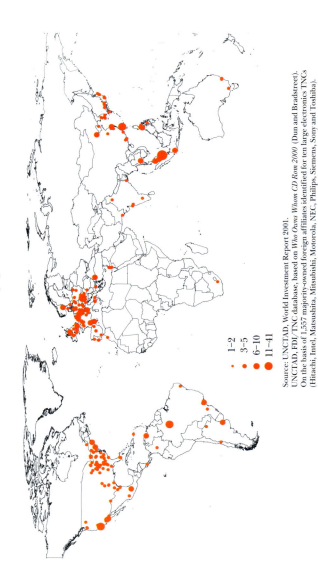

1–2
3–5
6–10
11–41

Source: UNCTAD, World Investment Report 2001.
UNCTAD, FDI/TNC database, based on *Who Owns Whom CD Rom 2000* (Dun and Bradstreet).
On the basis of 1,557 majority-owned foreign affiliates identified for ten large electronics TNCs
(Hitachi, Intel, Matsushita, Mitsubishi, Motorola, NEC, Philips, Siemens, Sony and Toshiba).

Map 4: Distribution of Foreign Affiliates in the Textile and Clothing Industry, 1999

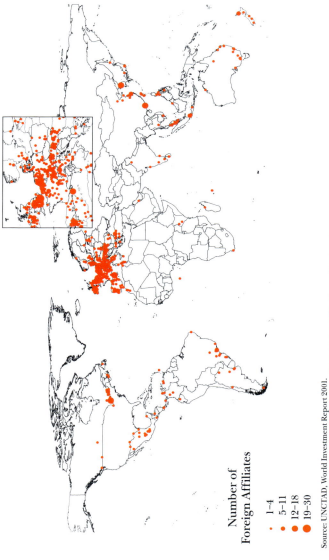

Number of
Foreign Affiliates

- 1–4
- 5–11
- 12–18
- 19–30

Source: UNCTAD, World Investment Report 2001.
UNCTAD, FDI/TNC database, based on *Who Owns Whom CD Rom 2000* (Dun and Bradstreet).
On the basis of 1,455 majority-owned foreign affiliates identified.

Map 5: Average Annual GDP per Capita Growth, 1980–2000

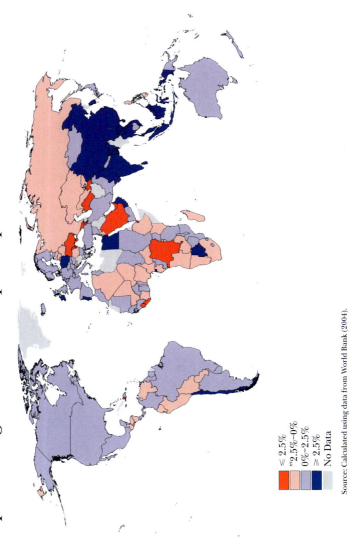

≤ 2.5%

−2.5%–0%

0%–2.5%

≥ 2.5%

No Data

Source: Calculated using data from World Bank (2004).

Map 6: Western Europe

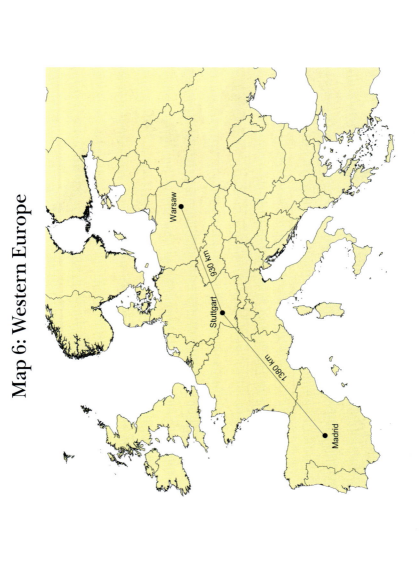

Map 7: Distribution of FDI Stock in China, by Province and Major City, 1999

(millions of dollars)

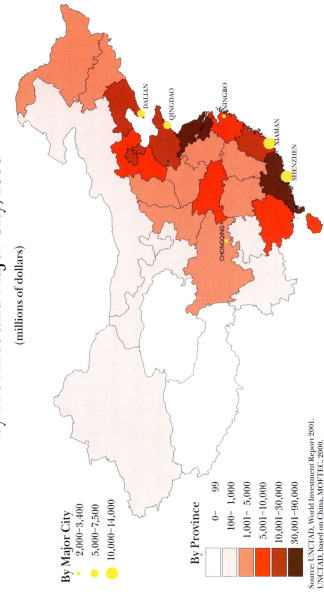

By Major City
- 2,000–3,400
- 5,000–7,500
- 10,000–14,000

By Province
- 0– 99
- 100– 1,000
- 1,001– 5,000
- 5,001–10,000
- 10,001–30,000
- 30,001–90,000

DALIAN
QINGDAO
NINGBO
XIAMAN
SHENZHEN
CHONGQING

Source: UNCTAD, World Investment Report 2001.
UNCTAD, based on China, MOFTEC, 2000.

Map 8: Variation in Life Expectancy Around the World

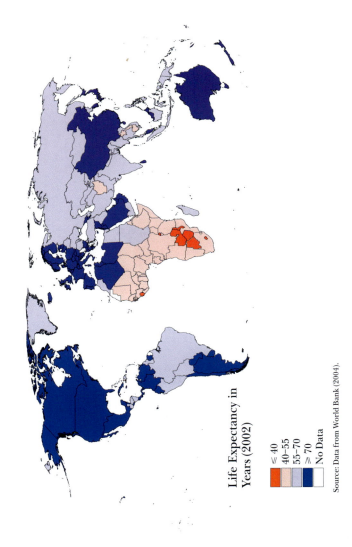

Life Expectancy in
Years (2002)

≤ 40
40–55
55–70
≥ 70
No Data

Source: Data from World Bank (2004).

Map 9: Low-Income Countries

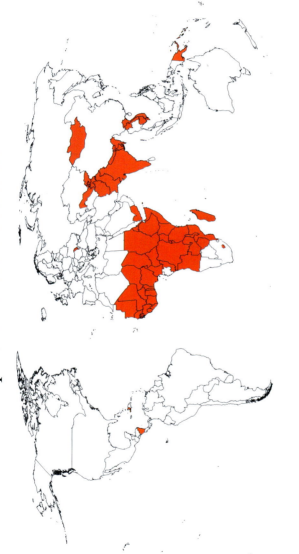

Low-income countries by World Bank
classification (income below
$765 per capita)

Source: Data from World Bank (2004).

Map 10: Malaria Risk in 1946, 1965, and 1994

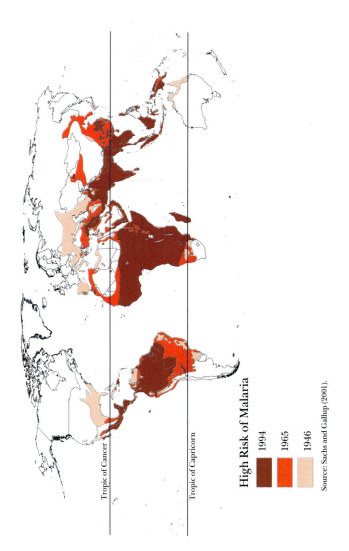

Tropic of Cancer

Tropic of Capricorn

High Risk of Malaria

- 1994
- 1965
- 1946

Source: Sachs and Gallup (2001).

Map 11: Malaria Ecology Index

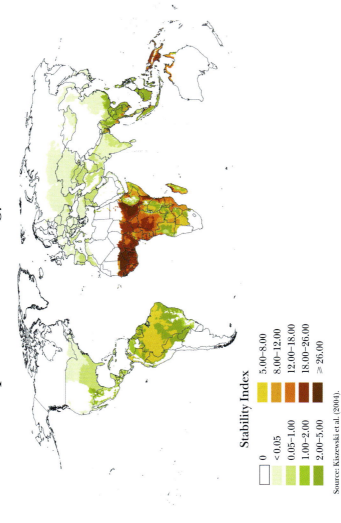

Stability Index

0	5.00–8.00
< 0.05	8.00–12.00
0.05–1.00	12.00–18.00
1.00–2.00	18.00–26.00
2.00–5.00	≥ 26.00

Source: Kiszewski et al. (2004).

ting malaria was not understood until 1898. (It was a great British scientist based in India, Ronald Ross, who first elucidated the life cycle of the malaria parasite, independently from the Italian scientist Giovanni Battista Grassi.) Britain's failure was its response to famine. The British repeatedly failed to organize food relief and other social services in the face of mass suffering. Davis quotes Lord Curzon, the British viceroy, lecturing starving Indians as follows:

> [A]ny Government which imperiled the financial position of India in the interests of prodigal philanthropy would be open to serious criticism; but any Government which by indiscriminate alms-giving weakened the fibre and demoralized the self-reliance of the population, would be guilty of a public crime.

In the end, millions died as the imperial authority passively stood by.

Notably, India's last major famine was in 1943 in Bengal, in the waning years of imperial rule. The monsoons failed to come again in the 1960s, but this time a sovereign Indian state came to the rescue of the hungry masses through large-scale distributions of emergency food rations. This rescue from disaster led Amartya Sen to his great insight that famines have as much or more to do with authoritarian politics as they do with climate fluctuations and crop yields. (Sen's insight is sometimes carried too far, however, with the claim that democracies never have famines. In the extreme climatic and demographic conditions of Africa, where highly vulnerable populations rely on rain-fed agriculture in arid regions, droughts can cause famines even in democracies.)

Some recent historical accounts, most notably *Empire,* by historian Niall Ferguson, praise the British Empire's spread of technology and knowledge to India and other colonies. These are misleading accounts in my view, for although empire did extend infrastructure and technology, it did so to Britain's advantage. Without empire, the same technologies could have diffused in many other ways: trade in capital goods, imitation and reverse engineering, the purchase of technical advice (always available at a price), and the spread of scientific knowledge through textbooks, global conferences, student exchanges, and scientific academies. Japan, for example, did not fall prey to empire to achieve the technological benefits of the industrial age. By keeping its sovereignty, Japan enjoyed an even quicker ascent into industrialization than did the colonies. Indeed, as Maddison notes, "Indian industrial efficiency was hampered by the British administration's neglect of technical education, and the reluctance of British firms and managing agencies to provide training or managerial experience to Indians."

The overall record of economic performance under the British Raj was pretty dreadful. Using Maddison's data, India experienced no per capita growth from 1600 to 1870. Per capita economic growth during the period 1870 to independence in 1947 was a meager 0.2 percent per year, compared with 1 percent in the UK.

INDEPENDENCE AND INDIA'S ECONOMIC CHOICES

India, like the rest of the colonized world, chafed under foreign domination. When Europe bled itself to exhaustion in two world wars and the intervening Great Depression, the European colonies were ready to assert their independence. India went first, at the stroke of midnight, August 15, 1947. Thus began India's "tryst with destiny," in Nehru's evocative phrase, as well as its rendezvous with its own twin demons—colonial rule, which left India allergic to international trade and to foreign investment, and extreme social divisions, which left India weakened internally as well as competitively vis-à-vis the rest of the world.

When Nehru became the first prime minister, he quickly introduced a strategy of democratic socialism. Like other postcolonial nation builders of his era, Nehru looked for a path of self-sufficient economic development, one that would not rely on global markets, international trade, and foreign direct investments. After a long and hard-won struggle against colonial rule, Nehru and his fellow nation builders had no taste for risking a new period of subjugation to foreign economic forces. They had other reasons as well for choosing an inward-looking (autarkic) development strategy. World markets were hardly functioning in 1947, and the Great Depression had left the feeling that market forces were unreliable. Moreover, the apparent triumphs of Soviet industrialization, much exaggerated by phony data and hidden repression, added to the view that scientific state planning had come of age.

For these reasons, Nehru opted for a system of strong state controls. Licenses were needed for everything in India: to trade, to invest, to expand factory capacity. Large industrial units were held back, ostensibly to preserve room for small and technologically backward enterprises.

Hand-loom operators were protected from industrial looms. Industrial workers could not be laid off. Urban land could not be converted into new industrial uses without permission. Bank accounts, money transfers, and foreign investments all required licenses. The economy, in summary, was tied up in horrendous knots so tight that it could hardly grow, giving rise to the "Hindu" growth rate of around 3.5 percent per year, or just 1.9 percent per capita, during the period 1950 to 1970.

India's first major economic breakthrough came in the late 1960s and early 1970s with the introduction of the Green Revolution into the country. Scientific plant breeders were able to breed new varieties of maize, wheat, and rice in which the plant's growth was channeled into the grain rather than the stalk. The resulting rise in food yields freed India from the chokehold of famine. After the Green Revolution, India was able to feed itself even in years when the monsoons failed. The seemingly endless saga of India's fighting mass starvation came to an abrupt end, well before its market reforms triggered a sustained acceleration in economic growth.

The Green Revolution created pockets of rising income, especially in Punjab, where irrigation and the existing railways supported the rapid introduction of the new high-yield crop varieties. More generally, though, India remained trapped with low and erratic growth. In the late 1980s, Rajiv Gandhi introduced some limited market reforms that seemed to speed economic progress, but unsustainable foreign borrowing, in fact, fueled much of that acceleration. The foreign borrowing cycle ended in mid-1991, when foreign investors realized that India's foreign debt levels were rising quickly without a commensurate rise in its exports. As investors began to withdraw funds and demand a repayment of their loans, India's foreign exchange reserves fell sharply. A balance of payments crisis loomed. Enter Manmohan Singh, who understood clearly that it was time to end the License Raj. From mid-1991 onward, India became part of the global wave of market reforms, joining China, the Soviet Union, Eastern Europe, and Latin America in their globalization.

THE LAUNCH OF REFORMS

Singh's first steps were to end the most crippling bureaucratic restrictions on international trade and investment. Businesses that could find profitable opportunities were suddenly allowed to pursue them. The government lowered tariff barriers and lifted import quotas from thousands of goods. Noneconomists feared that these measures would simply open the floodgates of imports, further drowning Indian producers in a sea of low-cost imports. They did not understand that by liberalizing imports, the government was also promoting exports. Suddenly, Indian producers could buy capital goods and intermediate inputs on world markets at competitive prices, making it possible for them to sell their own finished goods on world markets at lower prices as well. More gingerly and then gradually, the government also began to make it easier for foreign firms to invest in India. To encourage foreign investors, the government liberalized the number of approvals needed, the percentage of a company that could be foreign owned, and the range of sectors in which foreigners were permitted to invest.

Perhaps not surprisingly, when I arrived in India in mid-1994, just three years after the start of these major changes and with India still shaking off the remnants of a financial crisis, the academic economists were still pessimistic. How could India possibly compete in world markets? How could India avoid domination by a new East India Company? My protestations that trade liberalization works—that India's exports were bound to grow—were met with repeated warnings that "India is different." In which sectors would India compete? they asked me repeatedly. Thank goodness the choice was made by the markets, not me! I would have placed my bets on labor-intensive manufactures—footwear, toys, apparel, electronics—just as in China. While those sectors did achieve some notable gains, they were not destined to be the engines of growth for India in the first decade of reforms. To nearly worldwide astonishment, India became a hub of large-scale service-sector exports in the new information technologies.

By the mid-1990s, with Microsoft asserting its dominance in computer software and the Internet coming into its own as a revolutionary tool of business as well as education and entertainment, the fact of the large numbers of Indian software engineers in the cutting-edge businesses slowly started to become apparent. Silicon Valley, the epicenter of the information technology (IT) revolution, was filled with highly trained and motivated Indians. Small Indian-owned and Indian-led IT businesses were quickly becoming big Indian-owned businesses with considerable cachet in the industry, including Sycamore and Infosys. Microsoft itself began to invest heavily in Indian software engineers, who were already legion in the company, and in India itself, as a place to write software, often at the cutting edge.

The factors underpinning India's ability to compete effectively in the IT industry were increasingly obvious. First, for more than a generation India had been turning out high-quality entrepreneurs and engineers from the Indian Institutes of Technology (IITs), a collection of seven world-class, loosely affiliated campuses around the country. Because of India's relatively stagnant economy, IIT graduates migrated in large numbers to the United States. By the mid-1990s, they were becoming the business leaders of their generation, taking leadership positions at Microsoft, McKinsey & Company, Citigroup, numerous investment banks, IT firms, and other major international companies.

Second, many of these overseas Indians had begun to establish business relations back in India, a process greatly facilitated by the new information technologies. Decades of economic closure and sluggish growth had left India's physical infrastructure in a fairly decrepit state, especially when it came to exports. The port facilities were crowded, poorly managed, and hard to access. Roads were clogged and riddled with chassis-breaking potholes. But the IT revolution meant that exports of information, by way of satellite linkups in the mid-1990s and fiber optic cables a few years later, could bypass the logjams on the roads and ports. A satellite dish on the roof of the building was all that was needed to make nearly instantaneous contact halfway around the world.

In 1994, I made my first visit to an offshore back-office operation, a visit that I have repeated innumerably since then. We visited the Santa Cruz Electronics Export Processing Zone in Mumbai and the office of Swiss Air. There were rows of young women sorting through boarding passes and frequent flyer claim forms, entering into the computer the mileage awards of last month's travels. Swiss Air simply gathered its paper records in Zurich and Geneva, put them on a Swiss Air flight to India, and processed them in this office at a tiny fraction of the costs back in Switzerland. The data were entered into spreadsheets and beamed back to headquarters through a dedicated satellite line. By the late 1990s, India's centers of IT operations, in the cities of Bangalore, Chennai, Hyderabad, and Mumbai, were the new destinations for major companies looking for software engineering, data transcription services, computer graphics, back-office processing, computer-aided design, and a myriad of other IT-based activities.

From the point of view of economic reforms, it was clear that India was internationally competitive. An export boom, albeit initially in services rather than the manufactures that many of us had expected, was fueling the most rapid economic growth in India's history. The fear that a wave of multinational companies would conquer India was looking rather silly. On the contrary, India's great success in attracting U.S. outsourcing contracts had become a political issue back in the United States, with ill-founded charges that India was somehow unfairly taking jobs from Americans. In a time-hallowed way, the country's entrepreneurs were using the forces of globalization to help close the technological gap with the world's leading economies. And they were succeeding.

The result of India's reforms, therefore, involved another step up in India's growth rate trend. Looked at from the long-term perspective, India passed through four phases of growth in the twentieth century: low growth under the British Raj (1900–47), low growth under Nehru's License Raj (1947–70), faster growth with the advent of the Green Revolution (1970–91), and sustained high growth with market liberalization in the 1990s (1991–2000). These steps are shown in figure 1.

The fears about globalization were vastly overblown, but there are good reasons to remain vigilant about the politics of multinational companies. A striking example of this came during one of my visits to Delhi at the end of the second Clinton administration. The U.S. ambassador to India invited me to pay a courtesy call at the embassy a day or so before I was to meet with the Indian prime minister. The ambassador looked me in the eye and said, "Please urge your friends to resolve their dispute with Enron." He was referring to an ongoing commercial disagreement between the U.S. company and the Indian state of Maharashtra over electricity pricing at an Enron-built plant. "If they don't settle, this will jeopardize India's standing with many other U.S. companies." I have always resented such heavy-handed lobbying by a senior U.S. official on behalf of a U.S. company, and I resent it even more, in retrospect, now that Enron has become the poster child for U.S. corporate sleaze.

INDIA'S ECONOMIC CHALLENGES

India faced four major challenges in 1994, and they remain the main challenges a decade later, albeit in somewhat less acute form. First, the reforms needed to be extended. Liberalization had begun, but key sec-

Figure 1: Economic Growth in India Since 1900

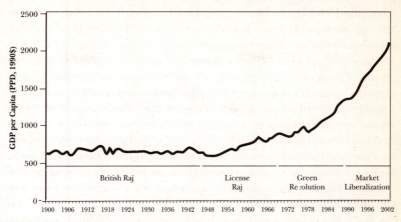

Source: Data from Maddison (1995).

tors of the Indian economy remained hamstrung by the systems put in place a half century earlier. Second, India needed to invest heavily in basic infrastructure—roads, ports, power, water and sanitation, telecommunications—to reduce production costs and deepen India's integration domestically and with world markets. Third, India needed to invest much more in the health and education of its own people, especially the lower castes and outcastes who faced continuing extreme social exclusion. Fourth, India needed to figure out how to pay for the infrastructure and social investments, since by 1994 the budget was in a perilous state, with large deficits both at the central (union) government as well as the state levels.

Following my 1994 visit, I left behind a detailed report about these challenges; this work, in turn, led to further intensive discussions with the government and academics. In 1996, my colleague Nirupam Bajpai and I became advisers to the central government as well as to the government of Tamil Nadu, a fast-growing state in southeast India. We have had the satisfaction of seeing many of our recommendations adopted in recent years. Our basic argument has been that India could achieve the growth rates seen in China if India broadened and deepened its reforms. Events have not disappointed us. By 2004, India was growing at around 7 percent per year, approaching the growth rate of China. The favorable results were also evident in the reduction of extreme poverty.

By national measures, the poverty rate declined from 42 percent of the population in 1990 to an estimated 35 percent of the population in 2001. As shown in figure 2, strong economic growth came hand in hand with the decrease in the poverty rate.

India's export boom has continued to deepen, extending from traditional IT operations (basic software, data transcription, telephone call centers) to increasingly sophisticated business process outsourcing (BPO). U.S. and European firms in the health, insurance, and banking sectors are increasingly resorting to the BPO route to cut their costs. And the export boom is not just in IT. One of the most dynamic new export sectors is automotive components, where India is becoming the location of choice for many major global producers of automobiles. Components are now produced in India, then shipped to assembly plants all over the world.

India has not yet matched China in the depth and breadth of economic modernization, but it is easy to underestimate what has already

Figure 2: Economic Growth and Poverty Reduction in India

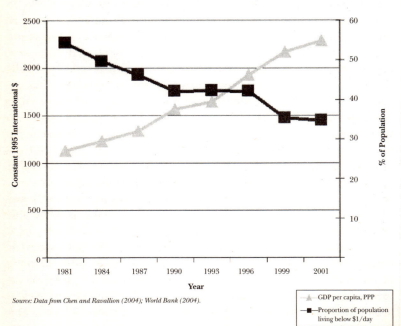

Source: Data from Chen and Ravallion (2004); World Bank (2004).

GDP per capita, PPP
Proportion of population living below $1/day

been accomplished. China gives the aura of a unified, well-oiled reform engine, but under the surface are the powerful tensions of clashing ethnicities, regional inequalities, large-scale migration, and extensive corruption. In India, nothing is under the surface. The politics are exuberantly in the open. On any day in India, an English-speaking visitor can choose among a dozen newspapers, each carrying full-throated political criticism as well as lurid crime stories. During any given month, it seems, a state government is tottering or the national coalition government is looking fragile. Political crisis is always at hand, yet somehow India stumbles forward. Each coalition government since 1991 (and there have been five governments at the union level) has endorsed and furthered the reform process. The Indians themselves have described their country as an Asian elephant, lumbering thunderously—and ponderously—through the jungle, rather than an Asian tiger, the favored metaphor for India's neighbors in East Asia.

DECADE OF DEVELOPMENT

By the year 2000, the reforms had advanced sufficiently that Nirupam Bajpai and I recommended to Prime Minister Vajpayee that India set its sights still higher for the new decade. We urged the prime minister to declare the coming ten years a decade of development, in which India would double its per capita income and make breakthroughs in literacy, education, health, and basic infrastructure. A doubling of per capita income in a decade, as had been achieved by Japan in the 1960s, Korea in the 1970s, and China in the 1980s and 1990s, requires an average annual growth rate of 7 percent per capita for a decade, a rate of growth that we believed to be within India's reach. We were delighted when the prime minister proclaimed these objectives in his message to the nation on August 15, 2000. The goal of at least 8 percent per year economic growth (and therefore around 7 percent in per capita terms) was subsequently endorsed by India's Planning Commission.

Despite rapid economic growth during 2001–3, elections in the spring of 2004 turned Prime Minister Vajpayee's government out of office. The result was a great surprise, reflecting a massive vote for change emerging from India's countryside. It was, in part, a reflection of short-run factors. Widespread drought in 2003 had left many farm communities financially strapped and hungry, though large-scale famine was easily avoided. But the results went deeper than that. The evidence showed clearly that India's economic growth was urban led, with the gaps in living standards between the cities and the countryside widening in recent years. My studies with Nirupam Bajpai had found that the rate of urbanization at the state level was the strongest predictor of the relative growth rates among the Indian states, with the most urbanized states, as of 1981, the places where growth was the most rapid. Figure 3 shows the relationship of state-level growth during 1981 to 1991, in relation to each state's extent of urbanization as of 1981. Clearly, the urbanized parts of India have been the fastest growing. This is not surprising. The Green Revolution had its largest impact in boosting rural incomes in the 1970s, whereas the economic growth since then had been in the urban-based IT industry as well as in urban-based manufacturing. In the 2004 elections, the rural sector was saying that enough was enough, that rural areas should reap more of the benefits of India's rapid growth.

With Manmohan Singh as the new prime minister, the government is turning its policies to redress the shortfall in rural growth. The basic approach, which I believe is strongly merited, is to boost public invest-

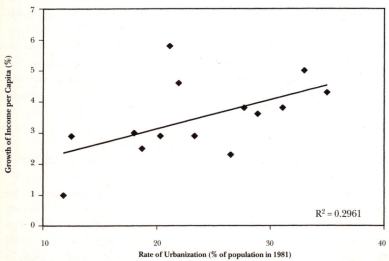

Figure 3: Growth Rate, 1981–1991, and
1981 Urbanization by State

$R^2 = 0.2961$

Source: Data from Sachs, Bajpai, Ramiah (2002).

ments in rural areas in order to ensure that every village in India will soon have the benefits of basic infrastructure and social services. The government has boldly proclaimed "electricity for all," as well as essential health services and safe drinking water for everyone. In the Indian context, these are not mere populist slogans. They are achievable goals, and the basis for much-needed investments. They cut to the core of Indian social divisions as well by committing the state to ensure that every Indian, not just the upper castes, receives the benefits of basic social services and essential infrastructure. The government's new commitments are a necessary part of a successful decade of development, and even more, of India's historic escape from poverty. Finance Minister P. Chidambaram concluded his 2004 budget speech with the following inspiring commitment:

> The countries of the world, India included, have set for themselves the Millennium Development Goals. Our date with destiny is not at the end of the millennium, but in the year 2015. Will we achieve those goals? In the eleven years that remain, it is in our hands to shape our destiny. Progress is not always on a linear path, nor is it inevitable. Two thousand years ago, Saint Tirvalluvar said:
>
>> "Aran Izhukkathu Allavai Neeki Maran Izhukka Maanam Udayathu Arasu."
>> ("They are good rulers who observe ethics, commit no crime and walk the path of honour and courage.")
>
> If we bring thought and passion to our governance, and walk the path of honour and courage, we can make the future happen. And this century will be India's century.

LESSONS FROM INDIA

Finance Minister Chidambaram is right. As with China, the twenty-first century is likely to be the era when centuries of relative economic decline in India are substantially reversed. I have made that optimistic point since the early 1990s, and events have proven it correct. The pessimistic argument that I first read in the 1970s and heard again in the first half of the 1990s—that India is somehow condemned by culture, history, or geopolitics to continued poverty—is wrong. Contrary to the pessimists, India did not have an irreparable "Hindu" growth rate. The Green Revolution and then market reforms overrode the slow growth of the 1950s and 1960s. Even the deep-seated rigidities of caste, which have impeded social mobility and kept large parts of the Indian population bereft of adequate health, nutrition, and education, are proving malleable in the face of powerful economic and political forces. As economic development has proceeded, and India has become increasingly urbanized, many of the caste distinctions that still loom large in the villages have fleeting significance in the urban labor market. Democracy, too, is wearing away at age-old social hierarchies. One person, one vote transformed the political scene in mid-2004, when India's villages spoke loud and clear for a greater share of public investments.

India is also teaching the world a lot about the richness of the international division of labor, and how it changes in response to technological possibilities. Who would have guessed twenty-five years ago that impoverished India would burst upon the world economy in the 1990s through high-tech information services? Nobody. The technological possibilities of Internet-empowered software programming, offshore business processing, long-distance data transcription, and a host of other IT-based industries had not even reached the concept stage. I saw firsthand, repeatedly, how India's ability to take advantage of the new IT possibilities resulted from its long-standing investments in higher education, especially in the Indian Institutes of Technology. These have become the hubs for the newly established IT-based industries. In my visits around India I have often met outstanding scientists who are making important contributions to India's economic development through their superb educations and decades of scholarship.

India's varied geography also further deepened my understanding of how the physical environment helps to shape economic activity. As in China, India's Green Revolution led to a short period in the 1970s and 1980s of rural-led development, with the Green Revolution state of Punjab becoming India's fastest growing and richest state. But this phase of rural-led growth was relatively short-lived. Since the 1980s, and especially since the 1990s, urban-based manufacturing and services have led the way. As a result, the large coastal port cities—Mumbai, Kolkata (formerly Calcutta), Chennai—have been the stars of Indian economic growth. The hinterland, especially in the Gangetic plains, has lagged behind, in the same way that China's western hinterland lagged behind the coastal provinces. Geography—with its attendant rainfall, temperature, soil, natural resources, and disease vectors—continues to affect Indian regional development in countless subtle ways through disease ecology, tourism, crop production, and other factors.

The return of China and India to global economic prominence in the twenty-first century is likely to reshape global politics and society. The overwhelming dominance of the West, which lasted half a millennium, is probably passé. We should view these developments not only with awe, but with anticipation. Adam Smith viewed the uniting of Europe and Asia via sea-based trade and the discovery of America as "the two greatest and most important events recorded in the history of mankind." He argued that "[b]y uniting, in some measure, the most distant parts of the world, by enabling them to relieve one another's wants, to increase one another's enjoyments, and to encourage one another's industry, their general tendency would seem to be beneficial." Smith was painfully aware, however, that Europe's "superiority of force" had enabled the Europeans "to commit with impunity every sort of injustice in those remote countries." He looked forward to the day when an equality of courage and force would lead instead to "respect of the rights of one another," and he believed that "extensive commerce" would hasten that day. If we act wisely, an era of mutual respect and beneficial exchange between the East and West will, at long last, be at hand.

Ten

THE VOICELESS DYING:

AFRICA AND DISEASE

I had never been to sub-Saharan Africa before 1995. After working in every other part of the world, I felt an increasing urgency to understand the development challenges in the world's most distressed region. What I found was a crisis much more severe than I had expected, with causes quite different from what is commonly assumed. A decade of work in Africa has taught me a considerable amount about extreme poverty, the power and limits of globalization, and the indomitable strength of the human spirit in the face of adversity.

By the time I had begun to work in Africa, I was prepared to see things more clearly than I would have a few years earlier. An intensive decade of economic advising from 1985 to 1995 taught me something of the art of differential diagnosis, so I could better appreciate how Africa's development crisis reflected the interactions of history, geography, domestic policies, and geopolitics. These interactions had left Africa stuck in a poverty trap. Worse, as of the mid-1990s, Africa was careening headlong into an HIV/AIDS pandemic, one of the most ferocious disease contagions in history.

LOOK WHO'S LECTURING WHOM ON GOVERNANCE

The outside world has pat answers concerning Africa's prolonged crisis. Everything comes back, again and again, to corruption and misrule. Western officials, including the countless "missions" of the IMF and World Bank to African countries, argue that Africa simply needs to behave itself better, to allow market forces to operate without interference by corrupt rulers. An American talk show host, Bill O'Reilly, reflected a common view when he recently declared that Africa "is a corrupt continent; it's a continent in chaos. We can't deliver a lot of our systems that we send there. Money is stolen. Now when you have a situation like that, where governments don't really perform consistently, where there's just corruption everywhere, how can you cut through that?"

Western governments enforced draconian budget policies in Africa during the 1980s and 1990s. The IMF and World Bank virtually ran the economic policies of the debt-ridden continent, recommending regimens of budgetary belt tightening known technically as structural adjustment programs. These programs had little scientific merit and produced even fewer results. By the start of the twenty-first century Africa was poorer than during the late 1960s, when the IMF and World Bank had first arrived on the African scene, with disease, population growth, and environmental degradation spiraling out of control.

When it comes to charges of bad governance, the West should be a bit more circumspect. Little surpasses the western world in the cruelty and depredations that it has long imposed on Africa. Three centuries of slave trade, from around 1500 to the early 1800s, were followed by a century of brutal colonial rule. Far from lifting Africa economically, the colonial era left Africa bereft of educated citizens and leaders, basic infrastructure, and public health facilities. The borders of the newly independent states followed the arbitrary lines of the former empires, dividing ethnic groups, ecosystems, watersheds, and resource deposits in arbitrary ways.

As soon as the colonial period ended, Africa became a pawn in the cold war. Western cold warriors, and the operatives in the CIA and counterpart agencies in Europe, opposed African leaders who preached nationalism, sought aid from the Soviet Union, or demanded better terms on Western investments in African minerals and energy deposits. In 1960, as a demonstration of Western approaches to African independence, CIA and Belgian operatives assassinated the charismatic first prime minister of the Congo, Patrice Lumumba, and installed the tyrant Mobutu Sese Seko in his stead. In the 1980s, the United States supported Jonas Savimbi in his violent insurrection against the government of Angola, on the grounds that Savimbi was an anticommunist, when in fact he was a violent and corrupt thug. The United States long backed the South African apartheid regime, and gave tacit support as that regime armed the violent Renamo insurrectionists in neighboring Mozambique. The CIA had its hand in the violent overthrow of President Kwame Nkrumah of Ghana in 1966. Indeed, almost every African political crisis—Sudan, Somalia, and a host of others—has a long history of Western meddling among its many causes.

The one thing that the West would not do, however, was invest in long-term African economic development. The die was cast in the 1960s, when senior U.S. policy makers decided that the United States would not support a Marshall Plan type of policy for Africa, even though such an effort was precisely what was needed to build the infrastructure for long-term growth. It was not that U.S. officials rejected the diagnosis—they knew it was needed—but the political leadership was not willing to pay the price.

In April 1965, the director of the Central Intelligence Agency submitted a National Intelligence Estimate on the "Problems and Prospects in Sub-Saharan Africa." The estimate accurately concluded the following about Africa's growth prospects:

> Economic growth in most areas will be very slow; indeed, setbacks are probable in a number of countries. There is a desperate shortage of virtually all kinds of technical and managerial skills; indeed, the basic institutions and staff for economic development are often inadequate or absent. *Moreover, it is highly unlikely that most African countries will obtain external assistance or investment on anything approaching the scale required for sustained economic development.* (Emphasis added.)

As a National Security Council staffer noted in June 1965 in briefing McGeorge Bundy, President Lyndon Johnson's special assistant for national security affairs, the president's mandate to the State Department "cautions that substantial increases in U.S. foreign assistance expenditures [to Africa] are not envisaged."

DEEPER CAUSES OF AFRICAN POVERTY

Both the critics of African governance and the critics of Western violence and meddling have it wrong. Politics, at the end of the day, simply cannot explain Africa's prolonged economic crisis. The claim that

Africa's corruption is the basic source of the problem does not with-stand practical experience or serious scrutiny. During the past decade I witnessed close at hand how relatively well-governed countries in Africa, such as Ghana, Malawi, Mali, and Senegal, failed to prosper, whereas societies in Asia perceived to have extensive corruption, such as Bangladesh, India, Indonesia, and Pakistan, enjoyed rapid economic growth. Table 1 compares the Transparency International "corruption perception" rank for these African and Asian countries and their re-spective economic growth rates. We see that African countries lag be-hind in economic growth even when they are perceived to be less corrupt than their Asian counterparts. Using formal statistical tests, it turns out that Africa's per capita economic growth is significantly lower, by around 3 percentage points per year, than in other developing coun-tries with comparable levels of corruption and income.

Table 1: Corruption and Economic Growth			
		Corruption Perception Rank*	Average Yearly GDP per Capita Growth, 1980–2000
Sub-Saharan Africa	Ghana	70	0.3
	Senegal	76	0.5
	Mali	78	-0.5
	Malawi	83	0.2
East Asia	India	83	3.5
	Pakistan	92	2.4
	Indonesia	122	3.5
	Bangladesh	133	2.0

* Source: Transparency International, Global Corruption Report 2004 (London: Pluto Press, 2004). A higher rank indicates greater perceived corruption.

At the same time, Africa's harsh colonial legacy and the West's very real depradations in the postcolonial period also do not explain the long-term development crisis. Other regions of the world that are now growing rapidly also experienced severe damage from decades or cen-turies of colonial rule and postcolonial meddling. Vietnam is a case in point, a country that had to fight for independence for decades and yet emerged from that brutal experience to achieve very rapid economic growth.

In sub-Saharan Africa, therefore, a good differential diagnosis is ur-gently needed. The political story lines of both the left and the right reflect platitudes and prejudices, with little explanatory power about economic development. I was intent on finding a better approach. My work in Africa has been both an intellectual as well as a human adventure, and I think the effort has paid off in helping to uncover some of the deeper roots of Africa's predicament, as well as some promising solutions.

FIRST ENCOUNTERS

From my first drive across the border from Zimbabwe into Zambia, and during innumerable visits since, what has impressed me most is the distinctive physical ecology, and how it has helped to shape Africa's recent economic history. The great biologist E. O. Wilson is correct, I believe, when he argues that human beings are "hard-wired" to feel a special resonance ("biophilia") with the African savannah, the place where our species arose some 150,000 years ago. Yet however captivating these savannahs are, they pose innumerable and unique challenges for modern economic development: disease, drought, and distance from world markets, to name just three. Adam Smith, I noted earlier, had already pointed out the third of this trilogy in *The Wealth of Nations,* when he observed in 1776 that Africa had been poor from time immemorial because it lacked the navigable rivers and natural inlets that afford the benefits of low-cost, sea-based trade.

Driving past the adobe huts in sparsely populated rural areas of southern Zambia, I was struck by the extreme economic isolation of these rural households, even those relatively close to the paved road on which we drove. The settlements were typically a few huts circled around an area for chickens and some fuel wood. The settlements had no electricity or telecommunications, but more than that, there was no motorized transport whatsoever or even animal-drawn carts. The low population densities reflected the meager yields of the farms, the food output of which could support only a small population. (And this region was one of relatively stable rainfall and reasonable soils; other parts of Africa that I visited soon thereafter were even more disadvantaged.) The soils of these farms were depleted of nutrients, I would come to learn, and the homesteads were too disconnected from organized markets to sell crops or buy fertilizers. My detailed understanding of these problems, though, was still years away, and I certainly did not glean that knowledge from economics commentaries!

I came to appreciate that isolation and lack of basic infrastructure are the prevailing conditions of most of rural Africa, and that rural Africa is where most Africans live. Perhaps these facts should have been obvious to me from the start. Relevant information on population densities, roads, motor vehicles, access to electricity and telecommunications, and the like was certainly available from published data. But without the benefit of visiting Africa's rural communities, I would not have known what to look for in the data, or what the data really meant.

By the time I reached Lusaka on that first visit to Africa, I knew that things were very different, but I still did not begin to fathom just how different. One omnipresent force, which would overwhelm me for the coming decade, had still not made its presence felt. I was in the Bank of Zambia on the second or third day after my arrival, when my colleague from Harvard University explained to me that a Zambian coworker in the financial reform project had recently died. "How old was he?" I asked. "Oh, our age," came the reply. "But why?" I asked. "AIDS, Jeff, AIDS."

That was my firsthand introduction to the realities of AIDS in Africa. A team at Harvard had been leading a project for the past three years to help Zambia get back on its feet after a disastrous financial crisis. Sadly, Zambians were not getting back on their feet at all; instead, they were dying in remarkable numbers, including the highly trained Zambians in the project. This project was meant to be "capacity building," but Zambia was clearly losing trained capacity much faster than it was being gained.

AIDS was already relentless by the mid-1990s, but much worse was yet to come: endless work absences, funerals, and hushed conversations. Death was at the door. AIDS was not alone in its devastating impact on African society. Soon I became vividly aware of another insidious killer: malaria. At first I thought malaria was little more than a concern to be addressed with my once-a-week dose of mefloquine. Then I slowly grew aware of the obvious. Every African colleague, almost without exception, lost a few days per year to a flulike spell of malaria. Every now and then I would hear that one of our African graduate students who had returned to his country for a visit had come down with a much more serious bout of malaria. Several ended up in the hospital, some near death. What surprised me most, though, was malaria's grip on children. Everyone's children—rich and poor alike—contracted malaria. And all risked grave complications.

Married to a doctor, I have grown accustomed to frequent discussions about disease. But beyond anything I had experienced or could imagine, disease and death became the constant motif of my visits to Africa. Never, not even in the highlands of Bolivia, where illness is rife, had I confronted so much illness and death. India had never evoked the same sense of death in the air. By the turn of the new millennium, sub-Saharan Africa's life expectancy stood at forty-seven years, more than two decades lower than in East Asia (sixty-nine years) and thirty-one years lower than the average age in developed countries (seventy-eight years). In parts of Africa life expectancy was plummeting by almost twenty years as a result of the spread of AIDS. The worldwide map of life expectancy in map 8 highlights Africa's unique and extraordinary situation.

I began to suspect that the omnipresence of disease and death had played a deep role in Africa's prolonged inability to develop economically. The unsolved challenge for development economists is to understand why economic development in Africa has been so hard to achieve, not just in modern times but for centuries, and not in some places but in virtually all of tropical Africa (not including the five countries of North Africa or South Africa). Even before the Industrial Revolution, Africa had the lowest urbanization rate of any part of the world, and apparently the world's lowest living standards on the eve of the era of modern economic growth. According to economic historian Angus Maddison, Africa's growth rate has been among the lowest of any world region during each major subperiod since 1820. That includes a long stretch before Africa fell to European colonial rule in the 1880s and the period since independence. Could the exceptional burden of illness be a significant reason?

I decided to take on the question of Africa's lack of economic development in a series of research projects and advisory roles. Part of the answer, to be sure, lay in the governance choices made by African regimes. I visited Zimbabwe several times, and saw Robert Mugabe's depredations firsthand. Zimbabwe is a case where the traditional explanation of miserable rule is a sufficient explanation for a country's ills (although the nation no doubt also suffers from other serious problems as well). In 1997, I was invited to address a national forum in Harare, Zimbabwe, the only foreign speaker invited for the occasion. I gave a firm warning that Zimbabwe was veering off a cliff financially. Fittingly, perhaps, the lights promptly went out in the hotel and convention center. I descended seventeen flights of stairs by candlelight when the backup generator also failed. Sadly, the painful metaphor of Zimbabwe's lights going out has proved only too true in the ensuing years.

Another part of the answer, it is true, lay in implementing traditional market reforms, especially regarding export promotion. Asia had begun its ascent up the development ladder through garment exports. I was deeply puzzled about why African countries were not doing the same. One country was the exception that proved the rule: Mauritius, an Indian Ocean island off the coast of East Africa. During the colonial era, the island was a British slave colony for sugarcane production, but after independence, Mauritius began to export clothing. At the time of the country's independence in 1968, an ethnic-Chinese academic on the island happened to visit his brother in Taiwan. The brother was playing a leading role in the new export processing zones that were just then being established in Taiwan and other parts of Asia. The academic carried the concept back to the first prime minister, Seewoosagur Ramgoolam, who established a Mauritius free-trade zone in 1971. The rest is history. In 1996, I briefed U.S. Treasury Secretary Robert Rubin on the notion of expanding the number of African free-trade zones by offering Africa ensured access to the U.S. market for textile exports. This concept fed directly into the early Treasury Department drafts of new trade reform legislation for Africa, which became the African Growth and Opportunity Act in late 2000. The AGOA is now helping to create urban-based manufacturing employment in several countries in Africa.

Yet the more I saw, the more I realized that although predatory governance can soundly trounce economic development, good governance and market reforms are not sufficient to guarantee growth if the country is in a poverty trap. I visited and worked in many places with good governments that were struggling mightily against the odds. Botswana, Ethiopia, Ghana, Malawi, Mozambique, Nigeria (under President Olusegun Obasanjo), Senegal, Tanzania, Uganda, to name just a few, all have better governance than might have been expected given the burdens of extreme poverty, illiteracy, lack of financial resources, massive debt overhang, AIDS, malaria, and repeated droughts. In all of those cases, but especially in the landlocked countries (which number a whopping fifteen in Africa, by far the most of any continent), free-trade zones would not suffice, nor would they relieve extreme poverty on any kind of realistic timetable.

What, then, could be done for such places, where the struggle against poverty and disease was more elemental than choices about privatization, budget deficits, or trade policy? To understand—and over-come—such crises, it would be necessary to unravel the interconnec-tions between extreme poverty, rampant disease, unstable and harsh climate conditions, high transport costs, chronic hunger, and inade-quate food production. My first foray into this complex mix was via dis-ease—mainly AIDS and malaria—which I began to study in detail in 1997. More recently, especially in the context of the UN Millennium Project, I have also focused my attention on the issues of infrastructure and increased food production.

The Malaria Mystery

I had a lot to learn about disease and public health. It took me a while to understand the dire state of affairs. I still remember asking, "What do you mean they are not going to doctors? They have AIDS but they are not seeing doctors? Their children suffer from malaria-induced anemia but are not treated? How can this be?" "You know, there are treatments for AIDS and malaria," I sputtered. "What do you mean, there are no medicines here? What do you mean, there's no treatment program? What do you mean, USAID is doing nothing? What do you mean that the World Bank hasn't had an AIDS or malaria program in this country for years?" These were basic questions that I had never asked before coming to Africa. Strangely, neither had other economists, including those leading the IMF and World Bank missions to Africa.

Malaria became my first target of study. Malaria is a potentially fatal protozoan disease transmitted by a specific kind of mosquito, the genus anopheles. Malaria is utterly treatable, yet, incredibly, it still claims up to three million lives per year, mostly young children, about 90 percent of whom live in Africa. The rest of the deaths occur in tropical regions of the Americas and Asia. In fact, there are four types of human malaria. The malaria caused by the pathogen *Plasmodium falciparum* is by far the most lethal variant and is responsible for the vast proportion of malaria cases in Africa. The malaria due to *P. vivax* is very widely distributed in tropical and subtropical regions outside of Africa and is much less lethal. It is worth restating the central fact: malaria is utterly treatable, yet it still claims around three million lives per year, overwhelmingly in Africa. Low-cost treatments exist, but they do not reach the poor. These statistics boggled my mind, as does the current estimate that malaria causes up to five billion clinical cases per year. Virtually everybody in tropical Africa contracts the illness at least once a year. In some places, the entire population lives year-round with the malaria parasite in their bodies (although without clinical symptoms much of the time).

I overlaid two world maps, one of low GDP per capita and one that shows malaria transmission at three points in time: 1946, 1966, and 1994 (one can see the areas where malaria has been eliminated during those fifty years). The poor regions were largely the same as malarious ones, as shown in maps 9 and 10. This prompted four questions: First, does malaria contribute to poverty, or does poverty cause higher malaria incidence, or is it both? Second, why was the malaria situation so much worse in Africa? Third, what was being done to break the malaria-poverty linkage? And fourth, of course, what more could be done? Addressing these questions opened my eyes to a host of issues that I had hardly imagined in the mid-1990s. They led me from malaria to AIDS to public health, and then to the Millennium Development Goals.

The first finding I tried to establish was whether malaria and poverty were intertwined because poor countries lacked the means to fight malaria, or also because malaria contributes to extreme poverty. The evidence suggests both directions of causation. Poverty certainly exacerbates malaria by leaving impoverished households and governments without the financial means to fight the disease. Richer households and governments can afford to spray homes with insecticide, a highly effective intervention in many contexts; they can afford to install screen doors and windows to help keep the mosquitoes from entering the houses in the first place; they can afford insecticide-treated bed nets, which can substantially reduce the transmission of malaria in a village; and they can ensure access to health care and effective medications when the need arises.

Yet malaria also causes poverty, and for reasons that go well beyond the obvious ones of causing absenteeism from work and school. It is worth remembering how malaria and yellow fever delayed the construction of the Panama Canal for more than thirty years. The first attempt, led by the great French engineer Ferdinand de Lesseps, ended in tragedy when these two mosquito-borne diseases struck down the workforce. Only after the United States invested heavily in a mosquito-control effort guided by Colonel William C. Gorgas was the canal constructed. Malaria to this day can stop a good investment project in its tracks, whether a new mine, farm region, or tourist site.

Malaria also has extremely pernicious effects on the investments in human capital. Children who suffer repeated bouts of malaria can suffer lifetime ill effects caused by chronic anemia and the aftermath of complicated cases. With so many repeated disease episodes, they may drop out of school early because of poor attendance and a poor ability to learn. But there is an even deeper, if indirect, channel straight to poverty. In highly malarious regions, malaria impedes the demographic transition and the investment in human capital. When children die in large numbers, parents overcompensate and have more children, with devastating results. Too poor to invest in the education of all of their children, the family might educate just one child, usually the elder son. If children in malarious regions manage to survive, they enter adulthood without the proper education they need to succeed.

Why, though, was Africa so much more vulnerable to malaria than other regions? I was frequently asked how it was that malaria had not crippled the United States, which had had malaria until the 1940s (as map 10 showed), whereas it arguably had crippled Africa. It took me a while to understand some basic disease ecology, but once I did, the answer became clear. Malaria in the United States, and indeed in every other place in the world outside of Africa, was easier to control. Africa had it the worst, not because of poor governance and lack of public health services, but because of a unique disease environment. Malaria had coevolved with humans in Africa, and the result was a special intensity of transmission unequaled in any other part of the world.

I learned that malaria is transmitted when a female anopheles mosquito takes a blood meal from somebody already infected with malaria. After being ingested by the mosquito, the parasite finds its way to the mosquito's gut. There it undergoes a life-cycle transformation, after which the parasite migrates back to the mosquito's salivary glands, where it can be injected into another victim. But here is the catch. The life-cycle change, called sporogony, takes about two weeks, roughly the life span of the mosquito itself. If the mosquito dies before sporogony is completed, the mosquito never becomes infective. The central ecological point is that the warmer the temperature, the faster the sporogony— and the more likely it is that the mosquito will live to become infective. Malaria is largely a tropical disease, and if warm weather is a prerequisite, Africa has it!

Another important point is that some types of mosquitoes prefer to bite people, whereas others feed off cattle. Transmitting malaria requires two consecutive human bites: the first for the mosquito to ingest the parasite and the second for the mosquito to infect another person, roughly two weeks later. If the mosquito feeds frequently on cattle rather than on people, the odds are that at least one of the two bites, if not both, will be taken from cattle. In India, for example, the predominant type of anopheles tends to bite humans about one third of the time, and cattle the rest. Africa, sadly, has another predominating mosquito type which prefers human biting nearly 100 percent of the time. Mathematically, the chance that an Indian mosquito will feed off two humans in a row is about one out of nine, whereas in Africa it's about one out of one, or nearly certain. The force of transmission of malaria in Africa is therefore roughly nine times that of India because of the difference of mosquito species.

Thus Africa is really unlucky when it comes to malaria: high temperatures, plenty of breeding sites, and mosquitoes that prefer humans to cattle. When all these factors were put into a formal mathematical model, map 11 emerged. The darker shades in Africa signify that the disease transmission is higher simply because of the ecology. Africa's crisis is unique, with only a few other scattered parts of Asia (notably Papua New Guinea) sharing the same high ecological burden.

All of this helps to explain why Africa is burdened with malaria like no other part of the world, but it does not mean that the situation is hopeless. Far from it. Household spraying, insecticide-treated bed nets, and antimalarial medicines all work in Africa just as they do in other parts of the world. Although these technologies will not eliminate the disease in the way that it was eliminated in Europe and the United States, they will control the disease, reducing decisively the number of deaths from malaria. No children need to die, and none will if they have access to all of the modern tools of disease prevention and treatment! Yet malaria sets the perfect trap: it impoverishes a country, making it too expensive to prevent and treat the disease. Thus malaria continues and poverty deepens in a truly vicious circle.

This knowledge led me to the third question: what to do? I have to admit, I could not even begin to imagine what I would find when I first looked into possible solutions. There I was, a macroeconomist, reasonably proficient in issues of trade, budget deficits, inflation, and exchange rates. I understood quite a bit, I believed, about market reforms and globalization. And I believed these issues were quite important.

Nonetheless, I presumed malaria to be an even more urgent issue, a truly life-and-death concern. I fully expected to find that whatever could be done to fight malaria was already being done. Surely, I thought, the world community would not simply be standing by while millions of children were dying each year. But when my colleague Amir Attaran and I began to run the numbers on the levels of donor assistance to fight malaria, we barely found any numbers. The level of rich-country help to Africa to fight malaria was minimal, in the tens of millions of dollars per year when $2 to $3 billion was needed.

I was shocked. I started to scour the World Bank and USAID Web sites and project descriptions. Surely we had overlooked a massive effort to help Africa fight the disease. But no, the original calculations were correct. Malaria was not on the policy radar screen. The IMF and World Bank were apparently too busy arguing for budget cuts and privatization of sugar mills to have much time left to deal with malaria.

Africa's AIDS Cataclysm

From these lessons, it was but a small step to HIV/AIDS. The same three questions applied for AIDS as for malaria. What does the disease do to economic growth and poverty? What accounts for Africa's special circumstances? And what must be done? The answers are similar, but they have one important difference: as of today there is no solid explanation for why Africa's AIDS prevalence is at least an order of magnitude higher than anywhere else in the world.

The simplest answer, widely believed, is that in Africa there is more sexual activity outside of long-term stable relationships. The data, however, repeatedly cast doubt on that widely believed hypothesis. Perhaps the sexual networking is different in Africa (for example, there are more relationships between older men and younger women and more concurrent relationships, although not more lifetime partners). Perhaps HIV/AIDS is transmitted more easily in Africa because the population has other untreated ailments (malaria, other sexually transmitted diseases), or because men are much less frequently circumcised, or because condoms are less frequently used in casual sexual relations. Perhaps the viral subtypes (known as clades) are different in Africa. The truth is that nobody is sure. The only certainty is that HIV/AIDS is an unmitigated tragedy and a development disaster throughout Africa, especially in the hardest hit regions of eastern and southern Africa.

As for the economic costs of the disease, these certainly rival or exceed malaria's in the disaster at hand. Africa is losing its teachers and doctors, its civil servants and farmers, its mothers and fathers. There are already more than ten million orphaned children. Business costs have soared because of disarray from massive medical costs for workers, relentless absenteeism, and an avalanche of worker deaths. Foreign investors are deterred from stepping into Africa's AIDS morass. And millions of households are battling the illness of the head of household, resulting in an incredible toll in time and expense, to say nothing of the emotional trauma for the family.

Once again I looked at what was being done and what could be done. By the late 1990s, AIDS in the rich countries was being treated, with growing success, by antiretroviral medicines given in three-drug combinations, so-called highly active antiretroviral therapy (HAART) or simply antiretroviral therapy (ARV). This therapy was changing the face of the disease in the rich countries. Individuals infected with HIV now had hope. Others who thought they might be infected were willing to come forward for testing. The prospect of drug treatment, and therefore the readiness of more people to submit to voluntary counseling and testing, meant that prevention and treatment programs worked in a mutually supportive manner.

Certainly, I thought, the same must be happening in the low-income world. With all the worldwide attention on AIDS, and all the hand wringing and speeches, surely the donor world was gearing up to help the impoverished world to fight this terrifying epidemic. But once again my presumptions were wrong. Attaran and I went to work on the donor figures, and we were blown away by what we found. Could it really be true that the world was giving just $70 million to all of Africa to fight AIDS? Was this even conceivable? As we started circulating these data, shown in table 2, there was no statement of correction or complaint from the donors. These estimates were, stunningly, the right numbers, and soon afterward Attaran and I published them in one of Britain's leading medical journals, *The Lancet*.

Over and over again I saw the difference between spin and reality in how the world community faced AIDS and malaria. At one point, for example, an IMF official published a letter in the *Financial Times* noting that health and education spending in poor countries with IMF programs was actually up 2.8 percent per year between 1985 and 1996. The fact is, however, that although the IMF official was correct in a strictly

Table 2: Overseas Development Budgets for Sexually Transmitted Disease Control, Including HIV/AIDS, in Sub-Saharan Africa (1990–1998)

Year	All Sources Total	Grant Sources				Loans from World Bank Total
		Total	Tied	Untied	Tech Coop	
1990	28.9	28.9	10.8	18.1	9.9	0.0
1991	38.4	38.4	18.8	9.3	10.3	0.0
1992	53.7	53.7	14.8	22.6	2.6	0.0
1993	39.1	39.1	28.1	3.4	3.1	0.0
1994	162.5	86.2	46.4	28.3	28.1	76.3
1995	139.3	99.3	25.7	43.1	28.2	40.0
1996	43.7	43.7	25.6	10.5	8.9	0.0
1997	88.3	88.3	49.0	22.3	18.1	0.0
1998	73.9	73.9	24.7	20.6	17.2	0.0

Millions of US$.

Source: Attaran and Sachs (2001).

technical sense, health spending was disastrously, indeed shockingly, low in African countries with IMF programs. In most cases, public health spending in 1996 was below $10 per person, so the increase had been from almost nothing to almost nothing. I was initially amazed that the IMF would play such tricks with the public, but I came to realize that the fund had no special feel for these numbers. The IMF management and staff know very little about public health, and traditionally they pay almost no attention to whether health spending in their client countries is $10 or $100 or $1,000 or more per person (as it is for the rich countries that dominate the Executive Board of the institution).

Around the same time, I made a speech noting that the World Bank had made no grants or loans during 1995–2000 for controlling AIDS in Africa. A bank spokesman attacked me vigorously. "You don't know what you're talking about. We had several program countries with AIDS programs." "That can't be; I've checked, and I did not find a single loan." Again they were technically correct, in a way that utterly distorted the truth. There were probably a few dozen countries where AIDS was mentioned in a sentence or maybe a paragraph in a loan for the health sector. The AIDS component was usually tiny, perhaps a few million dollars over several years. Up to the year 2000, these minimal efforts never even contemplated the use of antiretroviral drugs to treat AIDS.

In the late 1990s, in the wake of my public spats with the IMF over their mismanagement of the 1997–98 East Asian financial crisis, I went on the warpath with the international financial community over AIDS and malaria. I called for an end to the international community's gross negligence regarding the diseases ravaging Africa. I complained that the IMF and World Bank had been in Africa for decades, but had remained blind to the most basic realities there, and to the growing human and economic catastrophe.

At that point, I teamed up with President Olusegun Obasanjo of Nigeria to help prepare a major Africa-wide summit on malaria in Abuja, Nigeria, in April 2000. My colleagues, including several world-class malariologists at Harvard—Andy Spielman, Awash Teklehaimanot (visiting from WHO), and Anthony Kiszewski—and I wrote a key background report that demonstrated the massive burden of malaria on economic development in Africa and also stressed the opportunities at hand to control the disease.

At about this time I received a call from Dr. Gro Harlem Brundtland, who had recently been appointed director general of the World Health Organization. Brundtland was former prime minister of Norway and, without doubt, one of the world's most skilled political leaders. In the mid-1980s she had chaired the famous Brundtland Commission, which had launched the concept of sustainable development. She said to me, "If you want to get someone's attention about the health crises in Africa, 'show them the money.' Help them to understand the economic costs of the disease pandemics, as well as the economics of disease control. Above all, propose practical solutions based on a rigorous emphasis on economic costs and benefits."

Brundtland suggested that I chair a commission of macroeconomists and public health specialists to do just that. The WHO Commission on Macroeconomics and Health (CMH) was born. I chaired the commission for two years, from the start of 2000 to the end of 2001. In December 2001, the CMH published its report, *Investing in Health for Economic Development.* This was the work of eighteen commissioners, including Harold Varmus, Nobel laureate and former director of the National Institutes of Health; Supachai Panitchpakdi, who would go on to lead the World Trade Organization; Robert Fogel, the Nobel laureate economic historian at the University of Chicago; and Manmohan Singh, the former finance minister and future prime minister of India. In addition to this stellar commission, we drew upon six task forces that included more than a hundred specialists from around the world. The commission and task forces had senior representation of the IMF, the World Bank, and several donor agencies.

The commission gave me a wonderful opportunity to test my favorite hypothesis about collective rationality, which is that if you put people of strongly opposing views in a room together, and infuse their discussion with data, background studies, and unhurried time for debate, it is possible to bridge seemingly irreconcilable positions among the members of the group. I have come to call this process analytical deliberation. It works. The commission was deeply divided at the start about who was "to blame" for Africa's roiling disease crisis: Africans for their mismanagement, the pharmaceutical industry for its greed, the rich world for its malign neglect. Did Africa need more aid, or just better use those resources that it had at hand? Could anti-AIDS drug treatment be applied in Africa? On these and a dozen other issues, the first day of the two-year process was contentious, to say the least. On the last day, when the report was issued, we had reached a consensus that extended not only to the eighteen commissioners and hundred or so experts in the working groups, but also to major representatives of the pharmaceutical industry and the NGO community. We had worked diligently and assiduously to bring forward evidence and a consensus on three basic issues:

First, is disease a cause of poverty, a result of poverty, or both? The commission concluded that causation runs strongly in both directions. Poor health causes poverty and poverty contributes to poor health.

Second, why do poor countries have a life expectancy several decades shorter than rich countries? Why, especially, is Africa's life expectancy, at forty-seven years in 2000, more than three decades less than the seventy-eight years of the rich countries? The commission identified eight areas that accounted for the vast proportion of the gap in disease burden: AIDS, malaria, TB, diarrheal disease, acute respiratory infection, vaccine-preventable disease, nutritional deficiencies, and unsafe childbirth.

Third, how much should the rich world help the poor world to invest in health? The commission calculated that donor aid ought to rise from around $6 billion per year to $27 billion per year (by 2007). With the combined GNP of the donor countries equal to around $25 trillion dollars as of 2001, the commission was advocating an annual investment of around one thousandth of rich-world income. The commission showed, on the best epidemiological evidence, that such an investment could avert eight million deaths per year.

The report of the Commission on Macroeconomics and Health had quite a notable reception. Reports come and go. This one, I think it is fair to say, came and stayed. It made the important point that we, as a generation, can do something dramatic to improve our world. The report found a wide audience, in part, because it was based on a broad and surprising consensus. It was launched with the kind of pizzazz that it deserved, with Brundtland; UK Secretary of State for International Development Clare Short; Ray Gilmartin, the CEO of Merck; and Bono as enthusiastic supporters.

Around the same time that the commission began meeting, I started to push the idea of a "global fund" to fight AIDS and malaria. At the International AIDS Conference in Durban in July 2000, I gave a speech calling for such a global fund. Word spread of the speech and the idea of a new global fund took hold. I met with UN Secretary-General Kofi Annan, whom I consider the world's finest statesman, to discuss the practicalities and design of such a fund. He was very interested and asked me to work closely with his staff in the coming months to refine the concept.

One more piece of the puzzle was needed. As of early 2001, the donor world still shunned the idea of using anti-AIDS drugs in low-income countries to save the lives of people with late-stage AIDS disease. The donor world viewed anti-AIDS drugs as hugely expensive and technically impractical—in short, not cost-effective. Getting global financing for them in Africa was still a huge uphill struggle. The most common claim was that anti-AIDS treatment wouldn't work anyway. Impoverished and illiterate patients would not be able to comply with complicated drug regimens.

My colleague Paul Farmer put those arguments to rest for me and, in some ways, for the world. A professor of medicine at Harvard, and a saint of global health, Paul had been running a clinic in the impoverished central plateau of Haiti since 1985. Using charitable contributions and drug donations from HIV-infected patients whose regimens had changed (leaving the patients with unneeded pills), Paul had begun introducing anti-AIDS drug treatment among his AIDS patients. He was getting marvelous clinical results. In January 2001, he invited my wife and me to his clinic to see the results. We went out to the villages to meet mothers and fathers who had been at death's door, but who were now standing tall with their children. Wherever we went, we were greeted with gracious hospitality by people who would have been dead but for a few pills per day.

Birth of the Global Fund to Fight AIDS, TB, and Malaria

It was time to bring these benefits to the poorest of the poor all over the world and, most urgently, to Africa. Together with two other colleagues in the struggle against AIDS—Bruce Walker, of the Harvard Medical School, and Max Essex, of the Harvard School of Public Health—Paul Farmer and I decided that we would prepare a document to show that treatment of dying AIDS patients was possible and could be scaled up to millions of people within a few years. In the end, the four of us guided the Consensus Statement by Members of the Harvard Faculty. One hundred twenty-eight faculty members signed the document that outlined how large-scale anti-AIDS drug treatment was possible in the impoverished world.

One of our key points was that drug treatment for the poor would actually cost the donor world much less than appeared to be the case from drug prices in the rich countries. Under the patent system, antiretroviral medicines are priced far above their actual cost of production. The companies can price in this manner because the patent gives them a temporary monopoly. The economic theory is that the profits that result from high patent-protected prices are the incentive for the companies to engage in research and development in the first place. Still, with the actual production costs of an antiretroviral regimen at $500 per year or less (compared with U.S. market prices of around $10,000 per year), it would be possible to provide access to the poor with donor help, assuming that drug companies would supply the low-income markets at production cost rather than monopoly prices. This turned out to be the case. The patent holders agreed to cut their prices in the low-income markets, while various generic drug manufacturers provided additional competition by offering low-priced competitor drugs in countries where patents did not apply or where they were circumvented by special procedures.

The consensus statement therefore showed that it would be possible to treat millions of poor people per year for a few billion dollars of donor support each year. The statement circulated immediately around the world, to Anthony Fauci at the National Institutes of Health, the White House, the Commission on Macroeconomics and Health, the WHO, the foundations, the presidents in Africa, and, of course, UN Secretary-General Kofi Annan.

I worked very closely with the secretary-general and his staff in the weeks leading up to the Abuja Summit on AIDS in April 2001, refining the concepts of a new global fund as well as the economics that would underlie the fund. The secretary-general announced his support for a plan for the Global Fund to Fight AIDS, TB, and Malaria at the summit in a marvelous and historic speech. By the next month, the secretary-general was standing at the Rose Garden next to President Obasanjo to hear President Bush announce that the United States would subscribe to the Global Fund. In June, the General Assembly endorsed the fund, followed by the G8 leaders in July. By the end of 2001, the fund had begun.

As always, these battles are never won, just pushed forward to new terrain. Since the fund started, the continuing battle has been to get the resources the fund needs on a long-term reliable basis, and to help the low-income countries to prepare and implement plans that are commensurate with their challenge. Still, after years of extreme neglect, the battle against AIDS, malaria, and TB has finally been joined.

SOME LESSONS LEARNED

A decade of intensive work in Africa has added to my determination to fight against the prejudices and misperceptions that leave hundreds of millions of impoverished people stranded in unnecessary suffering. Africa gets a bad rap as the "corrupt continent." Even when such sentiments are not racist in intent, they survive in our societies as conventional wisdom because of existing widespread racism. Many African governments are desperately trying to do the right thing, but they face enormous obstacles of poverty, disease, ecological crisis, and geopolitical neglect or worse.

Since the issuance of the Macroeconomics and Health Report and the launch of the Global Fund, I have turned my own attention in Africa to issues beyond public health. Africa needs solutions not only for disease control, but also for chronic hunger, rural isolation, and growing environmental degradation, often the result of still-booming populations. As in the case of disease, there are special reasons why Africa is particularly hard pressed in each of these areas. In other words, geography has conspired with economics to give Africa a particularly weak hand. I have noted that Africa lacks navigable rivers with access to the ocean for easy transport and trade. Moreover, much of Africa's population lives in the interior of the continent rather than at the coast. Indeed, sub-Saharan Africa's highest population densities are in the highland regions, such as Ethiopia and Rwanda, because rainfall reliability and soils tend to be a bit better there than in the interior lowlands and coast. Yet these highland populations are isolated from the international division of labor. In general, Africa lacks irrigation, and more than 90 percent of the food crops are rain fed. Rainfall tends to be highly variable in the subhumid savannah and the arid Sahel near the Sahara. Farmers lack access to roads, markets, and fertilizers. Soils have been long depleted of nutrients as the result of repeated harvests without the benefit of chemical or organic nutrient inputs. Without transport, telecommunications, clinics, and fertilizers, the hunger-disease-poverty nexus has only deepened.

The combination of Africa's adverse geography and its extreme poverty creates the worst poverty trap in the world. Yet the situation in Africa is not hopeless. Far from it. Just as my malaria-expert colleagues taught me about bed nets, indoor spraying, and effective antimalarial medicines, and just as my HIV/AIDS-knowledgeable colleagues taught me what can be accomplished through effective prevention programs linked to access to anti-AIDS drugs, so my colleagues in tropical agriculture, rural electrification, road building, and safe water and sanitation began to teach me what could be done in these other areas of vital concern.

Africa's problems, I have come to understand, are especially difficult but still solvable with practical and proven technologies. Diseases can be controlled, crop yields can be sharply increased, and basic infrastructure such as paved roads and electricity can be extended to the villages. A combination of investments well attuned to local needs and conditions can enable African economies to break out of the poverty trap. These interventions need to be applied systematically, diligently, and jointly, since they strongly reinforce one another. With focused attention by African countries and the international community, Africa

THE VOICELESS DYING   209

could soon have its own Green Revolution, and achieve a takeoff in rural-led growth, thereby sparing the coming generation of Africans the continued miseries of drought-induced famine. Sooner than I expected, I received an important new opportunity to put these ideas into practice.

Eleven

THE MILLENNIUM, 9/11,
AND THE UNITED NATIONS

The new millennium opened on a hopeful note. The world survived the widely feared Y2K computer crisis without incident. Celebrations the world over went off without a hitch. The U.S. economy continued to surge ahead. Economic progress in China, India, and finally even Russia gave the sense that globalization might yet fulfill its promise. The IT boom was still in its full glory. We marveled at the dizzying progress of the new Internet age, the new global interconnectivity, and the seemingly endless flow of new products, new ways of organizing business, and new ways of linking people and production systems around the world. Although Africa remained a place of unrelieved crisis, even there the spread of democracy and the possibility of mobilizing new technologies to fight AIDS, malaria, and other diseases gave hope.

Perhaps the most vivid geopolitical reflection of this hope was the Millennium Assembly, which took place at the United Nations in September 2000. It was the largest gathering of world leaders in history. One hundred forty-seven heads of state and government came to New York, and did more than create a colossal traffic jam. At their historic UN meeting, the world leaders convincingly expressed a global determination to end some of the most challenging and vexing problems inherited from the twentieth century. They conveyed the hope that extreme poverty, disease, and environmental degradation could be alleviated with the wealth, the new technologies, and the global awareness with which we had entered the twenty-first century.

For the occasion, Secretary-General Kofi Annan presented the world with a remarkable document. *We the Peoples: The Role of the United Nations in the 21st Century* reflected the secretary-general's strong conviction that the UN represents not only its 191-member governments but also the peoples of the world as individuals, who are endowed with rights and responsibilities that have a global reach. *We the Peoples* laid out a discerning view of the great challenges facing global society: extreme poverty, pandemic disease, environmental harm, war and civil conflict. The document moved from a panoramic view of these great challenges through a powerful diagnosis of their root causes to a set of recommendations on how these challenges could be met through global cooperation and action.

The document became the basis for an important global statement, the Millennium Declaration, adopted by the assembled leaders. It is worthy and important reading for all of us. Despite our travails in the intervening years, the Millennium Declaration still inspires hope that the world, complicated and divided as it is, can come together to take on great challenges. The Declaration, like the secretary-general's report, surveys the issues of war and peace, health and disease, and wealth and poverty, and commits the world to a set of undertakings to improve the human condition. Specifically, it sets forth a series of quantified and time-bound goals to reduce extreme poverty, disease, and deprivation. Those goals were subsequently excerpted from the Millennium Declaration to become the eight Millennium Development Goals, or MDGs.

Table 1 lists the eight goals and eighteen targets that are bold commitments to achieve sustainable development for the world's poorest

Table 1: The Millennium Development Goals	
1. Eradicate extreme poverty and hunger	Halve, between 1990 and 2015, the proportion of people whose income is less than one dollar a day
	Halve, between 1990 and 2015, the proportion of people who suffer from hunger
2. Achieve universal primary education	Ensure that by 2015 children everywhere, boys and girls alike, will be able to complete a full course of primary schooling
3. Promote gender equality and empower women	Eliminate gender disparity in primary and secondary education, preferably by 2005, and to all levels of education no later than 2015
4. Reduce child mortality	Reduce by two thirds, between 1990 and 2015, the under-five mortality rate

5. Improve maternal health	Reduce by three quarters, between 1990 and 2015, the maternal mortality ratio
6. Combat HIV/AIDS, malaria and other diseases	Have halted by 2015 and begun to reverse the spread of HIV/AIDS
	Have halted by 2015 and begun to reverse the incidence of malaria and other major diseases
7. Ensure environmental sustainability	Integrate the principles of sustainable development into country policies and programs and reverse the loss of environmental resources
	Halve by 2015 the proportion of people without sustainable access to safe drinking water and basic sanitation
	By 2020 to have achieved a significant improvement in lives of at least 100 million slum dwellers
8. Develop a global partnership for development	Develop further an open, rule-based, predictable, nondiscriminatory trading and financial system. Includes a commitment to good governance, development, and povery reduction—both nationally and internationally
	Address the special needs of the least developed countries. This includes: tariff- and quota-free access for least developed countries' exports; an enhanced program of debt relief for HIPC and cancellation of official bilateral debt; and more generous ODA for countries committed to poverty reduction
	Address the special needs of landlocked countries and small island developing states (through the Program of Action for the Sustainable Development of Small Island Developing States and the outcome of the twenty-second special session of the General Assembly)
	Deal comprehensively with the debt problems of developing countries through national and international measures in order to make debt sustainable in the long term
	In cooperation with developing countries, develop and implement strategies for decent and productive work for youth
	In cooperation with pharmaceutical companies, provide access to affordable, essential drugs in developing countries

> In cooperation with the private sector,
> make available the benefits of new
> technologies, especially information and
> communications

people. The first seven goals call for sharp cuts in poverty, disease, and environmental degradation. The eighth goal is essentially a commitment of global partnership, a compact of rich and poor countries to work together to achieve the first seven goals. The Millennium Development Goals wisely recognize that extreme poverty has many dimensions, not only low income, but also vulnerability to disease, exclusion from education, chronic hunger and undernutrition, lack of access to basic amenities such as clean water and sanitation, and environmental degradation such as deforestation and land erosion that threatens lives and livelihoods.

The Millennium Development Goals could, no doubt, engender some cynicism as well as hope. In many cases, the goals repeated long-held commitments of the international community that had not been fulfilled in the past. After all, one of the famous commitments of the past century was the international community's 1978 pledge of "Health for All by the Year 2000." Yet the world arrived in 2000 with the AIDS pandemic, resurgent TB and malaria, and billions of the world's poor without reliable, or sometimes any, access to essential health services. At the World Summit for Children in 1990, the world pledged universal access to primary education by the year 2000, yet 130 million or more primary-aged children were not in school by then. The rich world had famously committed to the target of 0.7 percent of GNP devoted to official development assistance (ODA), direct financial aid to poor countries, yet the share of financial aid as a proportion of rich-world GNP had actually declined from 0.3 to 0.2 percent during the 1990s.

Still, when the world leaders adopted the Millennium Declaration, and the Millennium Development Goals within the Declaration, there was a palpable sense that this time—yes, this time—they just might be fulfilled. The world felt that with the strength of the ongoing economic boom, the vast new power of modern technologies, and the uniqueness of our global interconnectedness, this time we would follow through.

How quickly that optimism was shattered. There were small things that dented the optimism—the U.S. trauma of a tied national election, the end of the stock market boom, and a spate of high-profile corporate scandals—but these look insignificant now in the shadow of September 11. Much changed that day, partly because of the unwise ways in which the U.S. government reacted. More than ever, we need to return to the purpose and hope of the Millennium Development Goals.

As it has for almost everyone else in the world, 9/11 remains as vivid to me as if it were just moments ago. The way I experienced that morning continues to impress on me the nature of our global society. I was in my office at Harvard University, on a live videoconference feed to South Africa, giving a lecture on AIDS to a group of community leaders and business people in Durban. As I was speaking, I saw the people at the podium in South Africa begin whispering to each other. I was shocked when one turned to the video camera and said, "Professor Sachs, I regret to inform you that your country is under attack and we have to end this conference immediately." With that, the transmission went down, and I walked out of the room to see dozens of shocked and dazed colleagues milling in the halls. People congregated in front of a giant television screen in the central foyer. Within minutes, we watched in horror as the towers collapsed before our eyes.

For all of us, those are events that we will not forget. The meaning of those events, however, remains to be decided. Within hours it became the immediate presumption in the United States that everything had changed, that what we experienced that day was a great turning point in history. One of the leading journalists in the United States, Thomas Friedman, immediately declared that September 11 was the start of World War III, a notion that found wide resonance among the horrified American population. President Bush himself said then, and many times since, that September 11 changed everything about his view of his job, the United States itself, its vulnerabilities, and its place in the world. Indeed, September 11 marked the start of the Bush administration's self-proclaimed war on terrorism. The president declared that hereafter his whole presidency would be devoted to the extirpation of terror.

The ease with which the pundits talked about World War III stunned me deeply. They were playing with fire, or much worse, with the destruction of our world in a new conflagration. Were they not aware, I asked myself, of the way that World War I had destroyed globalization a century before? In that case, too, the pundits had been only too happy to see the soldiers march off to war, sure that that tidy affair would be wrapped up in a month. The demons unleashed by that war, however, stalked the planet until the end of the twentieth century, having their hand in the Great Depression, World War II, the Bolshevik revolution, and much more.

For me, the 9/11 attacks were harrowing events, but they did not change everything—unless the United States acted recklessly in response. After all, Americans had experienced terrorist acts before, and will experience them again. We have seen repeated terrorist acts throughout the Middle East, in Kenya and Tanzania, and on U.S. soil at the World Trade Center in 1993 and in Oklahoma City in 1995. Terrorism is a scourge that can be fought, but it cannot be eliminated entirely, just as the world will not eliminate entirely the scourge of infectious disease. President Bush made the same point during the 2004 election campaign—"I don't think you can win it [the war on terrorism], but I think you can create conditions so that those who use terror as a tool are less acceptable in parts of the world"—but then reversed himself the next day.

Terrorism is not the only threat that the world faces. It would be a huge mistake to direct all our energies, efforts, resources, and lives to the fight against terrorism while leaving vast and even greater challenges aside. Almost three thousand people died needlessly and tragically at the World Trade Center on September 11; ten thousand Africans die needlessly and tragically *every single day*—and have died every single day since September 11—of AIDS, TB, and malaria. We need to keep September 11 in perspective, especially because the ten thousand daily deaths *are* preventable.

Moreover, terrorism has complex and varying causes, and cannot be fought by military means alone. To fight terrorism, we will need to fight poverty and deprivation as well. A purely military approach to terrorism is doomed to fail. Just as a doctor fights disease by prescribing not only medication, but also by bolstering a person's immune system through adequate nutrition and by encouraging a healthy lifestyle for his patient, so, too, we need to address the underlying weaknesses of the societies in which terrorism lurks—extreme poverty; mass unmet needs for jobs, incomes, and dignity; and the political and economic instability that results from degrading human conditions. If societies like Somalia, Afghanistan, and western Pakistan were healthier, terrorists could not operate so readily in their midst.

The appropriate response to September 11 was therefore two tracks, not one. Civilized nations needed surely to take up the challenge to cripple the networks of terrorism that carried out the attacks. The financial controls and direct military actions against Al-Qaeda were a necessary response, but hardly sufficient. In addition, we needed to address the deeper roots of terrorism in societies that are not part of global prosperity, that are marginalized in the world economy, that are bereft of hope, and that are misused and abused by the rich world, as have been the oil states of the Middle East. The rich world, starting with the United States, needed to commit its efforts even more to economic development than to military strategies.

The great allied leaders of the fight against fascism in World War II understood that success in the war effort also required success in winning the confidence and trust of the world. Franklin Delano Roosevelt led the United States into World War II on the basis of defending four freedoms, not just the freedom from fear, but also the freedoms of speech and belief and, crucially, the freedom from want. His stirring words resonate today:

> In the future days, which we seek to make secure, we look forward to a world founded upon four essential human freedoms. The first is freedom of speech and expression—everywhere in the world.
>
> The second is freedom of every person to worship God in his own way—everywhere in the world.
>
> The third is freedom from want, which, translated into world terms, means economic understandings, which will secure to every nation a healthy peacetime life for its inhabitants—everywhere in the world.
>
> The fourth is freedom from fear, which, translated into world terms, means a worldwide reduction of armaments to such a point and in such a thorough fashion that no nation will be in a position to commit an act of physical aggression against any neighbor—anywhere in the world.

When Roosevelt and British Prime Minister Winston Churchill met to announce the Atlantic Charter, the joint statement of the war aims of the United States and the United Kingdom, they, too, put the focus on the hopes of the world for shared prosperity as one of the critical goals.

These war aims proved to be much more than empty rhetoric. They were also the successful bases for a peaceful postwar world. The United Nations was founded in 1945 to provide an institutional framework for global cooperation. The Marshall Plan proved the U.S. commitment to freedom from want, and that tradition was carried on in other development programs in Asia and Latin America. Over time, that effort has evaporated; U.S. aid fell from more than 2 percent of GNP during the heyday of the Marshall Plan to less than 0.2 percent of GNP today.

Soon after September 11, I made these points in an article for *The Economist,* "Weapons of Mass Salvation." My point was that one cannot fight a war against weapons of mass destruction through military means alone. The weapons of mass salvation that I referred to—anti-AIDS drugs, antimalarial bed nets, borewells for safe drinking water, and the like—can save millions of lives and also be a bulwark for global security.

That fall it seemed that the Bush administration would pursue more than a military approach. In November 2001, it promoted the launch of a new global trade round, in Doha, Qatar. The resulting Doha Declaration placed emphasis on reform of the trading system in order to meet the needs of the poorest countries. An even more important event followed in March 2002, in Monterrey, Mexico, at an international conference on financing for development. This conference dedicated itself to the challenge of providing the financial means for economic progress. The Monterrey Consensus that emerged from the conference usefully highlighted both the role of private investment and official development assistance.

The Monterrey Consensus made clear that the poorest countries cannot really be expected to receive large inflows of private capital because they lack the basic infrastructure and human capital that can attract international and even domestic private investment. On the other hand, for countries that are much further along in economic development—the so-called emerging markets—aid may play a small role, whereas private capital can fuel a great deal of development. The Monterrey Consensus puts it this way:

> Official development assistance (ODA) plays an essential role as a complement to other sources of financing for development, especially in those countries with the least capacity to attract private direct investment . . . For many countries in Africa, least developed countries, small island developing States and landlocked developing countries, ODA is still the largest source of external financing and is critical to the achievement of the development goals and

targets of the Millennium Declaration and other internationally agreed development targets.

The United States and the other signatories agreed to something much more dramatic in the following paragraph of the Monterrey Consensus, to "*urge all developed countries that have not done so to make concrete efforts toward the goal of 0.7 percent of gross domestic product as official development assistance.*" As of 2002, aid equaled $53 billion, just 0.2 percent of rich-world GNP. If rich countries met the target, aid would reach $175 billion per year, equal to 0.7 percent of the $25 trillion rich-world GNP in 2002. For the United States, foreign aid would rise from around $15 billion per year in 2004 (0.14 percent of GNP) to around $75 billion (0.7 percent of U.S. GNP). Here indeed would be a breakthrough.

President Bush himself came to Monterrey to announce a surprising and welcome increase of U.S. foreign assistance in a new project known as the Millennium Challenge Account, or MCA. He pledged that the United States would increase its foreign assistance to countries that demonstrated the will and the capacity to use that increased funding effectively. He promised $10 billion over the coming three fiscal years, in increments of $1.6 billion, $3.2 billion, and $5 billion, respectively. When word of the U.S. program first spread among the conference participants, U.S. Ambassador to the UN John Negroponte came over to me, patted me on the back, and whispered in my ear, "You're getting what you've asked for."

For a brief moment, I was optimistic. Yes, I knew that the promised increase in U.S. foreign aid was really quite small relative to the size of the U.S. economy, so small that U.S. aid would remain less than 0.2 percent of U.S. GNP even after the first three years of the Millennium Challenge Account. While hardly a concrete step toward 0.7 percent of GNP, I thought it was just possible that the Bush administration would see in the tragedy of September 11 the need for a new relationship with the world, one in which the United States once again was an active champion of the quest to eliminate extreme poverty. Even if the challenge account was small at the start, I told myself, it could still grow to the 0.7 percent target to which the United States had agreed.

Alas, my hopes were deflated just a few months later. Once again, the world leaders had assembled for an international conference, this time in Johannesburg, South Africa, at the World Summit on Sustainable Development. The Summit was the tenth anniversary of the Rio

Earth Summit, at which critical decisions had been taken to protect the world's environment in the face of growing man-made threats. Most important, the Rio Summit had adopted the United Nations Framework Convention on Climate Change (UNFCCC), in which the world's governments committed to take steps to curb the emission of harmful greenhouse gases contributing to long-term global warming and other threatening climatic changes. The UNFCCC was the basis for negotiating the Kyoto Protocol to limit greenhouse gas emissions.

Ten years had not been kind to the Rio Summit. The Kyoto Protocol remained unratified and the Bush administration had walked away from the Kyoto agreement in its first months in office, an act that carried with it a special irony given that the first President Bush had originally signed the UNFCCC. Still, when the world assembled in Johannesburg, there were lingering hopes that just as in Monterrey, the world would get back on track with a clear global and U.S. commitment to the environmental agenda.

This was not to be the case. The Bush administration's neglect of this agenda and its waning interest in the overall development agenda was made vivid in Johannesburg in deeply ironic ways. First, President Bush skipped the meeting. More materially, just as the world gathered to take up the challenges of the global environment, the United States used the occasion to launch the public campaign for a war with Iraq.

As I stood in the pressroom in Johannesburg, all eyes were on the television screen, watching Vice President Dick Cheney, ten thousand miles away, speaking to the 103rd National Convention of the Veterans of Foreign Wars. This was the famous speech in which Vice President Cheney erroneously claimed that "there is no doubt that Saddam Hussein now has weapons of mass destruction. There is no doubt he is amassing them to use against our friends, against our allies, and against us." This new U.S. drumbeat of war immediately drained the attention from Johannesburg and marked the end of the two-track approach to fighting terrorism. From that point on, the United States put virtually all its emphasis, political energies, and finances behind the military approach.

In the month that followed Johannesburg, President Bush and his senior advisers gave literally hundreds of speeches, interviews, and presentations on Iraq, but they uttered few, if any, words about the challenges of extreme poverty, the message of Monterrey, and the commitments to the new Millennium Challenge Account. The sole exception to this abrupt change in focus was the president's State of the Union address in January 2003, in which the president announced his intention to scale up U.S. contributions to the fight against AIDS in Africa, an important and worthy initiative. I was pleased to hear the figure of $15 billion over five years—$3 billion per year—which was exactly the estimate that I had given to the White House in early 2001 (and which had been met with huge skepticism at the time). Otherwise, official Washington was completely focused on war rather than on development, the environment, and other issues of pressing human concern around the globe.

In the lead-up to the war, I wrote and spoke widely about my feeling that U.S. policy was veering wildly off track, that war in Iraq could not accomplish anything of lasting value but could do grave damage. Here is what I wrote in the *New Republic* on the eve of the war:

> [A] conventional army on the ground cannot suppress local uprisings or guerrilla warfare without tremendous bloodshed and years of agony. For decades, the British could not suppress the Irish Republican Army in Northern Ireland. The vast military might of Israel cannot suppress the Palestinian uprising. The Russians could not suppress the mujahedin in Afghanistan in the 1980s or the Chechens in the 1990s. The United States took casualties and quickly departed from both Lebanon and Somalia and even now is struggling to gain control in Afghanistan outside of Kabul. Under much worse circumstances, the United States is about to insert itself for years into the vicious internecine struggles of Iraq, where tens of thousands of angry young men will be keen to pick off the occupying force. Our smart bombs won't prove as helpful at ground level as they do at 35,000 feet.

I warned, too, about the illusions of a self-financing war:

> The Bush administration and many Americans seem to expect that Iraq's oil will pay for postwar occupation, reconstruction, and more— that there will be reconstruction contracts to tender, new reservoirs to develop, and lower world oil prices on the way. If only it were so. Iraq's new oil fields will take years to renovate and expand, probably under contentious political and security conditions. Iraq's existing

creditors hold claims for more than $150 billion. They will certainly insist on their place in the queue.

I concluded with another plea for the second track in the war against terrorism:

> In addition to our military power, therefore, we have to translate our economic wealth and technological prowess into a different kind of power—the power to help shape the global cooperation institutions on which we will depend for our livelihoods and our long-term prosperity. The much-maligned United Nations, the very institution we are doing so much to threaten by our current unilateralism, remains the single best hope for shaping a world to our liking in the twenty-first century. Through the United Nations and specialized agencies, such as the World Health Organization, UNICEF, or the Food and Agriculture Organization, we could deploy our economic strengths to overcome poverty, deal with climate-change problems, and fight debilitating diseases. We could help rid the world of the poverty that provides fertile ground for upheaval, dislocation, and terrorism. Over the long run, we would build international goodwill and shared values that would diminish the anti-American fury that threatens our lives and economic well-being. War with Iraq will, tragically, do the exact opposite.

The war in Iraq began on March 20, 2003, seven months after Cheney's speech in Nashville. The costs of that misadventure have been huge—at least $130 billion or so in direct military outlays in the first eighteen months, more than a thousand (and rising) U.S. lives lost, thousands of civilian dead in Iraq, and a devastation of U.S. credibility around the globe. All of these costs have been dramatically amplified by the lack of the second track of U.S. foreign policy. The war has been viewed worldwide as an unprovoked aggression, especially since the heated claims of Saddam's imminent threat to the world and his vast stockpiles of weapons of mass destruction proved to be completely wrong. The costs continue to mount, at roughly $5 billion a month, compared with just $1 billion for the Millennium Challenge Account for all of 2005.

From September 11 on, I was determined to redouble my own efforts to help preserve the spirit of global cooperation in any way that I could. I was nearing the end of the work of the Commission on Macro-economics and Health, with just two months left in the project. In that context, I had spoken frequently with Secretary-General Kofi Annan. In late 2001, I asked the secretary-general how I might assist him in his increasingly threatened and complex task of helping to lead the world in fulfillment of the hopes of the new millennium. He came back to me with the idea that I could play a role as his special adviser on the Millennium Development Goals themselves, and give him and the UN system advice on what actions to take to meet those goals. Specifically, he asked me not only to advise him on what needed to be done, but also to help lay out an operational plan in which the UN system, participating governments, and civil society could all contribute to the fulfillment of these bold objectives. I was honored and thrilled by this invitation to help the United Nations and especially the secretary-general in this moment of global peril, and immediately accepted his invitation to serve as his special adviser, and to launch a new UN Millennium Project, devoted to laying out a global plan for meeting the goals.

The secretary-general was interested in results. I think he was keenly aware of the fact that the United Nations system is much better at articulating goals than actually fulfilling them. He asked me to think out of the box. To do that, I drew upon the experience of the Commission on Macroeconomics and Health, but now in the context of a set of objectives that were even broader in range and more complex in their interconnections, and involved a greater extent of financial and global cooperative effort.

Analytical deliberation—the process of finding a cooperative approach to complex problems by building a consensus around a shared vision and understanding of the challenges—lies at the core of the UN Millennium Project. The Commission on Macroeconomics and Health had brought leaders and experts from many different perspectives around the table, and through a detailed process of debate, discussion, fact-finding, and research, had reached a consensus. In the same way, the UN Millennium Project was to bring the major policy makers and practitioners involved in poverty reduction around the table to search in a fact-filled process for a similar kind of consensus. This time, however, the number of challenges was simply too great for one table, so we organized our work into ten task forces that covered the very wide range of problems embodied in the Millennium Development Goals.

Each of these task forces brought together major thinkers, practitioners, policy experts, and other stakeholders to undertake that cooperative, intense, challenging deliberative effort. With ten task forces and roughly 25 members in each task force, we had an instant worldwide network of 250 central participants in this pathbreaking process. But that was not all. Facing a challenge of such enormous scale and requiring such complex interactions, our project engaged the entire UN system through a United Nations experts group composed of representatives of the leading specialized UN agencies—the World Health Organization, the Food and Agriculture Organization, UNICEF, the United Nations Environment Program, and so forth. That UN experts group ensured a connection between our deliberations and the actual, on-the-ground work of the United Nations around the world.

We similarly engaged with increasing intensity the UN country teams within several developing countries. In almost any part of the world, the poorest countries have a significant presence of experts from the specialized UN agencies advising on issues of health, water, sanitation, environmental management, agricultural productivity, and the like. Those UN experts sit together in a UN country team, which is led by a resident coordinator who in turn became a liaison for us between our New York-based effort and the on-the-ground realities of UN engagement within the developing countries.

In short, the secretary-general invited us to think big—and we did—by creating a global-scale effort that could begin to get its collective reach around problems of enormous scope and complexity. Through that process, we have been able to make great advances in analysis and a business plan for meeting the Millennium Development Goals that I describe in chapter 15.

No sooner had I begun the UN assignment than I received another call from New York, this time from Columbia University. Columbia President George Rupp and colleagues had heard about the UN work and were interested in exploring whether I might simultaneously take on the leadership of a major institute devoted to the challenge of sustainable development, Columbia's Earth Institute. Upon meeting with Rupp, I learned more about Columbia's bold and innovative initiative linking many major scientific departments at the university to take on the interconnected challenges of climate, environmental management, conservation, public health, and economic development.

By the end of two engaging hours of discussion, I had accepted Columbia's offer to become director of the Earth Institute, pending a discussion with incoming President Lee Bollinger. Bollinger later shared with me his vision that Columbia University would lead the way in the United States to become a truly global university. I was convinced. So ended thirty-two years of learning and teaching at Harvard University, and so began a new chapter in New York City with exciting new responsibilities at Columbia and the United Nations. I loved Harvard, but to combine these two activities and take on this new direction was incredibly good fortune.

All of the UN Millennium Project work has depended utterly on the Earth Institute. Fundamentally, progress on the MDGs rests on thorough scientific understanding of the underlying challenges of disease, food production, undernutrition, watershed management, and other related issues. These, in turn, require specialized expertise. Modern science has given us technological interventions, or specific techniques for addressing these problems, such as antimalarial bed nets or antiretroviral drugs. To name just a few examples, the Earth Institute is

- pioneering the use of geographic information systems (GIS) in rural Ethiopia to monitor, predict, and respond rapidly to malaria epidemics

- using specially programmed cell phones in remote rural Rwanda to provide real-time health data to the Ministry of Health

- introducing new agroforestry techniques to triple food crops in the nitrogen-depleted soils of Africa

- designing new efficient and low-cost battery devices to power lightbulbs in villages too poor and remote to join a power grid in the near future

- demonstrating how high-tech forecasting of El Niño fluctuations can be put to use in impoverished countries in the timing of crop planting and harvesting, the management of water reservoirs and fisheries, and in other ways

- applying state-of-the-art hydrology, geochemistry, and public health to devise solutions to the crisis of arsenic poisoning in Bangladesh's water supply.

The Earth Institute provides a unique academic base for garnering the science-based, cross-disciplinary understanding needed to confront the practical challenges of sustainable development. The institute is built on five clusters—earth sciences, ecology and conservation, environmental engineering, public health, and economics and public policy. By joining these disciplines under one roof, the Earth Institute can better connect the sciences with public policy to find practical solutions to problems at all scales, from local villages to global UN treaties. Bringing these five clusters together makes possible the kind of rigorous thinking about the challenges of the Millennium Development Goals that otherwise rarely takes place, even in partial perspective. One of the remarkable and deeply heartening aspects of directing this unique institute has been the enthusiasm with which the scientists have rallied to the cause of fighting extreme poverty. Their eagerness to use cutting-edge scientific knowledge to solve some of the most pernicious problems facing the most vulnerable people on the planet is inspiring.

Twelve

ON-THE-GROUND
SOLUTIONS FOR
ENDING POVERTY

The end of poverty will require a global network of cooperation among people who have never met and who do not necessarily trust each other. One part of the puzzle is relatively easy. Most people in the world, with a little bit of prodding, would accept the fact that schools, clinics, roads, electricity, ports, soil nutrients, clean drinking water, and the like are the basic necessities not only for a life of dignity and health, but also for economic productivity. They would also accept the fact that the poor may need help to meet their basic needs, but they might be skeptical that the world could pull off any effective way to give that help.

If the poor are poor because they are lazy or their governments are corrupt, how could global cooperation help? Fortunately, these common beliefs are misconceptions, only a small part of the explanation, if at all, of why the poor are poor. I have noted repeatedly that in all corners of the world, the poor face structural challenges that keep them from getting even their first foot on the ladder of development. Most societies with good harbors, close contacts with the rich world, favorable climates, adequate energy sources, and freedom from epidemic disease have escaped from poverty. The world's remaining challenge is not mainly to overcome laziness and corruption, but rather to take on geographic isolation, disease, vulnerability to climate shocks, and so on, with new systems of political responsibility that can get the job done.

In the next chapters, I lay out a strategy for ending extreme poverty by 2025. The strategy focuses on the key investments—in people and in infrastructure—that can give impoverished communities around the world, both rural and urban, the tools for sustainable development. We need plans, systems, mutual accountability, and financing mechanisms. But even before we have all of that apparatus—or economic plumbing—in place, we must first understand more concretely what such a strategy means to the one billion-plus people who can be helped. It is the bravery, fortitude, realism, and sense of responsibility of the impoverished and disempowered, for themselves and especially for their children, that give us hope, and spur us on to end extreme poverty in our time.

MEETING WITH THE RURAL POOR: SAURI, KENYA

Together with colleagues from the UN Millennium Project and the Earth Institute, I spent several days in July 2004 in a group of eight Kenyan villages known as the Sauri sublocation in the Siaya district of Nyanza Province, about forty-four kilometers from Kisumu, in western Kenya. We visited farms, clinics, a subdistrict and district hospital, and schools in Sauri and the environs. We met with international organizations working in the region, including ICRAF (the World Agroforestry Center), the UN Development Program, and the U.S. Centers for Disease Control and Prevention. The visit made vivid both why extreme poverty persists in rural areas and how it can be ended.

We found a region beset by hunger, AIDS, and malaria. The situation is far more grim than is described in official documents. The situation is also salvageable, but the international community requires a much better understanding of its severity, dynamics, and solutions if the crisis in Sauri and the rest of rural Africa is to be solved.

The situation is best understood through the voices of Sauri's struggling residents. In response to an invitation from our group, more than two hundred members of the community came to meet with us one afternoon (see photograph 2). Hungry, thin, and ill, they stayed for three and a half hours, speaking with dignity, eloquence, and clarity about their predicament. They are impoverished, but they are capable and resourceful. Though struggling to survive at present, they are not dispirited but determined to improve their situation. They know well how they could get back to high ground.

The meeting took place on the grounds of a school called the Bar Sauri Primary School, under the auspices of a remarkable school head-mistress, Ms. Anne Marcelline Omolo, who shepherds hundreds of hun-gry and impoverished schoolchildren, many of them orphans, through primary education and the travails of daily life. Despite disease, orphan-hood, and hunger, all thirty-three of last year's eighth-grade class passed the Kenyan national secondary school exams. On a Sunday in July, we saw why. On their "day off" from school, this year's class of eighth graders sat at their desks from 6:30 A.M. until 6:00 P.M. preparing months in advance for this year's national examinations in November. Unfortu-nately, many who will pass the exams will be unable to take a position in a secondary school because of lack of funds for tuition, uniforms, and supplies. Nonetheless, to boost the fortitude of the eighth graders dur-ing the critical examination year, the community provides them with a cooked midday meal, with the fuel wood and water brought from home by the students (shown in photographs 3 and 4). Alas, the community is currently unable to provide midday meals for the younger children, who must fend for themselves. Many go hungry the entire school day.

The village meeting got underway on a Monday afternoon, with the villagers arriving on foot from several kilometers away. I introduced my colleagues and told the community of the Millennium Project's assign-ment from UN Secretary-General Kofi Annan to understand the situa-tion of communities like Sauri, and to work with villagers to identify ways to help such communities to achieve the worldwide Millennium Development Goals of reducing extreme poverty, hunger, disease, and lack of access to safe water and sanitation. I also announced that thanks to a remarkable grant from the Lenfest Foundation in the United States, the Earth Institute at Columbia University would be able to put some of the ideas to work in Sauri and help the international commu-nity learn from the experience in Sauri for the benefit of villages in other parts of Africa and beyond. Several hours later, around 5:30 P.M., we all rose from a discussion that was distressing, uplifting, and pro-foundly challenging—challenging, most of all, for the rich world.

Whatever the official data may show about "stagnant" rural incomes in places like Sauri, stagnation is a euphemism for decline and early death. Food output per person is falling; malaria is pervasive and increasing; AIDS stalks the community and the region, with adult prevalence on the order of 30 percent, if not higher. Rudimentary springs for collecting water for household use are often dirty, especially later in the day after extensive morning use. An NGO from the UK helped install a few protected water points, but they are too few in number, far from many homesteads, and heavily congested, sometimes yielding little more than a trickle and therefore requiring several minutes to fill a jug. Rapid population growth in the past has made farm sizes small. Fertility rates are around six children per woman, and the villagers have no access whatsoever to family planning and reproductive health services or to modern contraceptives.

I canvased the group on the material conditions of the community, and received very perceptive accounts of the grim situation. Only two of the two hundred or so farmers at the meeting reported using fertilizer at present. Around 25 percent are using improved fallows with nitrogen-fixing trees, a scientific farming approach developed and introduced into Sauri by ICRAF. With this novel technique, villagers grow trees that naturally fix nitrogen, meaning that the trees convert atmospheric nitrogen, which most food crops cannot use directly, into a nitrogen compound that food crops can use as a nutrient. The leguminous (nitrogen-fixing) trees can be planted alongside maize or other food crops. By choosing the right timing for planting and the right combination of trees and crops, the farmer gets a natural substitute for chemical nitrogen fertilizer.

So far, just one fourth of Sauri farmers use the new method. It costs money to introduce the technique and one planting season is lost. Farmers may also need to add some nonnitrogen fertilizers, especially potassium, which is also costly, too costly for the impoverished farmers. All of these additional complications could easily be addressed, and the ICRAF technique could be scaled up throughout the village, if only there were additional financial resources available to ICRAF and the village to jump-start the process.

The rest of the community is farming on tiny plots, often no more than 0.1 hectares, with soils that are utterly exhausted of nutrients, and therefore biologically unable to produce an adequate crop. The soils are so depleted of nutrients and organic matter that even if the rains are good, with yields of around one ton of maize per hectare, the households still go hungry. If the rains fail, the households face the risk of death from immunosuppression because of severe undernutrition. Stunting, meaning low height for one's age, is widespread, a sign of the pervasive and chronic undernutrition of the children.

The real shocker came with my follow-up question. How many farmers had used fertilizers in the past? Every hand in the room went up. Farmer after farmer described how the price of fertilizer was now out of reach, and how their current impoverishment left them unable to purchase what they had used in the past. A fifty-kilo bag of diammonium phosphate (DAP) fertilizer sells for around 2,000 Ksh (Kenyan shillings) (US$25). At $500 a ton, that is at least twice the world market price. A proper application might require two to four bags per hectare, or $50 to $100 per hectare, a cost vastly beyond what the household can afford. Credits to buy fertilizer are neither available nor prudent for these farmers: a single failed crop season, an untimely episode of malaria, or some other calamity can push a household that has taken on debt into a spiral of unending indebtedness and destitution.

In my mind I started the calculations as the conversation progressed. Scaling up an appropriate combination of agroforestry and chemical fertilizer inputs would cost some tens of thousands of dollars. Yes, the amount was out of reach of the villagers themselves, but would represent a low cost per person in villages like Sauri if donors would rise to the occasion. Fortunately, on this occasion, the Earth Institute was able to respond.

As the afternoon discussion unfolded, the gravity of the community's predicament became more and more apparent. AIDS is ravaging the village, and nobody has yet had access to antiretroviral therapy. I asked how many households were home to one or more orphaned children left behind by the pandemic. Virtually every hand in the room shot up. I asked how many households were receiving remittances from family members living in Nairobi and other cities. The response was that the only things coming back from the cities were coffins and orphans, not remittances.

I asked how many households had somebody currently suffering from malaria. Around three fourths of the hands shot up. How many used antimalarial bed nets? Two out of two hundred hands went up. How many knew about bed nets? All hands. And how many would like to use bed nets? All hands remained up. The problem, many of the women explained, is that they cannot afford the bed nets, which sell for a few dollars per net, and are too expensive even when partially subsidized (socially marketed) by international donor agencies. How many in the community were using medicine to treat a bout of malaria? A few hands went up, but the vast majority remained down. A woman launched into an explanation that the medicines sell at prices well beyond what the villagers can afford.

A year or so ago, Sauri had a small clinic, as seen in photograph 5. The doctor has since left and the clinic is now padlocked. The villagers explained that they could not afford to pay the doctor and buy the medicines, so the doctor departed. Now they fend for themselves without health care or medicines. When malaria gets bad, and their children fall into anemia-induced tachycardia (rapid heartbeat), gasping for breath in small, ravaged bodies deprived of oxygen-carrying hemoglobin, they rush the child to the subdistrict hospital in nearby Yala. The mothers may carry the children on their backs or push them in wheelbarrows for several kilometers over dirt paths. Yet when we visited the Yala subdistrict hospital on our way from the village, we found a hospital with patients lying on cots in the halls—without running water, an in-house doctor (one visits only two afternoons per week), or even one complete surgical kit.

A few years back, Sauri's residents cooked with locally collected fuel wood, but the decline in the number of trees has left the sublocation bereft of sufficient fuel wood. The quarter or so households who are using the ICRAF system of improved fallows, based on leguminous trees, have a dedicated supply of fuel wood. Other farmer households do not. Villagers said that they now buy pieces of fuel wood in Yala or Muhanda (both a few kilometers away), a bundle of seven sticks costing around twenty-five shillings (thirty cents). These seven sticks are barely sufficient for cooking one meal. In our meeting with the villagers, I conveyed astonishment at the price, thirty cents per meal, for a community that earns almost no money at all. A woman responded that many villagers had in fact reverted to cooking with cow dung or to eating uncooked meals.

As this village dies of hunger, AIDS, and malaria, its isolation is stunning. There are no cars or trucks owned or even used within Sauri, and only a handful of villagers said they had ridden in any kind of motorized transport during the past year. Only three or four of the two hundred or so said that they get to the regional city of Kisumu each month, and about the same number said that they had been to Nairobi, Kenya's commercial and political capital, four hundred kilometers away, once during the past year. There are virtually no remittances reaching the village. Indeed, there is virtually no cash income of any kind reaching the village. Given the farmers' meager production, farm output must be used almost entirely for the household's own consumption, rather than for sales in the market. The community has no money for fertilizers, medicines, school fees, or other basic needs that must be purchased from outside of the villages. Around half of the individuals at the meeting said that they had never made a phone call in their entire lives. (Ironically, and promisingly, our own mobile phones worked fine in the village, relying on a cell tower in Yala. Extending low-cost telephony to the village, for example based on a mobile phone shared by the community, would therefore pose no infrastructure problems.)

This year the rains are failing again, another disaster in an increasingly erratic climate, quite possibly a climate showing the increasing effects of long-term man-made climate change emanating from the rich world. The two roof-water harvesting cisterns at the school are now empty, and the farmers fear disaster in the harvest next month. The Kenyan government has already put out a worldwide appeal for emergency aid to fight imminent starvation in several provinces, including Nyanza.

This village could be rescued, and could achieve the Millennium Development Goals, but not by itself. Survival depends on addressing a series of specific challenges: nutrient-depleted soils, erratic rainfall, holoendemic malaria, pandemic HIV/AIDS, lack of adequate education opportunities, lack of access to safe drinking water and latrines, and the unmet need for basic transport, electricity, cooking fuels, and communications. All of these challenges can be met, with *known, proven, reliable, and appropriate* technologies and interventions.

The crux of the matter for Sauri sublocation can be stated simply and directly:

Sauri's villages, and impoverished villages like them all over the world, can be saved and set on a path of development at a cost that is tiny for the world but too high for the villages themselves and for the Kenyan government on its own.

African safari guides speak of the Big Five animals to watch for on the savannah. The international development community should speak of the Big Five development interventions that would spell the difference between hunger, disease, and death and health and economic development. Sauri's Big Five, identified by the villagers as well as by the UN Millennium Project, are

- **Agricultural inputs.** With fertilizers, improved fallows (with ICRAF's proven technologies), green manures and cover crops, water harvesting and small-scale irrigation, and improved seeds, Sauri's farmers could triple the food yields per hectare and quickly end chronic hunger. In addition, storage facilities would allow the village to sell the grain over the course of months, rather than all at once, thereby getting more favorable prices. Grain could be protected in locally made storage bins using leaves from the improved fallow species tephrosia, which has insecticide properties. These improvements would be of particular advantage for the women, who do the lion's share of African farm and household work.

- **Investments in basic health.** A village clinic with one doctor and nurse for the five thousand residents would provide free antimalarial bed nets; effective antimalarial medicines; treatments for HIV/AIDS opportunistic infections (including highly effective and low-cost Bactrim); antiretroviral therapy for late-stage AIDS; and a range of other essential health services, including skilled birth attendants and sexual and reproductive health services.

- **Investments in education.** Meals for all the children at the primary school could improve the health of the schoolchildren, the quality of education, and the attendance at school. Expanded vocational training for the students could teach them the skills of modern farming (for example, using improved fallows and fertilizer), computer literacy, basic infrastructure maintenance (electrical wiring, use and maintenance of a diesel generator, water harvesting, borewell construction and maintenance), carpentry, and the like. With a mere thousand households in Sauri, villagewide classes once a month could train adults in hygiene, HIV/AIDS, malaria control, computer and mobile phone use, and a myriad of other technical and enormously pressing topics. Without doubt, the village is ready and eager to be empowered by increased information and technical knowledge.

- **Power, transport, and communications services.** Electricity could be made available to the villages either via a power line (from Yala or Nyanminia) or an off-grid diesel generator. The electricity would power lights and perhaps a computer for the school; pumps for safe well water; power for milling grain and other food processing, refrigeration, carpentry; charges for household batteries (which could be used for household illumination); and other needs. The villagers emphasized that the students would like to study after sunset but cannot do so without electric lighting. A village truck could bring in fertilizers, other farm inputs, and modern cooking fuels (for example, canisters of liquid petroleum gas [LPG], familiar from American backyard barbecues), and take out harvests to the market, transport perishable goods and milk for sale in Kisumu, and increase opportunities for off-farm employment for youth. The truck could rush women with childbirth complications and children with acute complications of anemia to the hospital. One or more shared mobile phones for the village could be used for emergencies, market information, and generally to connect Sauri with the outside world.

- **Safe drinking water and sanitation.** With enough water points and latrines for the safety and convenience of the entire village, women and children of the village would save countless hours of toil each day fetching water. The water could be provided through a combination of protected springs, borewells, rainwater harvesting, and other basic technologies. There is even the possibility of establishing links with an existing large-scale storage tank and pumping station a few kilometers away.

The irony is that the costs of these services for Sauri's five thousand residents would be very low. Here are some quick guesses, which colleagues at the Earth Institute are refining:

Fertilizers and improved fallows for the five hundred or so arable hectares would be roughly $100 per hectare per year, or $50,000 per year for the community.

A clinic, staffed by a doctor and nurse, providing free malaria prevention and care and additional free basic services other than antiretrovirals, would cost around $50,000 per year. (Antiretrovirals would be provided by the Global Fund to Fight AIDS, TB, and Malaria, the U.S. Emergency Plan, and other programs.) School meals could be paid for communally out of just a small part of the incremental grain yields achieved through the application of fertilizers.

A village truck would be an annual inclusive running cost of perhaps $15,000 per year if amortized over several years (or leased from a manufacturer). Modern cooking fuel for the primary and secondary school students (numbering about a thousand) in the entire sublocation would cost an additional $5,000 per year. A few village cell phones and a grain storage facility would add perhaps $5,000 per year, for a total of $25,000 per year.

A combination of protected springs (with improved access), borewells (with pumps), and community taps connected to the large-scale storage system would provide access to water at ten convenient locations and cost around $25,000 dollars.

Electricity could be provided to the school, the nearby clinic, and five water points by a dedicated off-grid generator or by a power line from Yala or Nyanminia for an initial cost of about $35,000. For another $40,000 in initial costs and recurring costs of $10,000, every household could be provided with a battery/bulb assembly to light a small bulb for a few hours every night with the battery charging station connected to the village generator. The annualized costs would be $25,000 per year.

Additional expenses would include scaling up educational activities, various costs of local management, technical advice from agricultural extension officers, and other related delivery services.

My Earth Institute colleagues and I estimated that the combined costs of these improvements would total around $350,000 per year, or roughly $70 per person per year in Sauri, for at least the next few years. The benefits would be astounding: decisive malaria control (with transmission reduced by perhaps 90 percent, judging from recent CDC bednet trials in a neighboring area), a doubling or tripling of food yields per hectare with a drastic reduction of chronic hunger and undernutrition, improved school attendance, a reduction of water-borne disease, a rise in incomes through the sale of surplus grains and cash crops, the growth of cash incomes via food processing, carpentry, small-scale clothing manufacturing, horticulture, aquaculture, animal husbandry, and a myriad of other benefits. With anti-AIDS drugs added to the clinic's services, the mass deaths from AIDS, as well as the deluge of newly orphaned children, could also be stanched.

Sooner rather than later, these investments would repay themselves not only in lives saved, children educated, and communities preserved, but also in direct commercial returns. Consider the case of fertilizers, which are currently unused, since households lack access to storage, transport, credit, and a financial cushion against the risk of crop failures even if credit is made available. A fertilizer application of $100 per hectare (such as two hundred kilos of DAP), combined with or substituted by improved fallows (as appropriate), could raise crop yields in a normal season from one ton per hectare to three tons per hectare, with a marketable value of the increment of roughly $200 to $400 dollars per hectare, assuming that transport is available and there is a stable price for the maize crop. In a drought year, fertilizer and/or improved fallows would mean the difference between harvesting one ton and a failed crop (with attendant acute hunger, if not starvation). In the first few years, *fertilizers and improved fallows should be given largely for free to the villagers* to boost their own nutrition and health, and to build a small financial cushion. Later on it will be possible to share the costs with the community and, eventually, perhaps in a decade, to provide the fertilizer and improved fallows on a full commercial basis.

INTERNATIONAL DONORS AND VILLAGES LIKE SAURI

The international donor community should be thinking round the clock about one question: *how can the Big Five interventions be scaled up in rural areas like Sauri?* With a population of some thirty-three million people, of whom two thirds are in rural areas, Kenya would require annual investments on the order of $1.5 billion per year for its Sauris, with donors filling most of that financing gap, since the national government is already stretched beyond its means. (More precise estimates of cost would have to be worked out in the context of detailed development plans as described in chapter 14.) Instead, donor support to Kenya is around $100 million, or a mere one fifteenth of what is needed. Kenya's debt servicing to the rich world is around $600 million per year, so its budget is still being drained by the international community, not bolstered by it.

This is all the more remarkable since Kenya is a new and fragile democracy that should be receiving considerable help from its development partners. Kenya, ironically, is also a victim of global terrorism, caught in a war not of its own making. U.S. and Israeli targets on Kenyan soil have been hit in recent years, sending Kenya's tourist industry into a downward spiral and causing hundreds of deaths of Kenyans and massive property damage.

The UN Millennium Project is working with the government of Kenya to ensure that its poverty reduction efforts are bold enough to achieve the Millennium Development Goals. This strategy will require much greater development assistance and deeper debt cancellation from the rich world to enable Kenya to invest in the Big Five—agriculture, health and education, electricity, transport and communications, and safe drinking water—not only in Sauri villages, but across impoverished rural Kenya. Yet when the Kenyan government recently proposed a national social health insurance fund, the very thing needed to scale up access to basic health care, donors quickly objected rather than jumped at the opportunity to examine how it could actually be accomplished.

The issue of corruption overshadows donor relations with the Kenyan government. Much of the corruption reflects holdouts from the earlier regime of more than two decades, corrupt officials who have not yet been weeded out. Part of the corruption is new and completely avoidable, but only if donors help Kenya to improve the functioning of the public administration, not by moralizing and finger pointing but by the installation of computer systems, published accounts, job training and upgrading, higher pay for senior managers so that they do not have to live off bribes and side payments, continued support for the government's already major efforts to improve the judicial system, empowerment of local villages to oversee the provision of public services, and some humility on the part of donors. Most donor governments have corruption inside their own governments and even in the provision of foreign aid (which is often linked to powerful political interests within the donor countries). The affliction is widespread, and needs to be attacked systematically and cleverly, but without useless and false moralizing.

Donors should sit down with the government leadership and say, "We'd like to help you scale up the Big Five in Kenya's villages to enable you to ensure that all of Kenya's rural poor have access to agricultural inputs, health, education, electricity, communications and transport, and safe water and sanitation. Together, let's design a budgetary and management system that will reach the villages and ensure a monitorable, governable, and scalable set of interventions across the country. We're prepared to pay if you are prepared to ensure good governance on such a historic project." Private international consulting firms could be brought in to help design these systems and to lend credibility to their implementation and performance.

With a little more forethought, donors and governments could take advantage of the crucial fact that villages like Sauri have a group monitoring and enforcement mechanism automatically built into village life that can help to ensure that aid to the village is well used. Just as experience with group lending in microfinance has been highly successful, projects that empower village-based community organizations to oversee village services have also been highly successful. Recent experiences with village governance in India, based on the *panchayats* (local councils), are but one notable example. In Sauri, the villagers jumped with eagerness at the invitation to form various committees (schooling, clinics, transport and electricity, farming) to help prepare for the actual investments and to ensure proper governance as they are put into place. Headmistress Omolo, who oversaw the formation of the committees, also ensured that the village women, with their special needs and burdens and even legal obstacles, would be well represented in each of the committees.

If donor officials would join the government of Kenya in meeting with the villagers and brainstorming with government officials, they could come up with dozens of fruitful approaches to ensure that aid actually reaches the villages. We need to be more creative in order to save the lives of millions of people now struggling to survive—and often failing—in the impoverished villages around the world. The donors and the government of Kenya can and should agree on a suitable and bold strategy. Kenya's new democracy, from the national government down to the villages, is prepared to govern the use of international help with transparency, efficiency, and equity if we can get the delivery mechanisms right and invest in the supporting information and reporting technologies.

MEETING WITH THE URBAN POOR: MUMBAI, INDIA

Several thousand miles from Sauri, Kenya, an impoverished community in Mumbai, India, struggles with the urban face of extreme poverty. A group that I met in June 2004 comes from a community that lives near the railway tracks. By near, I do not mean within range of the railway whistle as the train rolls through the city; I mean a community that lives within ten feet of the tracks. It may seem impossible, but the shacks of poster board, corrugated sheet metal, thatch, and whatever else is at hand are pushed right against the tracks, as seen in photograph 6. Children and the old routinely walk along the tracks, often within a foot or two of passing trains. They defecate on the tracks, for lack of alternative sanitation. And they are routinely maimed and killed by the trains.

An energetic and charismatic social worker, Sheela Patel, who left academic research years earlier to work with communities like this one, has brought me to meet the group. She has pioneered the cause of community organization within the very poorest slums, such as those shown in photographs 7 and 8. The NGO that she founded, the Society for the Promotion of Area Resource Centres (SPARC), is our host today. The fifty or so people assembled around the room are mostly women in their thirties and forties, but they look much older after decades of hard physical work and exposure to the elements. They have come to meet with me, and also a group of visitors from Durban, South Africa, who are there to learn about community organization for slum dwellers and squatters.

The overarching theme of our discussion is not latrines, running water, and safety from the trains, but empowerment: specifically, the group is discussing how slum dwellers who own virtually nothing have found a voice, a strategy for negotiating with the city government. In the past few years, this particular group, with SPARC's support, has been negotiating arrangements to relocate away from the tracks to safer ground, in settlements with basic amenities like running water, latrines, gutters, even roads. Thousands have already been relocated, though thousands more wait to find new living quarters.

The notion of large communities of people living within a few feet of the train tracks is startling enough for me this morning. It is, to be sure, a measure of the desperation of the poorest of the poor who arrive in cities to escape rural impoverishment, even famine, and then struggle to establish survivable conditions for themselves and for their children. But I'm even more startled to learn that there is actually a Railway Slum Dwellers Federation (RSDF), which has been organized by the community members, with the aid of SPARC, to negotiate with the municipality and the Indian Railways concerning their needs and interests. In addition to SPARC and the RSDF, a third NGO is represented at the meeting, Mahila Milan (Women Together), which focuses specifically on the needs of women slum dwellers.

As the women begin to talk, the realities of extreme urban poverty and the range of solutions come vividly to the fore. Each woman begins with a kind of testimonial to the power of group action. This testimony might have seemed staged but for the genuine smiles, calm demeanor, and straightforward, matter-of-fact approach of the group. They explain how they have had no schooling—perhaps two or three years of fitful attendance several decades ago. They cannot read or write, but they know full well that their children need and deserve better. Before they came together in the joint initiative of SPARC, the RSDF, and Mahila Milan, they were resigned to their dreadful circumstances, living in constant danger, noise, disruption, and squalor.

But group action has taught them that in fact they have legal rights within the city and even the possibility of access to public services if they act together. The city government and Indian Railways, for their part, have been only too happy to try to relocate the group away from the railway tracks, since the presence of the slum right up against the track leads to frequent accidents and forces the trains to slow down markedly, raising costs and limiting service. The city and the railway company have learned the hard way that any forcible actions to relocate individual families can trigger an uproar, as occurred in February 2001 when two thousand huts were demolished along the Harbour railway line and the federation mobilized its members to shut down the city's railways.

As in the villages of Sauri, what this community needs are investments in individuals and basic infrastructure that can empower people to be healthier, better educated, and more productive in the workforce. These impoverished families want basic amenities—to live away from the railway tracks, with access to water, sanitation, roads, and even electricity. They will need to have new ration cards for the government-supplied subsidized food and cooking oil in the new neighborhoods where they will live. Their children will need access to a school and clinic. They would like to be able to reach their jobs on public transport or by foot if they are close enough. All are hard workers, earning their meager incomes as maids, cooks, sweepers, guards, launderers, or in other low-skilled, labor-intensive services. The younger and more literate members of the group have actually begun to gain, or regain, basic literacy, empowered and motivated by their political activism. Those who become literate have a chance to find work at two or three times their current salaries, perhaps in the garment factories.

One recent report from the slums of Mumbai and Pune, India, speaks plainly to how the lack of basic infrastructure, in this case safe drinking water, has devastating consequences on the dignity and physical well-being of women:

It is typically women who collect water from public standpipes, often queuing for long periods in the process and having to get up
very early or go late at night to get the water. It is typically women
who have to carry heavy water containers over long distances and on
slippery slopes. It is typically women who have to make do with the
often inadequate water supplies to clean the home, prepare the
food, wash the utensils, do the laundry and bathe the children. It is
also women who have to scrounge, buy or beg for water, particularly
when their usual sources run dry. It is important not to underestimate this side of the water burden. There are no compelling international statistics, comparable to health statistics, documenting the
labour burdens related to inadequate water provision. It is difficult
for those who have never had to rely on public or other peoples' taps
to appreciate how humiliating, tiring, stressful and inconvenient this
can be. Not having toilets, or having to wait in long queues to use
filthy toilets, carries health risks and is also a source of anxiety.

In many ways, the logistical and investment needs of the squatters
will be easier to address than the comparable needs of the villagers in
Sauri. Water taps can be provided from the main city pipes. Electricity
can be tapped into from the power grid rather than supplied by a stand-
alone generator. In densely populated urban areas, access to schools
and clinics can also be easier to arrange. Doctors and nurses abound in
Mumbai in comparison with the scarcity of trained medical personnel
in rural Kenya. The problems in urban areas revolve around empowerment and finance. How can an impoverished squatter community, without its own land, find a collective voice and the security to raise that
voice, and how can the financial burdens be shared among the city government and the slum dwellers in a realistic manner?

With SPARC's initiative, the new Slum Rehabilitation Act has given
added power to the communities: slum-dweller organizations are now
legally empowered to act as land developers if they can demonstrate
that they have agreements to represent at least 70 percent of the eligible
slum dwellers in a particular location. As land developers, the slum-
dweller organizations can tap into special municipal programs to gain
access to real estate for community resettlement or for commercial development that can finance resettlement elsewhere. SPARC is also negotiating with the Kolkata Municipal Authority to help set up lavatories in
Kolkata's slums, under an arrangement in which the costs of construc-

tion would be borne jointly by the municipality and the slum dwellers, and maintenance would be the responsibility of the slum dwellers' organization.

As Sheela Patel explains, adding an organized slum dwellers' voice at the table will make possible future solutions that were undreamed of in the past. Recently the World Bank has creatively joined the mix, helping to finance some of the upgrading of Mumbai's urban transport based on a major role for the NGOs in the design and implementation of the resettlement programs. The NGOs, for their part, have made important advances in organizing and documenting the community members to facilitate the process. Sheela Patel and her colleagues have said that these programs are "steps on the journey towards citizenship for the urban poor, where rights are translated into reality because of the favorable confluence of a supportive policy environment and grassroots democracy in action."

THE PROBLEM OF SCALE

The end of poverty must start in the villages of Sauri and the slums of Mumbai, and millions of places like them. The key to ending poverty is to create a global network of connections that reach from impoverished communities to the very centers of world power and wealth and back again. Looking at the conditions in Sauri, we can see how far $70 per person can go in changing lives—not as a welfare handout, but as an investment in sustained economic growth. Looking at the conditions in Mumbai, we can see how a stable and safe physical environment for a community can enable its households to get a foothold in the urban economy, one that is already linked to global markets. For a sum similar to that in Sauri, it will be possible to establish that foothold.

The starting points of that chain are the poor themselves. They are ready to act, both individually and collectively. They are already hard working, prepared to struggle to stay afloat and to get ahead. They have a very realistic idea about their conditions and how to improve them, not a mystical acceptance of their fate. They are also ready to govern themselves responsibly, ensuring that any help that they receive is used for the benefits of the group rather than pocketed by powerful individuals. But they are too poor to solve their problems on their own. So, too, are their own governments. The rich world, which could readily provide the missing finances, wonders how to ensure that money made available would actually reach the poor and be an investment in ending poverty rather than an endless provision of emergency rations. This question can be answered by showing how networks of mutual accountability can run alongside the networks of financing.

In short, we need a strategy for scaling up the investments that will end poverty, including a system of governance that empowers the poor while holding them accountable. In each low-income country, it is time to design a poverty reduction strategy that can meet this challenge.

Thirteen

MAKING THE INVESTMENTS NEEDED TO END POVERTY

At the most basic level, the key to ending extreme poverty is to enable the poorest of the poor to get their foot on the ladder of development. The development ladder hovers overhead, and the poorest of the poor are stuck beneath it. They lack the minimum amount of capital necessary to get a foothold, and therefore need a boost up to the first rung. The extreme poor lack six major kinds of capital:

- Human capital: health, nutrition, and skills needed for each person to be economically productive

- Business capital: the machinery, facilities, motorized transport used in agriculture, industry, and services

- Infrastructure: roads, power, water and sanitation, airports and seaports, and telecommunications systems, that are critical inputs into business productivity

- Natural capital: arable land, healthy soils, biodiversity, and well-functioning ecosystems that provide the environmental services needed by human society

- Public institutional capital: the commercial law, judicial systems, government services and policing that underpin the peaceful and prosperous division of labor

- Knowledge capital: the scientific and technological know-how that raises productivity in business output and the promotion of physical and natural capital

How to overcome a poverty trap? The poor start with a very low level of capital per person, and then find themselves trapped in poverty because the ratio of capital per person actually falls from generation to generation. The amount of capital per person declines when the population is growing faster than capital is being accumulated. Capital is accumulated, in turn, in a balance of two forces, one positive and one negative. On the positive side is the capital accumulated when households save a part of their current income, or have a part of their income taxed to finance investments by the government. Household savings are either lent to businesses (often through financial intermediaries such as banks) or invested directly in family businesses or equities traded in the market. Capital is diminished, or depreciated, as the result of the passage of time, or wear and tear, or the death of skilled workers, for example, because of AIDS. If savings exceed depreciation, there is positive net capital accumulation. If savings are less than depreciation, the capital stock declines. Even if there is positive net capital accumulation, the question for growth in per capita income is whether the net capital accumulation is large enough to keep up with population growth.

HOW THE POVERTY TRAP WORKS AND HOW FOREIGN AID HELPS OVERCOME IT

Figure 1 shows the basic mechanics of saving, capital accumulation, and growth, and figure 2 shows how a poverty trap works. In figure 1, we start on the left-hand side with a typical household. The household divides its income into consumption, taxation, and household savings. The government, in turn, divides its tax revenues into current spending and government investment. The economy's capital stock is raised by both household savings and by government investment. A higher capital stock leads to economic growth, which in turn raises household income through the feedback arrow from growth to income. We show in the figure that population growth and depreciation also negatively affect the accumulation of capital. In a "normal" economy, things proceed smoothly toward rising incomes, as household savings and government investments are able to keep ahead of depreciation and population growth.

In figure 2, the process breaks down into a poverty trap. We start again on the left-hand side, but now with a household that is impoverished. All of its income goes to consumption, just to stay alive. There are no taxes and no personal savings. Nonetheless, depreciation and population growth continue relentlessly. The result is a fall in capital per person and a negative growth rate of per capita income. That leads to still further impoverishment of the household in the future. The figure depicts a vicious circle of falling incomes, zero savings and public investment, and falling capital per person as a result.

The solution is shown in figure 3, where foreign help, in the form of official development assistance (ODA), helps to jump-start the process of capital accumulation, economic growth, and rising household incomes. The foreign aid feeds into three channels. A little bit goes directly to households, mainly for humanitarian emergencies such as food aid in the midst of a drought. Much more goes directly to the budget to finance public investments, and some is also directed toward private businesses (for example, farmers) through microfinance programs and other schemes in which external assistance directly finances private small businesses and farm improvements. If the foreign assistance is substantial enough, and lasts long enough, the capital stock rises sufficiently to lift households above subsistence. At that point, the poverty trap is broken, and figure 1 comes into its own. Growth becomes self-sustaining through household savings and public investments supported by taxation of households. In this sense, foreign assistance is not a welfare handout, but is actually an investment that breaks the poverty trap once and for all.

A Numerical Illustration

Economists like to use numerical models because it helps them to calibrate more specifically how much it will cost to accomplish a particular goal, in this case the goal of breaking a poverty trap. Here's a numerical illustration of how the poverty trap works, and though a bit tedious, it shows how financial planning can be used to identify the overall magnitude of official development assistance that will be needed to end poverty. To keep things simple, I use an illustration based entirely on household savings and investment, without worrying about taxation and public investment.

Figure 1: The Basic Mechanics of Capital Accumulation

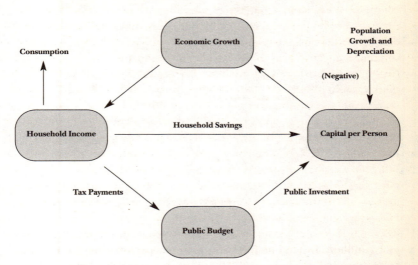

Suppose that an economy requires $3 of capital for every $1 of annual production. Suppose also that the capital stock depreciates at a rate of 2 percent per year. For each $1 million of capital this year, about $835,000 will remain at the end of a decade, after ten years of depreciation. We'll suppose that the economy currently has 1 million poor people, each with capital of $900. This results in annual income of $300 per person ($900 capital divided by three). The total GNP is therefore $300 million ($300 per person times 1 million people). The population is growing at 2 percent per year, so at the end of the decade there will be about 1.2 million people.

Suppose now that the society is too poor to save. Each year the population lives hand to mouth, consuming whatever meager amount is produced. The starting income of $300 is just barely enough to meet basic needs. At the end of a decade, the capital stock will have partly worn out. Instead of $900 million in capital, there will be only $750 million in capital. In the meantime, the population will have grown from 1 million

Figure 2: The Poverty Trap

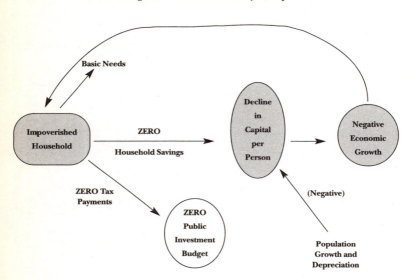

to 1.2 million. Instead of $900 of capital per person, there is now only $628 of capital per person ($750 million in capital divided by 1.2 million population). Instead of each person being able to produce $300, each person will now produce only $209 ($628 of capital divided by three). Households will be sinking into extreme poverty, without the income to meet basic needs.

In another illustration, suppose now that for whatever reason, the economy begins with the same population, but with a capital stock that is twice as large, equal to $1.8 billion. Per capita income is also twice as large, $600 per capita. As before, households need $300 per person per year to meet their basic needs, and do not save anything out of incomes of $300 or below. On all income *above* $300 per person, they save 30 percent. Thus a household earning $600 per capita saves 30 percent of $300 ($600 income minus $300 basic needs), or $90 in annual saving. Economywide saving is therefore $90 million.

This year, the capital stock is $1.8 billion, or $1,800 per capita. What about next year? I have assumed that 2 percent of this year's capital stock, or $36 million, will depreciate by next year. But there is also new savings of $90 million. The net change of the capital stock is a rise of $54 million ($90 million minus $36 million). Next year's capital stock is therefore

Figure 3: The Role of ODA in Breaking the Poverty Trap

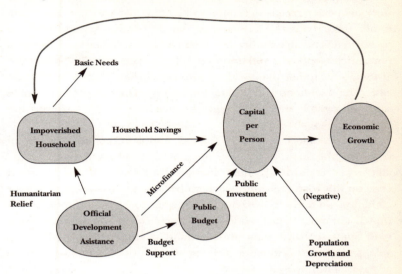

$1.854 billion ($1.8 billion plus $54 million). This amount of capital produces a GNP of $618 million ($1.854 billion divided by 3). The population also grows by 2 percent, and so stands at 1.02 million. Per capita income is equal to $606 ($618 million divided by 1.02 million). Per capita income has increased by 1 percent (in comparison with $600), and will increase each year through the decade. Actually, the growth rate will rise gradually over time, reaching more than 2 percent per annum toward the end of the decade as household incomes rise further above the $300 threshold of basic needs. If you use a spreadsheet to repeat the calculations for ten years rather than one year, the GNP per person at the end of the decade is $687, up 15 percent during the decade.

Voilà. With the same economic structure as the first economy, but starting with twice the capital stock, the economy grows rather than declines. The reason is that at an income of $600 per person, the economy is wealthy enough to save for the future; at $300 per person, it is not. Therefore, starting at $600 per capita, the economy finds its way onto a sustainable growth path, whereas starting at $300 per capita, the economy sinks into further misery.

This is not all. As capital accumulates from the income base of $600 per person, and the ratio of capital per person increases, not only does the economy grow, but the economy is likely to get an *extra* boost from increasing returns to scale of capital. An economy with twice the capital stock per person means an economy with roads that work the year-round, rather than roads that are washed out each rainy season; electrical power that is reliable twenty-four hours each day, rather than electrical power that is sporadic and unpredictable; workers who are healthy and at their jobs, rather than workers who are chronically absent with disease. The likelihood is that doubling the human and physical capital stock will actually *more* than double the income level, at least at very low levels of capital per person.

A graphic illustration of increasing returns to capital is the case of roads like the one that connects the port at Mombasa, Kenya, with the landlocked countries Uganda, Rwanda, and Burundi. The transport costs on this road are extremely high because the road is in very poor condition on various stretches. From time to time, transport is disrupted entirely when the rains wash away bridges and sections of the road. Suppose that, at some point, around half the road is paved and usable, and the rest is unpaved and impassable, with alternating sections of paved and unpaved roadway. Repairing the missing sections would amount to doubling the kilometers of paved road, but would much more than double the economic benefits of the road, since it would become usable along its entire length. This is an example of a threshold effect, in which the capital stock becomes useful only when it meets a minimum standard.

Thus targeted investments backed by donor aid lie at the heart of breaking the poverty trap. Donor-backed investments are needed to raise the level of capital per person. When the capital stock per person is high enough, the economy becomes productive enough to meet basic needs. Households can thus save for the future, putting the economy on a path of sustained economic growth. In my illustration, foreign aid (over several years) that raises the capital stock from $900 per person to $1,800 per person would enable the economy to break out of the poverty trap and begin growing on its own. It would also enable the economy to benefit from increasing returns to capital.

Without donor funding, alas, the necessary investments simply cannot be financed. No matter how hard a government might try—through taxes, user fees, or privatization—the poor households at $300 per person simply do not have enough income to meet their basic needs and at the same time finance the accumulation of capital. They need the $300 just to eat and provide clothing, shelter, and other basics.

Differential Diagnosis and Capital Accumulation

In a simple illustration, or model, as economists call it, it is easy enough to talk about capital as a single item, something that can be doubled or halved fairly straightforwardly. Much of the complexity of real economic strategy, however, is that capital comes in numerous, almost unlimited, forms. Suppose that an economy successfully negotiates an extra $1 billion in foreign aid. Should that go to building roads, or schools, or power plants, or clinics, or to pay doctors, or teachers, or agricultural extension officers? The answer, in general, is yes to all of the above. The mix will differ markedly country by country. At the core of an effective investment strategy is a rigorous differential diagnosis. The differential diagnosis should build on the appropriate division of labor between the public sector and the private sector, as shown in figure 4.

The public sector should be mainly focused on five kinds of investments: human capital (health, education, nutrition), infrastructure (roads, power, water and sanitation, environmental conservation), natural capital (conservation of biodiversity and ecosystems), public institu-

Figure 4: Private and Public Investments in Capital

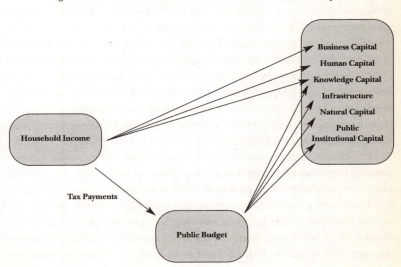

tional capital (a well-run public administration, judicial system, police force), and parts of knowledge capital (scientific research for health, energy, agriculture, climate, ecology).

The private sector (funded largely through private savings) should be mainly responsible for investments in businesses, whether in agriculture, industry, or services and in knowledge capital (new products and technologies building on scientific advances), as well as for household contributions to health, education, and nutrition that complement the public investments in human capital. Occasionally the public sector will want to provide direct financing for some private-sector activities, for example, to help farmers adopt new technologies, or to help impoverished rural families to start small businesses or buy critical inputs for the farm, or to encourage the start-up of new urban industries. The general lesson of successful economies is that governments are wise to stick mainly to general kinds of investments—schools, clinics, roads, basic research—and to leave highly specialized business investments to the private sector.

Why should government finance schools, clinics, and roads, rather than leave those to the private sector? There are five kinds of reasons, all compelling in the proper context. First, there are many kinds of infrastructure, especially networks like power grids, roads, and other transport facilities—airports and seaports—which are characterized by increasing returns to scale. If left to private markets, these sectors would tend to be monopolized, so they are called natural monopolies. If such capital investments are left to the private sector, the privately owned monopolies would overcharge for their use, and the result would be too little utilization of this kind of capital. Potential users would be rationed out of the market. It is more efficient, therefore, for a public monopoly to provide network infrastructure and set an efficient price below the one that would be set by a private monopolist.

A second category of publicly provided capital goods includes those that are nonrival, when the use of the capital by one citizen does not diminish its availability for use by others. A scientific discovery is a classic nonrival good. Once the structure of DNA has been discovered, the use of that wonderful knowledge by any individual in society does not limit the use of the same knowledge by others in society. Economic efficiency requires that the knowledge should be available for all, to maximize the social benefits of the knowledge. There should not be a fee for scientists, businesses, households, researchers, and others who want to utilize the scientific knowledge of the structure of DNA! But if there is no fee, who will invest in the discoveries in the first place? The best answer is the public, through publicly financed institutions like the National Institutes of Health (NIH) in the United States. Even the free-market United States invests $27 billion in publicly financed knowledge capital through the NIH.

Third, many social sectors exhibit strong spillovers (or externalities) in their effects. I want *you* to sleep under an antimalarial bed net so that a mosquito does not bite you and then transmit the disease to *me*! For a similar reason, I want you to be well educated so that you do not easily fall under the sway of a demagogue who would be harmful for me as well as you. When such spillovers exist, private markets tend to undersupply the goods and services in question. For just this reason, Adam Smith called for the public provision of education: "An instructed and intelligent people . . . are more disposed to examine, and more capable of seeing through, the interested complaints of faction and sedition. . . ." Smith argued, therefore, that the whole society is at risk when any segment of society is poorly educated. Natural capital is another area where externalities loom large. Private actions—pollution, logging, overfishing, and the like—can lead to species extinction, deforestation, or other kinds of environmental degradation with serious adverse consequence for the whole society, or even the whole world. Governments therefore have a crucial role to play in conserving natural capital.

Fourth, societies around the world want to ensure that everybody has an adequate level of access to key goods and services (health care, education, safe drinking water) as a matter of right and justice. Goods that should be available to everybody because of their vital importance to human well-being are called merit goods. The rights to these merit goods are not only an informal commitment of the world's governments, they are also enshrined in international law, most importantly in the Universal Declaration of Human Rights, as follows:

• Everyone has the right to a standard of living adequate for the health and well-being of himself and of his family, including food, clothing, housing and medical care and necessary social services, and the right to security in the event of unemployment, sickness, disability, widowhood, old age or other lack of livelihood in circumstances beyond his control.

- Everyone has the right to education. Education shall be free, at least in the elementary and fundamental stages. Elementary education shall be compulsory. Technical and professional education shall be made generally available and higher education shall be equally accessible to all on the basis of merit.

Moreover, according to Article 28 of the Universal Declaration, "Everyone is entitled to a social and international order in which the rights and freedoms set forth in this Declaration can be fully realized." A follow-through on commitments to the Millennium Development Goals would mark a major practical application of that article.

Fifth, government will want to help the poorest of the poor not only by providing infrastructure and social investments, but also by providing productive inputs into private businesses if that, too, is required to help impoverished households get started in market-based activities. Thus government might want to provide subsidized fertilizers to subsistence farmers so that they can produce enough to eat or microcredits to rural women so that they can start microbusinesses. Once these households successfully raise their incomes above subsistence, and begin to accumulate savings on their own, the government subsidies can be gradually withdrawn.

At the same time, except in the case of the poorest households, governments generally should *not* provide the capital for private businesses. Experience has shown that private entrepreneurs do a much better job of running businesses than governments. When governments run businesses, they tend to do so for political rather than economic reasons. State enterprises tend to overstaff their operations, since jobs equal votes for politicians, and layoffs can cost a politician the next election. State-owned banks tend to make loans for political reasons, rather than on the basis of expected returns. Factories are likely to be built in the districts of powerful politicians, not where they can best serve the broader population. Moreover, governments rarely have the in-house expertise to manage complex technologies, and they shouldn't, aside from sectors where the government's role is central, such as in defense, infrastructure, health, and education.

It is one thing to identify the general checklists of public investments and another to apply the checklist to specific contexts. In Sauri, Kenya, and thousands of villages like it, the priorities include the Big Five: agriculture, health, education, infrastructure (power, transport, and communications), and water and sanitation. Natural capital needs bolstering, especially land reclamation, pollution control, and limits on overfishing, logging, and deforestation generally. Support should come both as direct public provision of services and as public support for private capital accumulation via microfinance and provision of critical farm inputs for smallholder farmers.

A distinct package of public investments will be needed in the urban areas. The higher urban population density makes it feasible, and indeed necessary for public health and economic reasons, to reach households through infrastructure grids for water, sewerage, and power. It is often claimed that in urban areas, private markets can provide these infrastructure services on the basis of market prices. This claim typically overlooks the fact that a sizable proportion of low-income households will be unable to purchase their basic needs at market prices, and will therefore require significant subsidies. One successful model for combining a market approach with subsidies is through lifeline-tariff pricing. In this approach, all households (or all poor households, if they are easy to identify) are guaranteed a given supply of free infrastructure services, for example six thousand liters of water per household per month in South Africa's program. Above that amount, the household pays by the meter.

Urban areas are also vulnerable to intense environmental damage, though in ways quite different from rural areas. Urban environmental hazards include outdoor air pollution (especially from fossil fuel combustion), the release of toxic chemicals into the environment from factories, excessive mining of water aquifers, urban garbage, coastal erosion and destruction of fragile marine ecosystems close to urban centers, and the transmission of airborne infectious diseases (such as tuberculosis) in the crowded living conditions of urban slums. These conditions need to be ameliorated by targeted environmental investments, though impoverished cities rarely have the financial means to undertake these investments on their own.

Why Good Investments Come in Packages

One of the weaknesses of development thinking is the relentless drive for a magic bullet, the one decisive investment that will turn the tide. Alas, it does not exist. Each one of the six identified types of capital is needed for an effective, well-functioning economy. Each one is needed to escape the poverty trap. Even more to the point, success in any single area, whether in health, or education, or farm productivity, depends on investments across the board.

Let me focus on child survival to make the point. The solutions for child survival will not be found in the health sector alone, although investing in the health sector is crucial overall. Here are ways that each of the six forms of capital contribute to healthier children and reduced child mortality (the list is hardly comprehensive):

- Business capital. Higher household incomes on the farm and in the cities allow households to invest in safer shelter (with screen doors to keep out mosquitoes), piped water, modern cooking fuels, access to doctors, improved diets, and the like.

- Human capital. Key human capital investments include nutrition (micronutrient and macronutrient supplementation), health care (immunizations, routine monitoring, emergency interventions, preventative interventions like antimalarial bed nets), family planning (birth spacing and smaller family size), mother's literacy, and public health awareness.

- Infrastructure. This includes safe drinking water and sanitation, power supplies for safer cooking, emergency transport to clinics, and information and communications technology to underpin routine and emergency health services.

- Natural capital. Investment in natural capital includes protection against natural hazards such as El Niño–induced droughts, control of disease vectors and pests, conservation of ecosystem services to support crop productivity, and avoidance of toxic wastes in the air and water.

- Knowledge capital. Investments here are for improved organizational procedures for fighting epidemic diseases, development of new drugs and immunizations, development and diffusion of improved seed varieties to improve food intake, and low-cost energy sources for the household for food preparation and storage.

- Public institutional capital. These investments provide the operation and extension of public health services, nutrition programs, and community participation schemes involving public health.

The same approach would apply in addressing each of the Millennium Development Goals. Fighting hunger, disease, lack of education, environmental degradation, and urban slums all require *packages* of investments to attack these ills from a variety of directions.

Investing in Technological Capacity

In both rural and urban areas, increased investments not only increase the amount of capital per person but also the quality of the technology embedded in the capital. A cell phone, or personal computer, or high-yield variety seed brings the latest in science to the benefit of the poor. Yet using these new technologies requires training and technical competence. Even in the poorest societies, primary education alone is no longer sufficient. All school-aged youth should be provided a minimum of nine years of schooling, and most should have more than that. The society as a whole should promote a significant cohort of university-trained graduates. These teachers, medical officers, agricultural extension officers, and engineers will be needed to harness technologies for local use.

Indeed, rapid economic development requires that technical capacity suffuse the entire society, from the bottom up. But how can we accomplish that task in a setting of widespread illiteracy, where most adults have very few years if any of formal education? The trick, I believe, is to train very large numbers of people at the village level in creative and targeted ways, specifically for the main tasks at hand. For example, every village should aim to have a group of village experts, who, like the barefoot doctors of China, have enough formal training to address basic technical needs at the village level.

A literate community health worker, trained for one year, could be taught to prescribe antimalarial medicines, observe patients taking their daily anti-AIDS drugs, distribute and explain the use of antimalarial bed nets, give children medicine for helminthic (parasitic) infections, give immunizations, track the body weight and size of the community's children, explain the use of oral rehydration solutions, and with colleagues, keep track of all of this. Ideally, the community health worker would be a member of the community selected to be trained for this purpose, so that the problem of attracting a trained worker from outside the village would not arise—nor would the problem of brain drain of doctors and nurses, since one year of training would not qualify the individual for a health career outside the village.

Similarly, we could also imagine in each village a community-based agricultural extension worker with much less formal training than a traditional agricultural extension officer. The community-based worker would understand the basics of soil chemistry (measuring the adequacy of nitrogen, phosphorus, potassium, soil pH, and structure) and related soil tests, as well as the basic techniques of agroforestry, seed selection, and water management. One year of training for a high school graduate could suffice. A community-based engineer could similarly be trained in the operation—and routine maintenance—of diesel generators, electrical wiring, hand pumps, road grading, and the village truck.

Villages of several hundred to a few thousand people have an added advantage: the ability to gather together on the village green for discussions of village issues. With some planning, villages around the world could be helped to engage in continuing adult education on issues of pressing, life-and-death concern, such as, for example, how AIDS is contracted and spread, how malaria can be controlled, the role of hygiene in food preparation, the use of fertilizers, and so forth. Such relevant knowledge, if suitably presented, could inform rural societies on a massive scale. The nearly costless production and distribution of CDs and DVDs with educational materials prepared for village discussions could make it easy to disseminate such information.

In addition to training technical workers and educating villagers, national governments should promote scientific research activities as well. It used to be thought that research could be left to the rich countries while poor countries focused on raising their basic education and literacy levels. When India created its Indian Institutes of Technology in the 1950s and 1960s, development experts expressed skepticism that such advanced and rarified educational programs really belonged in such an impoverished country. Decades later we see the remarkable fruit of those investments in scientific research capacity. The institutes not only produced the generation of information technology engineers that are now powering India's IT boom, but they also created teams of scientists able to harness that technology specifically to meet India's needs. Dr. Ashok Jhunjhunwala, a professor at the IIT, Chennai, for example, designed appropriate local-loop wireless technology that has helped millions of Indian villagers to get online. In any developing country, similar homegrown technologies will be needed to adapt global processes to local needs in areas ranging from energy production and use, construction, natural hazard mitigation, disease control, and agricultural production.

India and China are both on the verge of technological break-throughs from technology importers to technology producers and exporters on a large scale. This rise of homegrown high technology will fuel the growth of these countries for decades to come. Similar efforts are needed to create scientific capacity in sub-Saharan Africa and other very low-income regions. The task is particularly difficult, since it is swimming against the powerful current of brain drain. The few scientists trained in Africa go abroad in search of laboratory equipment, colleagues, and grant support. The infrastructure for science—well-financed universities, laboratories, and a critical mass of research funding and collegial support—will have to be built, and just like other infrastructure, this one will require the backing of rich-country donors. They will have to understand the critical importance of investment in higher education alongside primary education.

EXAMPLES OF SCALING UP IN THE FIGHT AGAINST POVERTY

The world is filled with pilot projects showing that one intervention or another has proven successful time and again. It has been shown repeatedly that antimalarial bed nets save lives in rural Africa, that anti-AIDS drugs can be administered in low-income settings, and that immunizations can be delivered in the most difficult places in the world, even in the middle of war zones. The main challenge now is not to show what works in a single village or district—though these lessons can be of great importance when novel approaches are demonstrated—but rather to scale up what works to encompass a whole country and even the world.

There are several significant examples of programs that have been scaled up massively to remarkable success. Here are ten dramatic examples that prove the naysayers wrong:

The Green Revolution in Asia

The Green Revolution is one of the most important triumphs of targeted science in the past century. Fearing the possibility of massive hunger because of a rapidly rising global population, the Rockefeller Foundation took the initiative in developing and promoting high-yield varieties (HYVs) of staple crops, first in Mexico, and then in Asia and more broadly elsewhere. The start was in 1944, when the Rockefeller Foundation set up an institute to develop HYVs of wheat for Mexico, under the lead of Dr. Norman Borlaug. Scientific breeding, using crosses of strains brought from Japan after World War II, led to a breakthrough. Mexico went from a large net importer of grain to a significant net exporter between 1944 and 1964. Borlaug then persuaded donors to invest in similar crop-breeding efforts for South Asia, and also helped to introduce the resulting technologies to local crop breeders who successfully developed new strains. As the result of its Green Revolution, India went from eleven million metric tons of wheat production in 1960 to twenty-four million tons in 1970, thirty-six million tons in 1980, and fifty-five million tons in 1990, far outstripping the increase in population. High-yield varieties were similarly developed for other crops and locations through a network of international institutions, such as the International Rice Research Institute in the Philippines and the International Potato Center in Peru.

The Eradication of Smallpox

A concerted global effort ended the scourge of smallpox after thousands of years of epidemics that claimed the lives of hundreds of millions of people. In 1796, Edward Jenner demonstrated the use of a cowpox vaccine to prevent smallpox; that breakthrough provided the technological basis for eventual eradication. By the 1950s, most of the rich world had already become free of smallpox, but the disease continued to rage in poor countries, where vaccine coverage was very low. As recently as 1967, the disease struck around 10 to 15 million people each year, and claimed 1.5 to 2 million lives. That year, the World Health Organization established the Smallpox Eradication Unit, and began to implement a campaign of mass vaccination worldwide, backed by strong efforts on surveillance and containment. In 1980, the World Health Organization declared the world free of smallpox. The campaign had successfully reached the farthest corners of the world, including impoverished regions in the hinterlands of Asia and Africa, and regions in the midst of violent conflict.

The Campaign for Child Survival

In 1982, the executive director of UNICEF, James Grant, launched the Campaign for Child Survival. The campaign promoted a package of interventions known as GOBI: growth monitoring of children; oral rehydration therapy to treat bouts of diarrhea; breastfeeding for nutrition and immunity to diseases in infancy; and immunization against six childhood killers: tuberculosis, diphtheria, whooping cough, tetanus, polio, and measles. As in the smallpox eradication effort, the campaign depended on standardized technologies that could be massively scaled up in low-income settings. During the decade, particularly in the latter years, dozens of poor countries conducted all-out campaigns to introduce these measures, especially to reach at least 80 percent coverage with the immunization package. The results were striking. Child mortality rates fell sharply in all parts of the low-income world, including Africa, where the rates were (and are) by far the highest. The campaign was estimated to have saved around twelve million lives by the end of the decade.

The Global Alliance for Vaccines and Immunization

By the late 1990s, the campaign for childhood immunizations needed fortifying in two major ways. First, many new immunizations had been developed and adopted in the rich countries, but because of costs and lack of training and facilities, they had not been introduced into poor countries. Second, coverage rates achieved by the early 1990s had slipped, often the result of intensifying poverty and economic crisis in sub-Saharan Africa and other regions. Bill Gates stepped up to the effort, announcing an initial gift of $750 million from the Bill and Melinda Gates Foundation to reenergize the effort. The Global Alliance for Vaccines and Immunizations was launched in 2000 to guide the new effort. In the first years of its operation, the alliance made commitments of $1.1 billion to poor countries, and it has achieved a series of striking results. As of 2004, the alliance reported 41.6 million children vaccinated against hepatitis B; 5.6 million children vaccinated against Haemophilus influenzae type b (Hib); 3.2 million children vaccinated against yellow fever; and 9.6 million children vaccinated with other basic vaccines. Once again, its strategy has depended on the coupling of standardized technologies with systems of mass distribution, in this case based on proposals developed and submitted by the recipient countries.

The Campaign Against Malaria

During the 1950s and 1960s, the World Health Organization launched a series of efforts directed at eradicating malaria. Sometimes judged to have been a failure, since malaria was certainly not eradicated, these efforts can be seen as a stunning success for certain parts of the world where the scourge of malaria was eliminated or brought dramatically and decisively under control. Well over half of the world's populations living in endemic regions in the 1940s were largely freed of malaria transmission and mortality as a result of WHO's concentrated efforts, mainly in the areas where disease ecology favored the control measures. Africa, alas, was neither part of the program at the time, nor a beneficiary of its results until today. The standardized technologies that produced these regional, if not global, successes were two: the use of DDT and other pesticides to reduce the transmission of the disease and the use of chloroquine and other new antimalarial drugs to treat cases of it. (Newer technologies, especially antimalarial bed nets and artemisinin-combination therapies to treat the disease, combined with DDT where appropriate, can dramatically reduce the burden of the disease in Africa but will not eliminate the transmission entirely.)

The Control of African River Blindness

The Onchocerciasis Control Program (OCP) was launched in 1974 as a collaboration of WHO, the World Bank, Merck, the Food and Agriculture Organization (FAO), and the United Nations Development Program (UNDP). OCP aimed to reduce the transmission of African river blindness (onchocerciasis), a disease transmitted by a species of black fly. The program adopted a multipronged, scaled-up strategy in eleven hard-hit countries of West Africa based on a combination of prevention activities (including airborne spraying of insecticides to reduce the black fly abundance) and treatment. In the 1980s, Merck and WHO scientists realized that one of Merck's drugs used in veterinary medicine, ivermectin (Mectizan by trade name), could also effectively treat African river blindness. Merck agreed to donate ivermectin in a massive effort to control the disease. The OCP now reports the following accomplishments: an estimated six hundred thousand cases of African river blindness prevented, twenty-five million hectares made safe for settlement and cultivation, and roughly forty million people protected from disease transmission. The economic benefits have been significant.

The Eradication of Polio

As there is for smallpox, an immunization technology is also available to achieve global eradication of polio. There are technical differences between the two diseases, which make the polio effort a bit harder. Still, polio eradication is feasible and well on its way to being achieved. In 1988, the World Health Assembly (the governing board of the World Health Organization), voted to launch the Global Polio Eradication Initiative. At the time, polio was still endemic in more than 125 countries. Today, thanks to massive efforts by official institutions such as WHO, UNICEF, and the U.S. Centers for Disease Control and Prevention, as well as actions within poor countries and a remarkable and tireless effort by Rotary International, polio remains in only six countries (Nigeria, India, Pakistan, Niger, Afghanistan, and Egypt); and it is being contained. Only 784 cases were reported worldwide in 2003, compared with 350,000 in 1988. An estimated two billion children have been immunized since 1988, with the cooperation of twenty million volunteers and international funding on the order of $3 billion.

The Spread of Family Planning

Modern contraception has contributed to a dramatic reduction in total fertility rates, from a world average of 5.0 children per woman in the period 1950 to 1955 to 2.8 children per woman in the period 1995 to 2000. Family planning programs have played an enormous role in providing advice and information, advocating and assisting in the empowerment of women, and promoting modern contraception, although many other factors (women's literacy, women's entry into the nonfarm labor force, reduced child mortality, and urbanization) have played important roles. The United Nations Population Fund (UNFPA) was established in 1969 to help coordinate this effort, and it currently operates in 140 countries. It has helped to spur a massive increase in the use of modern contraceptives among couples in developing countries, rising from an estimated 10 to 15 percent of couples in 1970 to an estimated 60 percent in 2000.

This program has been an example of scaling up par excellence, but the unmet needs are still massive, since funding for contraceptive availability in the poorest countries is far below needed levels.

Export Processing Zones in East Asia

To a remarkable extent, the early industrialization of East Asia after World War II depended on a new organizational technology, the Export Processing Zone (EPZ), or free-trade zone. The free-trade zone is an industrial zone (sometimes a whole region or country) in which special tax, administrative, and infrastructure conditions are applied in order to encourage foreign companies to set up export-oriented manufacturing facilities. The general key has been physical security within the zone, ample land for manufacturing operations, easy connections to reliable water and power, low-cost proximity to a seaport or airport, tax holidays on profits, and tax-free imports of inputs and exports of finished products. Free-trade zones have been the basis for East Asia's leap into global production in garments, footwear, toys, automotive components, electronics, and semiconductors. In almost all cases, the East Asian countries began with very low-skilled, labor-intensive operations (such as the manual assembly of components onto electronics motherboards or the cutting and stitching of fabrics into ready-made garments), and then progressed to higher technology parts of the value chain, including product design. The result was an export boom at national, indeed global, scale. *Asiaweek* magazine once referred to free-trade zones as "Instant Industry." Manufactured exports from East Asia rose at an astounding compound rate of 12 percent per annum between 1978 and 2000, or in dollar terms, from $37 billion to $723 billion (in 1995 dollars).

The Mobile Phone Revolution in Bangladesh

Bangladesh's Grameen Bank, already justly famous for its microfinance lending, has also opened the world's eyes to expanding the use of modern telecommunications technologies in the world's poorest places. Grameen Telecom went into the business of mobile phones in 1997, reaching half a million subscribers by 2003, roughly equal to the total number of landlines. It used that mainly urban base of operations to launch a village phones program, whereby a village woman borrows funds for a mobile phone that is then used throughout the village at a small charge. With the fees she collects, the woman gradually repays the loan. Grameen estimates that each phone reaches an average of about 2,500 people in the village. With 9,400 villages covered by early 2004, the estimated access would be on the order of 23 million villagers. The model is being widely adopted now in dozens of other countries.

These cases demonstrate some common themes. First and foremost, scaling up is possible when it is backed by appropriate and widely applicable technology, organizational leadership, and appropriate financing. In many cases—such as smallpox or polio eradication—the technologies had long existed, but had not been applied in the poorest settings. In other cases, such as with the high-yield varieties of food crops at the core of the Green Revolution, the appropriate technologies had to be developed and then promoted through a targeted effort. In almost every case, technologies had to be adapted to local conditions (for example, solving the problems in tropical settings of maintaining the "cold chain" for immunizations that must remain cold until used, or adapting crop-breeding technologies to the local conditions of land, climate, and labor).

In the case of the Millennium Development Goals, the promising technologies exist, but have not yet been scaled up. Antimalarial bed nets, just to name one pertinent example, are used by fewer than 1 percent of rural Africans living in endemic malaria regions. It is time for that to change. Next, I consider the operational ways to get the job done.

Fourteen

A GLOBAL COMPACT
TO END POVERTY

Ending global poverty by 2025 will require concerted actions by the rich countries as well as the poor, beginning with a "global compact" between the rich and poor countries. The poor countries must take ending poverty seriously, and will have to devote a greater share of their national resources to cutting poverty rather than to war, corruption, and political infighting. The rich countries will need to move beyond the platitudes of helping the poor, and follow through on their repeated promises to deliver more help. All of this is possible. Indeed, it is much more likely than it seems. But it needs a framework. My colleagues and I in the UN Millennium Project have proposed just such a framework, focused on the period until 2015, called the Millennium Development Goals-Based Poverty Reduction Strategy.

A SHADOW PLAY

Today's situation is a bit like the old Soviet workers' joke: "We pretend to work, and you pretend to pay us!" Many poor countries today pretend to reform while rich countries pretend to help them, raising the cynicism to a pretty high level. Many low-income countries go through the motions of reform, doing little in practice and expecting even less in return. The aid agencies, on their part, focus on projects at a symbolic rather than national scale, just big enough to make good headlines. In 2002, the United States Agency for International Development (USAID) proudly trumpeted its West African Water Initiative, noting that "a reliable supply of safe water, along with adequate sanitation and hygiene, are on the front line in the combat against water-related disease and death." Fair enough, but what was USAID's actual contribution? A pitiful $4.4 million over three years. If West Africa has a population of some 250 million people, $4.4 million over three years would be *less than a penny per person per year,* enough perhaps to buy a Dixie cup, but probably not enough to fill it with water!

The chronic lack of donor financing robs poor countries of their poverty-fighting zeal. In 2003, Prime Minister Meles Zenawi and I cohosted an event in Addis Ababa to launch the Human Development Report in Ethiopia, one of the world's poorest countries. The prime minister made a powerful and insightful presentation about Ethiopia's potential to expand food production, and thereby to overcome pervasive hunger. A question came from the floor. "Mr. Prime Minister, we agree with you on the importance of agriculture, but what about health care?" To my surprise, the prime minister responded, "I'm afraid that health care is going to take more time. We will be able to expand health care only later, once we are richer." Back in his office, I said that I did not agree with his answer, "Ethiopia needs expanded health care now." He looked back at me plaintively and agreed. But then he told me that IMF officials had recently told him, "There's no more money available for health."

A reasonable estimate, based on the work of the UN Millennium Project, is that Ethiopia needs about $70 per person per year in development assistance (or $5 billion in total for a seventy-million person economy) compared with the $14 per person per year it receives today (or $1 billion in total). About half of that sum would be devoted to the scaling up of public health. The balance would go to infrastructure and raising rural productivity, especially in the food sector.

As soon as I returned to New York from Addis, I telephoned a senior IMF official. "Jeff, what are you complaining about now?" the official said good-naturedly. I repeated the story and noted that Ethiopia lived, in essence, without modern health care, enduring a life expectancy rate of forty-two years, child mortality of 170 for every 1,000 born, a one-third chance of living to sixty-five years, one doctor for every 30,000 people, and public spending on health of $2 per person per year. "So what do you want me to do?" said the official. "I want the IMF to support a major increase of public health spending in Ethiopia." "But Jeff, there's no donor money for that." "The donor world is awfully rich," I retorted. "Jeff, the donors are not offering to give more to Ethiopia." "But then there's absolutely no way for Ethiopia to meet the Millennium Development Goals." "You're right, those goals are unreachable." Exasperated, I said, "Well, then, at least say that publicly—that Ethiopia will fail to meet the MDGs unless the donors give more. The world needs to hear that. Perhaps that would get the donors to move."

We are stuck in a shadow play. In public, the IMF says how well things are going in Ethiopia; in private, it recognizes that aid for Ethiopia is insufficient for the country to achieve the Millennium Development Goals. The March 2004 IMF–World Bank Joint Staff Assessment of Ethiopia's Poverty Reduction Strategy (on the IMF's Web site) does not breathe a word about the need to scale up donor financing significantly if the MDGs are to be achieved. Even more distressing, but par for the course, the IMF–World Bank document contains no data whatsoever about the country's public health emergency. How could the IMF and World Bank executive directors even know that the country program they have approved cannot even achieve the goals that have been promised?

I believe that the senior IMF official was wrong: there is more money available for Ethiopia, but only after we cut through the thicket of excuses and platitudes about aid, some of which the IMF itself propagates. In public, all of the standard reasons why aid to Ethiopia is at just the right level are marshaled: Ethiopia is doing fine (says the IMF–World Bank Staff Assessment), it has all the donor resources it needs, it could not absorb any more, corruption and mismanagement would undermine greater assistance. This is the standard litany of excuses used to justify the status quo. In private, virtually the entire development community knows that Ethiopia is starved for cash. Apparently, it is too embarrassing to the political bosses in the United States and Europe to make the point. This is a mistake. If we explain patiently and honestly to the taxpayers in the rich world that more money is needed and can be well used, it is much more likely to become available.

TWO SIDES OF THE COMPACT

So that I am not misunderstood, let me underscore that a global compact, like any contract, has at least two parties, and therefore responsibilities on both sides. Poor countries have no guaranteed right to meet the Millennium Development Goals or to receive development assistance from the rich countries. They only have that right if they themselves carry through on their commitments to good governance. The expansion of aid is predicated on a serious plan of action, combined with a demonstrated will to carry it out in a transparent and honest manner. Not all governments will want to, or be able to, make such a commitment, and those nations need not apply. Our compact, our commitment, in the rich countries should be to help all poor countries where the collective will is present to be responsible partners in the endeavor. For the others, where authoritarian or corrupt regimes hold sway, the consequences for the population are likely to be tragic, but the responsibilities of the rich world are also limited. Perhaps the most important action that rich countries can take in those circumstances is to help the well-governed neighbors of such countries to prove that there is help available for those that are organized politically to help themselves. The biggest problem today is not that poorly governed countries get too much help, but that well-governed countries get far too little.

PLANNING FOR SUCCESS

Boring as it may seem, we need to fix the "plumbing" of international development assistance in order to be effective in helping the well-governed countries. Aid flows through certain pipes—bilateral donors, the World Bank, the regional development banks (such as the African Development Bank)—but these pipes are clogged or simply too narrow, not able to carry a sufficient flow of aid. If we are to get agreement by the rich world's taxpayers to put more aid through the system, we first have to show that the plumbing will carry the aid from the rich countries right down to where the poorest countries need it most—in the villages, slums, ports, and other critical targets. Let me describe how that plumbing can be put right. I focus my attention on the period until 2015, when the Millennium Development Goals are to be met. Similar principles will apply for the second decade, from 2015 to 2025.

The UN secretary-general, overseeing the UN agencies and the Bretton Woods Institutions (which are also part of the UN family), should oversee the entire effort. Working through the United Nations Development Program—the economic development arm of the UN system—the secretary-general, on behalf of the member nations, should ensure that the global compact is put into operation. Much of the work will take place at the level of the individual country, where plans will be devised and investments made on the basis of national financial resources and increased donor aid.

To organize country-level work, each low-income country should adopt a poverty reduction strategy (PRS) specifically designed to meet the Millennium Development Goals. Most poor countries today already have some form of a poverty reduction strategy—usually a poverty reduction strategy paper or plan—that it has developed in cooperation with the IMF and World Bank. The existing World Bank poverty reduction plan lays out the country's goals, targets, policies, and strategies to cut poverty. Introduced a few years ago to give more coherence to each country's efforts to fight poverty, and to provide a framework for official debt relief, the existing plans are not yet designed with enough rigor or ambition to enable the countries to achieve the MDGs.

The poverty reduction strategy papers, incidentally, are all publicly available on the IMF and World Bank Web sites, so one can read for oneself what the countries have deemed to be their poverty reduction strategies. The programs are often ingenious, but are all chronically underfunded compared with what is needed to achieve the Millennium Development Goals. As a result they are often forced to shortchange entire areas of public investment (such as public health). Five recent poverty reduction strategy plans of notable quality in Africa are:

- Ghana's Poverty Reduction Strategy (GPRS)

- Ethiopia's Sustainable Development and Poverty Reduction Program (SDPRP)

- Kenya's Economic Recovery Strategy for Wealth and Employment Creation (ERS)

- Senegal's Poverty Reduction Strategy Paper (PRSP)

- Uganda's Poverty Eradication Action Plan (PEAP)

Why Today's System Is Incoherent

Alas, the international community's approach remains incoherent in practice. On the one side, it announces bold goals, like the Millennium Development Goals, and even ways that the goals can be achieved, such as the pledge of increased donor assistance made in the Monterrey Consensus. Yet when it comes to real practice, where the rubber hits the road, in the poverty reduction plans, the Millennium Development Goals are expressed only as vague aspirations rather than operational targets. Countries are told to go about their business without any hope of meeting the MDGs. The IMF and World Bank reveal split personalities, championing the MDGs in public speeches, approving programs that will not achieve them, and privately acknowledging, with business as usual, that they cannot be met!

Here is how the aid actually makes its way through the plumbing today. When Prime Minister Meles Zenawi or his counterparts in Africa, Asia, and Latin America lead their country's preparation of the poverty reduction plans, they are told to be "realistic," meaning that they should take as a given the limits of today's constricted donor resources.

Operationally, the IMF and World Bank staffs make rounds of calls to canvas the "bilateral" donor community, that is, the aid agencies of the rich countries. They contact the aid agencies to get a forecast of the level of aid that each agency is likely to provide in the coming year. These sums are totaled up and then conveyed to the recipient country. Ethiopia is told, for example, "You can expect around $1 billion next year. Please tell us what you plan to do with that aid."

Knowing that a certain amount of aid is likely, the recipient country is expected to engage in a broad-based public consultation to prepare the poverty reduction plan, including how the aid will be deployed. The international community's insistence on broad public participation in the design of these plans is designed to achieve four main goals: (1) better prioritization of investment plans, (2) increased public awareness about poverty reduction programs, (3) mobilization of NGOs and community groups in the fight against poverty, and (4) fostering more political "antibodies" against corruption.

All of this is fine; indeed, it is reasonably successful in eliciting public participation. What is missing in the process are the practical linkages between the Millennium Development Goals and the poverty reduction plans. In today's arrangements, the country is presented with a fait accompli—"Here's the amount of aid you will receive." Instead, the process should be turned around. The first step should be to learn what the country actually needs in foreign assistance. After that, the IMF and World Bank should go out to raise the required amount from the donors!

To show how straightforward it would be to adopt this approach, let me provide another recent example, Ghana's poverty reduction plan.

Ghana is one of the best governed and managed countries in Africa. It is a stable, multiparty democracy with relatively high literacy (92 percent of youths aged fifteen to twenty-four) and modest levels of corruption compared with other countries at a comparable income level. Ghana suffers from considerable extreme poverty. Like other African countries, Ghana has been unable to diversify its export base beyond a narrow range of primary commodities, mainly cocoa beans. It lacks the domestic resources needed to finance critical investments in health, education, roads, power, and other infrastructure. It fell into a sharp debt and financial crisis in the early 1980s, and since then the government has been hard pressed to pay its monthly bills, much less to expand the levels of public investment.

The government of Ghana reached these same conclusions when it presented the Ghana Poverty Reduction Strategy (GPRS) in 2002, its version of the poverty reduction plan. Ghana took seriously the Millennium Development Goals and presented a strategy based on the investments that it would need to achieve the MDGs. The plan called for a major scaling up of public investments in the social sectors and infrastructure, estimated to require donor aid of around $8 billion over five years, or roughly $75 per Ghanaian per year during the five-year period. The Ghana strategy was exceptionally well designed and argued, but the donors balked. The first draft was rejected by the donors. The government cut back on its ambitions, and slashed the aid request to just $6 billion over five years. The donors balked again. The plan was slashed again. By the end of this excruciating process, the poverty reduction plan was funded at around $2 billion for the five-year period.

When I was recently in Accra, Ghana, a very pleasant representative of the European Commission said to me, "But Professor Sachs, the original plan was simply not realistic." "What do you mean by realistic?" I responded. "Do you mean that it was not realistic because the program was poorly designed, or do you mean that it was not realistic because the donors wouldn't foot the bill?" "Oh, I mean only the latter, Professor Sachs. The strategy was fine, but we couldn't come close to the $8 billion request." Realism, it seems, is in the eye of the beholder. I would have thought that the original plan was realistic because it aimed to accomplish the very goals that the world had endorsed. The final plan seemed *unrealistic* to me, because it can no longer achieve the MDGs. The donors, evidently, meant something else about realism. For the donors, realism meant convenience, and specifically shoehorning Ghana's financial needs into the tight fit of an insufficient aid package.

A MILLENNIUM DEVELOPMENT GOALS-BASED POVERTY REDUCTION STRATEGY

Still, I am not despairing. Ghana could soon have a strategy based on the Millennium Development Goals. One reason is that creative work by the World Bank, the UN agencies, and the bilateral donors has actually prepared the plumbing system to handle a much greater flow of resources. Ghana's donors have already reached important agreements to coordinate (or "harmonize") their efforts around the Ghana strategy. They have agreed to simplify their own aid procedures, and in fact to pool their financial resources to support the plan.

In the alphabet soup of donor aid, the new donor program for Ghana is called the Multi-Donor Budget Support (MDBS) policy. Under this new arrangement, the donors have agreed to give their money directly to Ghana's budget so that the government of Ghana can carry out the public investments it has identified as the highest priorities for poverty reduction. In Ghana's case, a viable development plan (GPRS) and the financial plumbing to support the plan are now in place. What Ghana now needs is an adequate flow of cash.

A true MDG-based poverty reduction strategy would have five parts:

- A *Differential Diagnosis,* which identifies the policies and investments that the country needs to achieve the Millennium Development Goals

- An *Investment Plan,* which shows the size, timing, and costs of the required investments

- A *Financial Plan* to fund the Investment Plan, including the calculation of the Millennium Development Goals Financing Gap, the portion of financial needs that the donors will have to fill

- A *Donor Plan,* which gives the multiyear donor commitments for filling the Millennium Development Goals Financing Gap

- A *Public Management Plan* that outlines the mechanisms of governance and public administration that will help implement the expanded public investment strategy

In combination, these five sections would put to rest the current favorite explanation of donors for not doing more to help the poorest countries: the alleged lack of "absorptive capacity" to use more aid. How can we scale up the health sector, the donors ask, if the countries lack the doctors, nurses, and clinics to provide health services? Such a question misjudges the whole purpose of aid. Sure there are not enough doctors and nurses now. What about in four, or six, or ten years? With more aid, there can be more doctors, nurses, and clinics. Getting from here to there is a matter of routine planning, not heroics.

With a lead time of a couple of years, for example, doctors from the country who have relocated abroad could be attracted home with improved salaries, covered partly by donor aid. Within two or three years, tens of thousands of community health workers could be trained, with the training financed by donor aid. With a lead time of five years, the graduating class of the existing medical schools could be enlarged, with the expenses covered in part with donor aid. And with a lead time of ten years, several new medical schools could be built within the country, with the new schools financed by donor aid. Limited absorptive capacity is not an argument against aid. It is the very reason that aid is needed! The key is to invest that aid over the course of a decade, so that absorptive capacity can be increased step by step in a predictable manner.

In the previous chapter we discussed the essence of the differential diagnosis and the investment plan, specifically the areas of priority investments in infrastructure and social services that can lift a country out of a poverty trap. Let me therefore turn directly to the last three elements of the MDG-based poverty reduction strategy: the financial plan, the donor plan, and the public management plan.

The Financial Plan and Millennium Development Goals Financing Gap

A proper financial plan begins with an estimate of the unit costs of providing the key investments: teachers, classrooms, kilowatt hours of electricity, health clinics, kilometers of road, and so forth, and then examines the increased populations to be covered by these interventions. These costs of scaling up can be estimated with considerable detail, and they should cover not only the capital costs of the projects, but also the costs of operations and maintenance. In the past, donors often have helped countries to build clinics, but then rejected the plea to help cover the salaries of doctors and nurses to staff the clinics. The predictable result has been the construction of empty shells rather than operating health facilities. Donors need to be prepared to finance not only the physical infrastructure, but also the salaries of public-sector workers.

During the structural adjustment era of the 1980s and 1990s, the IMF, World Bank, and donor community often accepted the need for larger funding for health or education, but said that the poor should pay their own way. Similar arguments are heard today concerning the privatization of water and sanitation services. "Yes, let's mobilize new investments in water and sanitation, but let's do it through the private sector. The poor can pay for improved services." In some cases, donors have supported a compromise formula called social marketing, in which the poor are asked to pay part, not all, of the cost of the service, with the donors picking up the balance. Social marketing has been applied, for example, to the sale of contraceptives and antimalarial bed nets. These recommendations have failed repeatedly. They have been unrealistic about what the poor can actually afford to pay, which is usually little or nothing. The extreme poor don't even have enough to eat, much less to pay for electricity or water or bed nets or contraceptives. The history of user fees imposed on the poor is a history of the poor being excluded from basic services.

The financial plan, therefore, must include a realistic picture of what the poor can actually pay and what they can't pay. The UN Millennium Project, following the similar recommendations of the WHO Commission on Macroeconomics and Health (CMH) recommends that user fees should be dropped entirely for essential health services and primary education in poor countries. As for water, sanitation, and power, the project strongly endorses the use of lifeline tariffs, explained earlier. In that system, every household gets a guaranteed fixed supply of electricity and safe water; above that amount, they pay by the meter.

The financial plan should also estimate the share of GDP in tax revenues that can be devoted to the Millennium Development Goals. Here again realism is vital. Poor countries can only raise limited amounts in taxation. The poor cannot be squeezed by taxes any more than they can be squeezed through user fees. Attempting to raise taxes too high results in widespread evasion and serious economic distortions. When the

Commission on Macroeconomics and Health considered this issue, the IMF representative on the commission suggested that it assume that a low-income country could mobilize an additional 1 percent of GDP in tax revenues for the health sector by 2007 and an additional 2 percent of GDP by 2015. The UN Millennium Project adopted the same approach, assuming that low-income countries can raise an additional 4 percent of GDP by 2015 for *all* MDG-related investments.

With these assumptions, it is possible to calculate a Millennium Development Goals financing gap, which measures how much the donor community would have to contribute to enable the low-income country to finance the investment plan. The following chapter details these calculations. One point to stress here is that help will be needed not just for a few years, but for most (or all) of the period until 2025. Funding plans cannot realistically expect that poor countries will suddenly pick up the full tab for expanded projects after just a few years. Sustainability of the investment plans will require sustained large-scale donor financing for at least a decade to come, and in many cases for two decades.

The Donor Plan

The donors have put great stress on the need for countries to improve their governance, but much too little stress on how donors themselves need to improve their own performance. As part of every MDG-based poverty reduction strategy, we need a donor plan that spells out in a transparent manner the way that donor commitments will be fulfilled. A donor plan should focus on four aspects of aid flows:

- *Magnitude.* Aid must be large enough to enable the recipient country to finance its investment plan.

- *Timing.* Aid must be long term enough to enable the recipient country to follow through on a ten-year program of scaling up.

- *Predictability.* Aid must be predictable enough so that stops and starts in the aid flows do not jeopardize the investment program or the macroeconomic stability of the recipient country.

- *Harmonization.* Aid must support the MDG-based poverty reduction strategy, and specifically the investment plan, rather than the pet projects of the aid agencies.

Let me underscore why predictability of aid will be almost as important as the overall amount of aid. If poverty is to be ended, aid of around $60 per person per year will have to flow to the poorest countries. But that level of aid will constitute around 20 to 30 percent of GDP when per capita incomes are in the range of $200 to $300 per person per year. When aid flows are such a large part of GDP, unexpected fluctuations in aid can be a huge shock to the economy. If, one year, the donors give 30 percent of GDP, but the next year only 15 percent of GNP, the result would be massive layoffs, closures of government facilities, huge budget deficits, and inflation. To guard against this threat, donor aid must be highly predictable over a period of at least a few years.

The issue of aid harmonization is also crucial. A discussion in 2000 about aid to Tanzania noted that there are "thirty agencies involved in providing development funds, 1,000 projects, 2,500 aid missions a year [and] all with separate accounting, financial and reporting systems. . . ." World Bank President Jim Wolfensohn has commented, "I think that we are now in a situation where everybody recognizes that to have countries burdened with innumerable visits from good-hearted people like us and all the bilateral donors, and innumerable reports that they have to complete quarterly and little coordination in terms of some of the mechanics of the implementation, that there is a large pick-up to be had in just coordinating and better implementing what the development community are doing already."

In order to harmonize aid, the various aid agencies should operate on the basis of their true comparative advantage. When it comes to large-scale aid to help countries expand their public investment programs, the money should flow through multilateral donors such as the World Bank and the regional development banks. Why should Ghana negotiate with twenty-three bilateral donors when what Ghana really needs is budget support to scale up public investments? The twenty-three bilateral donors should agree, beforehand, to pool their money at the World Bank or the African Development Bank, and then let those institutions make a single grant. The bilateral agencies are much better when it comes to matters that require individual small-scale projects, such as specific kinds of technical assistance (for example, to treat AIDS patients or to mobilize solar power), or small-scale experiments, or people-to-people exchanges.

A Public Management Strategy

Financing is necessary, but hardly sufficient, for success. Money will be wasted or sit idly in a bank account if the government is unable to implement its investment plan. Implementation requires time, of course, for planning, construction, training, and improved oversight. But beyond the necessary time, a sound public management plan should have six components:

- *Decentralization.* Investments are needed in hundreds of thousands of villages and thousands of cities. The details will have to be decided at the ground level, in the villages and cities themselves, rather than in the capitals or in Washington. Decentralized management of public investment is therefore a sine qua non of scaling up.

- *Training.* The public sector at all levels—national, district, village—lacks the talent to oversee the scaling-up process. This is not a case for evading the public sector, which will not work, but for building the capacity of the public sector. Training programs (or capacity building) should be part of the overall strategy.

- *Information Technologies.* If the aid plumbing is going to carry much larger flows of aid each year, we will need better meters, which will mean the use of information technologies—computers, e-mail, mobile phones—to increase dramatically the amount of information transmitted in the public sector and accessible to all parties.

- *Measurable Benchmarks.* Much clearer targets of what is to be achieved must accompany a major increase of spending. Every MDG-based poverty reduction strategy should be supported by quantitative benchmarks tailored to national conditions, needs, and data availability.

- *Audits.* Let's face it: the money has to reach the intended recipients. No country should receive greater funding unless the money can be audited.

- *Monitoring and Evaluation.* Right from the start, the MDG-based poverty reduction strategy should prepare to have the investments monitored and evaluated. Budgets and mechanisms for monitoring and evaluation should be essential parts of the strategies.

Regional Infrastructure

Many important investments are regional in nature and involve several countries at once. Consider, as I did earlier, the road that links the Kenyan port of Mombasa with the four countries that depend on that port: Kenya, Uganda, Rwanda, and Burundi. The road is a two-lane, semipaved road that services more than a hundred million people. It is poorly maintained and imposes extremely high costs for freight shipments to and from the coast. One part or another of the road frequently gives way. The road should be repaired in a shared four-country project, rather than as piecemeal haphazard projects within each of the four countries. The problem is that the World Bank and other donors are not good at managing multicountry projects, since they are used to thinking about one country at a time. Various regional economic groups have sprung up around the world, including several in Africa, that could help to achieve coordination of investments across neighboring countries. Multicountry investments will become more common, not only in roads and rail, but also in port services, telecommunications, financial market regulations, biodiversity conservation (of forests and river sheds), control of air and water pollution, energy development (including hydropower, geothermal power, electricity transmission), and other areas.

Regional groupings can also play another significant role: shared responsibility for governance. Countries respond to peer pressure. The African Union is utilizing that basic insight to launch a policy known as the African Peer Review Mechanism (APRM), in which countries voluntarily subscribe to a systematic governance review by their peers. As the African Union describes it, the primary purpose of the APRM is

> To foster the adoption of policies, standards and practices that lead to political stability, high economic growth, sustainable development and accelerated sub-regional and continental economic integration through sharing of experiences and reinforcement of successful and best practice, including identifying deficiencies and assessing the needs of capacity building.

The experience of many other regional efforts, from the Marshall Plan to the European Union, shows that these hopes have great merit. Group pressure from outside can help to keep a reform-minded government on track, just as Poland's hopes to join the European Union helped to insulate Poland's economic reform policies from enormous and inappropriate short-term pressures and populist enticements.

GLOBAL POLICIES FOR POVERTY REDUCTION

Poor countries also have critical needs that cannot be solved by national or regional investments or by domestic policy reforms. There are concerns that must be addressed at the global level. Four are most important:

- The Debt Crisis
- Global Trade Policy
- Science for Development
- Environmental Stewardship

The Debt Crisis

This issue should have been resolved years ago. For at least twenty years we have known that heavily indebted poor countries (HIPCs) are unable to repay their debts, or at least do so and achieve the MDGs at the same time. The debts should simply have been canceled, but the debtors have insisted for far too long that the poorest countries of the world continue to pay debt service, often in amounts that were greater than national spending on health and education. In fact, rich countries should have given the poorest countries grants rather than loans, so that the poor countries would never have been indebted in the first place.

The behavior of the creditor countries in recent decades compares very poorly with the U.S. commitment and practice during the formulation of the Marshall Plan, when it decided to help rebuild Europe with grants rather than loans. The post–World War II planners knew well the disastrous experience after World War I, when, as Keynes had foretold, allied war debts and post–World War I reparations claims entangled creditor and debtor nations in a prolonged political and financial crisis that contributed to the Great Depression and indirectly to the rise of fascism. After World War II, U.S. strategists chose a different course, ensuring that postwar debts would not encumber Europe's fragile democracies. We would do well to emulate that wisdom today. It is time for the debts of the highly indebted poor countries to be cancelled outright as part of the financing package for the Millennium Goals-based poverty reduction strategies.

Global Trade Policy

Sustained economic growth requires that poor countries increase their exports to the rich countries, and thereby earn the foreign exchange to import capital goods from the rich countries. Yet trade barriers in rich countries hamper export growth. The ongoing Doha Trade Round, launched in November 2001, is committed—on paper at least—to improving market access for poor countries. This commitment is vitally important, especially in low-skill, labor-intensive sectors such as garment manufacture. Still, two caveats are in order.

The first is that although trade is important, the popular slogan "trade not aid" is wrong. Poor countries will need "trade plus aid," since trade reforms alone are not nearly powerful enough to enable the poorest countries to escape from extreme poverty. The "trade not aid" lobby seeks to use the undoubted importance of open trade to undermine the case for aid. Even if trade reforms would raise the incomes of the poorest countries by billions of dollars per year, only a small fraction of that would be available for funding the vitally important public investments needed to escape from the poverty trap. When huge gains are attributed to trade reforms (hundreds of billions of dollars), we need to look at the fine print: almost all of those gains accrue to the richest countries and the middle-income countries, not the poorest countries, and especially not the poorest countries in Africa. How, after all, could trade alone enable isolated rural villages in Africa to meet their basic needs?

The second caveat is to warn against hyperbole vis-à-vis agricultural trade liberalization. There is no doubt that liberalization of world agricultural trade would be a good thing. Europe, for example, wastes incredible amounts of money subsidizing its high-cost farmers, and could accomplish other goals (environmental preservation) much more cheaply. But it is wrong to conclude that the end of agricultural subsidies would be a great boon for least developed countries in Africa and other parts of the world. If Europe cuts back on its subsidies for staple crops (wheat, maize), the results for Africa could well be negative, not positive, since Africa is a net food-importing region: consumers of food would pay higher prices for food, whereas farmers would benefit. The net effects on poverty could be either positive or negative, but are very unlikely to be hugely beneficial. Africa will unambiguously benefit from the liberalization of trade in tropical products (for example, cotton, sugar, bananas), but the subsidies for tropical products are only a very small part of the widely reported $300 billion in artificial support for farmers in the rich countries. In short, liberalize trade in agriculture, but do not believe it to be a panacea. The benefits will accrue over-whelmingly to the large food exporters: the United States, Canada, Argentina, Brazil, and Australia.

Science for Development

Many of the core breakthroughs in long-term economic development have been new technologies: the Green Revolution for food produc-tion, vaccines and immunizations, antimalarial bed nets, oral rehydra-tion therapies, agroforestry to replenish soil nutrients, antiretroviral medicines. In almost all of these cases, the technologies were first de-veloped for the rich-country markets, or were sponsored for the poor nations in a special donor-led process. It is very rare, alas, that technolo-gies are developed by the private sector to meet specific challenges in the poor countries (for example, for tropical foods or diseases). The poorest of the poor simply do not provide enough of a market incentive for private-sector-led research and development.

Recognizing that the poor are therefore likely to be ignored by the international scientific community—unless special efforts are made—it is critical to identify the priority needs for scientific research in relation to the poor, and then to mobilize the requisite donor assistance to spur the research and development. Here are a few areas of special impor-tance, drawing on work by various scientific bodies in recent years that have explored this issue:

- Diseases of the poor: new preventive, diagnostic, and therapeu-tic measures for diseases specific to low-income countries, espe-cially tropical diseases

- Tropical agriculture: new seed varieties, water management techniques, and soil management techniques

- Energy systems in remote rural areas: special technologies for off-grid power, including renewable energy sources (for example, photovoltaic cells), power generators, improved batteries, and low-watt illumination

- Climate forecasting and adjustment: improved measurement of seasonal, interannual, and long-term climate changes, with a view toward prediction as well as adjustment to climate changes

- Water management: improved technologies for water harvesting, desalination, small-scale irrigation, and improved management of aquifers being depleted by overuse. Water will rise in importance as population densities and climate change interact to produce more regions in acute water stress.

- Sustainable management of ecosystems: fragile ecosystems around the world (coral reefs, mangrove swamps, fisheries, rainforests, to name a few) are succumbing to anthropogenic forces, often with dire consequences. In many cases, poor communities do not have the technical capacity to monitor changes or to respond in an effective an sustainable manner.

The UN Millennium Project recommends global donor support on the order of $7 billion per year to address priority R&D needs for health, agriculture, energy, climate, water, and biodiversity conservation in the poorest countries. Targeted scientific efforts have had huge benefits in the past. The Rockefeller Foundation financed the research leading to the yellow fever vaccine in 1928 and much of the plant breeding research leading to the Green Revolution. In recent years the Bill and Melinda Gates Foundation has financed extensive research into AIDS, TB, malaria, and other diseases that afflict the poor. GlaxoSmithKline, working together with the Gates Foundation, has recently announced promising advances toward a malaria vaccine, though a proven vaccine for use in Africa is still years off. In order to stimulate the needed research and clinical testing of new vaccine candidates, I have recommended together with Harvard economist Michael Kremer that donor agencies and the Global Fund to Fight AIDS, TB, and Malaria commit ahead of time to purchasing a successful vaccine on a large scale for distribution in Africa, thereby creating a financial incentive for vaccine research and development.

Environmental Stewardship

Even though the local effects of global climate change are extremely hard to forecast, we can be sure that many of the world's poorest places are at risk of being overwhelmed by climate shocks coming from outside their borders. Rising ocean levels associated with long-term warming will likely inundate impoverished regions such as Bangladesh and small island economies. Shifting patterns of rainfall, such as the declines in precipitation evident in Africa's Sahel and those associated with long-term warming in the Indian Ocean, are likely to be experienced elsewhere. An increasing frequency and intensity of El Niño climate cycles could become an important disturbance for hundreds of millions of people in Asia, Latin America, and Africa. Changes in ocean chemistry associated with rising atmospheric concentrations of carbon dioxide could poison the coral reefs, with attendant disastrous effects on coastal ecosystems and coastal economies.

The poorest of the poor are mostly innocent victims in this drama. The major cause of long-term climate change, fossil fuel combustion, is disproportionately the result of rich-country actions. Any responsible global approach to poverty reduction should include much greater attention to three things. First, the rich countries themselves, and particularly the United States, will have to live up to their longstanding commitment under the United Nations Framework Convention on Climate Change to the "stabilization of greenhouse gas concentrations in the atmosphere at a level that would prevent dangerous anthropogenic interference with the climate system." Second, the rich countries will have to give added financial assistance to the poor countries to enable them to respond effectively to, or at least to cope with, the changes ahead. Third, as I noted earlier, the rich countries will have to invest more in climate science to gain a clearer understanding of how the changes already under way are likely to affect the world's poorest people, as well as the rest of us.

WHO CONDUCTS THE
INTERNATIONAL SYSTEM?

The poor countries refer euphemistically to the UN agencies, bilateral donors, and Bretton Woods institutions as their "development partners." In the best of circumstances, these agencies and counterpart governments really act as partners. Often, however, they can be as much nuisance as help. Aid flows are often small and unpredictable, while hundreds of small-scale aid projects eat up the time and attention of overstretched and impoverished governments. Harmonization of aid in support of a single MDG-based poverty reduction strategy is vital.

In order to harmonize aid, however, the partners themselves need to do a better job in dealing with each other. The key, I believe, is to use the United Nations system to its best advantage. The UN secretary-general is the best placed official in the world to help coordinate the various stakeholders who must contribute to the achievement of the Millennium Development Goals. The UN agencies offer vitally important expertise in every aspect of development. A partial listing of these agencies and their core areas of competence is shown in table 1. With the lead of the secretary-general, and operating through the UN Development Program (UNDP), each low-income country should have the benefit of a united and effective United Nations country team, which coordinates in one place the work of the UN specialized agencies, the IMF and the World Bank. In each country, the UN country team should be led by a single United Nations resident coordinator, who reports to the administrator of the United Nations Development Program, who in turn reports to the UN secretary-general. This UN country team is vital to providing every poor country with the best of international evidence and science addressed to the challenges of escaping the poverty trap and achieving sustainable development.

Why do I belabor such an obvious housekeeping point? Because the current system is surprisingly dysfunctional, to the point where the IMF and the World Bank sometimes hardly speak with the UN agencies, even though they all depend on one another. For the past twenty years, the rich countries have assigned the IMF and the World Bank a privileged position in relation to the other UN agencies, so much so that the other agencies would sometimes have to call me simply to find out what the IMF was actually doing in a particular country. They lacked the direct access to find out on their own.

Why the IMF and the World Bank were given this privileged position is easily explained. As the old advice puts it, Follow the money. The rich countries hold sway in the IMF and the World Bank much more than in the UN agencies. Unlike the UN General Assembly, and most of the

Agency	Abbreviation	Core Areas of Concern in Developing Countries
Table 1: UN Agencies in Development (partial list)		
Bretton Woods Institutions		
International Monetary Fund	IMF	Provides assistance to developing countries on finance and budgetary issues, and temporary financial assistance to help ease macroeconomic adjustments
World Bank		Provides loans and grants, policy advice, and technical assistance to help low- and middle-income countries fight poverty
Food and Agriculture Organization	FAO	Leads fight on hunger, providing policy advice and technical assistance
International Fund for Agricultural Development	IFAD	Finances agricultural development projects to increase food production and improve nutrition
United Nations Development Program	UNDP	Serves as the UN's global development network; also has programs to strengthen democratic governance in developing countries, fight poverty, improve health and education, protect the environment, and deal with crises
United Nations Environment Program	UNEP	Helps countries care for the environment through projects and technical scientific support
United Nations Human Settlements Program	UN–HABITAT	Promotes socially and environmentally sustainable towns and cities with the goal of providing adequate shelter for all
United Nations Population Fund	UNFPA	Helps countries establish population and reproductive health programs
United Nations Children's Fund	UNICEF	Improves children's lives, particularly through programs promoting education, health, and child protection
World Food Program	WFP	Frontline agency in the fight against global hunger, feeding over 100 million people in 81 countries in 2003, including most of the world's refugees and internally displaced people.
World Health Organization	WHO	Provides vital technical assistance to countries on investing in health

boards of the specialized agencies, where it's "one country, one vote," in the IMF and the World Bank, it's "one dollar, one vote." Each member of the IMF and the World Bank joins with an assigned quota, which determines the voting rights of the country and the size of the country's subscription. In this way, the rich countries have kept a voting majority. This voting majority has led the United States, in particular, to rely more heavily on the IMF and the World Bank, which it more easily controls, than on the UN agencies, over which it has much less influence.

The problem is that the IMF and the World Bank simply cannot do their jobs without much closer cooperation with the UN agencies. The IMF and the World Bank are generalist institutions, the IMF for macroeconomic (budget, financial, exchange rate) issues and the World Bank for development issues. The UN agencies are specialized institutions. UNICEF, for example, has great knowledge in child health and education; the United Nations Population Fund (UNFPA) has unrivaled expertise in family planning; the Food and Agriculture Organization (FAO) is unmatched in agriculture; the World Health Organization (WHO) has unique capacity in public health and disease control; the United Nations Development Program (UNDP) is unequaled in capacity building and governance; and so on. On the other hand, the specialized agencies rarely have the macroeconomic overview that is an important part of the IMF–World Bank perspective. Without a much closer partnership of the specialized UN agencies with the IMF and the World Bank, none of these institutions can do their work properly.

NEXT STEPS

Extreme poverty is a trap that can be released through targeted investments if the needed investments are tested and proved and the investment program can be implemented as part of a global compact between rich and poor countries, centered on a Millennium Development Goals-based poverty reduction strategy. That is all great news. But can we afford to do all of this? Would helping the poor in fact bankrupt the rich? I answer this underlying question, in some detail, in the next chapter.

Fifteen

CAN THE RICH AFFORD TO HELP THE POOR?

It may seem highly imprudent to ask the rich world to take responsibility for helping the poorest of the poor to escape from the poverty trap. Not only is the task thankless and endless, it may also break the bank—or so the thinking goes. After all, haven't the rich world's own welfare programs proven to be too much to handle? Aren't the rich countries in enough of a fiscal mess with the problems that they have already taken on? How could the rich world possibly take responsibility for billions of people outside of their borders, in countries with rapidly growing populations? These are all reasonable questions. Happily, they have reasonable answers. The more one looks at it, the more one sees that the question isn't whether the rich can afford to help the poor, but whether they can afford not to.

The truth is that the cost now is likely to be small compared to any relevant measure—income, taxes, the costs of further delay, and the benefits from acting. Most important, the task can be achieved within the limits that the rich world has already committed: 0.7 percent of the gross national product of the high-income world, a mere 7 cents out of every $10 in income. All of the incessant debate about development assistance, and whether the rich are doing enough to help the poor, actually concerns less than 1 percent of rich-world income. The effort required of the rich is indeed so slight that to do less is to announce brazenly to a large part of the world, "You count for nothing." We should not be surprised, then, if in later years the rich reap the whirlwind of that heartless response.

There are five reasons why the level of required effort is, in truth, so modest. First, the numbers of extreme poor have declined to a relatively small proportion of the world's population. The World Bank estimates that some 1.1 billion people live in extreme poverty today, a bit less than one fifth of the world's population. A generation ago, the proportion was roughly one third. Two generations ago, the proportion was closer to one half. The proportion of the world's population still mired in extreme poverty is, relatively speaking, manageable.

Second, the goal is to end *extreme* poverty, not to end all poverty, and still less to equalize world incomes or to close the gap between the rich and the poor. This may eventually happen, but if so, the poor will have to get rich on their own effort. The rich can help most by giving the extreme poor some assistance to extricate themselves from the poverty trap that now ensnares them.

Third, success in ending the poverty trap will be much easier than it appears. For too long, too much economic thinking has been directed at the wrong question—how to make the poor countries into textbook models of good governance or efficient market economies. Too little has been done to identify the specific, proven low-cost interventions that can make a difference in living standards and economic growth. When we get practical, and speak of investments in specific areas— roads, power, transport, soils, water and sanitation, disease control—the task is suddenly a lot less daunting.

Fourth, the rich world today is so vastly rich. An effort to end extreme poverty that would have seemed out of reach even a generation or two ago is now well within reach because the costs are now such a small fraction of the vastly expanded income of the rich world. Especially for the United States, part of the solution to getting donors to honor their commitment to the world's extreme poor is to assign more responsibility to the richest of the rich, not the average taxpayers, but taxpayers with incomes at the very top of the charts. The rich can manage to pay for a significant proportion of what needs to be done, either through a modest increase in taxation or a burst of large-scale philanthropy commensurate with their vast wealth.

Fifth, our tools are more powerful than ever. Mobile phones and the Internet are ending the information famine of rural areas in Asia and Africa. Improved logistics systems now enable global industries to operate profitably in far-flung regions. Modern agronomic practices, including improved seed breeding, agrobiotechnology, and science-based management of soil nutrients, are restoring lands that were long degraded or opening new lands that were previously considered infertile. New approaches to disease prevention and control offer the prospect of breakthroughs in medical practice. It is true that these investments still reach only a small fraction of the poorest of the poor. At the core of poverty reduction lies the strategy of scaling up critical investments in infrastructure, health, and education, investments that have been rendered vastly more effective through rapid technological progress.

Here are some calculations of what it will cost to get the job done, and who should pay.

THE SIMPLEST CALCULATION

The first cut at the problem—the simplest but still eye-opening—is to ask how much income would have to be transferred from rich countries to poor countries to lift all of the world's extreme poor to an income level sufficient to meet basic needs. Martin Ravallion and his colleagues on the World Bank's poverty team have gathered data to address this question, at least approximately. The World Bank estimates that meeting basic needs requires $1.08 per day per person, measured in 1993 purchasing-power adjusted prices. Using household surveys, the Ravallion team has calculated the numbers of poor people around the world who live below that threshold, and the average incomes of those poor.

According to the Bank's estimates, 1.1 billion people lived below the $1.08 level as of 2001, with an average income of $0.77 per day, or $281 per year. More important, the poor had a shortfall relative to basic needs of $0.31 per day ($1.08 minus $0.77), or $113 per year. Worldwide, the total income shortfall of the poor in 2001 was therefore $113 per year per person multiplied by 1.1 billion people, or $124 billion.

Using the same accounting units (1993 purchasing power adjusted U.S. dollars), the income of the twenty-two donor countries of the Development Assistance Committee (DAC) in 2001 was $20.2 trillion. Thus a transfer of 0.6 percent of donor income, amounting to $124 billion, would in theory raise all 1.1 billion of the world's extreme poor to the basic-needs level. Notably, this transfer could be accomplished within the 0.7 percent of the GNP target of the donor countries. That transfer would not have been possible in 1980, when the numbers of the extreme poor were larger (1.5 billion) and the incomes of the rich countries considerably smaller. Back in 1981, the total income gap was around $208 billion (again, measured in 1993 purchasing power prices) and the combined donor country GNP was $13.2 trillion. Then it would have required 1.6 percent of donor income in transfers to raise the extreme poor to the basic-needs level.

THE NEEDS ASSESSMENT APPROACH

Except for humanitarian emergencies, direct cash transfers are rarely an attractive way to deliver official development assistance (ODA). Cash transfers can raise the poor above desperate income levels, but are not likely to unlock the poverty trap if they merely fill a consumption gap. To end the poverty trap, as I have explained, direct foreign assistance should be used for *investments* in infrastructure and human capital (through public services in health, nutrition, and education), thereby empowering the poor to be more productive on their own account, and putting the poor countries on a path of self-sustaining growth.

To estimate the costs of the investments needed to end extreme poverty, a straightforward approach with six specific steps has proven extremely useful for the WHO Commission on Macroeconomics and Health and for the UN Millennium Project. The key is to identify a core package of public infrastructure and social investments to meet basic needs and to end the poverty trap. These investments include roads, power, water and sanitation, health care, education, and the like.

This approach to costing these investments has the following six steps:

- Identify the package of basic needs
- Identify, for each country, the current unmet needs of the population
- Calculate the costs of meeting the unmet needs through investments, taking into account future population growth
- Calculate the part of the investments that can be financed by the country itself
- Calculate the Millennium Development Goals Financing Gap that must be covered by donors

- Assess the size of the donor contributions relative to donor income

These calculations will show the worldwide cost of ending extreme poverty. They are not meant to suggest that money in such amounts should automatically be levied on the rich and turned over to the poor. As I have stressed repeatedly, the actual transfer of funds must be based on rigorous, country-specific plans that are developed through open and consultative processes, backed by good governance in the recipient countries, as well as careful monitoring and evaluation. For these reasons, the actual flow of resources could, alas, be much smaller than the needs assessment will show. If areas of extreme poverty remain, it would not be because of a lack of donor will, but a lack of recipient-country ability to use donor support effectively.

THE PACKAGE OF BASIC NEEDS

The WHO Commission on Macroeconomics and Health identified 49 essential health services that constitute the basic package of health interventions. The UN Millennium Project expanded that list of health interventions and complemented it with interventions in other critical areas—food production and nutrition, education, infrastructure—to enumerate some 150 interventions or public services that should be universally accessible. The standards of need are minimum standards, consistent with the interpretation that lack of access to these interventions constitutes extreme poverty. These interventions include, for example:

- Primary education for all children, with designated target ratios of pupils to teachers

- Nutrition programs for all vulnerable populations

- Universal access to antimalarial bed nets for all households in regions of malaria transmission

- Access to safe drinking water and sanitation

- One-half kilometer of paved road for every thousand of population

- Access to modern cooking fuels and improved cooking stoves to decrease indoor air pollution

In the high-income countries, these and other needs are already 100 percent fulfilled, even for the relatively poor in those societies. This underscores the point that extreme poverty (a lack of access to basic needs) is very different from the relative poverty (occupying a place at the bottom of the income distribution) within the rich countries. In the middle-income countries, these interventions are also generally available for most, if not all, of the population.

To meet these needs for an entire population requires a decade or more of investments in physical and human capital. The next step of the analysis is to estimate the proportion of the population in each country that lacks access to the relevant service, and to propose an investment profile that closes the gap within a specific period of time. The UN Millennium Project calculated an investment profile to the year 2015 of sufficient scope to achieve the Millennium Development Goals. Of course, such calculations require intensive country-specific knowledge that can only be carried out with a high degree of accuracy within each country itself, but for the UN Millennium Project, and our purposes here, we can make some rough approximations.

For five developing countries—Bangladesh, Cambodia, Ghana, Tanzania, and Uganda—the UN Millennium Project calculated the costs of scaling up infrastructure and social services by the year 2015 to have a price tag of roughly $100 per person per year during the period 2005 to 2015. (All prices in the UN study were expressed in constant 2000 U.S. dollars). Since cost data were unavailable for some critical interventions,* the true needs are likely to be at least $110 or higher. For the rich world, with its annual income of some $27,000 per person per year, and government revenues of $7,000 per person per year or more, $110 is a very small sum. For the poorest countries, however, $110 per capita is a very large sum, equal to the income per capita of Ethiopia in 2001, and one third of the average income per capita of these five developing countries. Most of the services, moreover, are to be provided by

---

*The interventions that have not yet been quantified include: higher education; storage and distribution infrastructure for water and fuel; irrigation systems; ports and railroads; information and communication technologies; and specific investments in environmental sustainability.

government. But government revenues in low-income countries are generally around 10 percent of national income. For a country at $300 per capita, therefore, domestic revenues for the national budget might total around $30 per capita, less than one third of the cost of providing the basic package of infrastructure and social services.

Once the cost of the basic package is identified, the next step is to figure out who can pay for what. To at least a small extent, households themselves can pay out of household income for some of their basic needs, for example, through purchases from private-sector providers. The government can provide a larger fraction out of domestic public revenues. The rest constitutes the "financing gap" that international donors would have to pay. To allocate these proportions of the $110 per year, the UN Millennium Project made the following assumptions. First, it assumed that government revenues directed at poverty reduction could be raised substantially as a share of GDP, specifically by 4 percentage points as of the year 2015. Second, it assumed that for certain sectors—such as health and education—the basic package would be paid entirely by the public sector (using domestic revenues or donor aid) rather than by households. Third, it assumed that households could pay for part of their energy consumption, water supply, sanitation services, and investments in agricultural productivity, but with payments graduated according to household income: the households in extreme poverty would receive the services with full subsidy, the next richer group would pay a part of the cost, and the high-income households would cover their full costs.

Sharing the Investment Costs

Using this approach, the UN Millennium Project identified the total costs of meeting the goals and the allocation of those costs among the national government, the households (paying out of pocket), and the donors. The costs differ by region for two reasons. First, the needs differ. Second, the costs of meeting those needs differ. In general, a given package of investments is slightly cheaper to implement in poor countries because the costs of labor are lower.

With these assumptions, the findings for the five developing countries were the following: Of the $110 per person per year, households will be able to pay around $10 per person per year, whereas the government could be expected to cover another $35 per person per year out of budget revenues. The remainder, roughly $65 per person per year, constitutes the financing gap, which donors will have to finance.

When the same calculation is made for middle-income countries, the situation is completely changed. Countries such as Brazil, Chile, or Mexico are able to provide the complete package of services out of domestic resources. They do not need donor assistance to end extreme poverty, since they have sufficient domestic resources to accomplish the task. Of course, they may still have many extremely poor citizens, but according to this analysis, that is mainly because of the lack of internal efforts. China, too, is largely able to cover its needs. India is just straddling the divide, requiring a significant amount of help—roughly $4 to $5 per person per year—but it is an amount that will decline over time as India's rapid economic growth continues.

As a general matter, the middle-income countries are able to cover their own needs, whereas the low-income countries generally will require at least some modest assistance from abroad to meet basic needs by 2015. Although a precise costing on a global scale really requires a detailed country-by-country assessment, some rough extrapolations from a small number of detailed country estimates allow us to approximate the global donor effort required. A rough guess puts the donor needs until 2015 at around $40 billion for sub-Saharan Africa, and perhaps twice that, or $80 billion for the entire developing world. This estimate corresponds with an even simpler route to the number. With roughly 1.1 billion people in extreme poverty, and each requiring roughly $65 per capita in annual assistance, the donor price tag would be around $72 billion per year until 2015, in addition to costs for global initiatives such as vaccine development and for managing the large increase in assistance. The actual outlay of funds, to repeat, is likely to be lower since it would cover only those countries with sufficiently good planning and governance to justify the aid.

Table 1 shows the regional breakdown of the donor assistance to finance the investments needed to meet the Millennium Development Goals. This table makes clear that Africa and Asia remain the two epicenters of extreme poverty and the two regions where large-scale donor aid is still most urgently needed. Of course, individual countries in other regions are also found to require donor aid, so a calculation of this kind needs to be made on a country-by-country basis.

Table 1: Regional Breakdown of Annual Budget Support Required from Donors to Meet the MDGs

(in billions of 2003 US$)

	in 2006	in 2015
East Asia and Pacific	11.1	8.9
Europe and Central Asia	2.0	2.9
Latin America and Caribbean	0.7	1.3
Middle East and North Africa	0.9	1.4
South Asia	22.4	36.8
Sub-Saharan Africa	36.4	83.4
Total	**73.5**	**134.7**

Source: UN Millennium Project (2005).

The sector breakdown of the external finance needed for the investment program is shown in table 2, taking the case of three sub-Saharan African countries for these detailed calculations. The table helps to clarify where the foreign assistance should be directed: some 35 percent of total assistance should go to the health sector, 35 percent to energy and road infrastructure, another 15 percent to education, 2 percent to water and sanitation; and the rest to other components of the core package.

HOW MUCH TOTAL OFFICIAL DEVELOPMENT ASSISTANCE IS NEEDED?

Even if we know that around $70 to $80 billion per year would be needed within poor countries by 2006, it is still tricky to determine the total amount of development assistance that the rich world should provide to the poor for three reasons. First, a considerable proportion of official donor assistance is not for development at all, but for other purposes such as emergency relief, care and resettlement of refugees, geopolitical support of particular governments, and help for middle-income countries that have already largely ended extreme poverty. Second, of the portion of foreign aid directed to development, only a fraction of that aid currently comes in a form that can help to finance the intervention package. Much of the aid, for example, is technical assistance, which is not counted in the Millennium Project's cost estimates. Some aid is for cancellation of debts that were not being paid

Table 2: Sector Breakdown of ODA for the MDGs in Ghana, Tanzania, and Uganda
(in 2003 US$)

Ghana

Required Total External Budget Support	Over the Full Period 2006–2015			
	Average per Year ($m)	Average per Capita ($)	Average % GDP	As % of Total Required Budget Support
Hunger	74	3.0	0.9%	5.6%
Education	266	11.0	3.2%	20.2%
Gender Equality	40	1.6	0.5%	3.0%
Health	375	15.4	4.5%	28.5%
Water Supply and Sanitation	33.1	1.4	0.4%	2.5%
Improving the Lives of Slum Dwellers	16.0	0.7	0.2%	1.2%
Energy	115	4.7	1.4%	8.7%
Roads	154	6.3	1.9%	11.7%
Other	243	10.0	2.9%	18.5%
Total*	1,317	54.1	15.9%	100.0%

Tanzania

Required Total External Budget Support	Over the Full Period 2006–2015			
	Average per Year ($m)	Average per Capita ($)	Average % GDP	As % of Total Required Budget Support
Hunger	163	3.8	1.1%	5.8%
Education	327	7.7	2.1%	11.7%
Gender Equality	70	1.6	0.5%	2.5%
Health	920	21.7	5.9%	33.0%
Water Supply and Sanitation	52.5	1.2	0.3%	1.9%
Improving the Lives of Slum Dwellers	44.3	1.0	0.3%	1.6%
Energy	201	4.7	1.3%	7.2%
Roads	586	13.8	3.8%	21.0%
Other	424	10.0	2.7%	15.2%
Total*	2,788	65.4	18.0%	100.0%

Uganda

Required Total External Budget Support	Over the Full Period 2006–2015			
	Average per Year ($m)	Average per Capita ($)	Average % GDP	As % of Total Required Budget Support
Hunger	78	2.3	0.7%	4.2%
Education	222	6.6	2.0%	12.0%

Uganda (continued)

Required Total External Budget Support	Over the Full Period 2006–2015			
	Average per Year ($m)	Average per Capita ($)	Average % GDP	As % of Total Required Budget Support
Gender Equality	50	1.5	0.4%	2.7%
Health	634	18.8	5.6%	34.2%
Water Supply and Sanitation	25.9	0.8	0.2%	1.4%
Improving the Lives of Slum Dwellers	19.8	0.6	0.2%	1.1%
Energy	90	2.7	0.8%	4.8%
Roads	394	11.7	3.5%	21.3%
Other	337	10.0	3.0%	18.2%
Total*	1,852	54.9	16.4%	100.0%

* Includes $10 per capita for large infrastructure projects, higher education, and environmental sustainability.

Source: UN Millennium Project (2004).

anyway. While debt cancellation may be very important for enabling a country to regain access to credit markets, or to regain hope, it does not add to actual resource flows if the debts could not be serviced anyway. Third, there is need for direct assistance to support investments at the global level that are above and beyond the financial needs of specific poor countries.

To clarify the first reason, consider the following breakdown of current official development assistance: total gross foreign aid from all donors to all developing countries in 2002 was $76 billion (all numbers in 2003 dollars). Of that, $6 billion were debt relief grants, which do not correspond to any actual flow of resources. Moreover, developing countries paid close to $11 billion in loan repayments to rich countries, leaving a net flow of foreign aid of $59 billion. Of that amount, $16 billion went to middle-income countries Of the $43 billion that went to low-income countries, $12 billion at the most were devoted to direct support of the government. The remainder consisted mostly of emergency assistance and technical cooperation, which mostly pays for expensive foreign consultants rather than local experts.

Roughly speaking, only $12 billion out of the $43 billion went to low-income countries in a form that could be deemed budgetary support, and thus helped support the package of basic needs interventions. For all developing countries, only around $15 billion of the $48 billion in net ODA flows in 2002 could be considered to be the kind of support for financing investments in basic needs. The remaining $33 billion reflects other considerations and costs that are not available for making the investments I have been discussing. Some go to emergency relief and technical cooperation that funds in parts the building of capacity. Other important needs are regional infrastructure and global research, which currently receive roughly $4 billion. Finally, the operating and other cost of bilateral and multilateral agencies account for $9 billion.

In addition to the $73 billion (rising to $135 billion per year in 2015) for the scaling up of basic needs at the country level, $48 to $54 billion will be required each year to finance other needs. These include the costs of running the aid agencies themselves, in essence, the costs for operating an international system of donor assistance. The UN Millennium Project estimated an additional $2 to $5 billion per year in such costs to increase technical assistance capacity of international and donor organizations plus an additional $1 to $3 billion in increased costs to bilateral donors. The added expenses reflect the increased operational responsibilities of the specialized UN agencies, the IMF and World Bank, the regional development banks, and the bilateral donors. There are also the costs of greater investments in global science directed at the needs of the poor, on the order of an estimated $7 billion per year by 2015.

If we put the pieces together and make further adjustments for poorly governed countries that won't qualify for aid and for rechanneling some existing aid, total global foreign aid would amount to something like what is shown in table 3. Net ODA flows in 2006 come to $135 billion per year (up from $65 billion) and increase gradually to $195 billion by 2015. Clearly, there is not a high degree of precision in these estimates. The exact costs of meeting the Millennium Development Goals cannot be determined until each country conducts its own detailed costing following the Millennium Project methodology. Still, the estimates show one compelling fact. The bottom line of about $135 to $195 billion per year for the period 2005 to 2015 is about .44 to .54 percent of the rich-world GNP each year during the forthcoming decade, significantly less than the 0.7 percent of GNP promised in ODA, which would be closer to an average of $235 billion per year (in constant 2003 dollars). *The point is that the Millennium Development Goals can be financed within the bounds of the official development assistance that the donor countries have already promised.*

Table 3: Estimated Cost of Meeting the MDGs in Every Country

(in billions of 2003 US$)	2002	2006	2010	2015
I. MDG Investment Needs in Low-Income Countries				
• MDG Financing Gap	12	73	89	135
• Capacity Building to Achieve the MDGs	5	7	7	7
• Grants in Support of Heavy Debt Burden	–	7	6	1
• Debt Relief to Poor Countries	4	6	6	6
Minus: Repayments of Concessional Loans	–5	0	0	0
Subtotal	*15*	*94*	*108*	*149*
II. MDG Investment Needs in Middle-Income Countries				
• ODA Provided Directly to Government	4	10	10	10
• Capacity Building to Achieve the MDGs	5	5	5	5
Minus: Repayments of Concessional Loans	–6	–3	–4	–6
Subtotal	*3*	*12*	*11*	*9*
III. MDG Investment Needs at the International Level				
• Regional Cooperation and Infrastructure	2	3	7	11
• Funding for Global Research	1	5	7	7
• Implementing the Rio Conventions	1	2	3	5
• Technical Cooperation by International Organizations	5	5	7	8
Subtotal	*10*	*15*	*23*	*31*
Estimated Cost of Meeting the MDGS in Every Country	**28**	121	143	189

Plausible ODA Needs to Meet the MDGs				
(in billions of 2003 US$)	**2002**	**2006**	**2010**	**2015**
Baseline ODA for the MDGs in 2002	27	27	27	27
+ Incremental MDG Investment Needs		94	115	161
– Adjustment for Nonqualifying Countries Due to Inadequate Governance		–21	–23	–25
– Reprogramming of Existing ODA		–6	–7	–9
+ Emergency and Distress Relief	4	4	5	6
+ Other ODA*	34	36	34	35
Total Indicative Net ODA Needs for the MDGs†	**65**	135	152	195
as % of OECD-DAC Countries' GNI	*0.23%*	*0.44%*	*0.46%*	*0.54%*
ODA to Least-Developed Countreis (as % of OECD-DAC Countries' GNI)	*0.06%*	*0.12%*	*0.15%*	*0.22%*
Absolute Increase in Net ODA Required (compared to 2002)		70	87	130
Difference Between Total Net ODA Needs and Existing Commitments		48	50	**74**

* Includes ODA that does not contribute directly to the MDGs and operating expenditures of donor agencies.

† This estimate does not include several important ODA needs, such as responding to crises of geopolitical importance, such as Afghanistan or Iraq; mitigating the impact of climate change; protecting biodiversity and conserving global fisheries; and so forth.

Source: UN Millennium Project (2005).

Assuming that high-income countries will meet the specific commitments they have already made to increasing aid, gross ODA volumes will need to rise by approximately $48 billion in 2006 *beyond* the level of existing commitments in order to meet the MDGs. I hasten to add that the donor countries should not plan to land short of their 0.7 percent commitment. Table 3's $195 billion estimate of net ODA flows in 2015 leaves out one potentially large expense: help for the poorest countries to adapt to long-term climate change that is under way and caused, in significant part, by the rich countries. With rising temperatures and ocean levels, changes in precipitation patterns, and an increasing frequency of extreme weather events, some highly populous parts of the developing world will require substantial assistance adjusting to climate change. Other kinds of ODA needs not yet foreseen will likely arise as well.

HOW THIS NEEDS ASSESSMENT COMPARES WITH OTHERS

The UN Millennium Project is not alone in estimating the need for a doubling of ODA. Many estimates in recent years have converged around a similar level. In 2001, in the lead-up to the Monterrey Summit, a high-level commission chaired by former Mexican president Ernesto Zedillo estimated $50 billion per year, or a doubling of then-current official development assistance. The World Bank, using a very simplified methodology in the same year, also forecasted incremental aid needs at around $50 billion per year. In September 2003, the World Bank noted that low-income countries could immediately absorb some $30 billion per year of additional aid, given their absorptive capacity at the time, the concept we visited last chapter. In 2004, leaders of the UK and France called for a significant increase of foreign aid to achieve the Millennium Development Goals, roughly a doubling of ODA from 0.25 percent of donor GNP to around 0.5 percent of donor GNP. UK Chancellor Gordon Brown in particular has shown great leadership in proposing ways to coordinate such an increase among the donor countries.

WHICH DONORS SHOULD PAY?

Let's examine the implications of expanded aid on a country-by-country basis. Suppose that foreign assistance for *all* purposes will have to rise to 0.5 percent of donor income during the period 2005 to 2015, roughly $140 billion per year at today's GNP. To give a sense of what that would imply for each donor country, figure 1 shows the change in net foreign aid from today's level, assuming each donor in the Development Assistance Committee moves this year to 0.5 percent of GNP. For the G-0.7 (the countries already at foreign assistance or above 0.7 percent of GNP), this would mean a drop in funding (certainly not recommended!).

For the rest, it would mean a significant increase. The key point is that a few big countries would account for 90 percent of the increase. Of the total $75 billion or so rise in foreign aid (in 2003 dollars), 51 percent (roughly $38 billion) would be due from the United States. Japan would account for 18 percent (roughly $13 billion), and Germany, France, Italy, and the UK would account for 20 percent (roughly $15 billion).

Figure 1: Additional ODA Required to Reach 0.5% of GDP

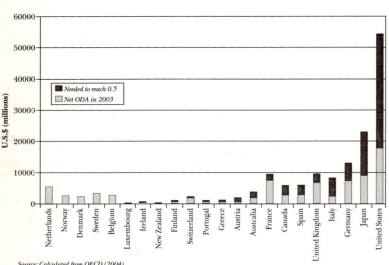

Source: Calculated from OECD (2004).

The United States is the largest missing element in financing the Millennium Goals, almost half of the total foreign assistance shortfall.

The U.S. government has argued recently that development assistance from private U.S. citizens and the nonprofit sector (faith-based organizations, philanthropies, foundations, NGOs) makes up for much of the shortfall in official aid. The evidence at hand does not bear this out. The Development Assistance Committee of the OECD has compiled cross-country data on nongovernmental development assistance. The estimate for the United States is about $3 billion per year, an amount that raises the total U.S. development assistance from 0.15 percent of GNP to 0.18 percent of GNP, still leaving the United States at the very bottom of the donor list. The U.S. government also tried to argue, incredibly, that remittances of foreign workers in the United States back to their home country should somehow count as a form of aid. This is ridiculous. The remittances are the returns for work. They are no more a form of aid than are the remittances of U.S. profits from Mexico a form of aid from Mexico to the United States.

THE COSTS AFTER 2015

These calculations calibrate the needs through 2015 in order to achieve the Millennium Development Goals. The needs after 2015 would fall, quite significantly in many cases, and surely as a share of donor GNP. The reasons are straightforward, even if the post-2015 foreign aid needs cannot be calculated with any precision. By 2015, most of the developing world will have been freed from the poverty trap onto a path of self-sustaining growth. These countries will therefore "graduate" from the need for ODA to cofinance investments in basic needs. Extreme poverty will have been eliminated from China, and will encompass less than 20 percent of the population in India. In sub-Saharan Africa, the rate of extreme poverty will have declined from around 40 percent of the population today to under 20 percent.

Many of the key infrastructure investments will have been made, with massive improvements in roads, power grids, telecommunications, seaports, and airports. The extent of new investments needed to eliminate the remaining poverty will be much less than during the Millennium Development Goals phase. Although many public investments will still be needed, the key thresholds to operate infrastructure networks should already have been met.

As the rich countries continue to get richer, the share of the extreme poor in the world population continues to decline, and the income of poor countries rises so that they can cover more of their own needs, there will gradually be a declining need for foreign assistance. In the Millennium Project's calculation, the ODA needed to meet the Millennium Development Goals will be 0.5 percent of donor income in 2015. It will fall further in the following decade, and will therefore remain below the key political threshold of 0.7 percent during the entire period between 2005 and 2025.

CAN THE UNITED STATES AFFORD 0.7 PERCENT OF GNP?

The question is silly on its face. Can the United States manage an aid target that five other donor countries have already achieved, six more have scheduled, and all donors—including the United States—have promised "concrete efforts" to achieve? Of course it can, especially since I am speaking of much less than 1 percent of income. Think of it. To go from today's donor assistance level of 0.15 percent of GNP to 0.7 percent of GNP would be an extra tax of 0.55 percent of GNP. With U.S. per capita GNP rising by around 1.9 percent per year, the extra amount represents less than one third of a single year's growth of GNP. So, if the United States were on track to reach a $40,000 disposable income by, say, January 1, 2010, it would instead reach the same income on May 1, 2010, one third of a year later. This four-month lag in attaining a higher level of consumption would mean that a billion people would be given an economic future of hope, health, and improvement rather than a downward spiral of despair, disease, and decline.

People would hardly be weighed down by an extra 0.55 percent of income collected in taxes. But to make the increase in ODA truly imperceptible for the vast majority of Americans, the richest of the rich in the United States should be asked to pay their fair share to help the poorest of the poor in the world. Most of the world, including most Americans, does not appreciate how rich the superrich have become, and how disproportionately they have benefited from the economic and tax changes of the past two decades. The vast incomes of the superrich hit home for me a couple of years ago in the months preceding President Bush's 2003 trip to Africa.

Some months before the trip, the Internal Revenue Service issued a special report on the richest taxpayers of the year 2000. It turned out that the top four hundred taxpayers had a combined income of $69 billion dollars, or $174 million dollars per taxpayer. As President Bush prepared to visit Africa, I made a back-of-the-envelope calculation, shown in table 4, to confirm that the four hundred richest U.S. taxpayers had a combined income in 2000 that exceeded the combined incomes of four of the countries on Mr. Bush's tropical tour. The difference was astounding: the $57 billion in combined income of Botswana, Nigeria, Senegal, and Uganda in 2000 was the income of 161 million people, who average $350 in income per year, whereas the $69 billion was the income of four hundred individuals.

Table 4: Highest-Income Americans and African GDP

	Income in 2000	Population in 2000
	(GDP, in billions of current US$)	
Botswana	5	1,675,000
Nigeria	42	126,910,000
Senegal	4	9,530,000
Uganda	6	23,250,000
Total	57	161,365,000
400 Highest-Income Americans	**69**	**400**

Source: Internal Revenue Service (2003); World Bank (2004).

The IRS reported that the superrich had enjoyed a sizable reduction in their tax payments as a percent of their incomes during the 1990s, but the best was yet to come. Three tax cuts from the Bush administration in 2001, 2002, and 2003 vitiated much of the progressivity of the tax code. The tax reform package signed into law scheduled the phase out of the estate tax, dropped the top tax bracket, and cut rates on dividends and capital gains. Together these changes enabled rich U.S. taxpayers with annual incomes above $200,000 to reap 37 percent of the total tax cut with an average $19,000 in annual tax savings. Since the total tax cut was on the order of $220 billion per year, the tax savings of the households above $500,000 per year, equal to 22.7 percent of the total tax savings, amounted to around $50 billion per year, more than enough for the United States to pay its share of the MDG needs! The details on the tax cut are shown in table 5.

Table 5: Tax Savings by Household Income in the Bush Administration Tax Cuts

	Number of Tax-Paying Households (thousands)	Percent of Total Households	Tax Savings per Household ($)	Total Tax Savings in the Income Category ($ billion)	Percent of Total Tax Savings
Bottom 80 Percent					
Incomes less than $75,000	114,151	79.5	533	60.87	28
Top 20 Percent	**28,799**	**20**	**5,610**	**156.66**	**72**
of which: (income in '000s)					
Incomes between $75–100	11,395	7.9	2,224	25.34	11.6
Incomes between $100–200	13,281	9.3	3,905	51.86	23.8
Incomes between $200–500	3,339	2.3	9,012	30.09	13.8
Incomes between $500–1,000	527	0.4	27,150	14.31	6.6
More than $1,000	257	0.2	136,398	35.05	16.1
All	143,509	100	1,520	218.13	100

Source: Calculated using data from Gale, William G., Peter Orszag, and Isaac Shapiro. "Distributional Effects of the 2001 and 2003 Tax Cuts and Their Financing," Tax Policy Center. Available at: http://www.taxpolicycenter.org/publications/template.cfm?PubID=8888.

One of the stunning, and politically surprising, aspects of the Bush tax cuts is that they came after a generation in which the shift in income distribution had been immensely favorable to the superrich. The share of income of the top 1 percent of U.S. taxpayers soared from 8.2 percent in 1980 to 14.6 percent in 1998 (signifying, of course, that the income of the top 1 percent was 14.6 times the average income). The reason for this dramatic shift toward the rich is not really known. The surprise is that the political system amplified the shift through tax cuts that favored the rich, instead of offsetting these shifts through greater progressivity of the tax system and income transfers toward the poor.

Achieving 0.7 percent of GNP in official development assistance in the United States would hardly be a stretch. On the spending side of the budget, the United States spent as much in Iraq for two weeks of support for the war (about $2.5 billion) as it does for an entire year of economic development assistance in Africa. In its first two years, the Iraq war cost about $60 billion per year, roughly the same increment needed to reach 0.7 percent of GNP. The overall rise in military spending has been on the order of $150 billion per year, comparing fiscal year 2001 as President Bush came into office and fiscal year 2005, an increase of 1.5 percent of GNP.

Having made little headway with the Bush administration in advocating the promised concrete efforts toward 0.7 percent, I used the occasion of the Bush trip to Africa to appeal directly to the richest Americans for their personal contributions. Writing in *The New York Times,* I suggested that the superrich could apply their tax savings in recent years to the Global Fund to Fight AIDS, TB, and Malaria. "For individuals who already have all the earthly possessions that can possibly be amassed," I wrote, "could there be a better way to give meaning to vast wealth?"

The top four hundred richest taxpayers, I suggested, could give 10 percent of their 2000 income, or $6.9 billion. This would be enough to save millions of lives per year, for example, through the comprehensive control of malaria in Africa. Casting the net more widely, the top 0.1 percent of taxpayers, roughly one hundred thousand in all, could in effect return their tax cuts in the form of personal giving, for a sum of around $30 billion per year. I noted in the op-ed that Bill Gates had, in effect, already done his part, with a stunning gift of $23 billion (which has since been augmented) to establish the Bill and Melinda Gates Foundation. The Gates Foundation spends around 70 percent of its annual outlays on fighting disease in poor countries, and is making history in the process. Other extraordinarily generous philanthropists—among them George Soros, Rob Glaser, Gordon Moore, and Ed Scott—have acted similarly.

This is a noble start, but not yet the groundswell that the world needs. Real solutions will no doubt require a balance of philanthropy and taxation. A practical proposal would be the following:

A 5 percent income tax surcharge on incomes above $200,000 directed toward the U.S. contribution to end global poverty, which in 2004 would yield around $40 billion. That surcharge could be paid as a tax to support U.S. gov-

ernment efforts, or it could be directed by the taxpayer to a qualifying charity or philanthropy that has registered programs in support of the Millennium Development Goals.

There are powerful reasons to take these steps, both out of enlightened self-interest of the rich nations and out of a deeper human need at the individual level. We will look at both of those powerful reasons in a later chapter.

Sixteen

MYTHS AND
MAGIC BULLETS

Everything up to this point is fine and good, except for one matter: it ignores the human factor. Take the case of Africa. Africa needs around $30 billion per year in aid in order to escape from poverty. But if we actually gave that aid, where would it go? Right down the drain if the past is any guide. Sad to say, Africa's education levels are so low that even programs that work elsewhere would fail in Africa. Africa is corrupt and riddled with authoritarianism. It lacks modern values and the institutions of a free market economy needed to achieve success. In fact, Africa's morals are so broken down that it is no surprise AIDS has run out of control. And here is the bleakest truth: Suppose that our aid saved Africa's children. What then? There would be a population explosion, and a lot more hungry adults. We would have solved nothing.

If your head was just nodding yes, please read this chapter with special care. The paragraph above repeats conventional rich-world wisdom about Africa, and to a lesser extent, other poor regions. While common, these assertions are incorrect. Yet they have been repeated publicly for so long, or whispered in private, that they have become accepted as truths by the broad public as well as much of the development community, particularly by people who have never worked in Africa. I use the case of Africa because prejudices against Africa currently run so high, but the same attitudes were expressed about other parts of the world before those places achieved economic development and cultural prejudices could not hold up. Napoleon famously declared, "History is a fable often told." The same can be said about much of development thinking.

MONEY DOWN THE DRAIN

Former U.S. Secretary of the Treasury Paul O'Neill expressed a common frustration when he remarked about aid for Africa: "We've spent trillions of dollars on these problems and we have damn near nothing to show for it." O'Neill was no foe of foreign aid. Indeed, he wanted to fix the system so that more U.S. aid could be justified. But he was wrong to believe that vast flows of aid to Africa had been squandered. It is no surprise that there is so little to show for the aid to Africa, because there has in fact been so little aid to Africa!

Contrary to popular perception, the amount of aid per African per year is really very small, just $30 per sub-Saharan African in 2002 from the entire world. Of that modest amount, almost $5 was actually for consultants from the donor countries, more than $3 was for food aid and other emergency aid, another $4 went to servicing Africa's debts, and $5 was for debt relief operations. The rest, $12, went to Africa. Is it really a surprise that we do not see many traces of that aid on the ground? If we want to see the impact of aid, we had better offer enough to produce results.

Since the "money down the drain" argument is heard most frequently in the United States, it is worth looking at the same calculations for U.S. aid alone. In 2002, the United States gave $3 per sub-Saharan African. Taking out the parts for U.S. consultants, food and other emergency aid, administrative costs, and debt relief, the aid per African came to the grand total of six cents. It's hardly shocking that Secretary O'Neill could find "nothing to show for it."

AID PROGRAMS WOULD FAIL IN AFRICA

Pessimism about Africans' ability to utilize aid is very deep, reflecting an amazing reservoir of deep prejudices. I have heard those prejudices for years and have come to expect them, always with sadness. Still, nothing prepared me for the amazing statements made by the new administrator of USAID, Andrew Natsios, a month after he took office in 2001. I had gone to Washington in the early weeks of the Bush administration to try to interest senior officials in a greatly expanded effort against AIDS in the developing world, especially Africa. I was propounding the idea, still highly controversial at the time, that antiretroviral treatment could be introduced effectively into a low-income setting. An enterprising *Boston Globe* reporter asked Mr. Natsios about these ideas. His answer stunned me.

Africans, he said, "don't know what Western time is. You have to take these [anti-AIDS] drugs a certain number of hours each day, or they don't work. Many people in Africa have never seen a clock or a watch their entire lives. And if you say, one o'clock in the afternoon, they do not know what you are talking about. They know morning, they know noon, they know evening, they know the darkness of night." He continued, "I'm sorry to say these things, but a lot of people like Jeffrey Sachs advocating these things [anti-AIDS drug treatment] have never worked in health care in rural areas in Africa or even in the cities."

This statement was extraordinary. The people of Sauri, Kenya, who arrived punctually at 2:30 P.M. for our Monday afternoon discussion, would have been chagrined to know how their lives had been compromised by such profound ignorance of a senior U.S. official. Not only did they know the time, they knew the nature of their predicament, whether it was the absence of anti-AIDS drugs or antimalarial bed nets, or fertilizers, or mobile phones. My colleagues and I battle these anti-African and antipoor attitudes regularly, even if they are rarely expressed in the unguarded terms that Andrew Natsios used. An argument on behalf of Africa must scale a sheer mountain of doubt before finding acceptance.

Corruption Is the Culprit

In the past, the overwhelming prejudices against Africa have been grounded in overt racism. Today the ever repeated assertion is that corruption—or "poor governance"—is Africa's venal sin, the deepest source of its current malaise. Both Africans themselves and outsiders level this charge. A senior human rights official of South Africa, speaking in full sincerity, stated the common view that "[poverty] is man made because poverty is the result of policy options that have been taken that impoverish some and enrich others. Inasmuch as poverty is man made, so also do I believe that poverty can be eradicated." Almost any account of African poverty these days begins with the same assertion: poor governance is the major stumbling block.

By almost any standard, Africa's quality of governance is low. Property rights are difficult to enforce, violence and crime are high, corruption is perceived to be extensive. Although there is an undoubted basis for putting an emphasis on improved governance, the focus on corruption and governance is exaggerated, and seriously overstates the causal role of corruption and poor governance in Africa's laggard growth performance. The point is that virtually all poor countries have governance and corruption indicators that are below those of the high-income countries. Governance and higher incomes go hand in hand not only because good governance raises incomes, but also, and perhaps even more important, because higher income leads to improved governance.

As a country's income rises, governance improves for two major reasons. First, a more literate and affluent society is better able to keep the government honest by playing a watchdog role over government processes. Newspapers, television, books, telephones, transport, and now the Internet, all of which are vastly more available in rich countries, enhance this watchdog function and empower civil society. Second, a more affluent society can afford to invest in high-quality governance. When governments are backed by ample tax receipts, the civil service is better educated, extensive computerization improves information flows, and the public administration is professionally managed.

Africa's governance is poor because Africa is poor. Crucially, however, two other things are also true. At any given level of governance (as measured by standard indicators), African countries tend to grow less rapidly than similarly governed countries in other parts of the world. There is distinctly slower growth in Africa even after controlling for the quality of governance. Something else is afoot; as I have argued at length, the slower growth is best explained by geographical and ecological factors. Second, Africa shows absolutely no tendency to be more or less corrupt than other countries at the same income level. There is no evidence whatsoever that Africa is distinctly poorly governed *by the standards of very poor countries.*

There is an easy way to check both claims. First, we can examine Africa's governance measures once we have controlled statistically for income levels. It turns out that some African countries are better than expected given their income; others are average, and some others are indeed worse. On average, however, Africa's governance is typical for countries at the same level of income. The ranking of performers is shown in table 1, taken from a study that my colleagues and I recently published. We see that Africa's well-governed countries (whose governance scores are relatively high given the country's income level) include: Benin, Burkina Faso, Ghana, Madagascar, Malawi, Mali, Mauritania, and Senegal. The poorly governed countries (whose governance scores are relatively low given the country's income level) include: Angola, Burundi, Democratic Republic of the Congo, Sudan, and Zimbabwe.

Table 1: Governance Ratings and Household Consumption in Tropical Sub-Saharan Africa

Country	Rating Based on World Bank Governance Indicators, 2002*	Rating Based in Transparency International Index, 2003*	Freedom House Rating, 2003	Household Final Consumption Expenditure per Capita, 2000 (1980 = 100)
Benin	Good	NA†	Free	98.9
Burkina Faso	Good	NA†	Partly Free	111
Ghana	Good	Average	Free	92.8
Madagascar	Good	Good	Partly Free	64
Malawi	Good	Good	Partly Free	111.2
Mali	Good	Good	Free	95.3
Mauritania	Good	Good	Partly Free	104.8
Senegal	Good	Good	Free	99.6
Cameroon	Average	Average	Not Free	102.5
Central African Republic	Average	NA	Partly Free	NA
Chad	Average	NA	Not Free	NA
Congo, Rep.	Average	Average	NA	80.5
Côte d'Ivoire	Average	Average	Not Free	78.2
Eritrea	Average	NA	Not Free	NA
Ethiopia	Average	Good	Partly Free	NA
Guinea	Average	NA	Not Free	NA
Kenya	Average	Average	Partly Free	100.7
Mozambique	Average	Good	Partly Free	79.4
Niger	Average	NA	Partly Free	NA
Nigeria	Average	Average	Partly Free	NA
Rwanda	Average	NA	Not Free	83.9

Sierra Leone	Average	Good	Partly Free	43.9
Tanzania	Average	Good	Partly Free	NA
Togo	Average	NA	Not Free	112.4
Uganda	Average	Average	Partly Free	NA
Zambia	Average	Good	Partly Free	47
Angola	Poor	Poor	Not Free	NA
Burundi	Poor	NA	Not Free	65
Congo, Dem. Rep.	Poor	NA	Not Free	45.1
Sudan	Poor	Average	Not Free	NA
Zimbabwe	Poor	Average	Not Free	88.4
Liberia	NA	NA	Not Free	NA
Somalia	NA	NA	Not Free	NA

* *Determined from the residuals of a regression of countries' governance indicators or scores on income per capita (at purchasing power parity); countries with residuals more than 1 standard deviation above or 1 standard deviation below the predicted value are categorized as "good" or "poor," respectively, and those with residuals within 1 standard deviation as "average."*

† *NA=not available.*

Source: Sachs et al. (2004).

Comparing growth rates and the quality of governance, we find that better governed countries grew faster, but the relationship is not all that strong. There is a tendency for countries with low governance scores to grow less rapidly than countries with high governance scores, but there is a huge range of growth outcomes even among well-governed countries or poorly governed countries. The problem for Africa, however, is that African countries on average grow less rapidly than other developing countries at the same level of income and the same quality of governance, but in different parts of the world. To test this proposition, I have estimated the relationship between economic growth during 1980 to 2000 and the quality of governance during that period, using a large sample of developing countries. The statistical test also took into account the initial income of each country in 1980. The idea was to check whether African countries grew faster or slower than other developing countries once we had taken into account the quality of governance and initial incomes. The results are clear: African countries on average grew around 3 percentage points less rapidly than other developing countries at the same levels of governance and income. This slower growth is caused, in my opinion, mainly by Africa's adverse geography and deficient infrastructure.

A Democracy Deficit

Another charge leveled against Africa and other poor regions is the absence of democracy. As with corruption, we need to "unpack" the evidence step by step. It is true that after achieving independence, most African countries fell into an authoritarian mold, as did most poor and newly independent countries around the world. In southern Africa, white minorities in South Africa and Rhodesia imposed authoritarian regimes on majority African populations. By the early 1990s, however, a little-heralded democratic revolution was sweeping the continent. One by one the long-ruling (and often highly corrupt and incompetent) founding generation gave way to multiparty elections. By 2003, Freedom House had categorized eleven African countries as "free," twenty as "partly free," and sixteen as "unfree." Africa's share of free and partly free countries, 66 percent, actually stands above the average for non-African low-income countries in 2003, 57 percent (thirteen countries out of twenty-three non-African low-income countries ranked by Freedom House).

Democratization, alas, does not reliably translate into faster economic growth, at least in the short term. The links from democracy to economic performance are relatively weak, even though democracy is surely a boon for human rights and a barrier against large-scale killing, torture, and other abuses by the state. The point is not that Africa will soar economically now that it is democratizing, but rather that the charge of authoritarian rule as a basic obstacle to good governance in Africa is passé.

Lack of Modern Values

Many people take for granted that poverty and wealth are simply a reflection of societal values. One recent study attributed African poverty to a dislike of work, suppression of individualism, and irrationality; another study identified the main obstacles to Mexican American upward mobility to be "resignation of the poor [to poverty]," "low priority of education," "fatalism," and "mistrust of those outside the family." The idea that whole societies are condemned to poverty because of their values has a long history, but one that is seldom useful.

Virtually every society that was once poor has been castigated for being lazy and unworthy until its citizens became rich, at which point their new wealth was "explained" by their industriousness. Japan is a case a point, a society that was viewed as doomed to poverty when foreigners first arrived in the 1870s. The foreign press in Japan, such as the *Japan Gazette,* cautioned that Japan would never be rich because of the indolence of the society: "Wealthy we do not think it [that is, Japan] will ever become: the advantages conferred by Nature, with the exception of the climate, and the love of indolence and pleasure of the people themselves forbid it." Indeed, the same newspaper opined that economic reforms were bound to fail because of the deep corruption found in Japanese society: "The national banking system of Japan is but another example of the futility of trying to transfer Western growth to an Oriental habitat. In this part of the world principles, established and recognized in the West, appear to lose whatever virtue and vitality they originally possessed and to tend fatally towards weediness and corruption."

Early in the twentieth century, sociological theories in the tradition of Max Weber tried to explain the lower incomes of Southern Europe and Ireland relative to Northern Europe on the basis of supposedly static values of Catholicism versus entrepreneurial values of Protestantism. After midcentury, the Catholic countries began to grow very rapidly, especially after malaria was controlled. By now, Catholic Italy and Ireland have overtaken the Protestant UK in per capita income. Similarly, Weber and his followers hypothesized that East Asian societies with Confucian values, notably China, would be unable to achieve economic progress. Later, when China and other countries of East Asia began to grow rapidly, "Asian values" were invoked as the explanation for success, turning the argument on its head. When Asia had a temporary economic crisis in 1997, Asian values were once again attacked as the culprit, but this interpretation quickly faded when economic recovery came a couple of years later. India's poverty was explained on the basis of Hindu social rigidities and mysticism, until of course, India became one of the fastest growing economies in the world in the 1990s.

In the wake of September 11, Islamic societies have been categorized by some Western observers to be unfit for modernity. The charges of cultural failure are legion: irrationality, fundamentalism, extreme bias against women, antipathy to science. Yet some of the fastest growing economies in the world in the past decade have been Islamic. Between 1990 and 2001, average annual per capita growth in Malaysia was 3.9 percent; in Bangladesh, 3.1 percent; Tunisia, 3.1 percent; and Indonesia, 2.3 percent. These countries also made great strides in equality of girls' education and literacy.

Culture-based predictions of social change are fragile and often incorrect even in the most culture-bound areas of human behavior, such as fertility choice. Consider the Iranian revolution, which by standard arguments should have led to massive discrimination against girls and women and a delay in the demographic transition to low fertility rates. Instead, since the revolution, Iran has achieved one of the world's fastest transitions to low fertility, with its total fertility rate falling from 6.6 in 1980 to 1985 to 2.5 in 1995 to 2000. This achievement was the result, in part, of a tremendous increase in girls' participation in school and in female literacy. One interpretation is that religiously conservative fathers had more confidence in sending their daughters to school after the revolution. Iran was not alone in the education and demographic transitions. Islamic countries such as Egypt, Jordan, Morocco, and Tunisia have all experienced tremendous increases in girls' schooling and significant declines in total fertility rates.

Cultural arguments hold two main problems. Most important, cultures change with economic times and circumstances. The role of women in the labor market, household fertility choices, school attendance of children, and other critical areas of economic behavior change dramatically as societies shift from villages to urban centers, farming to industry, and illiteracy to literacy. What look like immutable social values turn out to be highly malleable to economic circumstances and opportunities. Although not all cultural values change so easily, values deemed to be inimical to economic development are rarely, if ever, unalterable features of a society.

The second main problem with cultural interpretations is that they are usually made on the basis of prejudice rather than measurable evidence. The arguments tend to be circular. People are poor because they are lazy. How do we "know" they are lazy? Because they are poor. Promoters of these interpretations rarely understand that low productivity results not from laziness and lack of effort but from lack of capital inputs to production. African farmers are not lazy, but they do lack soil nutrients, tractors, feeder roads, irrigated plots, storage facilities, and the like. Stereotypes that Africans work little and therefore are poor are put to rest immediately by spending a day in a village, where backbreaking labor by men and women is the norm.

When social scientists try to measure cultural attitudes related to work, child rearing, and education, stereotypes tend to collapse. In the World Values Survey, households around the world are asked the same questions in order to permit serious comparisons of cultures and values. The answers are eye-opening. When asked in 2000, for example, whether it is especially important for children to be encouraged at home to learn "hard work," 61 percent of Americans said yes, whereas 80 percent of Nigerians, 75 percent of South Africans, and 83 percent of Tanzanians responded affirmatively. This answer and others hardly demonstrated social values of laziness in Africa and other poor countries.

THE NEED FOR ECONOMIC FREEDOM

If good governance has become the dominant mantra of those looking for instant solutions to development problems, its closest rival is surely economic freedom. Once again, a basically correct insight—that market economies outperform centrally planned economies—has been taken to the extreme, and then used as a substitute for analysis. When communism fell and free-market reforms swept Eastern Europe, the former Soviet Union, and China, free markets were hailed as the victor in the long-running battle between markets and state planning. So far, so good. But free-market ideologues took the argument to extremes that are utterly unsupportable by evidence or good economic reasoning. First, they maintained that markets should rule every nook and cranny of the economy, not just the basic productive sectors of farms, factories, and service trades, but also health, education, social security, and core infrastructure like water, energy transmission, roads, and rail. Second, they argued that all shortfalls in growth can be accounted for by the absence of free markets. Aid, they posited, becomes superfluous, even dangerous (as a delay to market reforms). All that is needed is the will to liberalize and privatize!

The Heritage Foundation and *Wall Street Journal,* which joined forces to produce the *Index of Economic Freedom,* put it this way:

> [A]chieving economic freedom is like building a car. What is the most important component of the car: the powerful engine, the transmission, the seats, the steering wheel, the brakes, or the tires?

The question defies an answer, because without any one of these components, the car is unlikely to reach the desired destination. In similar fashion, ignore any one of the 10 factors of economic freedom, and abundant prosperity is likely to remain elusive. For that reason, we often refer to the 10 factors of the *Index* as a "10-step plan to end dependency." The 10 factors provide a road map, and only by sticking to the highlighted route can a country achieve economic freedom, prosperity, and self-sufficiency.

In fact, countries moving down the road map toward economic freedom have higher growth rates. As long as they keep progressing along the road map, their growth rate tends to be above the average for all countries. The faster they move (the greater the improvement in score), the higher the growth rate. Once countries decide to stop by the roadside or to retrace their steps, growth plummets. So the important message to the countries of the world is that they can help themselves just by starting to adopt economic freedom. The more economic freedom they adopt, the faster they grow or the longer they have superior growth. More growth in turn means that the average level of prosperity is increasing.

Here again is magical thinking. Economic development is like moving down a road: only one direction to travel, and the only question one of speed. The more economic freedom, as measured by a ten-part index, the faster the progress down the road. Any deviation from the straight and narrow, and growth collapses.

The prescription has the virtue of simplicity, and as philosopher Karl Popper would say, falsifiability. In other words, the proposition can be tested. Here is how. Let us look at the countries in the Heritage Foundation/Wall Street Journal index, and ask whether the central claim is merited. Does the index explain the rate of growth of the countries, so that those with high scores (meaning bad governance in the case of this index) see their growth rates "plummet"? Figure 1 shows the average value of the *Index of Economic Freedom* during 1995 to 2003 on the horizontal axis and the annual growth of per capita GDP during 1995 to 2003 on the vertical axis. A "line of best fit" shows the relationship between the index score and economic growth. If better governance translated directly into faster growth, then as one moves to the right of the graph we would see countries growing faster. This is clearly not the case.

Figure 1: Growth and Governance

Index has been recalibrated so that higher values refer to better governance.
Source: Heritage/WSJ (2004); calculations from World Bank (2004).

Indeed, scoring well in the *Index of Economic Freedom* is not a ten-step plan to Nirvana, nor a very powerful explanation of differences in economic growth rates. There are many cases where the score on economic freedom is rather low, but economic growth is rather high, China being the notable case. On the other hand, there are many cases where the score on economic freedom is good, and yet economic growth is low, like Switzerland or Uruguay.

As for Africa, the same situation occurs as with governance. Africa grows less rapidly than would be explained by its score on economic freedom, indeed markedly so. As mentioned before, a formal statistical test of that proposition shows that African countries grew less rapidly than others at the same level of economic freedom, by about 3 percentage points per year. Once again, the factors of geography, disease, and levels of infrastructure, among others, none of which are captured in the "10-step plan" to prosperity, were taken into account. Economic freedom is definitely a plus for economic development, but alas, it is no magic bullet.

A Single "Mystery of Capital"?

Hernando de Soto, a Peruvian economist, has promoted and popularized one variant of the theme of economic freedom. De Soto argues that the security of private property, including the ability to borrow against land, represents the true "mystery of capital." The poor in most of the developing world hold their assets, such as housing and land, he says,

> . . . in defective forms: houses built on land whose ownership rights are not adequately recorded, unincorporated businesses with undefined liability, industries located where financiers and investors cannot see them. Because the rights to these possessions are not adequately documented, these assets cannot readily be turned into capital, cannot be traded outside of narrow local circles where people know and trust each other, cannot be used as collateral for a loan, and cannot be used as a share against an investment . . .
>
> [The poor] have houses but not titles; crops but not deeds; businesses but not statutes of incorporation. It is the unavailability of these essential representations that explains why people who have adapted every other Western invention, from the paper clip to the nuclear reactor, have not been able to produce sufficient capital to make their domestic capitalism work.

De Soto is on to something interesting. His recent study, entitled the *The Mystery of Capital,* and his earlier study, *The Other Path (El Otro Sendero),* have helped to focus policy attention usefully on squatters' rights, on formalizing the informal economy, and reducing the transactions costs of contracting and gaining access to public services.

The problem with de Soto's analysis, however, is that it relies on a single factor—the lack of titles and deeds—to explain single-handedly the failures of development. The subtitle to *The Mystery of Capital* claims that the book will explain "Why capitalism triumphs in the West and fails everywhere else." The problem is that capitalism is *not* failing everywhere else. Many developing countries are growing rapidly, but others are stuck. Many that are growing especially fast, such as China and Vietnam, have certainly not solved the problem of titles and deeds! Many non-Western countries now at high-income levels, such as Japan, Korea, and Taiwan, followed distinctive pathways of legal development.

Most important, all single-factor explanations fail the scientific test of accounting for the observed diversity of development experience. Dozens of recent statistical studies have shown that difference in economic growth rates across countries depends on a multiplicity of factors: initial incomes, education levels, fertility rates, climate, trade policy, disease, proximity to markets, and the quality of economic institutions, just to name a few of the relevant variables. The real challenge is to understand which of these many variables is posing particular obstacles in specific circumstances—what I mean precisely by "differential diagnosis."

A SHORTFALL OF MORALS?

The AIDS pandemic has ravaged Africa as it has no other place in the world. This tragedy has also unleashed long-standing assumptions about sexual licentiousness and irresponsibility in Africa that have led many to presume that a crisis of culture and morality lies at the core of Africa's problems. If men are so unfaithful to their spouses, and family life has broken down to such an extent, what future could there be for Africa no matter how much aid is given? This is a tough question to broach in public, but it is asked repeatedly in private. It merits an answer, if only to better understand and thereby better control the AIDS pandemic. The answer is surprising, far from what is commonly supposed.

As I noted in chapter 10, the reasons for Africa's extremely high prevalence rates are not well understood or agreed. The simplest explanations just do not work. A common view is that Africans have more sexual partners, and therefore more risk of transmitting the disease. But here is the conclusion of a recent survey of the most careful epidemiological studies from *The Lancet,* a leading UK medical journal:

> Although sexual cultures do vary from region to region, the differences are not so obvious. Demographic surveys and other studies suggest that, on average, African men typically do not have more sexual partners than men elsewhere. For example, a comparative study of sexual behaviour found that men in Thailand and Rio de Janeiro were more likely to report five or more casual sexual partners in the previous year than were men in Tanzania, Kenya, Lesotho, or Lusaka, Zambia. And very few women in any of these

countries reported five or more partners a year. Men and women in Africa report roughly similar, if not fewer, numbers of lifetime partners than do heterosexuals in many western countries.

There are many hypotheses, and few hard conclusions, about what can explain Africa's extraordinarily high transmission of the disease. Perhaps details of the sexual networks (such as the timing of having multiple sexual partners or the large number of African migrant male workers who are away from their families for long periods) account for some of the differences. The extent of male circumcisions may explain some of the difference (since circumcision seems to protect against transmission of the disease). The extent of other untreated diseases in the African population may be conducive to a faster transmission of AIDS. The viral type of HIV in parts of Africa may differ from the virus in other parts of the world. The fact is that nothing sure is known about the relative importance, or importance at all, of these possible factors. What is known is that the simple, broad-based attacks on African morals do not hold up to scientific scrutiny.

Saving Children Only to Become Hungry Adults?

I have been asked dozens of times if help for Africa would ultimately backfire in an even greater population explosion. Would greater child survival rates not translate directly into more adult hunger and suffering? Usually the questioner begins sheepishly, apologizing for what is to come. Then he or she explains that they do not want to sound callous, but that they really need to understand the issue. This is a very fair question. After all, Thomas Malthus asked almost the same one two hundred years ago.

The answer is that a concerted effort to end extreme poverty in Africa would be the best guarantor of ending today's population explosion, and doing so quickly, voluntarily, and in a way that empowers households to meet their personal objectives of human betterment. Poverty is the biggest risk factor in rapid population growth by far. Indeed, with a few exceptions in the Middle East, all of the places in the world where fertility rates remain very high—above 5.0—are in poor and largely rural countries. Fertility rates are the result of household circumstances. All of the basic factors that contribute to poverty tend to

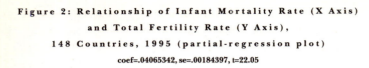

Figure 2: Relationship of Infant Mortality Rate (X Axis)
and Total Fertility Rate (Y Axis),
148 Countries, 1995 (partial-regression plot)
coef=.04065342, se=.00184397, t=22.05

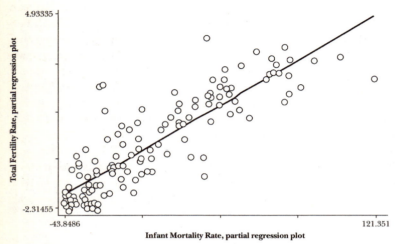

Infant Mortality Rate, partial regression plot

Source: CMH (2001).

contribute to high fertility rates. High fertility rates, in turn, are a factor in causing the poverty trap.

As I have noted before, fertility rates depend on several factors. First, when children die in large numbers, households tend to have many more children to compensate for the risk. Because the parents are risk averse, and want to ensure with very high probability at least one surviving child (and often at least one surviving son), they overcompensate in a statistical sense. The places with a high child mortality rate tend to be the places with a very high total fertility rate, as shown in the scatter plot in figure 2. For 148 countries in the year 1995, we plot one point per country, showing the child mortality rate on the horizontal axis and total fertility rate on the vertical axis. The strong upward line shows the strong tendency of societies with a high child mortality rate to have a high total fertility rate as well.

Figure 3 shows that the total fertility rate more than compensates. In this figure, we plot the child mortality rate on the horizontal axis to compare with the total population growth rate on the vertical axis. In-

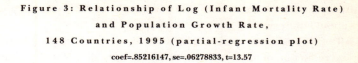

Figure 3: Relationship of Log (Infant Mortality Rate)
and Population Growth Rate,
148 Countries, 1995 (partial-regression plot)
coef=.85216147, se=.06278833, t=13.57

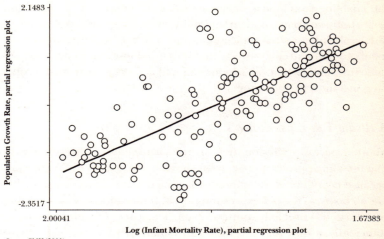

Source: CMH (2001).

deed, the places with high child mortality rates also have high overall population growth rates, contrary to conventional beliefs.

Fertility rates come down as economic development proceeds. As more children survive, households "risk" having fewer children, confident that each child is much more likely to survive. As households move from subsistence agriculture to commercial farming and especially to urban life, they also choose to have fewer children. This is partly because children are no longer so valuable as farmworkers. As households obtain modern amenities such as piped water or well water close to the home or a cookstove that uses gas canisters rather than fuel wood, children are not needed to fetch the water and wood. As households put their children in school, the expense of raising each child rises. Households decide to have fewer children and to invest more in each of them. As mothers find improved economic opportunities out of the household and off the farm, the time expense of raising children (in terms of lost wage income) rises as well. And, of course, as households are able to obtain modern health services, including family planning and modern contraceptives, they are able to follow through on their changing desires about family size.

All of these factors explain why most of the world has achieved a marked reduction of total fertility rates and a sharp slowdown in population growth. This phenomenon has not yet come to rural Africa, where the enabling conditions—child survival, girls' education, women's job opportunities, access to water and modern cooking fuels, and access to family planning and contraception—are not yet in place. The investments to end extreme poverty in Africa (and elsewhere) are the very same investments that will produce a rapid and decisive drop in fertility rates in a short period of time.

A Rising Tide Lifts All Boats

Another pervasive illusion, held by the champions of globalization, is that remaining problems of extreme poverty will take care of themselves because economic development will spread everywhere. A rising tide lifts all boats, as the old expression puts it. If the rising tide is not lifting your boat, it is probably your own fault. The forces of globalization are sufficiently strong that everyone can benefit if they can just behave themselves.

In real geographical terms, the rising tide of globalization has lifted most economies that lie at the water's edge. Those societies are, quite literally, the places that have boats in the water. The free-trade zones that fueled the initial industrialization of Asia, for example, were all on the coastline. But a rising tide does not reach the mountaintops of the Andes or the interior of Asia or Africa. Market forces, as powerful as they are, have identifiable limitations, including those posed by adverse geography. Even worse, when economic progress does not reach a country, the economic conditions can worsen as population growth and capital depreciation (including the depreciation of natural capital) lead to falling ratios of capital per person.

Nature Red in Tooth and Claw

The last myth worthy of mention is the social Darwinist myth, often the modern economist's myth, which warns against soft-hearted liberalism on the grounds that "real life" is competition and struggle, of "nature red in tooth and claw" in Tennyson's evocative phrase. Social Darwinism holds that economic progress is the story of competition and survival of the fittest. Some groups dominate; other groups fall behind. In the end, life is a struggle, and the world today reflects the outcome of that struggle.

Despite the fact that much of free-market economic theory has championed this vision, economists from Adam Smith onward have recognized that competition and struggle are but one side of economic life, and that trust, cooperation, and collective action in the provision of public goods are the obverse side. Just as the communist attempt to banish competition from the economic scene via state ownership failed miserably, so too would an attempt to manage a modern economy on the basis of market forces alone. All successful economies are mixed economies, relying on both the public sector and the private sector for economic development. I have explained the underlying theoretical reasons why markets and competition alone will not provide efficient levels of infrastructure, knowledge, environmental management, and goods. Just as that is true at the national level, it is also true internationally. Without cooperation, a collection of national economies will not provide efficient levels of investment in cross-border infrastructure, knowledge, environmental management, or merit goods among the world's poor.

There is broad consensus on the case for public goods at the national level, even if there are heated debates on exactly where to draw the line between public and private activities. Even the most hard-nosed conservatives in the United States support public financing of education, medical research, and many kinds of health care. Public spending in the United States is around 30 percent of GDP when expenditures at the local, state, and federal level are combined, and there is no serious prospect of any real reduction in that proportion. Yet when it comes time for countries to spend on the international level, suddenly even 0.7 percent of GDP looks burdensome and highly controversial. The same arguments that have prevailed at the national level—making the case for a mixed economy—will sooner or later, and hopefully sooner, prevail in international relations as well.

Eliminating poverty at the global scale is a global responsibility that will have global benefits. No single country can do it on its own. The hardest part is for us to think globally, but that is what global society in the twenty-first century requires. The philosophy of the Millennium Development Compact, which was both developed and ratified globally, can serve as an underpinning to this international effort.

MAKING THE CASE FOR ACTION

I reject the plaintive cries of the doomsayers who say that ending poverty is impossible. I have identified the specific investments that are needed; found ways to plan and implement them; shown that they can be affordable; and addressed the counsels of despair who claim that the poor are condemned by their cultures, values, and personal behaviors. But will the world act? What, after all, is in it for the rich countries? Why should they care? When has the world ever acted simply because it's the right thing to do? These are the final questions of my inquiry.

Seventeen

WHY WE SHOULD DO IT

Will the rich world act to help save the poor? The cynics say no. Why should we? Poverty is not our problem; it is theirs. What can the poor do to us, or for us? When has any country done anything out of altruism for others? How can we fight poverty when we have to fight terrorism? How can politicians ask the public to give more for Africa when the public is already feeling squeezed economically? These are questions I hear daily.

They are also particularly American questions these days. Many Americans do not see economic assistance as having much to do with their national security. For that they have put their faith in the military. The United States is spending thirty times more on the military than on foreign assistance in 2004, $450 billion compared with $15 billion. Only Greece comes anywhere close to that lopsided ratio, as figure 1 shows using the most recent available data for the year 2002 (before much of the current U.S. military buildup).

The American investment decision to back military rather than other approaches to international relations reflects several mistaken ideas. The first is that we are already doing all that we can do to help the poor. Public opinion research conducted over the past decade illustrates, time and again, that the American public greatly overestimates the amount of federal funds spent on foreign aid. In a 2001 survey, the Program on International Policy Attitudes (PIPA) at the University of Maryland reported that Americans, on average, believed that foreign aid accounts for 20 percent of the federal budget, roughly twenty-four times the actual figure. PIPA found essentially the same result in surveys in the mid-1990s.

Figure 1: Ratio of Military Expenditure to Official Development Assistant (2002)

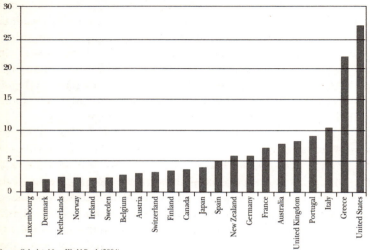

Source: Calculated from World Bank (2004).

President Bush seems to make the same error. In a press conference in April 2004, he said that as "the greatest power on the face of the Earth, we have an obligation to help the spread of freedom. We have an obligation to help feed the hungry." Yet how does the United States fulfill its obligation? U.S. aid to farmers in poor countries to help them grow more food runs at less than $1 billion per year, perhaps $1 per subsistence farmer in the world. Mind you, $1 billion comes to one penny of every hundred dollars of U.S. national income. The United States gives another $800 million in food itself, which helps to feed individuals in a crisis, but does nothing by itself to solve the more fundamental problem of unstable and insufficient food production.

The second fallacy is a widespread view that the U.S. military can achieve security for Americans even in the absence of a stable world. It is the same mistake that led Americans to believe that the United States would be greeted as liberators in Baghdad, that the capture of Saddam Hussein would stop the Iraqi violence, or that one more assault against al Qaeda will end the terror. Whether terrorists are rich or poor or middle class, their staging areas—their bases of operation—are unstable societies beset by poverty, unemployment, rapid population growth, hunger, and lack of hope. Without addressing the root causes of that instability, little will be accomplished in stanching terror.

The third fallacy is the "clash of civilizations," the belief that the world is entering a war of cultures. For many in America this is a literal war, the war of Armageddon. Millions of Americans, though just how many is unclear, believe that we are approaching the "end days" of biblical prophecy. This millennial belief has returned in waves in American history, but never before with the United States as a nuclear and global superpower. It is terrifying for those of us who would rather use rationality than scriptural prophecy to determine U.S. foreign policy.

Hard evidence has established strong linkages between extreme poverty abroad and the threats to national security. Poverty abroad can indeed hurt us at home, and has repeatedly done so. To answer the earlier question, yes, countries do occasionally act altruistically, helping other countries to address their basic economic and social challenges. Indeed, they have done so for generations, as with the magnificent U.S. Marshall Plan. Foreign policy strategists have long recognized that acts of altruism—ending the slave trade, supporting countries in their independence from empire, extending assistance for reconstruction and development, providing humanitarian relief after natural disasters—are also acts of enlightened self-interest. That self-interest does not diminish such generous acts. Moral precepts, after all, are rules of behavior that establish a basis for cooperation and reciprocity on which civilization depends.

It is also wrong to suppose that politicians are punished for supporting such actions. There is plenty of experience to show that the broad public will accept such measures, especially if they see that the rich within their own societies are asked to meet their fair share of the burden. The problem in the United States has not been public opposition to increased foreign assistance, but a lack of political leadership even to inform the public about its importance, and to ask the public for greater efforts. Americans have shown an overwhelming willingness to "share at least a small portion of its wealth with those in the world who are in great need," reaffirming the American public's strong support for giving foreign aid in principle. The PIPA survey also found that 54 percent rejected the idea that foreign aid "should be strictly a private matter taken care of by individuals giving donations through private organizations." Americans understand what must be done and why it is a public duty. What they do not appreciate is how little the United States is in fact following through.

U.S. SECURITY AND GLOBAL POVERTY

As a general proposition, economic failure—an economy stuck in a poverty trap, banking crisis, debt default, or hyperinflation—often leads to state failure as well. The most comprehensive study of state failure, carried out by the State Failure Task Force established by the Central Intelligence Agency in 1994, confirms the importance of the economic roots of state failure. The task force defines state failure as a case of revolutionary war, ethnic war, genocide, politicide, or adverse or disruptive regime change. Failed states, in turn, are likely to create problems not only for themselves, but also for the rest of the world. Throughout history they have been seedbeds of violence, terrorism, international criminality, mass migration, refugee movements, drug trafficking, and disease. If the United States, Europe, Japan, and other high-income countries want to spend less time responding to failed states, they will have to reduce decisively the number of failed economies.

Americans would dearly love to believe that the United States can be an island of stability and prosperity in a global sea of poverty and economic failure. History, however, proves otherwise. The examples are legion. The rise of the Bolsheviks to power in 1917 took place in the wake of the economic collapse of wartime czarist Russia. The rise of Hitler in 1933 occurred in the midst of the Great Depression that affected Germany especially hard because of its large foreign debt. More recently, Yugoslavia disintegrated into regional war not only because of interethnic conflicts, but also because of an economic collapse and the descent of the former federal state into hyperinflation in the late 1980s. Slobodan Milosevic used the economic collapse to grab power. Iraq's declining economic fortunes and rising debt burdens following the Iran-Iraq war of the 1980s prompted, at least in part, Saddam Hussein's invasion of Kuwait in 1990.

I certainly do not want to commit the simplistic fallacy of attributing all political failures to economic crises. The shah of Iran was knocked from power in 1979 in the midst of an oil boom. Tracing the rise of Lenin or Hitler to power on the basis of economics alone would be fatuous. And 9/11 and al Qaeda's existence weren't caused by poverty per se, although state collapse in Afghanistan and economic crises throughout South Asia and the Middle East certainly played their roles. Yet in practice, economic failure abroad undoubtedly matters greatly and can translate into very large costs for the United States in many spheres.

The findings of the CIA task force are compelling: it counted all cases of state failure between 1957 and 1994 in countries of half a million people or more, and identified 113 cases of state failure. Of all the explanatory variables examined, three were most significant:

- Infant mortality rates, suggesting that overall low levels of material well-being are a significant contributor to state failure

- Openness of the economy, in that more economic linkages with the rest of the world diminish the chances of state failure

- Democracy, with democratic countries showing less propensity to state failure than authoritarian regimes

The linkage to democracy has a strong economic dimension, however, because research has shown repeatedly that the probability of a country's being democratic rises significantly with its per capita income level. In refinements of the basic study, the task force found that in sub-Saharan Africa, where many societies live on the edge of subsistence, temporary economic setbacks (measured as a decline in gross domestic product per capita) were significant predictors of state failure. They also found that partial democracies, usually in transition from authoritarian to fully democratic institutions, were particularly vulnerable to collapse. Similar conclusions have been reached in studies on African conflict, which find that poverty and slow economic growth raise the probability of conflict.

State failures abroad are important to U.S. security, since they often lead to U.S. military engagements abroad. State failures have repeatedly dragged the United States into foreign imbroglios. If we compare the dates of U.S. military engagement with the timing of state failures according to the task force, as in table 1, virtually every case of U.S. military intervention abroad since 1960 has taken place in a developing country that had recently experienced a state failure. (For the purposes of the table, "military intervention" includes any use of U.S. troops abroad, whether for direct combat, peacekeeping, evacuation of civilians, or protection of U.S. property.) In many or most of these cases, the linkages from economic collapse to state failure to U.S. military engagements are vividly clear.

Table 1: State Failures and Subsequent
U.S. Military Involvement

(First date refers to U.S. military involvement, second refers to state failure; in chronological order by military intervention date)

Cuba (1962, 1956-1961)

Thailand (1962, 1957)

Laos (1962-1975, 1960-1979)

Congo (1964, 1960-1965)

Vietnam (1964-1973, 1958-1975)

Dominican Republic (1965, 1961-1966)

Congo (1967, 1960-1965)

Cambodia (1970, 1970-1979)

Cyprus (1974, 1963-1968, 1974)

Vietnam (1975, 1958-1975)

Lebanon (1976, 1965-1992)

Korea (1976, not applicable)

Zaire (1978, 1977-1979)

Iran (1980, 1977)

El Salvador (1981, 1977-1992)

Libya (1981, not applicable)

Lebanon (1982, 1965-1992)

Honduras (1983-1989, 1978-1990 state failure in Nicaragua)

Chad (1983, 1965-1996)

Liberia (1990, 1989-1997)

Zaire (1991, 1991)

Sierra Leone (1992, 1991 onward)

Somalia (1992, 1988 onward)

Bosnia–Herzegovina (1993, 1992-1996)

Somalia (1993, 1988 onward)

Source: The dates for state failure are taken from the State Failure Task Force data set; the dates of U.S. military intervention are taken from Ellen C. Collier, "Instances of Use of United States Forces Abroad, 1798-1993" (U.S. Congressional Research Service, October 7, 1993), located at http://www.history.navy.mil/wars/foabroad.htm

SINCE 9/11

The ideas that failed states threaten U.S. and European national security and that support for economic development is also support for national security are not wild-eyed left-wing propositions. They have become standard fare of strategic analysis. The problem lies not with the concept of linking poverty and national security, but with the follow-through. U.S. development policy in recent decades—in both Democratic and Republican administrations—can be measured more in sound bites than in assistance that is truly scaled to the size of the challenge.

Here is an example of the disconnect between foreign policy rhetoric and foreign policy follow-through. In a speech to the Inter-American Development Bank on the eve of the International Conference on Financing for Development in Monterrey, Mexico, President Bush said:

> Poverty doesn't cause terrorism. Being poor doesn't make you a murderer. Most of the plotters of September 11th were raised in comfort. Yet persistent poverty and oppression can lead to hopelessness and despair. And when governments fail to meet the most basic needs of their people, these failed states can become havens for terror.
>
> In Afghanistan, persistent poverty and war and chaos created conditions that allowed a terrorist regime to seize power. And in many other states around the world, poverty prevents governments from controlling their borders, policing their territory, and enforcing their laws. Development provides the resources to build hope and prosperity, and security . . .
>
> Successful development also requires citizens who are literate, who are healthy, and prepared and able to work. Development assistance can help poor nations meet these education and health care needs.

So far so good. Then, the president introduced a new aid program, the Millennium Challenge Account, that would increase U.S. annual aid by $5 billion per year:

> America supports the international development goals in the UN Millennium Declaration, and believes that these goals are a shared responsibility of developed and developing countries. To make

progress, we must encourage nations and leaders to walk the hard road of political, legal and economic reform, so all their people can benefit.

Today, I call for a new compact for global development, defined by new accountability for both rich and poor nations alike. Greater contributions from developed nations must be linked to greater responsibility from developing nations. The United States will lead by example. We will increase our development assistance by $5 billion over the next three budget cycles. This new money is above and beyond existing aid requests—is above and beyond existing aid requests in the current budget I submitted to the Congress.

The problem is the complete disconnect between the extent of the initiative—$5 billion more per year by the third year—and the needs of poor countries (on the order of $100 billion more per year between 2006–2015 to meet the Millennium Development Goals) and with the commitment of the United States to make "concrete efforts" to target 0.7 percent of GNP. The $5 billion represents less than 0.05 percent of U.S. GNP. Even more startling, not a single penny of the Millennium Challenge Account had been disbursed by late 2004.

Several months later the links of poverty abroad and security at home were enshrined in the new National Security Strategy of the United States of America:

A world where some live in comfort and plenty, while half of the human race lives on less than $2 a day, is neither just nor stable. Including all of the world's poor in an expanding circle of development—and opportunity—is a moral imperative and one of the top priorities of US international policy.

The strategy committed the United States to the following actions to promote development:

- Provide resources to aid countries that have met the challenge of national reform

- Improve the effectiveness of the World Bank and other development banks in raising living standards

- Insist upon measurable results to ensure that development assistance is actually making a difference in the lives of the world's poor

- Increase the amount of development assistance that is provided in the form of grants instead of loans

- Since trade and investment are the real engines of economic growth, open societies to commerce and investment

- Secure public health

- Emphasize education

- Continue to aid agricultural development

It is hard to understand the disconnect between these insights—which are absolutely valid—and the lack of a commensurate financial commitment by the U.S. government. Part of it is simply the frequent mistake of assuming that the United States is doing more than it is. The National Security Strategy, for example, asserts that "decades of massive development assistance have failed to spur economic growth in the poorest countries," apparently without realizing that the aid flows have neither been massive nor scaled in any way to the levels needed to "spur economic growth." Of the limited aid that the United States gives, a large proportion of it goes to pay for U.S. experts (technical assistance) or for emergency relief and food grains rather than for long-term investments in infrastructure or education or health. The aid, in other words, is not only very small compared to U.S. GNP and foreign needs, but is given in a form that offers little long-term help. The pattern is not confined to the current Bush administration. It has been a feature of U.S. aid policy for decades.

Acting Because We Promised

American political leaders and the broad public rarely recognize that the U.S. government has repeatedly made international commitments to do much more than the United States is doing, and even less do they realize that the lack of follow-through carries an enormous foreign policy cost. In speaking to the United Nations in September 2002, President Bush said the following:

The United States helped found the United Nations. We want the United Nations to be effective, and respectful, and successful. We want the resolutions of the world's most important multilateral body to be enforced.

Yet when it comes to the resolutions of the General Assembly, such as the Millennium Declaration, or to a series of agreements at UN conferences in the past twenty years, the United States often acts as if it were merely an innocent bystander, not a responsible government, much less a signatory. The 0.7 commitment is a case in point. The General Assembly voted on it thirty-five years ago, but U.S. officials long maintained that it did not apply to the United States. Nonetheless, the United States was a signatory of Agenda 21, the document adopted at the Rio Summit on Sustainable Development in 1992, which contained the following language in Chapter 33.13:

> Developed countries reaffirm their commitments to reach the accepted United Nations target of 0.7 per cent of GNP for ODA and, to the extent that they have not yet achieved that target, agree to augment their aid programmes in order to reach that target as soon as possible and to ensure prompt and effective implementation of Agenda 21.

A decade later, at Monterrey, the Monterrey Consensus, adopted by the United States and the other participating countries, stated:

> We urge developed countries that have not done so to make concrete efforts towards the target of 0.7 per cent of gross national product (GNP) as ODA to developing countries . . .

A few months after Monterrey, at the World Summit on Sustainable Development (WSSD) in Johannesburg, South Africa, the conferees agreed on the WSSD Plan of Implementation:

> Make available the increased commitments in official development assistance announced by several developed countries at the International Conference on Financing for Development. Urge the developed countries that have not done so to make concrete efforts towards

the target of 0.7 per cent of gross national product as official development assistance to developing countries . . .

I had an interesting exchange one day in a roundtable discussion with
senior U.S. State Department officials. One particular official was taking
great umbrage at my outspoken advocacy of official development assistance. At one point, he postulated that the United States was against aid
and, instead, was for the principles of the Monterrey Consensus. I was
perplexed, and responded that the Monterrey Consensus commits us to
urge all developed countries that have not done so—including us—to
make "concrete efforts" to 0.7. He stammered, "But we are for the parts
on private trade and investment!" This position is silly, of course, since
the document was negotiated in its entirety with the intensive participation of the U.S. team. Much of the Monterrey Consensus champions the
role of private-sector-led growth, but the document also skillfully describes why ODA is still needed in a world in which private capital flows
swamp official flows:

> Official development assistance (ODA) plays an essential role as a
> complement to other sources of financing for development, espe-
> cially in those countries with the least capacity to attract private di-
> rect investment. ODA can help a country to reach adequate levels
> of domestic resource mobilization over an appropriate time hori-
> zon, while human capital, productive and export capacities are en-
> hanced. ODA can be critical for improving the environment for
> private sector activity and can thus pave the way for robust growth.
> ODA is also a crucial instrument for supporting education, health,
> public infrastructure development, agriculture and rural develop-
> ment, and to enhance food security. For many countries in Africa,
> least developed countries, small island developing States and land-
> locked developing countries, ODA is still the largest source of exter-
> nal financing and is critical to the achievement of the development
> goals and targets of the Millennium Declaration and other interna-
> tionally agreed development targets.

The point is not to revisit the merits of the Monterrey Consensus, which
are significant, but to stress that policy commitments of the signatories
should translate into government action. The failure of the United States

to follow up on the Monterrey Consensus has no direct political fallout in the United States, of course, because not one in a million U.S. citizens even knows of the statement. But we should not underestimate the salience that is has abroad, where the terms of the Monterrey Consensus are a matter of life and death not only for other governments but also for their populations. Spin as we might in the United States about our generosity, the poor countries are fully aware of what we are *not* doing.

Rebalancing Foreign Policy

A vote for foreign aid has often been described as the toughest vote for a congressman. How can a congressman's constituency understand the case for giving money away to others? In fact, these political risks are ridiculously overstated. Politicians throughout the rich countries routinely vote aid for poor countries, and are perfectly safe in doing so. Indeed, every other Western democracy has found a way to vote more aid as a share of GNP than has the United States, despite the fact that the other countries are generally far below the United States in per capita income. But the U.S. experience is also clear: the public will support the president when the president explains that an issue like this is in the vital interest of U.S. foreign policy.

I have already noted that the American people vastly overestimate the amount of aid now being given, partly because no president in memory has spoken to the public about what the United States is and is not doing. The same opinion surveys demonstrate that the public is ready to do more, assuming that a tight case can be made that the aid will accomplish its assigned purposes. The public expresses dismay about foreign aid being wasted, used to support dictators, or spirited away to secret Swiss bank accounts. And yet the PIPA 2001 survey showed that Americans were willing, and indeed thought it an obligation of their government, to alleviate hunger in other countries. When aid was described as "giving food and medical assistance to people in needy countries," an overwhelming 87 percent of respondents favored the United States providing this support. Interestingly, and notably, a strong majority of respondents also said they preferred to give aid through multilateral institutions rather than bilaterally.

The fact is that aid programs can be passed through Congress, but they require presidential leadership to build a national coalition. And the coalition tends to reflect various constituencies and concerns. Some part of the public supports the programs for national security reasons; others for long-term economic benefits (richer countries will make better trade partners); others because it is the right thing to do; and still others because of religious precepts. History again offers four cases of the politics of aid to help us understand how and why major aid programs have been adopted in the past.

The Marshall Plan

Beyond its humanitarian mission, the Marshall Plan was a comprehensive economic development plan meant to ensure Europe's economic stability and strategic security in the postwar era. The framers of the Marshall Plan were motivated by the lessons of World War I, when a Carthaginian peace so embittered parts of German society that it contributed, if only indirectly, to the political rise of Hitler. Following World War II, President Truman and other leaders who took up the reconstruction of Europe were determined not to allow such economic suffering to reoccur. They believed that without properly functioning international trade and markets, and with the Soviet threat looming on the east of the continent, America's own economic progress and security interests would be undermined.

Supporters of the Marshall Plan campaigned systematically to convince the American people of the soundness of the plan. Their success in selling the Marshall Plan included four key steps, among many others: (1) establishing a bipartisan congressional committee, led by Congressman Christian Herter (R-Massachusetts), which took a crucial trip to Europe to study the problem on the ground and report back to Congress; (2) forming a blue ribbon commission of financial leaders, led by Averell Harriman, which confirmed the financial wherewithal of the United States to support a program with the scope of the Marshall Plan; (3) engendering high-level Republican support for a Democratic initiative that kept the plan from being tied up in partisan politics; and (4) alerting Americans to facts on the ground, especially the Soviet advance on Czechoslovakia in early 1948, which convinced the public that if the United States did not help Europe, its security and economic gain could be undermined by communist subversion.

These four elements, together with the concerted leadership of President Truman and a public information campaign that made the facts clear to the American people, enabled the U.S. Congress to pass the Economic Cooperation Act of 1948, which embodied the Marshall Plan. During the life of the Marshall Plan, the United States provided more than 1 percent of GNP, on average, from 1948 through 1952 to rebuild Western Europe, around ten times the current effort as a share of GNP.

Jubilee 2000 (Campaign to Drop the Debt)

The drop-the-debt campaign is a more recent initiative that grew out of the realization that the world's poorest countries were suffering under the crushing weight of debt repayments to international and bilateral lenders. The campaign was a more extensive call for action that responded to the IMF and World Bank's Heavily Indebted Poor Countries (HIPC) Initiative, launched in 1996. The HIPC initiative itself was a recognition that the structural adjustment era had failed to deliver its promises of economic development and growth to the world's poorest nations. The Jubilee 2000 campaign sought to cancel the debts of dozens of the world's poorest countries.

The Jubilee 2000 campaign ran up against stiff resistance from the donor countries and the Bretton Woods institutions, which did not share the sense of urgency about debt cancellation. The movement attracted a wide coalition of religious groups and NGOs, initially in Europe and especially the United Kingdom. In the late 1990s, it became a mass social movement: during a 1998 summit in Birmingham, the movement's leaders presented a global petition, which twenty-two million petitioners in sixty countries had signed, calling on rich-world leaders to drop the debt of poor nations. Leading entertainers, including Muhammad Ali and especially Bono, campaigned for the movement. Pope John Paul II, who linked the campaign to the Jubilee celebration of the year 2000 and the biblical call from Leviticus for a fresh start for the indebted in a Jubilee year, gave the movement vast reach.

As an economic adviser to Jubilee 2000, and working closely with Bono, I got a chance to see the shaping of the political coalition that ultimately carried the day. Bono and I were told, in no uncertain terms, that debt cancellation could not pass the U.S. Congress. That was the initial view across the political spectrum, from the Clinton White House and Treasury Department to the Republican-dominated House of Representatives. What the conventional wisdom failed to understand was the broad support for debt cancellation among a wide range of Americans. Conservatives thought it inevitable because they had no illusion about the creditworthiness of the poorest countries. Liberals thought it was the right thing to do. Many in the public were eager to find a sensible way to support the world's poor. And perhaps most important at the end of the day, many conservatives who might otherwise oppose foreign aid joined out of religious motivation.

When the movement finally gathered steam in the United States, leaders of the religious right, particularly Spencer Bachus (R-Alabama) took up the issue. Bachus authored key provisions of debt relief legislation and helped to shape a bipartisan coalition that reached across traditional liberal supporters of foreign assistance and representatives of the religious right who viewed the debt issue in religious terms. The U.S. Congress approved a generous debt relief package, even if it did not deliver all that was needed. As in many circumstances, the successful campaign to drop the debt achieved perhaps two thirds of what is truly needed, but it was two thirds more than what was deemed possible before we began.

The Emergency Plan for AIDS

A third example of broad coalition building is the five-year, $15 billion President's Emergency Plan for AIDS Relief (PEPFAR). I have already described some aspects of the campaign to bring anti-AIDS drug treatment to the world's poor, including my participation on the Commission on Macroeconomics and Health. Once again, I was lucky to have a front row seat in the shaping of a political coalition that delivered a package of aid initially derided as preposterous.

I had recommended the idea of a $3 billion per year program to the Bush administration, and had the opportunity to brief National Security Adviser Condoleezza Rice twice in the early days of the Bush administration. I discussed both the need and potential for a major expansion of AIDS treatment, and argued that it had become practical and affordable with the availability of powerful medicines with rapidly declining production costs. On my first visit to the White House, I stopped by to see Larry Lindsay, a former student and colleague, and the new economic adviser to the president. He gave me a warm reception, and also some advice on my way out of the office. "Jeff," he said with a smile. "That was very interesting, and important work. But don't hold your breath for $3 billion per year."

It turned out that the winning coalition for AIDS relief looked a lot like the victorious coalition on the debt issue: liberals, the religious right, NGOs, and a broad public far more sympathetic to action than the political leaders suspected. Once again, Bono played a unique role in pulling the coalition together, not just as a celebrity and entertainer, but as a rare individual who could reach deeply into the hearts and minds of a remarkable range of individuals. One day I was driving home when my cell phone rang. It was Bono. "What are you doing?" he asked. When I told him that I was driving home, he said that I had better pull over. "What's up?" "You won't believe what just happened. Senator Jesse Helms just blessed me and the effort on AIDS." Bono and the senator had read scripture together, and Helms had committed to help push AIDS legislation through the White House and Congress. Bono brilliantly brought the AIDS tragedy to the attention of several key leaders of the religious right, and this in turn showed the White House that AIDS legislation was not a political trap, but actually a political boon.

In the end, the coalition was even more inclusive than usual. It involved experts from the public health and biomedical community. Dr. Anthony Fauci of the National Institutes of Health played a decisive role. It involved celebrities, religious leaders, liberals and conservatives. And, ultimately, the president. On the evening of the 2003 State of the Union address, I got a phone call from UN Secretary-General Kofi Annan. He said that he had just been alerted that "the speech would be particularly interesting on AIDS." I rushed to the TV, and listened in amazement as President Bush said the following:

As our nation moves troops and builds alliances to make our world safer, we must also remember our calling, as a blessed country, is to make the world better.

Today, on the continent of Africa, nearly 30 million people have the AIDS virus, including 3 million children under the age of 15. There are whole countries in Africa where more than one-third of the adult population carries the infection. More than 4 million require immediate drug treatment. Yet across that continent, only 50,000 AIDS victims—only 50,000—are receiving the medicine they need.

Because the AIDS diagnosis is considered a death sentence, many do not seek treatment. Almost all who do are turned away. A doctor in rural South Africa describes his frustration. He says, "We have no medicines, many hospitals tell people, 'You've got AIDS.

We can't help you. Go home and die.'" In an age of miraculous medicines, no person should have to hear those words.

AIDS can be prevented. Anti-retroviral drugs can extend life for many years. And the cost of those drugs has dropped from $12,000 a year to under $300 a year, which places a tremendous possibility within our grasp.

Ladies and gentlemen, seldom has history offered a greater opportunity to do so much for so many. We have confronted, and will continue to confront, HIV/AIDS in our own country. And to meet a severe and urgent crisis abroad, tonight I propose the Emergency Plan for AIDS Relief, a work of mercy beyond all current international efforts to help the people of Africa.

This comprehensive plan will prevent 7 million new AIDS infections, treat at least 2 million people with life-extending drugs and provide humane care for millions of people suffering from AIDS and for children orphaned by AIDS. I ask the Congress to commit $15 billion over the next five years, including nearly $10 billion in new money, to turn the tide against AIDS in the most afflicted nations of Africa and the Caribbean.

This nation can lead the world in sparing innocent people from a plague of nature.

When the president finished these remarks, both houses of Congress rose for a standing ovation. So much for the risks of asking for foreign assistance!

TIME TO ASK FOR THE CONTRIBUTION OF OUR GENERATION

Political leaders throughout the rich democracies will soon have to go to the taxpayers and voters once again to accomplish what might seem to be impossible today. They will have to secure public support for 0.7 percent of GNP in development aid and explain that this commitment might be required for another twenty years. They will have to explain why the safety of global society, the value of their country's solemn word, the lives of millions of impoverished children, and the meaning and moral worth of our civilization all depend on what they are requesting. And, if they are clever, especially in the United States, they will explain that 0.7 won't hurt very much after all, especially if it is funded with two big wallops. The first will transfer part of an overgrown military budget to the agenda of global security through economic development. The second will call especially on the richest of the rich—whose incomes per year are tens of thousands of times those of the poorest of the poor—to do their special part.

I believe that the richest of the rich can comfortably make such a contribution, and that they will understand that it will be a profound and meaningful demonstration of our generation's unique moment to secure global well-being.

Eighteen

OUR GENERATION'S CHALLENGE

Our generation is heir to two and a half centuries of economic progress. We can realistically envision a world without extreme poverty by the year 2025 because technological progress enables us to meet basic human needs on a global scale and to achieve a margin above basic needs unprecedented in history. The technological progress has been fueled by the ongoing revolutions of basic science and spread by the power of global markets and public investments in health, education, and infrastructure. Remarkably, contrary to the dark vision of Thomas Malthus, we can accomplish all of this with a world population that is eight times larger than in 1750.

While our economic strengths are the product of 250 years of economic growth, our very concepts of economic and social progress are the product of social philosophies that emerged at roughly the same time as the Industrial Revolution. The Age of Enlightenment in Europe, throughout the eighteenth century, marked the introduction of new concepts of social progress. Until the onset of the Industrial Revolution, humanity had known only unending struggles against famine, pandemic disease, and extreme poverty, all compounded by endless cycles of war and political despotism. Yet with the early glimmerings of a new scientific and technological age, bold and brilliant Enlightenment thinkers throughout Europe and the emerging United States began to envision the possibility of sustained social progress in which science and technology could be harnessed to achieve sustained improvements in the organization of social, political, and economic life. All of us who work toward a brighter future are intellectually indebted to the awe-inspiring geniuses of the Enlightenment, who first glimpsed the prospect of conscious social actions to improve human well-being on a global scale.

Four overarching ideas of the Enlightenment inspire us today. Thomas Jefferson and other founders of the American Republic, who in turn were the disciples of English philosophers such as John Locke and David Hume, made clear that political institutions are human constructs that should be fashioned consciously to meet the needs of society. "Governments are instituted among Men," wrote Jefferson in words that have echoed ever since, to secure the rights of "Life, Liberty, and the Pursuit of Happiness." After the American Revolution and the French Revolution, political systems could no longer be justified on the basis of the divine rights of monarchs or claims of religious prophecy. Governments, increasingly, would have to meet a performance test: whether or not they could improve the human condition. As Jefferson wrote, "That whenever any Form of Government becomes destructive of these ends, it is the Right of the People to alter or to abolish it, and to institute new Government, laying its foundation on such principles and organizing its powers in such form, as to them shall seem most likely to effect their Safety and Happiness."

Adam Smith believed that the economic system could similarly be shaped to meet human needs, and his economic designs run parallel to Jefferson's political designs. *The Wealth of Nations* and the Declaration of Independence, in fact, both appeared in 1776. Although many remember Smith today mainly for his brilliant insight into how market forces could support a self-organizing division of labor—the invisible hand—he was anything but a laissez-faire ideologue. Smith spends much of Book V of *The Wealth of Nations* explaining in detail why the state has powerful responsibilities regarding defense, justice, infrastructure, and education, areas in which collective action is required to complement, or substitute for, private-market forces.

Immanuel Kant, the towering German Enlightenment philosopher, added a third plank to the foundations of our modern concept of human progress, calling for an appropriate global system of governance to end the age-old scourge of war. In 1795, Kant argued that perpetual peace between nations could be achieved if self-governing republics linked through international commerce replaced monarchies. Kant explained that monarchs have the incentive to launch wars because war does not require of the ruler "the least sacrifice of the pleasures of his table, the chase, his country houses, his court functions, and the like. He may, therefore, resolve on war as on a pleasure party for the most trivial reasons, and with perfect indifference leave the justification which decency requires to the diplomatic corps who are ever ready to provide it."

In a republic, by contrast, "the consent of the citizens is required in order to decide that war should be declared." "[N]othing is more natural than that they would be very cautious in commencing such a poor game, decreeing for themselves all the calamities of war," which include "having to fight, having to pay the costs of war from their own resources, having painfully to repair the devastation war leaves behind, and, to fill up the measure of evils, load themselves with a heavy national debt . . ."

Kant saw that international commerce would play a leavening role in international affairs. "The spirit of commerce, which is incompatible with war, sooner or later gains the upper hand in every state. As the power of money is perhaps the most dependable of all the powers (means) included under the state power, states see themselves forced, without any moral urge, to promote honorable peace and by mediation to prevent war wherever it threatens to break out." The findings of the CIA Task Force on State Failure that open economies are less likely to fall into state failure than are closed economies echo Kant's words.

To achieve the result of perpetual peace, Kant envisioned a "Federation of Free States," indeed a proto-United Nations exactly 150 years before it was established. Kant's federation or "league" would not have "any dominion over the power of the state but only to the maintenance and security of the freedom of the state itself and of other states in league with it." Over time, Kant argued, such a federation would "gradually spread to all states."

A fourth overarching Enlightenment vision joins Jefferson's vision of human-made political systems, Smith's rationally designed economic systems, and Kant's global arrangements for perpetual peace: that science and technology, fueled by human reason, can be a sustained force for social improvements and human betterment. Following the first modern philosopher of science, Sir Francis Bacon, who proposed in 1620 that science could "kindle a light in nature," the towering French Enlightenment philosopher Marie-Jean-Antoine Condorcet brilliantly foresaw the role that science and technology could play for sustained social betterment. Remarkably, and poignantly, he wrote his magnificent

Sketch for a Historical Picture of the Progress of the Human Mind in 1794 while hiding from Jacobin radicals of the French Revolution, who would soon capture and imprison him, leading to his early death in 1795.

Condorcet was able to see into the future as few individuals have in history. He accurately foretold that scientific discoveries would create a chain reaction of further discoveries so that "the real accumulation of truths forming the system of the empirical, experimental, and mathematical sciences can grow constantly." He argued that the progress of the "useful arts" is similarly "bound to follow that of the sciences upon which they depend for their theory, and to have no other limit." He envisioned, for example, that "an ever-smaller tract of land will yield a quantity of more useful and valuable commodities . . . It will be possible to select, for each kind of soil, the crop satisfying the greatest needs, and to choose, among crops satisfying similar needs, those satisfying a greater number of people with less work and less real consumption." He declared that "progress in medical care, healthier nutrition and accommodation, a mode of life developing strength through exercise . . . will inevitably extend the average life span and assure human beings more consistent health . . . It seems clear that advances in preventive medicine, rendered more efficacious by the progress of reason and of the social order, will in the long run extinguish transmissible and contagious illnesses, as well as the common illnesses caused by climate, foodstuffs, and working conditions."

Condorcet, like his fellow Enlightenment thinkers, put enormous stress on public education to accomplish all of these goals. Education enabled individuals to stand on their own feet, to avoid charlatans, to abandon useless or harmful superstitions, and to improve their ethics, human sympathies, and "moral goodness." The wider the education, including in social and political principles, the more peaceful, sound, and progressive the entire society would be. "Thus the constant expansion of elementary instruction in these [political] sciences . . . offers us an improvement in the destinies of the human species that can be regarded as indefinite." Condorcet, like Kant, believed that reason could lead to a reduction of warfare: "The most enlightened peoples, reclaiming the right to expend their blood and wealth, will gradually learn to see war as the deadliest scourge and the greatest of crimes."

One of the deepest and most abiding commitments of the Enlightenment was the idea that social progress should be universal, not restricted to a narrow corner of the world in Western Europe. All of the leading Enlightenment figures believed in the essential equality of humanity, and of the ability of societies in all parts of the world to share in economic progress. They all followed Adam Smith in believing that global trade, what we would now call globalization, would speed the process. But although Smith championed open trade, and indeed became the apostle of globalization itself, he understood its precariousness and risks. He had no illusions that globalization would automatically spread the benefits of technology and the division of labor.

With great eloquence, Smith described how the opening of sea trade between Europe and the East Indies (South and Southeast Asia) and the West Indies (the Caribbean) had certainly not benefited the non-European populations. As he put it: "To the natives, however, both of the East and West Indies, all the commercial benefits which can have resulted from [the new trade routes] have been sunk and lost in the dreadful misfortunes they have occasioned." Smith argued that the problem did not lie with international trade per se, but with the vast military advantage that Europe had over the native inhabitants in both the Americas and Asia: "At the particular time these [sea route] discoveries were made, the superiority of force happened to be so great on the side of the Europeans, that they were enabled to commit with impunity every sort of injustice in those remote countries." Smith looked forward to the day when the inhabitants of the East and West Indies would have sufficient power to resist these depredations, and he felt that globalization indeed would speed that day: "But nothing seems more likely to establish this equality of force than that mutual communication of knowledge and of all sorts of improvements which an extensive commerce from all countries to all countries naturally, or rather necessarily, carries along with it."

OUR GENERATION'S TURN

It is our breathtaking opportunity to be able to advance the Enlightenment vision of Jefferson, Smith, Kant, and Condorcet. Our generation's work can be defined in Enlightenment terms:

- To help foster political systems that promote human well-being, based on the consent of the governed

- To help foster economic systems that spread the benefits of science, technology, and the division of labor to all parts of the world

- To help foster international cooperation in order to secure a perpetual peace

- To help promote science and technology, grounded in human rationality, to fuel the continued prospects for improving the human condition

The agenda is broad and bold, as it has been for two centuries, but many of its sweetest fruits are just within our reach. The democratic revolution unleashed during the Enlightenment now covers more than half the world's population. Kant's vision of a federation of independent states is embodied in the United Nations, with its 191 member countries. Condorcet's image of a self-sustaining scientific revolution has proved to be on the mark, and science can now be harnessed to address some of humanity's greatest continuing perils. And Smith's concept of spreading economic wealth is the most immediate of the triumphs that can lie ahead: the elimination of extreme poverty itself in just two decades' time.

It became fashionable in many intellectual circles throughout the twentieth century and into our own to declare the Enlightenment a failure, even a threat to humanity itself. Man is not a rational species, declare one set of opponents, but a species subject to irrational passions. The Enlightenment, say these critics, offered the promise of progress, but instead brought devastating wars, the Holocaust, nuclear weapons, and environmental destruction. Some pundits argue today that "progress is an illusion—a view of human life and history that answers to the needs of the heart, not reason." These claims are wrong, dangerously so in my view. They are wrong empirically because progress in many crucial forms—scientific, technological, fulfilling human needs—has been real and sustained over the course of two centuries, notwithstanding the undoubted disasters and the yet-unmet challenges. The facts of global wars and continued extreme poverty do not invalidate the long, persistent, and continuing rise of global living standards and the fall in the share of the world population living in extreme poverty. The claim of progress is correct as long as it is not taken to be a claim of perfection.

The Enlightenment optimism did lead some thinkers astray into two kinds of fallacies. One was a fallacy of inevitability: the assumption that human reason would necessarily prevail over the passions. Nineteenth-century positivists such as Auguste Comte argued for the inevitability of progress and therefore cast doubt on the Enlightenment legacy when humanity nonetheless suffered major backsliding in wars and barbarism. The second was a fallacy of violence, that collective compulsion could speed the way to a society built on reason and progress. Lenin, Stalin, Mao, and Pol Pot were cruel promoters of violence in the name of social progress. They left tens of millions of their own countrymen dead, demoralizing and impoverishing their own societies.

The critics of progress should therefore be met partway. Progress is possible, but not inevitable. Reason can be mobilized to promote social well-being, but can also be overtaken by destructive passions. Human institutions, indeed, should be designed in the light of reason precisely to control or harness the irrational side of human behavior. In this sense, the Enlightenment commitment to reason is not a denial of the unreasonable side of human nature, but rather a belief that despite human irrationality and passions, human reason can still be harnessed—through science, nonviolent action, and historical reflection—to solve basic problems of social organization and to improve human welfare.

THE ANTIGLOBALIZATION MOVEMENT

At the start of the twenty-first century, Enlightenment hopes for progress embodied in the Millennium Declaration and the Millennium Development Goals have clashed head on with war, AIDS, and the still unmet challenge of extreme poverty in large parts of Africa, Latin America, and Asia. The clash of high rhetoric and poor results has led to the antiglobalization movement, which burst forth dramatically into public view on the streets of Seattle in November 1999.

I have intersected repeatedly with the antiglobalization movement from its very inception. I experienced the very first 1999 street demonstrations personally, having been in Seattle that day for a Gates Foundation conference on information technology for the poor that was running alongside the ministerial meeting of the World Trade Organization (WTO). It was the WTO event that brought the protesters to

Seattle. As I crossed Seattle's downtown streets filled with protesters of every variety—antiwar, antitrade, and especially anticorporate—I whispered to my walking companion, Bill Gates, Sr., the father of Microsoft founder Bill Gates, Jr., and president of the Gates Foundation, that it was probably just as well that he was not recognized by the crowds! The profound irony, of course, is that the Gates Foundation is the world's leading foundation for promoting public health in poor countries, yet to the antiglobalization movement, multinational companies like Microsoft are part of the problem, not the solution.

From Seattle onward, street demonstrations have greeted just about every major international conference. Street protesters have forced the G8 leaders, ostensibly the world's most powerful, to hold their annual conferences in the not-so-splendid isolation of islands, mountaintops, forests, and other sheltered venues as far away from protesters as possible. The World Social Forum in Porto Alegre, Brazil, now shares the stage with the Davos World Economic Forum. World business leaders compete with social activists for the upper hand in global reporting on

Figure 1: FDI and Income

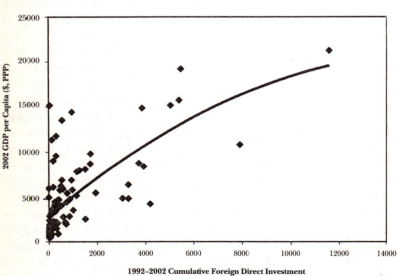

1992–2002 Cumulative Foreign Direct Investment
($ per capita)

Source: Data from World Bank (2004).

privatization. The IMF and World Bank have shortened their annual meetings from around a week to just a couple of days of business.

The antiglobalization movement has made its mark, and in my view, mostly for the good (except for the moments of violence that fringe elements of the movement incite). I applaud the overall movement for exposing the hypocrisies and glaring shortcomings of global governance and for ending years of self-congratulation by the rich and powerful. Before Seattle, the G8, IMF, and World Bank meetings were occasions for unqualified praise of globalization, and for the self-serving accolades of bankers and international financiers on their contribution to the spread of prosperity. Between the speeches and endless cocktail parties, there was little said about the world's poor, the AIDS pandemic, dispossessed minorities, women without rights, and human-made environmental degradation. Since Seattle, the agenda of ending extreme poverty, extending human rights, and addressing environmental degradation has been back on the international agenda and has attracted global media attention, albeit sporadically.

Nonetheless, I oppose many of the specific positions of antiglobalization leaders, even if I favor their moral fervor over the complacency of the rich. The antiglobalization movement has been fueled by legitimate moral outrage, but it has often been directed toward superficial targets, in my opinion. An anticorporate animus lies at the core of the movement, a belief that multinational corporations such as Microsoft, Coke, McDonald's, Pfizer, and Royal Dutch Shell, to name just a few, are the main villains in causing extreme poverty and environmental degradation. Policy recommendations of the movement have often prescribed classic protectionism, ostensibly to protect poor countries from the exploitative reach of rich corporations. The movement has especially targeted the World Trade Organization as the institution that allows the world's leading companies to go about their global business.

The views central to the antiglobalization movement are not new. They remind me very much of what I encountered in New Delhi in 1994, when Indian academics expressed grave reservations about the liberalization of trade and investment that had begun in India in 1991. Those views were passé then, and are more so today. By now the antiglobalization movement should see that globalization, more than anything else, has reduced the numbers of extreme poor in India by two hundred million and in China by three hundred million since 1990. Far from being exploited by multinational companies, these countries and many others like them have achieved unprecedented rates of economic growth on the basis of foreign direct investment (FDI) and the export-led growth that followed.

In my view, the antiglobalization movement leaders have the right moral fervor and ethical viewpoint, but the wrong diagnosis of the deeper problems. If they would ponder the data of figure 1, showing the amount of cumulative foreign direct investment per person from 1992 to 2002 in countries of Latin America, Africa, and Asia, they would see that countries with higher levels of FDI per person are also the countries with higher GNP per capita. Other studies confirm that high rates of foreign direct investment inflows have been associated with rapid economic growth. Africa's problems, I have noted repeatedly, are not caused by exploitation by global investors but rather by its economic isolation, its status as a continent largely bypassed by the forces of globalization. The same is true with trade, as we see in figure 2. Countries with open trade generally have grown more rapidly than countries with

Figure 2: Average Growth of Eight Always Open and
Forty Always Closed Economies 1966–1990

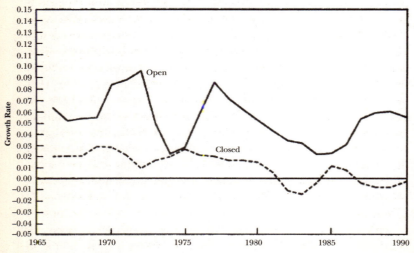

Source: Sachs and Warner (1995).

closed trade, and rising per capita incomes in most countries have generally been associated with a rise in the ratio of trade (exports plus imports) to GDP. Following the end of colonial rule after World War II, some countries chose open trade policies, whereas most developing countries chose protectionism. The open economies decisively outpaced the closed economies. By the early 1990s, almost all developing countries had opted for open trade, dropping decades of high-tariff and quota barriers. There is simply no evidence whatsoever that trade protectionism or the absence of multinational companies does a whit to end extreme poverty.

So why has the movement taken on trade and corporations as the first line of attack? First, because in truth many companies have behaved badly. The protesters have succeeded in illuminating and cleaning up bad or even corrupt corporate practices. U.S. and European companies that buy garments and apparel from low-wage plants no doubt treat their workers with greater civility and dignity today because of the protesters. Oil companies that once bribed African leaders with impunity think twice, or not at all, about doing so today, aware now of protesters' eyes upon them and the direct line between protesters' eyes, investor resistance, and bad corporate publicity. Drug company executives who at one time bellyached that they should have full freedom to price their patent-protected drugs as they saw fit, now give their drugs away or sell them on a zero-profit basis as a result of successful activism.

But the anticorporate, antitrade attitudes have also resulted from a knee-jerk antipathy to capitalism that reflects a more profound misunderstanding. Too many protesters do not know that even Adam Smith shared their moral sentiments and practical calls for social improvement, that even proponents of trade and investment can also believe in government-led actions to address the unmet needs of the poor and the environment. Too many protesters do not know that it is possible to combine faith in the power of trade and markets with understanding of their limitations as well. The movement is too pessimistic about the possibilities of capitalism with a human face, in which the remarkable power of trade and investment can be harnessed while acknowledging and addressing limitations through compensatory collective actions.

At a fundamental level, the global environmental crisis is not the fault of BP or Shell or ExxonMobil, and the AIDS pandemic is not the fault of Pfizer or Merck. Nor will the solutions to these crises be found by bloodying the leading energy or pharmaceutical companies. The solutions will be found in public policies, at national and international levels, that properly manage the emissions of climate-changing gases and that properly make life-saving medications available to the poor who cannot afford them. The antiglobalization movement is wrong to suppose that private companies are the ones to design the rules of the game. If governments would do their job in setting up the right rules, major international companies would play a vital role in solving problems. After all, these companies employ the world's best technologies, leading internal research units, and organizational and logistical operations that are superior to almost any public organizations in the world. They know, in short, how to get the job done when the incentives are in place for them to do the right thing.

Where the antiglobalization movement has a powerful point to stress is how multinational corporations often go well beyond their market demands to maximize shareholder wealth subject to the market rules of the game and, instead, expend substantial efforts, often hidden under the table, to make the rules of the game themselves. Economic reasoning justifies market-based behavior by companies if the rules of the game are sound. There is nothing in economic reasoning to justify letting the companies themselves set the rules of the game through lobbying, campaign financing, and dominance of government policies.

Toward an Enlightened Globalization

When all is said and done, however, the antiglobalization movement should mobilize its vast commitment and moral force into a proglobalization movement on behalf of a globalization that addresses the needs of the poorest of the poor, the global environment, and the spread of democracy. It is the kind of globalization championed by the Enlightenment—a globalization of democracies, multilateralism, science and technology, and a global economic system designed to meet human needs. We could call this an Enlightened Globalization.

What, then, would be the focus of a mass public movement aimed at an Enlightened Globalization? It would be, first and foremost, a focus on the behavior of the rich governments, especially the most powerful and wayward of the rich governments, the United States. It would insist that the United States and other rich countries honor their commitments to help the poor escape from poverty, as well as honor their commitments to limit environmental degradation including human-made climate change and the loss of biodiversity. Such a movement would continue to shine a spotlight on corporate responsibility, but would urge more rather than less investment by major multinational companies in the poorest countries. Instead of focusing on blocking trade and investment, it would insist that the World Trade Organization follow through on the political commitments made at Doha and elsewhere to ensure that the poorest countries have access to the markets of the richest.

Perhaps most important in the immediate future, such a movement would press the United States to end its reveries of empire and unilateralism and rejoin the world community in multilateral processes. The neoconservative calls for a U.S. empire are fantasies, but very dangerous ones. They misunderstand two basic points about our world. First, the United States is but 4.5 percent of the world's population and around 20 percent of its income when measured at purchasing power parity. By 2050, the share of population may decline slightly, but the share of GNP is likely to decline rather sharply, perhaps to a mere 10 percent of income. The United States simply does not hold a margin of economic advantage sufficient to sustain any real attempt at global empire, however good or bad such an idea might be. Ironically, the small-scale war in Iraq badly stretched U.S. military personnel and the public finances. And because the public was not at all interested in actually paying for the war through taxation, the Bush administration has had to finance the war through budget deficits.

Second, while the United States has vast military power, the use of that power for political advantage is rather small. As the Iraq war demonstrated, the United States can conquer, but it cannot rule. What the neoconservatives simply did not understand is that the era when foreign populations might conceivably tolerate U.S. rule ended a half century ago. The United States was not greeted in Iraq as a liberator, but rather as an occupier, a turn of events that was utterly predictable except, apparently, for neoconservatives divorced from modern realities. The leading political ideology of our time is nationalism and self-determination, and that ideology became vastly stronger throughout the twentieth century in the developing world as literacy spread and the arbitrary and cynical nature of colonial rule became painfully evident.

The unilateralism and militarism of the Bush administration has also been fueled by another powerful force. I alluded earlier to the fact that many millions of Americans apparently form their foreign policy beliefs not by assessing U.S. national interests but by interpreting biblical prophecy. As the United States invaded Iraq and Afghanistan, millions of U.S. fundamentalist Christians debated whether the rise of terrorism and Middle East conflict marked the end days of prophecy. The fictional *Left Behind* series of novels based on fundamentalist prophecy has sold tens of millions of volumes dramatizing a future Armageddon. Believers in these doctrines formed a powerful constituency within the Bush political coalition. If American foreign policy falls under the sway not only of unilateralism, or misconceived neoimperialism, but also irrational biblical prophecy as well, the risks for the world will multiply profoundly.

TAKING UP THE CHALLENGE

As global prosperity has accelerated in the past two centuries, each generation has been called upon to meet new challenges in extending the possibilities of human well-being. Some have faced the harrowing challenge of defending reason itself against the hysterias and mass brutalities of communism, fascism, and other totalitarianisms of the twentieth century. Others have been blessed with the opportunity to expand the ambit of human freedom and reason, spared from war and equipped with increasingly powerful tools to improve the human condition. Our own generation lives with a precarious peace, one threatened both by terrorism and by the overly militaristic response of the United States, but a peace on which we can build if we can sustain it. Ending poverty is the great opportunity of our time, a commitment that would not only relieve massive suffering and spread economic well-being, but would also promote the other Enlightenment objectives of democracy, global security, and the advance of science.

How, I am often asked, can I believe that inward-looking and materialistic societies such as those in the United States, Europe, and Japan could embrace a bold program of social improvement, especially one directed at the world's very poorest people? Aren't societies shortsighted and selfish, incapable of responding to the needs of others? I think not. Other generations have been triumphant in expanding the reach of human freedom and well-being through a combination of struggle, persuasion, patience, and the profound benefit of being on the right side of history. Three great generational challenges, in which the rights of the poor and weak were vindicated, come to mind. These examples offer inspiration and guidance for our own time.

The End of Slavery

In 1789, the year that the National Assembly of France adopted the Rights of Man and of the Citizen, proclaiming the Enlightenment vision that "men are born and remain free and equal in rights," slavery was still spreading around the globe, practiced throughout the French, British, Ottoman, and other empires. Across the Channel in London, a seemingly quixotic movement was just getting started: the formation of the Committee for Effecting the Abolition of the Slave Trade. Its founders, twenty-seven-year-old Thomas Clarkson and his friends, were Quakers who opposed the slave trade on moral and religious grounds. They established local abolitionist committees, and in the words of historian Hugh Thomas, "This was the first major public campaign in any country for a philanthropic cause." Clarkson soon met William Wilberforce, who would become the great parliamentary champion of the cause for the next quarter century.

Stunningly, the antislavery movement in Britain ran starkly against British commercial interests. Far from hastening the end of a declining industry, abolitionism grew at the same time the slave trade and slave-based industries were thriving. The opposition to slavery rested on moral, political, and ethical grounds, and on a vision of society, rather than on narrow self-interest. As always, opponents of ending the slave trade claimed that it would have exactly the opposite effect of what it intended, just as opponents of foreign assistance today claim erroneously and tendentiously that it does more harm than good. One of Wilberforce's parliamentary opponents put it this way: "If they [Africans] could not be sold as slaves, they would be butchered and executed at home." Others argued that even if meritorious in theory, the case for ending the slave trade had no practical prospect. "If abolition became law," suggested another of Wilberforce's foes, "all sensible merchants would go to France, where they would be well received."

As Thomas wryly notes, "Persistence is the most important quality in politics. It was possessed in heroic quantity by Wilberforce . . ." The next decades were filled with painful twists, turns, and prevarications, but they culminated in the successful abolition of the slave trade, and of slavery itself, in the European colonies. In 1807, in the midst of the Napoleonic Wars, the British Empire abolished the slave trade. At the end of the Napoleonic Wars in 1815, at the Congress of Vienna, the governments of Britain, France, Spain, Austria, Prussia, Russia, and Portugal committed themselves to the end of the slave trade, although without a date certain. During the 1820s, the abolition of slavery itself within the British Empire was debated vociferously in the British Parliament. Supporters of abolition cleverly used both moral and practical arguments. Yes, they acknowledged, Britain might suffer some financial inconveniences from abolition, but France, the competitor, would be hit even harder. Finally, after domestic political reforms in Great Britain, legislation abolishing slavery throughout the empire was adopted in 1833.

The End of Colonialism

Roughly one hundred years later, Mohandas Karamchand Gandhi led what seemed to be yet another quixotic quest: to wrest Indian independence from the grip of the British Empire. India was the jewel of the empire, and Winston Churchill and his imperial colleagues were hardly wont to concede India to a "seditious fakir," in Churchill's pungent judgment. Gandhi's campaign, which inspired dozens of independence movements throughout the colonial world, is now part of universal lore: the nonviolent struggle, the campaign for India's self-sufficiency to prove the capacity of the nation to stand on its own, and the call for political and social equality extended to the impoverished and disadvantaged lower castes of Indian society, whom Gandhi labeled *harijans,* or God's children. Gandhi's strategy rooted the independence movement in the broadest political, social, economic, and moral terms.

Who can say that mobilizing a mere 0.7 percent of rich world GNP to end extreme poverty is a major challenge in comparison with overthrowing the shackles of imperial rule to create more than fifty newly independent countries? As with the end of slavery, the end of colonial rule seemed a hopeless venture at the start and an inevitable outcome by the end. The precipitous end of colonial rule resulted partly from the devastating civil wars among the European colonial powers from 1914 to 1945, which literally bled the colonial powers, exhausted them economically, and discredited them morally. Still, the triumph was one of mass political action and the awakening of vast publics around the world to the ideals of self-rule. Without glossing over the tragic violence, cynicism, political failure, and despotism that often replaced imperialism, we can marvel at the phenomenal and positive spread of the Enlightenment ideal of government by consent.

The Civil Rights and Antiapartheid Movements

Gandhi's nonviolent struggle was a proof of concept for many struggles that followed. He demonstrated that the weak could break the oppression of the powerful by a massive and unrelenting appeal to universal values. Gandhi's political struggle for Indian independence was even more fundamentally a struggle for Indians' dignity and human rights, and thereby became the touchstone of the civil rights movement a generation later in the United States and the antiapartheid struggles after that. Martin Luther King, Jr., was the U.S. Gandhi, the pioneer in mass nonviolent mobilization who looked oppression in the eye and declared, "Enough!" In 1958, King wrote, "It was in this Gandhian emphasis on love and nonviolence that I discovered the method for social reform that I had been seeking." The following year, King made a pilgrimage to India to study the path of nonviolent protest. Three decades later, Nelson Mandela inspired the entire world by showing how moral courage and political deftness could end racist rule in South Africa in a peaceful transition to constitutional democracy.

In King's famous "I Have a Dream" speech, he harked back to the Enlightenment, and specifically to the U.S.' founding documents:

> When the architects of our republic wrote the magnificent words of the Constitution and the Declaration of Independence, they were signing a promissory note to which every American was to fall heir. This note was a promise that all men would be guaranteed the unalienable rights of life, liberty, and the pursuit of happiness.
>
> It is obvious today that America has defaulted on this promissory note insofar as her citizens of color are concerned. Instead of honoring this sacred obligation, America has given the Negro people a bad check which has come back marked "insufficient funds." But we refuse to believe that the bank of justice is bankrupt. We refuse to believe that there are insufficient funds in the great

vaults of opportunity of this nation. So we have come to cash this
check—a check that will give us upon demand the riches of freedom and the security of justice.

Our assertion today must be like King's forty years ago. The bank of international justice is not bankrupt. The world's poor cannot accept a
bad check marked insufficient funds, especially when it is painfully clear
that the funds are ample and even residing in the accounts of a few hundred of the U.S.' superrich, not to mention the four million or so American households with net worth in excess of $1 million, or the eight
million or so households worldwide, or the one billion people in total
who live in the high-income countries with a combined annual income
of some $30 trillion.

The movements against slavery, colonialism, and racism share some
basic features. They looked quixotic, perhaps even hopeless at the start,
as calls to the richest and most powerful in the world to extend justice for
the poorest and most helpless. They required a mix of political action,
real politics, and mass education to succeed. They appealed to enlightened self-interest as well as basic religious and ethical precepts. They
took decades to bring to fruition; perseverance was the key. They called
upon fundamental Enlightenment values of human rights and human
potentialities. Ultimately, with a sudden shift in public attitudes, they
transformed the impossible into the inevitable. In the same way, the end
of poverty will come quickly, marked by a rapid transition. The fact that
for thirty-five years rich countries have promised but not delivered something as basic as 0.7 percent of GNP in ODA is not a cause for despair,
but instead a basis for even greater social mobilization.

OUR NEXT STEPS

The time to end poverty has arrived, although hard work lies ahead. I
have diagnosed the reasons for continued extreme poverty in the midst
of great wealth. I have noted the specific steps that could address and
overcome this poverty. I have shown that the costs of action are small,
and indeed a tiny fraction of the costs of inaction. I have identified a
timetable to 2025, including the Millennium Development Goals as the
midway station in 2015. I have shown how key international institutions
can contribute to the process ahead. And yet we must carry out these

tasks in a context of global inertia, proclivities to war and prejudice, and understandable skepticism around the world that *this time* can be different from the past.

Yes, this time can be different, and here are nine steps to the goal.

Commit to Ending Poverty The first step is commitment to the task. Oxfam and many other leaders in civil society have embraced a goal, Making Poverty History. The world as a whole needs now to embrace that goal. We have committed to halving poverty by 2015. Let us commit to ending extreme poverty by 2025.

Adopt a Plan of Action The Millennium Development Goals are the down payment on ending poverty. They are specific, quantified, and already promised in a Global Compact of Rich and Poor. Not only should the world community recommit to those goals, but its leaders should adopt a specific global plan to meet the Millennium Development Goals of the sort outlined in chapter 15, and offered in detail by the UN Millennium Project.

Raise the Voice of the Poor Mahatma Gandhi and Martin Luther King, Jr., did not wait for the rich and powerful to come to their rescue. They asserted their call to justice and made their stand in the face of official arrogance and neglect. The poor cannot wait for the rich to issue the call to justice. The G8 will never champion the end of poverty if the poor themselves are silent. It is time for the world's democracies in the poor world—Brazil, India, Nigeria, Senegal, South Africa, and dozens of others—to unite to issue the call to action. The poor are starting to find their voice, in the G3 (Brazil, India, South Africa), the G20 (a trade grouping that negotiates within the WTO), and elsewhere. The world needs to hear more.

Redeem the Role of the United States in the World The richest and most powerful country in the world, long the leader and inspiration in democratic ideals, has become the most feared and divisive country in recent years. The self-professed quest by the United States for unchallenged supremacy and freedom of action has been a disaster, and it poses one of the greatest risks to global stability. The lack of U.S. participation in multilateral initiatives has undermined global security and progress toward social justice and environmental protection. Its own interests have been undermined by this unilateral turn. Forged in the crucible of the Enlightenment, the United States can become a champion of Enlightened Globalization. Political action within the United States and from abroad will be needed to restore its role on the road toward global peace and justice.

Rescue the IMF and the World Bank Our leading international financial institutions are needed to play a decisive role in ending global poverty. They have the experience and technical sophistication to play an important role. They have the internal motivation of a highly professional staff. Yet they have been badly used, indeed misused, as creditor-run agencies rather than international institutions representing all of their 182 member governments. It is time to restore the international role of these agencies so that they are no longer the handmaidens of creditor governments, but the champions of economic justice and enlightened globalization.

Strengthen the United Nations It is no use blaming the UN for the missteps of recent years. We have gotten the UN that has been willed by the powerful countries of the world, especially the United States. Why are UN agencies less operational than they should be? Not because of UN bureaucracy, though that exists, but because the powerful countries are reluctant to cede more authority to international institutions, fearing reduction of their own freedom of maneuver. The UN specialized agencies have a core role to play in the end of poverty. It is time to empower the likes of the UN Children's Fund, the World Health Organization, the Food and Agricultural Organization, and many others to do the job—on the ground, country by country—that they are uniquely qualified to lead, helping the poorest of the poor to use modern science and technology to overcome the trap of poverty.

Harness Global Science Science has been the key to development from the very start of the industrial revolution, the fulcrum by which reason is translated into technologies of social advance. As Condorcet predicted, science has empowered technological advances in food production, health, environmental management, and countless other basic sectors of production and human need. Yet science tends to follow market forces as well as to lead them. It is not surprising, I have noted repeatedly, that the rich get richer in a continuing cycle of endogenous growth, whereas the poorest of the poor are often left outside of this virtuous circle. When their needs are specific—by virtue of particular diseases, or crops, or ecological conditions—their problems are bypassed by global science. Therefore, a special effort of world science, led by global scientific research centers of governments, academia, and industry, must commit specifically to addressing the unmet challenges of the poor. Public funding, private philanthropies, and not-for-profit foundations will have to back these commitments, precisely because market forces alone will not suffice.

Promote Sustainable Development While targeted investments in health, education, and infrastructure can unlock the trap of extreme poverty, the continuing environmental degradation at local, regional, and planetary scales threatens the long-term sustainability of all our social gains. Ending extreme poverty can relieve many of the pressures on the environment. When impoverished households are more productive on their farms, they face less pressure to cut down neighboring forests in search of new farmland. When their children survive with high probability, they have less incentive to maintain very high fertility rates with the attendant downside of rapid population growth. Still, even as extreme poverty ends, the environmental degradation related to industrial pollution and the long-term climate change associated with massive use of fossil fuels will have to be addressed. There are ways to confront these environmental challenges without destroying prosperity (for example, by building smarter power plants that capture and dispose of their carbon emissions and by increasing use of renewable energy sources). As we invest in ending extreme poverty, we must face the ongoing challenge of investing in the global sustainability of the world's ecosystems.

Make a Personal Commitment In the end, however, it comes back to us, as individuals. Individuals, working in unison, form and shape societies. Social commitments are commitments of individuals. Great social forces, Robert Kennedy powerfully reminded us, are the mere accumulation of individual actions. His words are more powerful today than ever:

> Let no one be discouraged by the belief there is nothing one man or one woman can do against the enormous array of the world's ills—against misery and ignorance, injustice and violence . . . Few

will have the greatness to bend history itself; but each of us can work to change a small portion of events, and in the total of all those acts will be written the history of this generation . . .

It is from the numberless diverse acts of courage and belief that human history is shaped. Each time a man stands up for an ideal, or acts to improve the lot of others, or strikes out against injustice, he sends a tiny ripple of hope, and crossing each other from a million different centers of energy and daring, those ripples build a current which can sweep down the mightiest walls of oppression and resistance.

Let the future say of our generation that we sent forth mighty currents of hope, and that we worked together to heal the world.

Works Cited

"Americans on Foreign Aid and World Hunger: A Study of US Public Attitudes." February 2, 2001, Findings. Program on International Policy Attitudes, University of Maryland.

Angell, Norman. *The Great Illusion: A Study of the Relation of Military Power to National Advantage.* London: W. Heinemann, 1910.

Aslund, Anders. *How Russia Became a Market Economy.* Washington, D.C.: Brookings Institution, 1995.

Attaran, Amir and Jeffrey D. Sachs, "Defining and Refining International Donor Support for Combating the AIDS Pandemic," *The Lancet,* Vol. 357, January 6, 2001.

Bapat, Meera and Indu Agarwal, "Our Needs, Our Priorities; Women and Men from the Slums in Mumbai and Pune Talk About Their Needs for Water and Sanitation," *Environment & Urbanization,* Vol. 15, No. 2, October 2003.

Bredenkamp, Hugh. Letter to the Editor, *Financial Times,* June 29, 1999.

Bremen, Joel G., Martin S. Alilio, and Anne Mills, "Conquering the Intolerable Burden of Malaria: What's New, What's Needed: A Summary," *The American Journal of Tropical Medicine and Hygiene,* Vol. 71, August 2003, No. 2 Supplement.

Caritat, Marie-Jean-Antoine-Nicolas-de, Marquis de Condorcet. *Sketch for a Historical Picture of the Progress of the Human Mind.* Keith Michael Baker, tr., *Daedalus,* Summer 2004, 65–82.

Central Intelligence Agency, "National Intelligence Estimate 60/70-65, Washington, April 22, 1965." Source: Central Intelligence Agency: Job 79-R01012A, ODDI Registry of NIE and SNIE Files. Secret; Controlled Dissem. According to a note on the cover sheet, the estimate was submitted by Director of Central Intelligence John A. McCone and concurred in by the U.S. Intelligence Board on April 22.

Chen, Shaohua and Martin Ravallion, "How Have the World's Poorest Fared Since the Early 1980s?" World Bank Policy Research Working Paper 3341, June 2004.

Cheney, Richard. Remarks by Vice President Dick Cheney to the Veterans of Foreign Wars 103rd National Convention, August 26, 2002, Nashville, Tennessee.

Chidambaram, Palaniappan. Budget Speech, July 8, 2004. <http:www.deccanherald.com/deccanherald/july092004/n1.asp>

Commission on Macroeconomics and Health (CMH), *Macroeconomics and Health: Investing in Health for Economic Development.* Geneva: World Health Organization, 2001.

Davis, Mike. *Late Victorian Holocausts: El Niño Famines and the Making of the Third World.* London and New York: Verso, 2001.

Declaration of Independence, Action of the Second Continental Congress, July 4, 1776.

Donnelly, John, "Prevention Urged in AIDS Fight—Natsios Says Fund Should Spend Less on HIV Treatment," *Boston Globe,* June 7, 2001.

Eder, George. *Inflation and Development in Latin America—a Case of Inflation and Stabilization in Bolivia.* Ann Arbor: Program in International Business, Graduate School of Business Administration, University of Michigan, 1968.

Gray, John, "An Illusion with a Future," *Daedalus,* Summer 2004, p. 11.

Halperin, Daniel T., and Helen Epstein, "Concurrent Sexual Partnership Help to Explain Africa's High HIV Prevalence: Implications for Prevention," *The Lancet,* Vol. 364, July 3, 2004, p. 4.

Haynes, Ulric. "Memorandum from Ulric Haynes of the National Security Council Staff to the President's Special Assistant for National Security Affairs (Bundy), Washington, June 5, 1965." Source: Johnson Library, National Security File, Country File, Africa, General, Vol. II, Memos & Miscellaneous, 7/64-6/65.

Hu Jintao, Speech to Federal Parliament of Australia, October 23, 2003.

Inglehart, Ronald, et al. *Human Beliefs and Values.* Mexico: Siglo Veintiuno Editores, 2004. AO30.

Instituto Nacional de Estadística, www.udape.gov.bo/

International Monetary Fund, *A Study of the Soviet Economy.* Washington, D.C.: International Monetary Fund, 1991.

Kant, Immanuel. *Perpetual Peace.* Paris: 1795.

Keynes, John Maynard. *The Economic Consequences of the Peace.* London: Macmillan, 1919. <http:socserv2.socsci.mcmaster.ca/~econ/ugcm/3ll3/keynes/peace.htm>

———. "The Economic Possibilities for Our Grandchildren" in *Essays in Persuasion.* London: Macmillan, 1931.

Kiszewski, Anthony, et al., "A Global Index Representing the Stability of Malaria Transmission," *American Journal of Tropical Medicine and Hygiene,* 70, 5: pp. 486–98, 2004.

Maddison, Angus, *Monitoring the World Economy: 1820–1992.* Paris: OECD, 1995.

———. *The World Economy: A Millennial Perspective.* Paris: OECD, 2001.

Miles, Marc A., et al. *2004 Index of Economic Freedom.* Washington, D.C.: The Heritage Foundation and Wall Street Journal, 2004. <http:www.heritage.org/research/features/index/index.html>

Morales, Juan Antonio and Jeffrey D. Sachs, "Bolivia's Economic Crisis" in *Developing Country Debt and Economic Performance: Country Studies—Argentina, Brazil, Mexico,* vol. 2. Chicago: National Bureau of Economic Research, 1990.

OECD. Development Assistance Committee, Creditor Reporting System.

OECD. Development Assistance Committee, "Final ODA Data for 2003," 8–9 December 2004.

O'Reilly Factor, The, September 1, 2004.

Patel, Sheela, Celine d'Cruz, and Sundar Burra, "Beyond Evictions in a Global City: People-Managed Resettlement in Mumbai," *Environment & Urbanization,* Vol. 14, No 1, April 2002.

Pityana, Barney. Comments on December 8, 1998. http://www.wfn.org/1998/12/msg00181.html

Roosevelt, Franklin Delano. Address to the 77th Congress, January 6, 1941.

Sachs, Adam and Jeffrey D. Sachs. "Selling the Marshall Plan." n.p.

Sachs, Jeffrey D. and Wing Thye Woo, "Structural Factors in the Economic Reforms of China, Eastern Europe, and the Former Soviet Union," *Economic Policy,* Vol. 18, April 1994.

Sachs, Jeffrey D. and Andrew Warner, "Economic Reform and the Process of Global Integration," *Brookings Papers on Economic Activity,* 1995:1.

Sachs, Jeffrey D. and John Luke Gallup, "The Economic Burden of Malaria," *American Journal of Tropical Medicine and Hygiene,* 61 (1,2) S., 2001, pp. 85–96.

Sachs, Jeffrey D., Nirupan Bajpai, and Ananthi Ramiah, "Understanding Regional Economic Growth in India," *Asian Economic Papers,* Vol. 1:3, Summer 2002.

Sachs, Jeffrey D., et al., "Ending Africa's Poverty Trap," Brookings Papers on Economic Activity, No. 1, 2004.

Shameen, Assif, "Instant Industry," *Asiaweek.* Asiaweek.com, Asian of the Century, Ideas with Impact, December 10, 1999.

Smith, Adam. *The Wealth of Nations* (1776), Edwin Cannan, ed., 1904, London: Methuen and Co., Ltd.

Soto, Hernando de. *The Mystery of Capital: Why Capitalism Triumphs in the West and Fails Everywhere Else.* New York: Basic Books, 2000.

Thomas, Hugh. *The Slave Trade: The Story of the Atlantic Slave Trade, 1440–1870.* New York: Simon & Schuster, 1997.

Tomlinson, B.R. *The Economy of Modern India 1860–1970.* Cambridge: Cambridge University Press, 1993.

Transparency International, *Global Corruption Report 2004.* London: Pluto Press, 2004.

UNCTAD, *World Investment Report 2001.* New York and Geneva: United Nations, 2001.

UN Millennium Project, *Investing in Development: A Practical Plan to Achieve the Millennium Development Goals.* Report to the UN Secretary General. London: Earthscan, 2005.

———, "Millennium Project Goals Needs Assessments: Background Paper to 'Ending Africa's Poverty Trap,'" working paper, 2004. Available at: http://www.unmillenniumproject.org/html/backgroundpaper, shtm

Universal Declaration of Human Rights, United Nations General Assembly resolution 217 A (III), December 10, 1948, Article 25.

Wilson, Edward Osborne. *Biophilia.* Cambridge, Mass.: Harvard University Press, 1984.

Wolfensohn, James D. and the Utstein Group Proceedings. Prague, Czech Republic, September 24, 2000.

World Bank. *World Development Indicators.* Washington, D.C., 2004.

For Further Reading

The following readings include some of my academic studies on the subjects of this book. These articles may be downloaded at: www.sachs.earth.columbia.edu. I also mention some other outstanding recent books by others.

Much of my academic research has focused on the varied patterns of development in different parts of the world and on the roles of physical geography, international trade, history, and policy in shaping those differences. Among these studies I suggest the following for further reading (listed by year of publication):

Sachs, Jeffrey D. and Andrew Warner, "Economic Reform and the Process of Global Integration," *Brookings Papers on Economic Activity,* 1995:1.

Sachs, Jeffrey D., John Luke Gallup, and Andrew Mellinger, "Geography and Economic Development," in Boris Pleskovic and Joseph E. Stiglitz, eds., *Annual World Bank Conference on Development Economics 1998* (April), Washington, D.C.: The World Bank.

Sachs, Jeffrey D., "Twentieth-Century Political Economy: A Brief History of Global Capitalism," *Oxford Review of Economic Policy,* Vol. 115, No. 4, Winter 1999.

———, "Globalization and Patterns of Economic Development," *Review of World Economics,* Vol. 136(4), Kiel Institute of World Economics, 2000.

———, Andrew Mellinger and John Gallup, "Climate, Coastal Proximity, and Development," in *Oxford Handbook of Economic Geography,* Gordon L. Clark, Maryann P. Feldman, and Meric S. Gertler, eds., Oxford University Press, 2000.

———, "The Geography of Poverty and Wealth," *Scientific American,* March 2001.

Several of my studies have focused on the distinct geographical, historical, and institutional conditions in a particular region or country. Among these studies, I would suggest the following:

BOLIVA

Sachs, Jeffrey D., "The Bolivia Hyperinflation and Stabilization," *American Economic Review,* Vol. 77, No. 2, May 1987.

——— and Juan Antonio Morales, "Bolivia's Economic Crisis," Jeffrey D. Sachs, ed., *Foreign Debt and Economic Performance,* National Bureau of Economic Research and University of Chicago Press, 1989.

EASTERN EUROPE

Sachs, Jeffrey D. and David Lipton, "Creating a Market Economy in Eastern Europe: The Case of Poland," *Brookings Papers on Economic Activity*, 1990:1.

Sachs, Jeffrey D. *Poland's Jump to the Market Economy*. Cambridge: MIT Press, 1993.

RUSSIA

Sachs, Jeffrey D., "Russia's Struggle with Stabilization," *Annual Bank Conference on Development Economics*, World Bank, 1994.

—— and Wing Thye Woo, "Structural Factors in the Economic Reforms of China, Eastern Europe, and the Former Soviet Union," *Economic Policy*, Vol. 18, April 1994.

CHINA

Sachs, Jeffrey D., et al., "Geography, Economic Policy, and Regional Development in China," *Asian Economic Papers*, Vol. I, No. 1, Winter 2002, pp. 146–97.

Sachs, Jeffrey D. and Wing Thye Woo, "Understanding China's Economic Performance," *Journal of Policy Reform*, Vol. 4, Issue 1, 2000.

INDIA

Sachs, Jeffrey D. and Nirupam Bajpai, "India's Economic Reform—The Steps Ahead," *Journal of International Trade and Economic Development*, Vol. 6, No. 2, 1997.

——, "The Decade of Development: Goal Setting and Policy Changes in India," CID Working Paper No. 62, February 2001.

—— and Ananthi Ramiah, "Understanding Regional Economic Growth in India," *Asian Economic Papers*, Vol. 1, Issue 3, Summer 2002.

AFRICA

Sachs, Jeffrey D. and David Bloom, "Geography, Demography and Economic Growth in Africa," *Brookings Papers on Economic Activity*, 1998:2.

Sachs, Jeffrey D. et al., "Ending Africa's Poverty Trap," *Brookings Papers on Economic Activity*, 2004:1.

UNITED STATES (ECONOMIC GEOGRAPHY)

Sachs, Jeffrey D. and Jordan Rappaport, "The United States as a Coastal Nation," *Journal of Economic Growth*, Vol. 8, No. 1, March 2003.

During the past decade, I have studied extensively the links of disease and poverty, especially malaria and HIV/AIDS. Some of my studies in that area include:

Sachs, Jeffrey D. and John Luke Gallup, "The Economic Burden of Malaria," the Supplement to *The American Journal of Tropical Medicine and Hygiene,* Vol. 64, No. 1, 2, pp. 85–96, January/February 2001.

Sachs, Jeffrey D. and Amir Attaran, "Defining and Refining International Donor Support for Combating the AIDS Pandemic," *The Lancet,* Vol. 357, pp. 57–61, January 6, 2001.

Sachs, Jeffrey D., "A New Global Commitment to Disease Control in Africa," *Nature Medicine,* Vol. 7, No. 5, May 2001.

World Health Organization. *Macroeconomics and Health: Investing in Health for Economic Development.* Report of the Commission on Macroeconomics and Health. Geneva: World Health Organization, 2001.

Sachs, Jeffrey D. and Pia Malaney, "The Economic and Social Burden of Malaria," *Nature,* Vol. 415, No. 6872, February 7, 2002.

Sachs, Jeffrey D., "A New Global Effort to Control Malaria," *Science,* Vol. 298, October 4, 2002.

A few of my studies on the role of development assistance, debt relief, U.S. foreign policy, and international cooperation include:

Sachs, Jeffrey D., "The Strategic Significance of Global Inequality," *The Washington Quarterly,* Vol. 24, No. 3, Summer 2001.

———, "Resolving the Debt Crisis of Low-Income Countries," *Brookings Papers on Economic Activity,* 2002:1.

———, "Weapons of Mass Salvation," *The Economist,* October 26, 2002.

———, "Smart Money: What Military Power Can't Do," *The New Republic,* March 3, 2003.

Once a reader gets hooked on the compelling drama of global development, there is a treasure trove of wise and wonderful books to read, enjoy, and ponder. Some of the riveting analyses of global development in recent years that have shaped my own understanding include:

McNeill, William H. *Plagues and Peoples.* New York: Doubleday, 1977. A pathbreaking study of the links of disease and human history.

Braudel, Fernand. *Civilization and Capitalism* (3 volumes). New York: Harper-Collins, 1985. A magisterial history of the global economy and changing material conditions of human society during the past five hundred years.

Diamond, Jared. *Guns, Germs, and Steel: The Fates of Human Societies.* New York: W. W. Norton, 1997. A scintillating, highly original, and endlessly fascinating account of the relationship between ecology, human history, and economic development.

Landes, David S. *The Wealth and Poverty of Nations: Why Some Are So Rich and Some So Poor.* New York: W. W. Norton, 1998. A great economic historian's provocative views on the sweep of global economic history.

Smil, Vaclav. *Feeding the World: A Challenge for the 21st Century.* Cambridge, Mass.: MIT Press, 2000. A masterly interdisciplinary account of the interrelations of food, technology, demography, and development.

McNeill, J.R. et al. *Something New Under the Sun.* New York: W. W. Norton, 2001.

An original and deeply insightful study of the links of development and environment during the twentieth century.

Maddison, Angus. *The World Economy: A Millennial Perspective.* Paris: OECD, 2001. A remarkable quantitative analysis of economic growth during the past two hundred years.

Kidder, Tracy. *Mountains Beyond Mountains: Healing the World: The Quest of Dr. Paul Farmer.* New York: Random House, 2003. A biography of Dr. Paul Farmer, a pioneer in bringing essential health services to the poor.

Jones, Gareth Stedman. *An End to Poverty? A Historical Debate.* London: Profile Books, 2004. A marvelous intellectual history of the debates over ending poverty, especially during the Enlightenment era of the 1790s.

Notes

CHAPTER ONE: A GLOBAL FAMILY PORTRAIT

Page

18 **In Malawi, 84 percent:** World Bank, *World Development Indicators,* Washington, D.C.: World Bank, 2004.

20 **These measures feature:** Shaohua Chen and Martin Ravallion, "How Have the World's Poorest Fared Since the Early 1980s?" World Bank Policy Research Working Paper 3341, June 2004.

CHAPTER TWO: THE SPREAD OF ECONOMIC PROSPERITY

26 **Life expectancy in Western Europe:** Angus Maddison, *The World Economy: A Millennium Perspective* (Paris: OECD, 2001). Unless otherwise noted, all figures in this chapter are calculated from Maddison, 2001.

32 **"There is no record":** John Maynard Keynes, *The Economic Possibilities for Our Grandchildren* (London: Macmillan, 1930).

34 **". . . of manufactures for distant sale":** Adam Smith, *The Wealth of Nations.* 1776, Book III, Chapter 4, in paragraph III.4.20. London: Methuen and Co., Ltd., Edwin Cannan, ed., 1904. Available online at http://www.econlib.org/library/Smith/smWN.html.

45 **". . . and any deviation":** John Maynard Keynes, *The Economic Consequences of the Peace* (1919), Chapter 2. Available online at http://socserve2.socsci.mcmaster.ca/~econ/ugcm/3113/keynes/peace.

45 **"The projects and politics of militarism":** Ibid.

46 **". . . the gold standard and its "rules of the game":** Under the rules of the game, central banks were fearful of expanding the supply of money, as they should have in response to the Depression, because they were afraid to lose the gold reserves needed to back the currency. Only after coming off the gold standard did they have the freedom to maneuver to enact expansionary monetary policy.

CHAPTER THREE: WHY SOME COUNTRIES FAIL TO THRIVE

57 **Clearly, the poorest of the poor:** An economy needs to save roughly 15 percent of its GDP in order to keep up with population growth and capital depreciation according to the following equation:

*saving rate > (capital-output ratio) * (depreciation rate + population growth rate)*

Since the capital-output ratio is commonly assumed to be 3, the depreciation rate is about 3 percent and the population growth rate is about 2 percent, then the saving rate must be above 15 percent to keep up with depreciation and population growth. Figure 1 shows the least-developed countries as having a saving rate of 10 percent of GDP, which means that these economies are not saving enough to keep up with depreciation and population growth.

58 **". . . it is frequently":** Adam Smith, *The Wealth of Nations.* Book I, Chapter 3, in paragraph I.3.3, 1776.

62 **The top twenty countries:** Calculated using data from the U.S. Patent and Trademark Office.

66 **It is illuminating to divide:** Since countries were not yet officially classified by the World Bank into these categories back in 1980, I've defined low-income countries as those with a 1980 income per person below $3,000 per year (adjusted for purchasing power parity). Middle-income countries are those with per person incomes between $3,000 and $8,000, and high-income countries have incomes above $8,000.

CHAPTER FIVE: BOLIVIA'S HIGH-ALTITUDE HYPERINFLATION

95 **". . . a manner which":** John Maynard Keynes, "The Economic Consequences of the Peace" (1919). Chapter 6. Available online at http://socserve2.socsci.mcmaster.ca/~econ/ugcm/3113/keynes/peace.

98 **George Eder . . . advised:** George Eder, *Inflation and Development in Latin America: A Case of Inflation and Stabilization in Bolivia.* Ann Arbor: Program in International Business, Graduate School of Business Administration, University of Michigan, 1968.

102 **". . . it will, when it comes":** John Maynard Keynes, "The Economic Consequences of the Peace" (1919). Chapter 7. Available online at http://socserve2.socsci.mcmaster.ca/~econ/ugcm/3113/keynes/peace.

102 **". . . perhaps not in a way":** Ibid.

CHAPTER SIX: POLAND'S RETURN TO EUROPE

111 **. . . the leading strategists:** Kuron, sadly, died in 2004.

125 **the downward sloping line:** The graph excludes the oil-rich former Soviet Republics of Azerbaijan, Kazakhstan, and Turkmenistan, which received quite a bit of FDI for oil exploration and development despite their distance from Western Europe.

129 **. . . the seven richest countries:** The G7 included France, the United States, Britain, Germany, Japan, Italy and Canada until 1998, when Russia joined the group to become the G8.

CHAPTER SEVEN: REAPING THE WHIRLWIND:
RUSSIA'S STRUGGLE FOR NORMALCY

132 . . . **by 1989, debt:** Anders Aslund, *How Russia Became a Market Economy* (Washington, D.C.: Brookings Institution, 1995), Table 2.7, p. 49.

132 . . . **oil earnings had collapsed:** International Monetary Fund, et al., *A Study of the Soviet Economy* (Paris: OECD, 1991), p. 227.

135 **In 1989, for example:** Anders Aslund, *How Russia Became a Market Economy,* p. 45.

146 **". . . though some of the greatest rivers":** Adam Smith, *The Wealth of Nations,* Book I, Chapter 3, in paragraph I.3.8.

CHAPTER EIGHT: CHINA:
CATCHING UP AFTER HALF A MILLENNIUM

151 **". . . China . . . cannot":** Adam Smith, *The Wealth of Nations,* Book I, Chapter 9, in paragraph I.9.15.

158 **Only 20 percent of the population:** Jeffrey D. Sachs and Wing Thye Woo, "Structural Factors in the Economic Reforms of China, Eastern Europe, and the Former Soviet Union," *Economic Policy,* Vol. 18, April 1994.

158 **In the Soviet-style economy:** Ibid.

168 **". . . all countries must":** Hu Jintao, speech to the Federal Parliament of Australia, October 23, 2003.

CHAPTER NINE: INDIA'S MARKET REFORMS:
THE TRIUMPH OF HOPE OVER FEAR

174 **At the time of independence:** B. R. Tomlinson, *The Economy of Modern India 1860–1970* (Cambridge: Cambridge University Press, 1993), p. 7.

174 **Life expectancy in 1947:** Ibid.

174 **". . . many sectors of industry":** Angus Maddison, *The World Economy: A Millennial Perspective* (Paris: OECD, 2001), p. 116.

175 **"[A]ny Government which":** Mike Davis, *Late Victorian Holocausts: El Niño Famines and the Making of the Third World* (London and New York: Verso, 2001), p. 162.

176 **". . . the reluctance of British firms":** Angus Maddison, *The World Economy,* p. 116.

185 **"And this century":** Budget speech of P. Chidambaram, July 8, 2004.

187 **". . . their general tendency":** Adam Smith, *The Wealth of Nations,* Book IV, Chapter 7, in paragraph IV.7.166.

187 **". . . to commit with impunity":** Ibid.

CHAPTER TEN: THE VOICELESS DYING: AFRICA AND DISEASE

189 **". . . how can you cut through that?":** *The O'Reilly Factor,* September 1, 2004.

190 **National Intelligence Estimate:** National Intelligence Estimate 60/70-65, Washington, April 22, 1965. Source: Central Intelligence Agency: Job 79-R01012A, ODDI Registry of NIE and SNIE Files. Secret; Controlled Dissem. According to a note on the cover sheet, the estimate was submitted by Director of Central In-

telligence John A. McCone and concurred in by the U.S. Intelligence Board on April 22.

190 **". . . substantial increases":** Memorandum from Ulric Haynes of the National Security Council Staff to the president's special assistant for national security affairs (Bundy),Washington, June 5, 1965. Source: Johnson Library, National Security File, Country File, Africa, General, Vol. II, Memos & Miscellaneous, 7/64-6/65. Confidential. Copies were sent to Komer and Harold H. Saunders of the National Security Council Staff.

191 **Africa's per capita economic growth:** Jeffrey D. Sachs, et al., "Ending Africa's Poverty Trap," *Brookings Papers on Economic Activity,* No. 1, 2004.

192 **human beings are "hard-wired":** Edward Osborne Wilson, *Biophilia* (Cambridge, Mass.: Harvard University Press, 1984).

194 **(not including the five countries):** North Africa is significantly different from sub-Saharan Africa—its temperate and desert climate zones are less conducive to tropical diseases and its location gives it easy access to European markets, with most of the population concentrated along the Mediterranean coast. On the other hand, the Sahara restricts sub-Saharan Africa's access to Europe. The result is that North African populations are mostly coastal and close to Europe, leading to a very different economic structure compared to the rest of the continent. South Africa, meanwhile, has a mainly temperate ecology that also translates into a reduced tropical disease burden. Moreover, South Africa benefits from vast reserves of gold and diamonds and from ready sea trade with Asia and Europe.

194 **Africa's growth rate:** Angus Maddison, *The World Economy,* p. 226.

196 **Malaria is utterly treatable:** For an authoritative recent account of the epidemiology of malaria, see: Joel G. Bremen, Martin S. Alilio, and Anne Mills, "Conquering the Intolerable Burden of Malaria: What's New, What's Needed: A Summary," *The American Journal of Tropical Medicine and Hygiene,* Vol. 71 (August 2003, No. 2 Supplement), p. 10.

199 **Africa's crisis is unique:** Another piece of evidence of Africa's unique malaria burden is the high prevalence of sickle cell anemia. This terrible disease comes from a genetic mutation that is propagated in the population because it is partially protective against malaria in a child when the mutation is inherited from exactly one parent. When the trait is inherited from both parents, the condition is fatal in the absence of advanced medical treatments. The fact that such a dangerous genetic mutation has survived in Africa gives quantitative evidence that malaria has for a long time uniquely burdened African populations in comparison with other parts of the world.

200 **The level of rich-country:** World Health Organization, *Macroeconomics and Health: Investing in Health for Economic Development,* Report of the Commission on Macroeconomics and Health (Geneva: World Health Organization, 2001).

201 **health and education spending:** Hugh Bredenkamp, Letter to the Editor, *Financial Times,* June 29, 1999.

202 **. . . in the wake of my public:** During 1997, many of the East Asian middle-income countries were hit by a panicked withdrawal of international capital. For several months I became engrossed in a public debate with the IMF over how to handle such a crisis. My colleague Steve Radelet and I argued that the IMF had exacerbated rather than moderated the crisis by the IMF's own panicked response of closing banks and demanding sharp cuts in government

spending. Many of those critiques have since been vindicated, including by the IMF's own Office of Independent Evaluation.

203 **the massive burden:** The unpublished background paper showed that malaria has slowed economic growth in African countries by 1.3 percent per year. Further explained in Jeffrey D. Sachs and John Luke Gallup, "The Economic Burden of Malaria," *American Journal of Tropical Medicine and Hygiene,* Vol. 64: 1, 2, pp., 85–96. As a result of the compounded effect over thirty-five years, the GDP level for African countries is now up to 32 percent lower than it would have been in the absence of malaria.

CHAPTER ELEVEN: THE MILLENNIUM, 9/11,

AND THE UNITED NATIONS

215 **"I think you can create":** Interview with Matt Lauer, NBC News, August 31, 2004.

216 **". . . we look forward to":** Franklin Delano Roosevelt, address to the 77th Congress, January 6, 1941.

216 . . . **"ODA is still":** Monterrey Consensus of International Conference on Financing for Development, 2002, United Nations, paragraph 42.

217 . . . **one cannot fight a war:** Jeffrey D. Sachs, "Weapons of Mass Salvation," *The Economist,* October 26, 2002.

219 **This was the famous speech:** Remarks by Vice President Dick Cheney to the Veterans of Foreign Wars 103rd National Convention, August 26, 2002, Nashville, Tennessee.

220 . . . **$15 billion:** Unfortunately, as of September 2004, only twenty-five thousand Africans have been put under antiretroviral drugs under the new presidential initiative.

221 **". . . we have to translate":** Jeffrey D. Sachs, "Smart Money: What Military Power Can't Do," *The New Republic,* March 3, 2003.

224 . . . **the Earth Institute is:** With special thanks to Awash Teklehaimonot for his work on malaria throughout Africa and on economic development in Ethiopia, Jonathan Donner and Josh Ruxin for cell phones linked to public health, Pedro Sanchez and Cheryl Palm for research and practical breakthroughs on agroforestry, Mark Cane and Steve Zebiak on El Niño modeling, and Lex van Geen and Joe Graziano for the Bangladesh arsenic breakthroughs.

CHAPTER TWELVE: ON-THE-GROUND

SOLUTIONS FOR ENDING POVERTY

228 . . . **the Earth Institute at:** The project is headed by Dr. Cheryl Palm and Dr. Pedro Sanchez of the Earth Institute. They are both world-class soil scientists with extensive experience in East Africa. Pedro Sanchez directed the World Agroforestry Center for ten years and pioneered the use of nitrogen-fixing trees as a method for replenishing nitrogen in African soils. He won the World Food Prize in 2003 and the MacArthur Prize in 2004 for that and other work. Dr. Vijay Modi, also of the Earth Institute, is a professor of engineering at Columbia University and is working in Sauri on problems of core infrastructure—power,

transport, roads, water, and sanitation. Dr. Sonia Ehrlich is leading the effort to establish a new Sauri clinic and public health system. Dr. Daniel Hillel, professor emeritus at the University of Massachusetts, contributed advice on water management.

232 **. . . identified by the villagers:** Sachs, Jeffrey D., et al., "Ending Africa's Poverty Trap," *Brookings Papers on Economic Activity*, No. 1, 2004.

241 **". . . It is important":** Meera Bapat and Indu Agarwal, "Our Needs, Our Priorities; Women and Men from the Slums in Mumbai and Pune Talk About Their Needs for Water and Sanitation," *Environment & Urbanization*, 15, No. 2, October 2003.

242 **". . . the favorable confluence":** Sheela Patel, Celine d'Cruz, and Sundar Burra, "Beyond Evictions in a Global City: People-Managed Resettlement in Mumbai," *Environment & Urbanization*, 14, No. 1, April 2003.

CHAPTER THIRTEEN: MAKING THE INVESTMENTS NEEDED
TO END POVERTY

253 **"An instructed and intelligent people":** Adam Smith, *The Wealth of Nations*, Book V, Chapter 1, in paragraph V.1.189.

253 **"Everyone has the right":** Universal declaration of human rights, United Nations General Assembly resolution 217 A (III), December 10, 1948, Article 25.

254 **"Everyone has the right to education":** Ibid., Article 26.

254 **"Everyone is entitled":** Ibid., Article 28.

264 *Asiaweek* **magazine once referred:** Assif Shameen, "Asian of the Century, Ideas with Impact," *Asiaweek*, December 10, 1999, p. 1. <www.asiaweek.com>.

CHAPTER FOURTEEN: A GLOBAL COMPACT TO END POVERTY

267 **"a reliable supply of safe water":** Comments of Andrew Natsios regarding the U.S.AID West Africa Water Initiative, August 20, 2002. "$41 Million Public-Private Partnership to Provide Clean Water in West Africa," <http:www.usaid.gov/press/releases/2002/pr020820.html>.

277 **A discussion:** James D. Wolfensohn and the Utstein Group Proceedings, Prague, Czech Republic, September 24, 2000.

277 **". . . there is a large pick-up":** World Bank, press conference with James D. Wolfensohn, Washington, D.C., April 19, 2002.

279 **". . . the adoption of policies":** Thirty-Eighth Ordinary Session of the Assembly of Heads of State and Government of the OAU: African Peer Review Mechanism, July 8, 2002, Durban, South Africa, AHG/235 (XXXVIII), Annex II.

284 **". . . stabilization of greenhouse gas":** United Nations Framework Convention on Climate Change, 1992, Article 2: Objective, p. 9.

CHAPTER FIFTEEN: CAN THE RICH AFFORD TO HELP THE POOR?

289 **The World Bank estimates:** Shaohua Chen and Martin Ravallion, "How Have the World's Poorest Fared Since the Early 1980s?," World Bank Policy Research Working Paper 3341, June 2004.

290 **the numbers of poor people:** Ibid.

293 **Since cost data were unavailable:** For more details on the MDG needs assessment, refer to the background paper available at http://www.unmillenniumproject .org/html/secretariatdocs.shtm.

307 **"For individuals who":** Jeffrey D. Sachs, *New York Times,* July 9, 2003, Op-Ed page.

307 *A 5 percent income tax surcharge:* In 2004, there were an estimated 4.1 million taxpayers with cash income at or above $200,000. This is 2.9 percent of all taxpayers (143,500,000 taxpayers) and 25.3 percent of total cash income. Total adjusted gross income is around $6.3 trillion. Thus, total income of the taxpayers with incomes above $200,000 is 25.3 percent × 6.3 trillion, or $1.6 trillion. Total adjusted gross income above $200,000 is therefore $1.6 trillion minus (4.1 million × 200,000) or around 0.8 trillion. A 5 percent surcharge on 0.8 trillion is around $40 billion. In summary, a 5 percent surcharge on incomes above $200K would yield around $40 billion per year. Source: The numbers of taxpayers above $200K and their income shares are from Table "T04-0120—Distribution of AMT and Regular Income Tax by Cash Income, Current Law 2004 Calendar Year" of the Tax Policy Center, accessed online from http:taxpolicycenter.org on November 4, 2004. The estimate of adjusted gross income uses Internal Revenue Service data for 2002, which places AGI at approximately $6 trillion for 2002, and updates it to an estimate for 2004 of $6.3 trillion.

CHAPTER SIXTEEN: MYTHS AND MAGIC BULLETS

311 **"They know morning":** Quoted in John Donnelly, "Prevention Urged in AIDS Fight—Natsios Says Fund Should Spend Less on HIV Treatment," *Boston Globe,* June 7, 2001.

311 **"Poverty is the result of policy options":** Comments of Barney Pityana, December 8, 1998.

314 **This slower growth:** For more information about this analysis, see the Brookings paper: Jeffrey D. Sachs, et al., "Ending Africa's Poverty Trap," *Brookings Papers on Economic Activity,* No. 1, 2004.

315 **One recent study:** The study on Africa is Daniel Etounga-Manguelle, "Does Africa Need a Cultural Adjustment Program?" in Lawrence E. Harrison and Samuel P. Huntington, eds., *Culture Matters: How Values Shape Human Progress,* Basic Books, 2000, pp. 65–77. The reference on Mexican-Americans is Lionel Sosa, *Americano Dream* (New York: Plume, 1998), cited in Samuel P. Huntington, *Who Are We?* (New York: Simon & Schuster, 2004), p. 254.

316 **"Wealthy we do not think it":** *Japan Gazette.* Referenced in Junko Nakai, "Blessing or Curse: Characteristics of the Japanese Economy," *HKCER Letters,* Vol. 54, January 1999, <http:www.hku.hk/hkcer/articles/v54/nakai.htm>.

316 **"The national banking system":** Ibid.

318 **When asked in 2000:** Ronald Inglehart et al., *Human Beliefs and Values* (Mexico: Siglo Veintiuno Editores, 2004), AO30.

319 **"... In fact, countries":** Marc A. Miles, et al., *2004 Index of Economic Freedom* (Washington, D.C.: The Heritage Foundation and *Wall Street Journal*, 2004), <http:www.heritage.org/research/features/index/index.html>.

321 **"It is the unavailability":** Hernando de Soto, *The Mystery of Capital: Why Capitalism Triumphs in the West and Fails Everywhere Else* (New York: Basic Books, 2000), pp. 5–7.

321 **Many non-Western countries:** See, for example: Katharina Pistor, Jeffrey D. Sachs, and Philip Wellons, *The Role of Law and Legal Institutions in Asian Economic Development, 1960–1995* (New York: Oxford University Press, 1999).

322 **Dozens of recent statistical:** Some recent examples are: Robert J. Barro, "Economic Growth in a Cross-Section of Countries," *Quarterly Journal of Economics,* 106, No. 2, May, pp. 407–43; ——— and Xavier Sala-I-Martin, *Economic Growth,* 2nd ed. (Cambridge: MIT Press, 2003); ———, "Technological Diffusion, Convergence, and Growth," *Journal of Economic Growth* (2, No. 1, March 1997), pp. 1–26; Robert E. Hall and Charles I. Jones, "Why Do Some Countries Produce So Much More Output per Worker Than Others?," *Quarterly Journal of Economics,* 114, No. 1, February 1999, pp. 83–116; Andrew D. Mellinger, Jeffrey D. Sachs, and John L. Gallup, "Climate, Coastal Proximity, and Development," in *Oxford Handbook of Economic Geography,* Gordon L. Clark, Maryann P. Feldman, and Meric S. Gertler, eds. (Oxford: Oxford University Press, 2000); Jeffrey D. Sachs, "Globalization and Patterns of Economic Growth," forthcoming. In *Globalization: What's New?,* Michael M. Weinstein, ed., Columbia University Press/Council on Foreign Relations; Xavier X. Sala-i-Martin, "I Just Ran Two Million Regressions," *The American Economic Review* (87, No. 2, May 1997), Papers and Proceedings of the Hundred and Fourth Annual Meeting of the American Economic Association; ———, Gernot Doppelhofer and Ronal I. Miller, "Determinants of Long-Term Growth: A Bayesian Averaging of Classical Estimates (BACE) Approach," *The American Economic Review* (94, No. 4, September 2004).

322 **"Although sexual cultures":** Daniel T. Halperin and Helen Epstein, "Concurrent Sexual Partnership Help to Explain Africa's High HIV Prevalence: Implications for Prevention," *The Lancet,* Vol. 364, July 3, 2004, p. 4.

CHAPTER SEVENTEEN: WHY WE SHOULD DO IT

329 **In a 2001 survey:** "Americans on Foreign Aid and World Hunger: A Study of U.S. Public Attitudes." Program on International Policy Attitudes, University of Maryland, February 2, 2001.

331 **The PIPA survey:** Ibid.

335 **"Development assistance":** George W. Bush, speech to the Inter-American Development Bank, March 14, 2002, Washington, D.C.

336 **"The United States will lead by example":** Ibid.

336 **"Including all of the world's poor":** U.S. National Security Strategy, September 2002.

336 **The strategy committed:** Ibid.

337 **aid flows have:** Ibid.

338 **"We want the United Nations":** George W. Bush, speech to the United Nations, September 12, 2002.

338 **"We urge developed countries"**: Monterrey Consensus, paragraph 42.
338 **"Urge the developed countries"**: World Summit on Sustainable Development, WSSD Plan of Implementation, August 2002, paragraph 85 (a).
339 **"official development assistance"**: Monterrey Consensus, paragraph 39.
341 **Supporters of the Marshall Plan**: Adam Sachs and Jeffrey D. Sachs, "Selling the Marshall Plan" (n.p.).
345 **". . . This nation can lead"**: George W. Bush, State of the Union Address (January 28, 2003).

CHAPTER EIGHTEEN: OUR GENERATION'S CHALLENGE

348 **". . . Life, Liberty, and the Pursuit of Happiness"**: Declaration of Independence, Action of the Second Continental Congress, July 4, 1776.
348 **". . . it is the Right of the People"**: Ibid.
348 **Kant explained**: Immanuel Kant, *Perpetual Peace,* 1795, Section II, First Definitive Article for Perpetual Peace: "The Civil Constitution of Every State Should Be Republican," paragraph 2.
349 **". . . and, to fill up"**: Ibid.
349 **". . . states see themselves"**: Ibid., First Supplement to Perpetual Peace: "Of the Guarantee for Perpetual Peace," number 3.
350 **". . . It will be possible"**: Marie-Jean-Antoine-Nicolas Caritat, Marquis de Condorcet, *Sketch for a Historical Picture of the Progress of the Human Mind,* Keith Michael Baker, tr., *Daedalus,* Summer 2004, pp. 65–82, 80.
350 **". . . It seems clear"**: Ibid., p. 79.
350 **". . . The most enlightened peoples"**: Ibid., p. 77.
351 **"To the natives"**: Adam Smith. *The Wealth of Nations,* Book IV, Chapter 7, in paragraph IV.7.166.
351 **". . . the superiority of force"**: Ibid.
351 **". . . nothing seems more likely"**: Ibid.
352 **"progress is an illusion"**: John Gray, "An Illusion with a Future," *Daedelus,* Summer 2004, p. 11.
356 **Other studies confirm**: Eduardo Borensztein, Jose De Gregorio, and Jong-Wha Lee, "How Does Foreign Direct Investment Affect Economic Growth?," NBER Working Paper No. w5057, March 1995.
361 **"This was the first major"**: Hugh Thomas, *The Slave Trade: The Story of the Atlantic Slave Trade, 1440–1870* (New York: Simon & Schuster, 1997), p. 497.
361 **"If they [Africans]"**: Ibid., p. 513.
361 **"If abolition became law"**: Ibid., p. 514.
361 **"Persistence is the most important quality"**: Ibid., 537.
363 **". . . I discovered the method"**: Martin Luther King, Jr., "My Pilgrimage to Nonviolence," 1958. First appeared in September 1958 issue of *Fellowship.* Excerpted from *Stride Toward Freedom,* 1959.
364 **". . . So we have come to cash this check"**: Ibid., "I Have a Dream," delivered at the Lincoln Memorial, Washington, D.C., August 28, 1963.
368 **"It is from the numberless"**: Robert F. Kennedy, address on the Day of Affirmation, University of Capetown, South Africa, June 6, 1966.

Index

Credits